ANGLAIS Tle
B1/B2

Gaël Manescau
Chargé de mission d'inspection
Enseignant au Lycée Jean Monnet (78)
Auteur coordonnateur

Vincent Aufauvre
Campus scolaire de Coulommiers (77)

Laure Chourgnoz
Lycée Louis Armand (73)

Héliette Garcia-Fernandez
Lycée polyvalent La Saulaie (38)

Kathryn Hart
Lycée Berthollet (74)

Gaël Poirion
Enseignante au Lycée Assomption (35)

Yasmine Trouillard
Lycée Jules Hardouin-Mansart (78)

Anaïs Yeretzian
Lycée Notre-Dame Les Oiseaux (78)

Manuel Jobert
Professeur de linguistique anglaise
à l'Université Jean Moulin – Lyon 3 (69)
Grammaire, phonologie & Précis grammatical

Unité bonus numérique DNL
Mélanie Dubois
Enseignante d'histoire, Lycée Gambetta-Carnot (62)

Chers élèves,

Vous entrez en Terminale : **savourez votre dernière année au Lycée** en vous plongeant avec enthousiasme dans chacun de vos apprentissages.

Pour assurer votre réussite, **saisissez toutes les occasions pour vous investir dans votre travail** en classe d'anglais ou hors classe : communiquez, participez, lisez, écoutez, regardez des films et/ou des séries en VO, cultivez-vous !
Outre un grand nombre de documents qui vous étonneront et vous ouvriront de **nouveaux horizons**, *Hit the Road* vous **prépare efficacement aux épreuves de contrôle continu**, écrites et orales. ☺
C'est votre dernière année au lycée mais c'est aussi le début d'une belle aventure vers les études, les voyages et le monde professionnel !

À vous la joie de la **découverte d'autres pays et d'autres cultures** : prenez la route !

Hit the Road to success! We know you can!

Les auteurs

MAGNARD

Magnard remercie chaleureusement les **enseignant(e)s** ayant participé à des études sur notre méthode. Leurs avis nous ont été précieux !

Maeva Hau, Prades (66) ; **Laure Dauba**, Nantes (44) ; **Amandine De Faria**, Noyelles-Godault (62) ; **Morgane Gojard**, Ozoir-la-Ferrière (77) ; **Victorine Marie**, Saint-Raphaël (83) ; **Agnès Espaignet**, Auch (32) ; **Philomène Fernandes**, Charenton-le-Pont (94) ; **Maryline Berton**, Le Sourn (56) ; **Christine Serru**, Strasbourg (67) ; **Virginie Dernoncourt**, Bazas (33) ; **Kevin Plé**, Charleville-Mézières (08) ; **Rose Camara Cugliari**, Oullins (69) ; **Clotilde Viart**, Cergy (95) ; **Isabelle Colas Jalabert**, Mont-de-Marsan (40) ; **Joanna Alfonsi**, La Seyne-sur-Mer (83) ; **Ingrid Gouverneur**, Nantes (44) ; **Sophie Desprez Labourey**, Reims (51) ; **Séverine Convers**, Saint-Priest-en-Jarez (42) ; **Cécile Groult**, Salon de Provence (13) ; **Beatrice Mainguy**, Avranches (50) ; **Adèle Velly**, Les Andelys (27) ; **Maureen Dominé**, Lyon (69) ; **Marie-Sophie Leroueil**, Segré-en-Anjou-Bleu (49) ; **Mercedes Marcet Viñolas**, Asnières-sur-Seine (92) ; **Adeline Saverna**, Longwy (54) ; **Valérie Le Baut**, Le Chesnay (78) ; **Claire Bonnard**, Drap (06) ; **Anne-Catherine Al Abbas**, Compiègne (60) ; **Fatiha Abdou**, Roubaix (59) ; **Bouchra Karim** (Maroc) ; **Christine Toulouse**, Joué-les-Tours (37) ; **Jean-Luc Le Drogou**, Laval (53) ; **Corine Grillo**, Fontenay-le-Comte (85) ; **Aziza Benseddik** (Maroc) ; **Catherine Mahillon** (Belgique) ; **Lise Rubinstein**, Paris (75) ; **Kheira Atigui**, Vaujours (93) ; **Céline Maximilien**, Dax (40) ; **Charlotte Bateman**, Lyon (69) ; **Laura Dulong**, Bordeaux (33) ; **Angélique Caruso**, Hyères (83) ; **Véronique Catania**, Annemasse (74) ; **Florence Popelier**, Morangis (91) ; **Caroline Rozaire**, Luynes (13) ; **Jeanne Bénard-Poy**, Rouen (76) ; **Sonia Tuval**, Saint-Maur-des-Fossés (94) ; **Jean-Claude Lecointre**, Marcq-en-Baroeul (59) ; **Anne-Marie Mansard**, Thonon-les-Bains (74) ; **Jean-Cyrille Ly Van Tu**, Nogent-sur-Marne (94) ; **Olivia Maida**, Paris (75) ; **Laurence Dumont**, Royan (17) ; **Agnès Ourseyre**, Cournon d'Auvergne (63) ; **Emmanuelle Machiné**, Gleizé (69) ; **Laure Lagarde**, Trévoux (01) ; **Christine Lagarde**, Agen (47) ; **Nasséra Sahnoun**, Amiens (80).

Direction éditoriale : **Alexia Zoulas**
Édition : **Isabelle Breton** et **Audrey Poulat**
Assistante d'édition : **Anaëlle Goujon**
Création graphique & Mise en page : **Natacha Marmouget**
Mise en page liminaires et *Backpack* : **Nathalie Dudek**
Couverture : **Primo & Primo**
Iconographie : **Virginie Dauvet, Katia Davidoff, Valérie Dereux, Nadine Gudimard, Aurélie Teisseire**
Droits textes et vidéo : **Gabriella Marino**
Cartes : **Légendes Cartographie**
Chef de projet numérique : **Dominique Garrigues**
Édition du manuel numérique : **Alexia Labaste**
Enregistrements : **EuroDVD**
Relecture : **Lee Smart**
Remerciements à Marie Chochon

5, allée de la 2e D.B. 75015 Paris

www.magnard.fr

ISBN : 978-2-210-11391-6

VISITE GUIDÉE DU MANUEL

Une structure souple, pour traiter 6 axes sur 8, adaptée aux rythmes de Terminale

4 Unités CLASSIQUES

Pour les sujets fondamentaux

Documents : 4 à 7 double-pages
Langue : lexique, phonologie, grammaire + exercices
Projets : 2 projets au choix

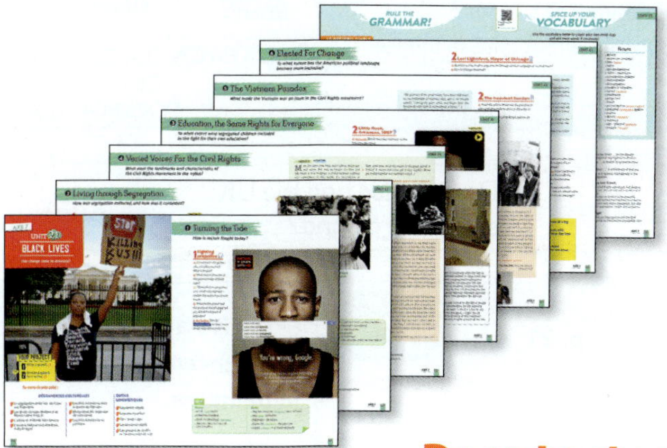

10 Unités MOYENNES ET 12 COURTES

Pour les sujets aux problématiques resserrées

Documents : 3 à 4 double-pages
Langue : exercices
Projets : 1 ou 2 projets au choix

Dans toutes les unités :

- Des documents adaptés à **toutes les classes**
- Des activités de production *« Your Turn »*
- Des activités en pairwork et en groupwork
- Des *« Have your say »* pour impliquer l'élève
- Des *« Go further »* pour pousser la réflexion
- Du lexique en contexte (*« Help! »*)
- Des activités variées, graduées et ludiques
- Un exercice **interactif de bilan**
- Des flashcodes pour accéder aux ressources élèves
- Une approche pragmatique pour **entraîner aux épreuves de Terminale**

En annexes :

27 P. Précis grammatical
6 P. Deux lectures suivies

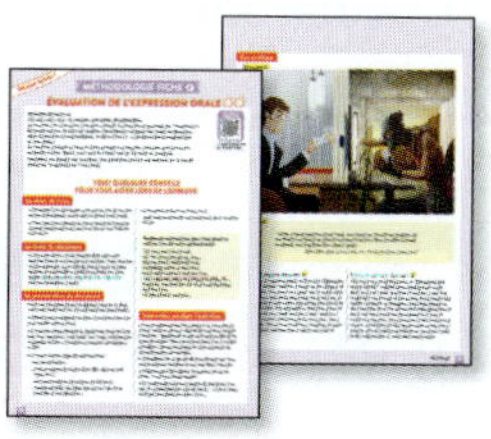

13 P. Dossier méthodologique spécial bac

[en lien avec chaque unité]

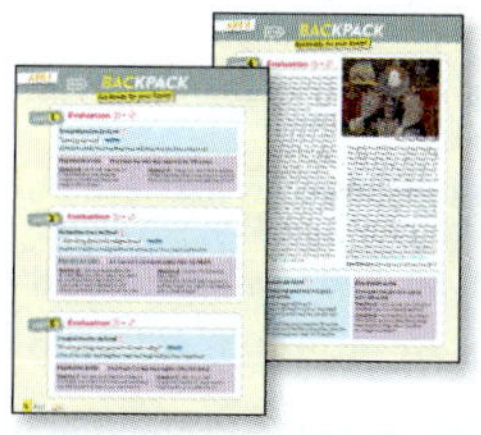

33 P. **Pages BAC** pour s'entraîner aux nouvelles épreuves de Tle

100% NUMÉRIQUE

Une unité bonus de **DNL** sur les affiches de propagande de la Seconde Guerre mondiale, en lien avec l'axe 3 **13 P.**

LES PICTOGRAMMES DES ACTIVITÉS LANGAGIÈRES

Compréhension de l'oral | Compréhension de l'écrit | Expression orale en continu | Expression orale en interaction | Expression écrite | Expression écrite en interaction | Médiation

LES SUPPORTS

MP3 n°138 **VIDEO n°51**
Documents audio et vidéo dans le manuel numérique et sur la clé USB de Ressources Classe.

Worksheet n°50
Fiches photocopiables distribuées par l'enseignant.

SOMMAIRE

Identities & Exchanges

p. 12-13

AXE 1

AXE 2 Private Space & Public Space
p. 38-39

Art & Power

AXE 3

UNIT 7 "ARTVERTISING"

How does advertising mirror the societies in the English-speaking world and their power?

Textes : 7
Icono. : 6
Affiches : 4
Audios/vidéos : 6

PROJECTS

- Present a spoof ad (radio commercial).
- Create an awareness campaign.

Grammaire
L'expression de la contrainte (*make sb do sth*)
Les quantifieurs
L'expression de l'indignation

Phonologie
La prononciation des mots : *ad*, *advertise*, *advertising*
L'intonation dans un spot publicitaire

Ressources élèves

UNIT 8 ONCE UPON A GUN

How is the power of culture used to influence public opinion on guns in the U.S.?

Textes : 2
Icono. : 3
Cartoons : 6
Audios/vidéos : 3

PROJECT

- Debate in an online forum.

Grammaire
Le *present perfect*
Le gérondif
L'expression du contraste

Phonologie
Le schéma intonatif des sigles

Ressources élèves

UNIT 9 MASTERS OF SPEECH

How powerful is oratory in the U.S.?

Textes : 3
Icono. : 5
Audios/vidéos : 6

PROJECTS

- Deliver a speech.
- Participate in a MOTH show.

Grammaire
Les connecteurs logiques

Phonologie
Les groupes de souffle
L'intonation

Ressources élèves

AXE 4 Citizenship & Virtual Worlds

UNIT 10 CRIME IN THE DIGITAL AGE

How are new technologies helping to solve crime?

Textes : 4
Icono. : 5
Vidéos : 5

PROJECTS

Write an essay.

Debate whether personal data should be used by the police.

Grammaire

Les modaux

Le *present perfect*

If clauses

Phonologie

La lettre « l »

La lettre « t » en anglais américain

Ressources élèves

UNIT 11 LOVE AT FIRST SWIPE

How have apps changed social bonds?

Textes : 4
Icono. : 4
Audios/vidéos : 5

PROJECT

In an online forum react to 21st century romance and courtship.

Grammaire

La comparaison

Be used to + -ing / used to + V

Le génitif

L'article Ø / *The*

Phonologie

La prononciation de « ou » et « our »

L'intonation des phrases

Ressources élèves

UNIT 12 HACKERS: FRIENDS OR FOES?

In the digital age, are hackers the new threat?

Textes : 2
Icono. : 2
Cartoons : 6 BD : 1
Audios/vidéos : 6

PROJECT

Read a graphic novel and sum up the main information.

Grammaire

Les modaux

La phrase interrogative

Phonologie

La terminaison « -ed »

Les accents britannique et américain

Ressources élèves

Fictions & Realities
p. 128-129

AXE 5

AXE 6 Scientific Innovations & Responsibility

Diversity & Inclusion

AXE 7 !

p. 228-229

UNIT 21 BLACK LIVES

Has change come to America? p. 230

Textes : 8
Icono. : 14
Audios/vidéos : 12

PROJECTS

Write a speech.

Choose a speech for a review.

Grammaire
Le prétérit ; Le *present perfect* ;
For / since / ago ; Les pronoms relatifs

Phonologie
Les terminaisons en « -ism », en « -age » et en « -ate »
L'intonation

Ressources élèves

BACKPACK CO › EE p.260
CE › EE p.261
POC › POI p.263

UNIT 22 BEYOND SIGHT

How does H.G. Wells manage to deal with difference and inclusion in "The Country of the Blind"? p. 246

SHORT CUT

Textes : 5
Icono. : 5
Audios : 3

PROJECT

Write the ending to H.G. Wells's short story.

Grammaire
Les temps du récit ; Le discours direct et indirect
L'expression de la simultanéité

Phonologie
La prononciation de « ea »

Ressources élèves

BACKPACK CO › EE p.260
CE › EE p.262
POC › POI p.263

UNIT 23 BARBIE GOES INCLUSIVE

How has the iconic doll evolved to embrace diversity in American society? p. 254

SHORT CUT

Texte : 1
Icono. : 5
Audios/vidéos : 5

PROJECT

Take part in a TV debate.

Grammaire
Les comparatifs / superlatifs ; Le *present perfect*
La place de l'adjectif ; Les adjectifs composés

Phonologie
Les mots en « -ic »
L'accent de phrase

Ressources élèves

BACKPACK CO › EE p.260
CE › EE p.262
POC › POI p.263

AXE 8 Territory & Memory

UNIT 24 GATEWAYS TO THE USA

Is the United States "the Land of Plenty" for everyone?

Poèmes : 8
Icono. : 8
Carte : 1
Audios/vidéos : 11

PROJECT
Write a poem.

Ressources élèves

Grammaire
L'obligation au passé (*had to*)
Le discours direct et indirect

Phonologie
Les accents américain et britannique
La prononciation du son /j/

UNIT 25 MĀORI MEMORY

How can New Zealand embrace the Māori memory?

Textes : 6
Icono. : 9
Audios/vidéos : 4

PROJECTS
Write and give a speech.
Write an article.

Ressources élèves

Grammaire
L'expression de l'exclamation et de l'emphase
For, *since* et *ago* ; Le passif ; Le *present perfect*

Phonologie
L'accent australien

UNIT 26 NEW ORLEANS: A LIVING MUSEUM

Which historical events have shaped New Orleans?

Texte : 1
Icono. : 7
Audios/vidéos : 10

PROJECT
Make a video proposing a new symbol for the city.

Ressources élèves

Grammaire
Le *past perfect* ; Les modaux au passé ;
L'expression de la suggestion (*What about... Let's...*)

Phonologie
La prononciation du « s » grammatical
La prosodie

ANNEXES

Unité Bonus **DNL** : "Propaganda in Times of War" (**unité numérique**, en lien avec l'axe 3)

Mayflower in Plymouth Harbour,
William Halsall, 1882

AXE 1

Identities & Exchanges

AXE 1

UNIT 1

SHORT CUT

BEING AMISH

How does an age-old community face 21st century challenges?

YOUR PROJECT

1 Put yourself in the shoes of an Amish teenager and tell your parents why you have decided to stay or leave.

OR

2 Write an article about young Amish people after their Rumspringa.

BEFORE CLASS!

Flash to watch!

Watch the video and be ready to talk about it in class.

Au menu de cette unité :

DÉCOUVERTES CULTURELLES

- Le mode de vie traditionnel des Amish et le rejet de la modernité
- L'ouverture des Amish aux autres (tourisme, échanges, nouvelles technologies…)
- Le rituel adolescent du *Rumspringa*
- Le départ de la communauté et le bannissement

OUTILS LINGUISTIQUES

- L'expression du contraste
- L'expression de la volonté, du souhait et de l'intention
- Le futur

LANGUAGE LAB

- Unit's vocabulary
- Audio words
- MP3
- Interactive Test

★ **1. Turn the following sentences into questions.**

A. The Amish will forever remain different from other American citizens.

B. You are going to try to live without technological tools for one month.

C. She's leaving this place for good.

D. Our community is to adapt if we want to survive.

★ **2. Fill in the blanks with the words below.**

still • while • though • different from • unlike • contrary to

A. ... Joe, Eirene enjoyed living in the Amish community.

B. ... received ideas, the Amish are very well aware of what's going on in the rest of the country.

C. The Amish way of life is ... the American way of life.

D. ... the Amish ... have horse-drawn buggies, some use the Internet.

E. Most Amish settlements are located in the East. You can find a few Amish communities in the West, ...

★★ **3. Give synonyms of these words and make a sentence for each one.**

A. limit (noun) = ...

B. way of life = ...

C. ancient = ...

D. prosperous = ...

★★ **4. Match each word with its definition.**

A. belief B. deeply-rooted C. commitment D. culture shock

1. A strong or firm belief shown by one's actions.
2. An opinion or conviction.
3. A feeling of confusion experienced by a person who is exposed to a different culture.
4. Firmly implanted, fixed, or established.

★★ **5. Fill in the blanks using the words below.**

comply with • conform to • pariahs • pious • ostracise • plain • outcasts • off the grid

A. The Amish are ... people who are often regarded as social ... or ....

B. They live ... lives and refuse to use modern technology. They live ... as they did two centuries ago.

C. The Amish do not hesitate to ... those who do not wish to ... the rules of the community.

D. Some Amish young people refuse to ... the traditions of their community and decide to leave.

★★★ **6. Translate into English.**

A. *J'aimerais pouvoir quitter cette communauté sans faire de mal à ma famille.* → I wish ...

B. *Nous aurions aimé que Levi ne soit pas parti sans dire au revoir.* → We wish ...

C. *Je suis désolé qu'il n'ait pas aimé mes parents.* → I'm sorry ...

7. Interactive test! What is your score?

OPEN YOUR EARS!

PHONOLOGY

• **Écoutez et classez ces mots en fonction de la prononciation de la graphie « ea ».**

MP3 N°02 | *leaving • bear • meant • dearest • tear* (larme) *• tear* (déchirer) *• heart • read • wear*

« ea »				
/iː/	/e/	/ɪə/	/eə/	/ɑː/

• **Récapitulons.**

- « ea » est généralement prononcé /iː/.
- « ea » est parfois prononcé /e/, par exemple dans le cas des verbes irréguliers (mean /iː/ → meant /e/, read /iː/ → read /e/).
- « ea » suivi de « r » se prononce régulièrement /ɪə/ (*dear, fear*, etc.) mais peut aussi se prononcer /eə/ (*bear*).

SHOWTIME

Écoutez cette phrase. Puis entraînez-vous à la répéter en accentuant les deux verbes.

Ici, les deux verbes sont mis en relief.

MP3 N°03 | *Are you* ***staying*** *and becoming a full member, baptised member of the church or are you* ***leaving****?*

Le tempo est plus rapide sur cette partie car elle est moins importante.

AUDIO MYSTERY

MP3 N°04

Listen to the recording and find the mystery word.

Picture challenge

★ 3 sentences
★★ 4 to 6 sentences
★★★ 7 sentences and +

How many sentences can you make using what you have learnt? Collect stars!

AXE 1

UNIT 2

JAMAICA AND THE UNITED KINGDOM

Do Jamaica and the UK still share a bond?

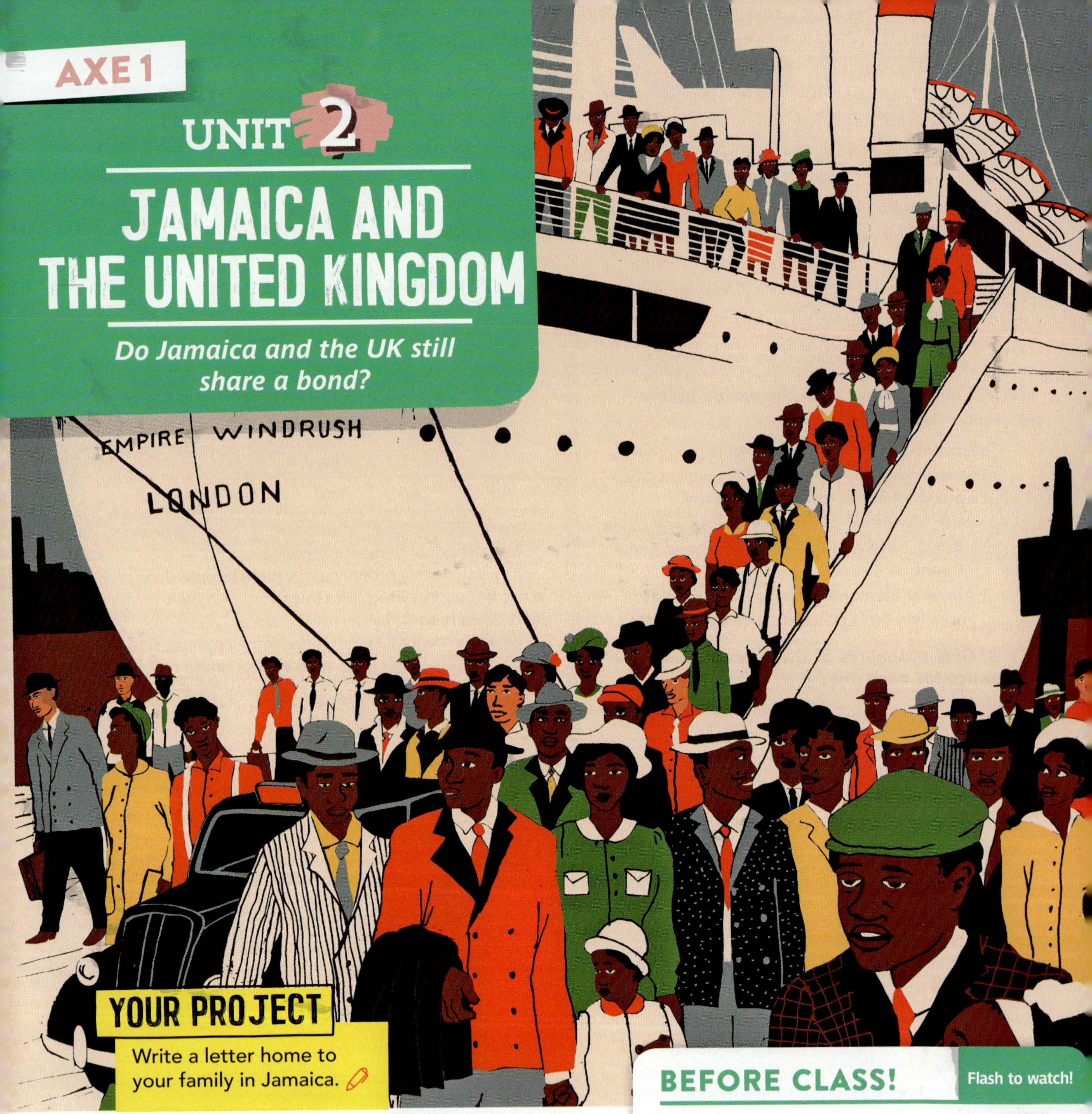

YOUR PROJECT

Write a letter home to your family in Jamaica.

Au menu de cette unité :

DÉCOUVERTES CULTURELLES

- Les attraits touristiques de la Jamaïque
- La *Windrush generation*
- Les échanges culturels et commerciaux entre la Jamaïque et la Grande-Bretagne
- Des extraits littéraires d'auteurs anglo-jamaïcains (*Small Island*...)

OUTILS LINGUISTIQUES

- Le *present perfect*
- La voix passive

BEFORE CLASS!

Flash to watch!

Watch the video and be ready to talk about it in class!

VIDEO N°05

❶ Reggae: The Heartbeat of a Nation

How has reggae forged Jamaican identity?

1 Jamaica's rebel music

A. Look at the picture. Who does the poster represent? Would you say he is an icon?

B. Read the text. Focus on:

- the role of reggae and its impact on Jamaica and the world;
- the Jamaicans' reaction following Unesco's decision (l. 1-2).

C. Find the main reason why *"Jamaican radio gave you no inkling that reggae was the 'heart and soul' of the country"* (l. 24-25).

D. Go further. Explain what the last sentence implies.

Don't you just know that Unesco's decision to add reggae to its list of the intangible cultural heritage of humanity will be the kiss of death for any remaining semblance of "rebel music" in Jamaica? While the island's delegation at the United Nations was skanking[1] in celebration the other night, there was no corresponding "jam out there" in the streets of Kingston, Spanish Town, Mo' Bay or Ochi. Once upon a time there would have been, but this recognition by the UN is at best too little too late and, at worst, somewhat suspect. [...] Jamaicans do not need the UN to endorse the soundtrack of their lives. They do not need Unesco to tell them that reggae is "cerebral, socio-political, sensual and spiritual". Jamaicans know that already. They have known for half a century that the reggae beat is their nation's heartbeat and that its lyrics are the soul and conscience of its people. [...] Wherever people were oppressed, reggae provided a battle cry for change: "Get up, stand up, stand up for your rights." In Jamaica especially, reggae was accusing the authorities of being the new "slave drivers". That message was tantamount[2] to sedition as far as the authorities were concerned and they came down hard on it. Back then, in the genre's 70s heyday[3], you couldn't hear a reggae tune on the state-controlled airwaves on the island. You could hear Abba and Jim Reeves, but Jamaican radio gave you no inkling[4] that reggae was the "heart and soul" of the country. [...]

The government — and Unesco —sanctioned "heart and soul" of Jamaica is that of the happy tourist on a beach with a few club sodas, meditating to the music of Bob Marley. Where the reggae doesn't point fingers at the establishment that sold you that all-inclusive holiday in the sun. It is not the gritty sufferer's heart and soul — that's one the tourists will never see. This is reggae without its teeth.

1 dancing • 2 /'tæntəmaʊnt/ = equivalent • 3 golden age • 4 indication

Dotun Adebayo, ***The Guardian***, 1 December 2018

YOUR TURN! 2 Holiday in Jamaica

Send an email to your British friend about your discovery of Jamaican music and people.
Use **Worksheet n°03** for help!

HELP!

Nouns & Adjectives	*Verbs & Expressions*
• deply-rooted • heritage /'herətɪdʒ/ = legacy • icon /'aɪkɒn/ • Jamaica /dʒə'meɪkə/ • rebel /'rebəl/ • rebellious /rɪ'beljəs/ = defiant /dɪ'faɪənt/ • The Caribbean /kærə'bi:an/	• keep traditions alive • preserve /prɪ'zɜ:v/ • rebel /rɪ'bel/ against sth/sb • stand up for sth = defend sth

❷ From One Island to the Other

How have Jamaicans managed to adapt to a new life in the UK?

1 An independent nation

A. Read the text. Use **Worksheet n°04** for help.
B. Go further. What does the last paragraph of the article show? What does it prove concerning Jamaican culture?

Since 1962 – when Jamaica first gained independence – the island's spirit, rhythm and passion for life has infected everything from the food we eat to the music we listen to. The cultural influence of this Caribbean gem is undeniable. Today Jamaicans all over the world will be gathering with family and friends – both at home and abroad – to celebrate the richness of their heritage. [...]

How did Jamaica become independent?

The drive for independence was largely born out of "homegrown" responses to economic, social, and political pressures on the island. Jamaica had been a British colony since 1655, and eventually became a hub of sugar production during the slave trade. After the Act of Emancipation went into effect in 1834, one of the colonial government's main form of control over newly freed slaves was through a carefully constructed education system which was meant to prepare them for employment as estate workers.

During the 1930s, Jamaica experienced an economic depression, which led to the labour riots in 1938 over working conditions. [...]

In 1961, a referendum was called to determine whether or not the people of Jamaica should remain part of the Federation.

The Jamaican people voted for Independence and on August 6, 1962, the British flag was lowered to make way for the new Jamaican flag. [...]

How to celebrate Jamaican Independence Day in London

For a slice of history, head down to the Black Cultural Archives in Brixton, the UK's only dedicated heritage centre for Black British history and culture. Whilst you're there, grab some jerk chicken[1] or goat[2] curry at Fish, Wings and Tings. And, for the vegans and veggies among us, visit Deserted Cactus in Peckham for some plant-based Caribbean flavour.

1 spicy chicken • **2** *chèvre*

www.standard.co.uk,
6 August 2019

2 The Windrush Generation

VIDEO N°06

A. Watch the video and find information about:
- when and why thousands of Jamaicans boarded a ship to Britain;
- the way they felt once they arrived in Britain;
- how they were considered by Britons.

B. Go further. Read the *Cultural fact* on **Worksheet n°05** and explain the "Windrush scandal" in your own words.

3 A new life

A. Read the text. Focus on the characters' emotions and reactions.

B. Why does Gilbert react badly to his wife's comments?

C. Go further. What does Gilbert imply when he tells his wife "*You are lucky*" (l. 53)?

London, 1948. England is recovering from war. Gilbert Joseph, a former Jamaican Royal Air Force pilot, now lives in England. When Hortense, his wife joins him to start a new life, she finds London far from the city she had imagined...

Chapter 1

This is the room,' he said.

All I saw were dark brown walls. A broken chair that rested one uneven leg on the Holy Bible. A window with a torn curtain and Gilbert's suit – the double-breasted one – hanging from a rail on the wall.

'Well,' I said, 'show me the rest, then, Gilbert.' The man just stared. 'Show me the rest, nah. I am tired from the long journey.' He scratched his head. The other rooms, Gilbert. The ones you busy making so nice for me you forget to come to the dock.'

Gilbert spoke so softly I could hardly hear. He said, 'But this is it.'

'I am sorry?' I said.

'This is it, Hortense. This is the room I am living.'

Three steps would take me to one side of this room. Four steps could take me to another. There was a sink in the corner, a rusty tap stuck out from the wall above it. There was a table with two chairs – one with its back broken – pushed up against the bed. The armchair held a shopping bag, a pyjama top, and a teapot. In the fireplace the gas hissed with a blue flame.

'Just this?' I had to sit on the bed. My legs gave way. There was no bounce underneath me as I fell. 'Just this? This is where you are living? Just this?'

'Yes, this is it.' He swung his arms around again, like it was a room in a palace.

'Just this? Just this? You bring me all this way for just this?'

The man sucked his teeth and flashed angry eyes in my face. 'What you expect, woman? Yes, just this! What you expect? Everyone live like this. There has been a war. Houses bombed. I know plenty people live worse than this. What you want? You should stay with your mamma if you want it nice. There been a war here. Everyone live like this.'

He looked down at me, his badly buttoned chest heaving.

Chapter 2

'This place is disgusting. I caan[1] believe you bring me all this way to live like this. You make me come here to live like an animal?'

Man, this woman is a barb under my skin – she irritates me so I lose me temper. I tell her, 'Yes, and you know what else, little Miss Stick-up-your-nose-in-the-air, you will have to wash your plate, your vegetable and your backside in that basin too. This room is where you will sleep, eat, cook, dress and write your mummy to tell her how the Mother Country is so fine. And, little Miss High-class, one thing about England you don't know yet because you just come off a boat. You are lucky.'

1 can't

Small Island,
Andrea Levy, 2004

YOUR TURN! 4 Write a letter

After the "Windrush scandal", you decide to send a letter to the Mayor of London to tell him/her about the need to grant British Jamaicans the same rights as British citizens.

❸ Maintaining Links with The United Kingdom

How strong are the links between Jamaica and the UK?

1 Celebrating the Windrush citizens

A. Read the text. Focus on what the Windrush generation has brought to the UK.
B. What were the obstacles that these men and women had to face in the UK?
C. Explain the sentence lines 14-16.
D. Go further. Browse the Internet to know more about the personalities mentioned lines 17, 22, 23 and 26. Then present them orally.

Each and every member of the Windrush generation showed enormous courage, in leaving their home, family and friends in search of a better life. Each and every one started out with almost no money to their name, but with the ambition and energy to work hard. And each and every one faced down barriers, structural and legal, that limited their ability to flourish in their adopted country.

[...] When no one else in Britain would, the Windrush generation did the low-grade and poorly paid jobs that kept Britain running. Seventy years on, we celebrate them. [...]

We also celebrate the accomplishments of those Windrush citizens who changed the shape of this country. A generation that brought us thinkers such as C. L. R. James, Stuart Hall and Paul Gilroy, without whom I[1] would never have been a politician. Their words gave me an understanding of my identity in Britain that no one else could, and a political voice to so many throughout this country. A generation like Benjamin Zephaniah, Andrea Levy and Zadie Smith – who have given us all evocative imagery of what it means to live in Britain today. Windrush gave this country Frank Bruno and Jessica Ennis: proud representatives of our country on the world stage.

1 David Lammy, the narrator born in London, is a Member of Parliament.

Mother Country: Real Stories of the Windrush Children,
Charlie Brinkhurst-Cuff, 2018

2 Strengthening links with Jamaica

A. Read the text and sum up the project initiated by Mayor Delroy Williams.
B. Say what the project may bring to both cities.

The Mayor of Kingston and St Andrew, Jamaica, has promised to increase his city's links to Bristol.

Mayor Delroy Williams says he is proud to see the success of Jamaica's diaspora in Bristol and is looking forward to strengthening economic and cultural ties between the two cities. [...] Mr Williams' comments were made at the close of the Global Parliament of Mayors conference, which was held in Bristol last week. [...] Speaking to *Bristol Live*, Mr Williams said: [...] "We have to connect with the Jamaican diaspora and Bristol has a strong Jamaican community, so it is part of my responsibility to connect with Jamaicans to encourage them and support them." [...]

Mr Rees[1] took the opportunity to say he "looks forward" to exploring a stronger relationship between Kingston and Bristol at the event.

"I first met Mayor Williams in Singapore when we were over there for the World Cities Summit. [...] I think there is a natural link [between Bristol and Jamaica] and not just for cultural benefits, but also economic. I really look forward to exploring those." Ms Craig[2] described the event as a "huge coup" for Bristol. "There are a lot of people who live in the city who come from Kingston and St Andrew who have family members there so he has shared his amazing vision for the city and has talked about trying to connect people in Jamaica and Bristol and how we can work together to look at investment opportunities."

1 Bristol Mayor • 2 Deputy Mayor

www.bristolpost.co.uk, 1 November 2018

3 Does Jamaica still need the Queen?

VIDEO N°07

A. Watch the video. On what occasion did Prince Harry go to Jamaica?
B. What is Jamaica's Prime Minister's position about the British monarchy?
C. Go further. What impact could the Prime Minister's position have on future relationships between Jamaica and the United Kingdom?

4 "Back to My Own Country"

A. Read the text with the help of Worksheet n°06.
B. What consequence did the writing course have on the narrator's life?
C. According to the narrator, how important is Jamaica to the United Kingdom?
D. Go further. Explain the last sentence in your own words.

I lived on a council estate in north London. I went to a local school. Spoke like a good cockney. I played outside with all the white kids who lived around my way – rounders, skipping and hide and seek. I ate a lot of sweets. Watched a lot of television [...] I lived the life of an ordinary London working-class girl.
But my parents had come to this country from Jamaica. [...] In my efforts to be as British as I could be, I was completely indifferent to Jamaica. None of my friends knew anything about the Caribbean. They didn't know where it was, or who lived there, or why. And they had no curiosity about it beyond asking why black people were in this country. It was too foreign and therefore not worth knowing. [...]
I had recently enrolled on an afternoon-a-week writing course at the City Lit in London, just as a hobby. Writing came to my rescue. The course had an emphasis on writing about what you know. So, nervously I began to explore what I knew – my family upbringing and background, and my complicated relationship with colour. [...] A few months into the course I had the urge to visit Jamaica for the very first time and stay with the family I had never met. I went for Christmas. It was an amazing experience. I discovered a family I had never really known I had. I realised that I meant something to people who lived on the other side of the world. I met my aunt and cousins and saw where my mum grew up. I realised for the first time that I had a background and an ancestry that was fascinating and worth exploring. Not only that, but I had the means to do it – through writing. [...] But there are still countless young Britons today of Afro-Caribbean descent who have as little understanding of their ancestry and have as little evidence of their worth as I did when I was growing up. And there are countless white Britons who are unaware of the histories that bind us together. Britain made the Caribbean that my parents came from. It provided the people – black and white – who make up my ancestry. In return my ancestors, through their forced labour and their enterprise, contributed greatly to the development of modern Britain. My heritage is Britain's story too. It is time to put the Caribbean back where it belongs – in the main narrative of British history.

"Back to My Own Country" in Six Stories and an Essay,
Andrea Levy, 2014

YOUR PROJECT

You are one of the passengers who came to Britain on the Windrush. Write a letter home to your family in Jamaica describing how people are treating you and what Britain is like compared to home.

HELP!

Nouns
- (cheap) workforce: *main-d'œuvre (bon marché)*
- hardships = difficulties

Adjectives
- economic
- strong-willed = determined

Verbs & Expressions
- be prejudiced against sth/sb
- discriminate against sth/sb
- fit in = adapt
- make a living
- start over
- overcome (obstacles)

SPICE UP YOUR VOCABULARY

Use the vocabulary below to create your own mind map and add more words if necessary!

Adjectives & Adverbs

- cultural /'kʌltʃərəl/
- deeply-rooted: *profondément ancré*
- economic /ekə'nɒmɪk/
- historical
- rebellious /rɪ'beliəs/ = defiant /dɪ'faɪənt/
- better off = preferable
- self-reliant
- inspirational
- outrageous /aʊt'reɪdʒəs/ = scandalous, revolting

Nouns

- bond: *lien*
- (the) Caribbean /kærə'biːən/
- citizen
- colonialism
- culture /'kʌltʃə/
- foreigner /'fɒrɪnə/: *étranger*
- hardship = difficulty
- heritage /'herətɪdʒ/
- homeland = motherland
- identity
- influence
- Jamaica /dʒə'meɪkə/
- obstacle /'ɒbstəkl/
- relationship
- tourism /'tʊərɪzəm/
- workforce: *main-d'œuvre*

Verbs & Expressions

- belong somewhere: *être à sa place qq part*
- contribute to sth
- discriminate against sb
- fit in = adapt
- fulfil one's dream = make one's dream come true
- grant rights to sb
- leave something behind
- make a living
- overcome (obstacles)
- pin one's hopes on sth/sb
- preserve (one's identity/traditions/culture)
- rebel /rɪ'bel/ against sth/sb
- stand up for sth = defend sth
- start over = start from scratch
- trade with sb = buy and sell

RULE THE GRAMMAR!

LA VOIX PASSIVE

- **Formation**

On utilise l'auxiliaire ***be*** et le verbe au participe passé.

Jamaica was granted independence in 1962.

- **Utilisation**

Le passif permet de mettre l'accent sur l'action plus que sur celui qui la fait (l'agent).

Comparez les deux phrases :

The English captured Jamaica from Spain in 1655. (voix active)

Jamaica was captured from Spain in 1655. (voix passive)

On peut toujours réintroduire l'agent, pour cela on utilise ***by***.

Jamaica was captured from Spain by the English in 1655.

→ P.316

LE *PRESENT PERFECT*

- **Formation**

Le *present perfect* se construit avec l'auxiliaire ***have*** au présent et le participe passé du verbe.

I / You / We	*have* + participe passé
He / She / It	*has* + participe passé

- **Utilisation**

On utilise le *present perfect* pour présenter le résultat dans le présent d'une action débutée dans le passé.

Jamaicans have managed to preserve their culture.

→ P.299

LANGUAGE LAB

- Audio words
- MP3
- Interactive Test

★ 1. Give synonyms of the words. Then, make a sentence for each one.

A. difficulties = ...
B. homeland = ...
C. adapt = ...
D. defend sth = ...
E. start over = ...
F. deny rights (to sb) ≠ ...

★ 2. Put the verbs in the present perfect (some past participles are irregular).

A. I ***(choose)*** Kingston for my summer holidays.
B. Jamaicans ***(not forget)*** their colonial past.
C. Andrea ***(not sing)*** reggae for months.
D. We ***(sail)*** from Kingston to Port-au-Prince.
E. Leroy ***(swim)*** along Yallahs Bay for thirty minutes.
F. You ***(decide)*** to visit Britain before going back home.

★★ 3. Match each word with its definition.

A. discriminate against B. deeply-rooted
C. colonialism D. trade E. foreigner

1. The policy by which a nation tries to extend its authority over other peoples or territories.
2. A person from another country.
3. To buy and sell.
4. The practice of treating one person or group differently from another in an unfair way.
5. Firmly implanted, fixed, or established.

★★ 4. Put the verbs in the appropriate tense (preterite or present perfect).

A. Since 1962, the island ***(develop)*** its own cultural specificities.
B. Jamaica ***(become)*** a hub of sugar production during the slave trade.
C. Reggae ***(be)*** always a battle cry for freedom.
D. In 1962, the Jamaican people ***(vote)*** for independence.
E. Bertha ***(love)*** the Caribbean islands since her first trip there.
F. The British flag ***(be lowered)*** yesterday morning.

★★★ 5. Translate the following sentences into English using the passive voice.

A. *Les Jamaïcains furent maltraités par les Anglais.*
B. *L'indépendance fut octroyée à la Jamaïque en 1962.*
C. *Les Jamaïcains sont souvent réduits* (pigeon-hole) *à l'image de chanteurs de reggae.*
D. *Les liens entre la couronne britannique et ses anciennes colonies sont compliqués.*

6. Interactive test! What is your score?

OPEN YOUR EARS!

PHONOLOGY

- **Écoutez le passage ci-dessous en faisant attention aux mots soulignés (non-accentués).**

MP3 N°05 | *They found that Britain was not as friendly to them as they had hoped.*

- **Écoutez le passage suivant en faisant attention aux syllabes accentuées (en gras).**

MP3 N°06 | *It was **cold** and **grey** and **Caribbean people** soon **experienced racism** and **discrimination**.*

- **Récapitulons.**

- En anglais, les **mots grammaticaux** sont généralement **non accentués** et leur voyelle est réduite (/ə/).
- Les **mots lexicaux** (noms, adjectifs, verbes, adverbes) quant à eux sont généralement **accentués**.

AUDIO MYSTERY

MP3 N°07

Listen to the recording and solve the mystery!

Picture challenge

★ 3 sentences
★★ 4 to 6 sentences
★★★ 7 sentences and +

How many sentences can you make using what you have learnt? Collect stars!

AXE 1

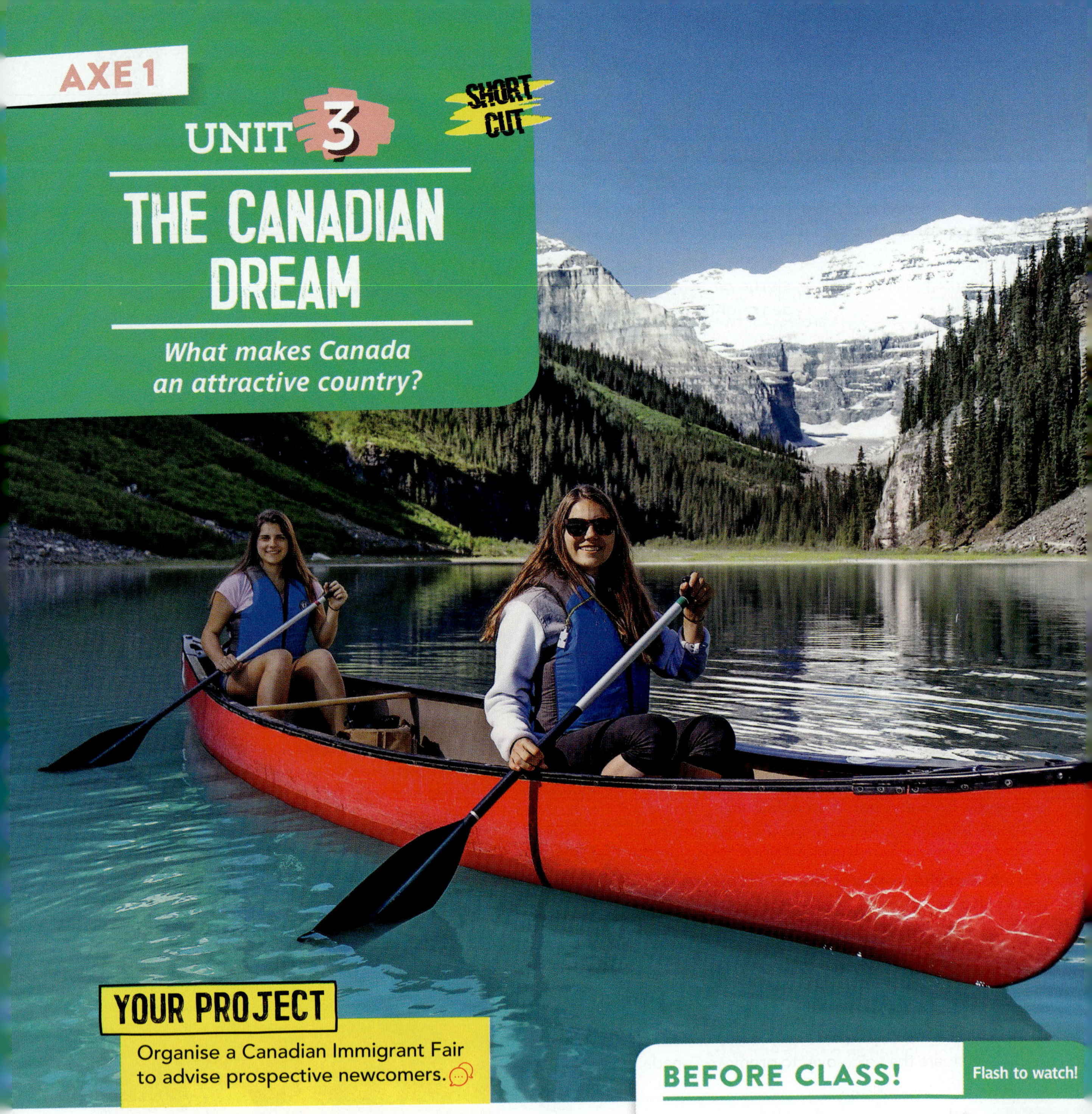

UNIT 3

SHORT CUT

THE CANADIAN DREAM

What makes Canada an attractive country?

YOUR PROJECT

Organise a Canadian Immigrant Fair to advise prospective newcomers.

BEFORE CLASS!

Flash to watch!

Watch the video and get ready to talk about it in class!

Au menu de cette unité :

DÉCOUVERTES CULTURELLES

- La politique en matière de tourisme
- L'importance d'attirer les étudiants étrangers
- L'offre de formules vacances-travail pour les étudiants
- Le choix d'une immigration sélective

OUTILS LINGUISTIQUES

- Les expressions du conseil et de la suggestion
- Les quantifieurs
- L'expression de l'intention (*I plan to, I intend to…*)
- Les adjectifs composés

❶ Destination Canada

How vital is tourism for Canada?

1 Visitors welcome!

A. Say what Canada is known for.

B. Explain Canada's project for tourism through its *Tourism Vision* plan.

C. Use figures to show that tourism is vital for the country.

D. Have your say. Say how important tourism is for Canada's national identity.

Tourism has always been a driving force in the building of Canada. [...] Today, tourism is a pillar of the Canadian economy, generating $102 billion in annual economic activity, 1.8 million jobs and accounting for over 2% of GDP. Since international visitors use foreign currency to buy Canadian services, tourism is Canada's largest service export, valued at over $22 billion in 2018 and close to 20% of all service export revenues. [...] Canada has built a powerful national brand, consistently ranking among the best countries on earth, with the highest quality of life, and topping the charts for happiness and inclusiveness. [...] Our dynamic, multicultural cities, like Calgary, Vancouver, Montreal and Toronto, are among the most liveable on the planet. [...] Beyond the metropolitan centres, Canada's smaller towns and communities offer their own singular experiences and attractions, including authentic Indigenous tourism experiences. They are also the gateways to globally famous national parks, heritage sites and the country's vast iconic wilderness.

The world is paying attention and coming to Canada in larger numbers than ever before, and from a widening range of countries. [...] That wave in tourism keeps rising with international visitation reaching a new height with the 150th anniversary of Confederation in 2017, only to be surpassed again in 2018 with over 21 million arrivals. [...] In 2017, the government released Canada's *Tourism Vision*, a plan to grow international visitation to Canada. Building on that vision, the new Minister of Tourism, Official Languages and La Francophonie was mandated in August 2018 to develop a federal Tourism Strategy to create tourism jobs for the middle class in communities across the country.

www.canada.ca

YOUR TURN!

2 Canada, a life-changing experience

VIDEO N°08

A. Watch the video and list the iconic images that make Canada attractive.

B. Prepare the voice-over to promote Canada through these images.

- Cut the video into parts and give a title to each one.
- For each part, prepare a script.

C. Practise several times and act out the voice-over.

HELP!

Nouns
- brand
- gateway /ˈgeɪtweɪ/
- heritage /ˈherɪtɪdʒ/
- inclusiveness /ɪnˈklu:sɪvnɪs/
- wilderness /ˈwɪldənɪs/

Adjectives
- iconic /aɪˈkɒnɪk/
- indigenous /ɪnˈdɪdʒɪnəs/

Verbs & Expressions
- account for /əˈkaʊnt/ = represent
- rank
- top the charts /tʃɑ:ts/ = come first
- welcome /ˈwelkəm/

❷ See Canada Before You're 30!

How beneficial are international students for Canada?

1 An international student speaks about her experience

A. Listen to **MP3 N°08**. Say what you learnt about Aishwarya Nair.

B. Explain why the University of Toronto is perfect for international students.

C. Have your say. How important are international students to improve foreign policies?

2 International students wanted!

Canada plans to attract more international students by expanding its presence overseas in an effort to advance classroom diversity and boost economic benefits that already amount to billions per year.

The economic effects of foreign students nearly doubled between 2010 and 2016, when they reached a total of $15.5 billion in Canada for everything from tuition fees to rent and groceries, according to a federal analysis.

To put that in perspective, the document says the sector supported nearly 170,000 jobs in 2016 and had greater economic impacts than Canada's exports of auto parts, aircraft and lumber.

[...] Canada has been an attractive place to study for years. In 2000, federal numbers show there were 122,665 valid study permits in Canada — a number that hit 572,415 last year for an increase of 467 per cent. Numbers compiled by Universities Canada say full-time international student enrolment at universities rose by about 15 per cent across Canada between 2017 and 2018.

[...] International Trade Minister Jim Carr said beyond the economic impacts, students from abroad often establish important, decades-long links with Canada.

"We believe that international students add value to our communities, that they experience Canada's fine institutions and take with them an appreciation of who we are as Canadians," Carr said in an interview. Denise Amyot, president and CEO of Colleges and Institutes Canada, said foreign students bring new perspectives that help their Canadian classmates better understand the world. Their higher tuition fees strengthen institutions and ensure a wider choice of programs are offered for all students, she added. [...]

She said immigration policy changes in Canada have helped it compete with other countries in attracting the world's increasingly mobile post-secondary students. The policies, she added, have sped up visa processing times, permitted foreign students to work in Canada while they study and improved a graduate's chance of obtaining permanent residency.

Andy Blatchford, ***www.globalnews.ca***, 14 April 2019

A. Give Canada's plan for its college education.

B. Explain the economic impact of college education in Canada (use figures).

C. Explain the social and cultural impacts international students have on Canada.

D. Say how immigration policies have helped develop post-secondary education.

E. Have your say. How profitable can post-secondary education be for the economy?

HELP!

Nouns
- oppor**tu**nity /ɒpə'tjuːnɪti/
- di**ver**sity /daɪ'vɜːsɪti/
- **be**nefit
- tuition fees /tju'ɪʃn 'fiːz/
- **stu**dy permit
- student en**rol**ment /ɪn'rəʊlmənt/
- **share** /ʃɛə/
- **po**licy /'pɒlɪsi/
- **life**style /'laɪfstaɪl/

Adjectives
- **pro**fitable /'prɒfɪtəbl/
- re**pu**ted /rɪ'pjuːtɪd/
- **fo**reign /'fɒrɪn/

Verbs
- **rise** by
- in**crease** by /ɪn'kriːs/
- **stren**gthen /'streŋθn/
- en**sure** /ɪn'ʃʊə/
- im**prove** /ɪm'pruːv/

3 Working Holiday Visa

VIDEO N°09

A. You are interested in an experience in Canada. While browsing the web you come across Claire's experience. Draw a mind map to select information.

B. Watch the video and split the tasks:

- **group A:** focus on Claire before she arrived (name, age, home country, current place of living, what she knew about Canada; reason for coming)
- **group B:** focus on how Claire ended up in Canada (agency, form of help, result, where she is now)
- **group C:** focus on Claire's contract (missions, work atmosphere and colleagues)
- **group D:** focus on how she feels about her experience (landscape ; human interaction)

C. Summarize: say if this experience makes you want to go to Canada or not. Justify.

4 WWOOFing Canada - essential tips from a host

A. Describe WWOOFing (definition, place of work, public targeted and motivations).

B. List the benefits of WWOOFing.

C. List advice given to future WWOOFers.

D. Have your say. Would you like to go WWOOFing? Why (not)?

WWOOF stands for World Wide Opportunities On Organic farms but it has become a general term. Many Canadian small farms, resorts and eco-businesses are dealing with WWOOFers.

[...] So you decided to volunteer on a ranch in Canada and WWOOFing is part of your travel plan. Working on Organic Farms is what you are looking for. You want to get away from the tourist route and experience the Canadian lifestyle and the culture.

[...] Who is WWOOFing Canada?

Most people who decide on WWOOFing Canada are college students spending a gap year abroad. Many still live at home in a protected environment, and now want to experience adventure. Spending money is limited, therefore WWOOFing seems attractive. Travelling in Canada can be expensive and WWOOFing is a great alternative and a money saver.

[...] You might argue that you work for free, that I don't pay you. I disagree, you don't work for free. You get to enjoy the comfort of my home, accommodation, and meals, how much is this worth? Check out accommodation and food prices and minimum wage in Canada and calculate the hours you have to work to make it fair.

[...] Farmers work hard and long hours, and if you want to team up with us, make sure you do your part. My hard-working WWOOFers were always rewarded with trips to rodeos, shopping trips, a day at a horse auction, hiking in the mountains, and lots more.

[...] Fit in and act like you are part of the team. It might be a culture shock first but might turn into the best travel experience ever.

Don't get annoyed if plans change daily, that's farm life. Farm work is mostly dirty, physical work, and you might not be used to it. Give your best and you will learn a lot and gain the respect of the host. Just think about all the stories you will have to tell when you get back home.

[...] All I can say now, enjoy, and tell me about your WWOOFing Canada experience when you get back!

www.backcountrycanadatravel.com, 28 January 2018

HELP!

Nouns
- accommodation /əkɒmə'deɪʃn/
- culture shock
- gap year
- hospitality /hɒspɪ'tælɪti/
- working holidays

Adjectives
- amazing /ə'meɪzɪŋ/
- awesome /'ɔ:səm/
- fair = just
- phenomenal /fɪ'nɒmɪnl/

Verbs & Expressions
- get the most out of
- provide /prə'vaɪd/ with
- reward /rɪ'wɔ:rd/
- team up with
- volunteer /vɒlən'tɪə/

❸ Selective Immigration

How does Canada boost its attractivity through selective immigration?

1 Recruiting skilled immigrant workers

A. Explain the figures of labour migrations in Canada.
B. Say what Express Entry is and why it is important.
C. Give other reasons for Canada's success.

D. Go further. How important is chosen immigration for both Canada and its immigrants?

Canada has not only the largest in terms of numbers, but also the most elaborate and longest-standing skilled labour migration system in the OECD. Largely as a result of many decades of managed labour migration, more than one in five people in Canada is foreign-born, one of the highest shares in the OECD. 60% of Canada's foreign-born population are highly educated, the highest share OECD-wide. The recent introduction of Express Entry, a two-step selection system based on an initial pre-screening of suitable candidates who enter a pool by Expression of Interest and subsequent selection of the most skilled candidates from the pool, has further enhanced the competitive edge of the selection system relative to other countries. It also ensures that those with the skills to succeed are admitted to Canada in a quick and efficient way. Core to Canada's success is not only the elaborate selection system itself, but also the innovation and infrastructure around it, which ensures constant testing, monitoring and adaptation of its parameters. This includes a comprehensive and constantly improving data infrastructure, coupled with the capacity to analyse it, and swift policy reaction to new evidence and emerging challenges.

www.OECD.org

Immigrants' top countries of origin (now permanent residents in Canada) in 2019

India	80, 685
China, People's Republic of	28, 560
Philippines	26, 200
Nigeria	11, 715
United States of America	10, 135
Pakistan	10, 075
Syria	9, 700
Eritrea	6, 555
Korea, Republic of	5, 765
Iran	5, 605
United Kingdom and Overseas Territories	5, 280
Brazil	5, 025
France	4, 500
Iraq	4, 330
Vietnam	3, 965

Percentage of immigrants to Canada by period of immigration

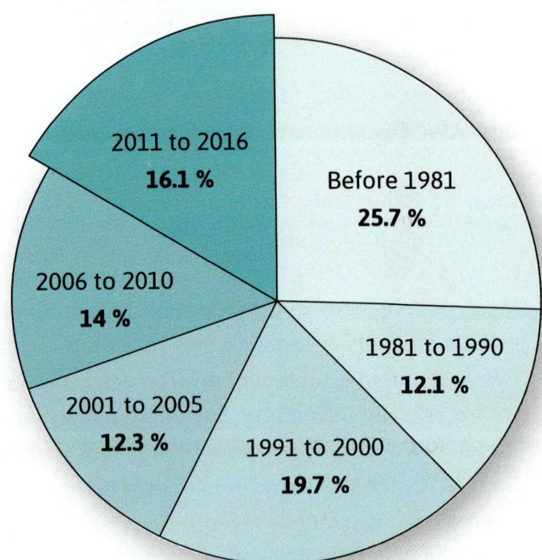

Statcan.gc.ca/census

HELP!

Nouns
- interview
- selection system
- selective immigration

Adjectives
- foreign-born
- managed
- skilled
- suitable /ˈsuːtəbl/

Verb
- recruit /rɪˈkruːt/

YOUR PROJECT

Organise a Canadian Immigrant Fair to advise prospective immigrants. Invite civil servants from the immigration and tourism services, former immigrants who share their experiences, and newcomers.

LANGUAGE LAB

- Unit's vocabulary
- Audio words
- MP3
- Interactive Test

★ 1. Fill in the blanks with *much, many, less* or *fewer*.

A. They welcome ... more students than they used to.
B. There are ... Americans in Canada than I expected. I didn't meet any!
C. There is ... snow in Vancouver than ten years ago.
D. Our presents were ... appreciated.
E. There are ... and ... caribous in British Columbia. It is an endangered species!

★ 2. Match these adjectives with their synonyms.

A. awesome	1. qualified
B. profitable	2. beneficial
C. skilled	3. terrific
D. suitable	4. appropriate

★★ 3. Put the verbs in the appropriate tense (preterite or present perfect).

A. Immigration figures *(increase)* in 2020.
B. Canada *(be)* an attractive place to study for decades.
C. In 2006, foreign students *(make up)* a 4% share of enrolment in the college system.
D. WWOOFing *(become)* very popular recently.
E. Obtaining a holiday visa never *(be)* easier.
F. The introduction of Express Entry *(enhance)* the competitive edge of the selection system.

★★ 4. Fill in the sentences with the words below.

attract • improve • expand • grow • strengthen

A. Canada also plans to ... its global image by offering quality hospitality to its visitors.
B. Through hospitality Canada intends to ... its global influence.
C. Moreover, the country will ... international students.
D. These international students will in turn ... the links with foreign countries.
E. Good foreign relations are important because they make a country ... .

★★★ 5. Translate into English.

A. *J'ai l'intention d'aller visiter le Grand Lac de l'Ours.*
B. *Si tu veux aller au Canada, tu devrais te renseigner sur les conditions d'entrée dans le pays pour les étudiants.*
C. *Pourquoi ne pas essayer la formule du WWOOFing ?*
D. *Au Canada, la distance la plus grande d'est en ouest est de 5 514 km.*
E. *Toronto est la ville canadienne la plus peuplée avec 5 429 524 habitants.*

6. Interactive test! What is your score?

OPEN YOUR EARS!

PHONOLOGY

1. Les pourcentages

• Lisez les chiffres suivants et vérifiez votre prononciation à l'aide de l'enregistrement. Attention, *percent* est accentué sur la deuxième syllabe /pə'sent/. De même, *percentage* se prononce /pə'sentɪdʒ/ (avec réduction de la voyelle finale).

MP3 N°09 | 25% • 63% • 34%

2. Les chiffres

• En anglais, les chiffres après le point se lisent individuellement contrairement au français.
Ex : 23.34 se lit « *twenty-three point three four* » (et non *thirty four*).

• Lisez ces chiffres et vérifiez votre prononciation.

MP3 N°10 | 3.345 • 2.45 • 63.345 • 7.87

• Attention à ne pas confondre les points et les virgules.
- 0,25 en français équivaut à 0.25 en anglais (le point remplace la virgule).
On dira « zéro vingt-cinq » en français mais « *zero point two five* » en anglais.
- 3 019 en français équivaut à 3,019 en anglais.
On dira « trois mille dix-neuf » en français et « *three thousand and nineteen* » en anglais.

• Pour l'heure et la monnaie :
- 3h45 se dit *three forty-five* ou *quarter to four.*
- £3.20 se dit *three pound(s) twenty.*

Quote challenge

★ 3 sentences
★★ 4 to 6 sentences
★★★ 7 sentences and +

Which quote best sums up what you have learnt? Justify.

"There is no such thing as a model or ideal Canadian. What could be more absurd than the concept of an "all Canadian" boy or girl? A society which emphasizes uniformity is one which creates intolerance and hate."

Pierre Trudeau, Former Prime Minister of Canada

"To be complex does not mean to be fragmented. This is the paradox and the genius of our Canadian civilization."

Adrienne Clarkson, Former Governor General

B1-B2

BACKPACK

Get Ready for your Exam!

UNIT 1 Évaluation

Compréhension de l'oral

"Leaving our land" MP3 n°11

Listen to the audio recording three times and recap what you have understood.

Expression écrite

Choisissez l'un des deux sujets (min. 120 mots).

Question A : An Amish man/woman is interviewed on the necessity to open up to the outside world. Imagine the interview.

Question B : Taking into account the subject of the recording, what consequences could it have on the Amish traditions and way of life?

UNIT 2 Évaluation

Compréhension de l'oral

"Celebrating Jamaica's Independence" MP3 n°12 VIDEO N°52

Listen to the audio recording three times and recap what you have understood.

Expression écrite

Choisissez l'un des deux sujets (min. 120 mots).

Question A : You have heard about the Jamaican festival in Birmingham. You write an email to a friend, asking him/her to join you to attend the festival, and convincing him/her that it is worth the visit.

Question B : Discuss the following statement:
"A festival is the best way to preserve and pass down the national or regional culture and heritage."

UNIT 3 Évaluation

Compréhension de l'oral

"What is guiding immigrants to Canada today?" MP3 n°13

Listen to the audio recording three times and recap what you have understood.

Expression écrite

Choisissez l'un des deux sujets (min. 120 mots).

Question A : As a young Australian immigrant to Canada, you write an article on your travel blog describing your first days in your host country.

Question B : Would you like to move to Canada for a few weeks, a few months or to settle there?

UNIT 1 Évaluation

Can the Amish resist the modern world?

Daniel Weaver does not vote, drive a car, read a paper, listen to music, watch sport of any kind, own a mobile phone or use a computer. But as we eat the food grown in his garden outside the window, he confesses that he did once see a film. He refuses to disclose what, brushing aside my questions as we sit talking around the dining table with his wife, five of his eight children and one grandson. […]
But this one-off incident, many years ago, speaks to the reasons why this 52-year-old sold his thriving Ohio clothing business, one that supplied hundreds of stores across North America, and moved his family to this idyllic farm in upstate New York three years ago. Daniel is Amish […] and he fears the impact of modernity and the temptations of technology on his children, his church and his traditional Christian world. […]
That evening, Daniel asks me to join his household for dinner, an unusual invitation. But the meal is punctuated by laughter, as the Weavers describe a way of life that revolves around faith, family and work. "I feel you can be trusted, so you are sitting at my table," Daniel says. "But on a friendship level, our values are very different. We would not want to mix with you, because if our children came to your home, they might sit and watch television."
[…] The Amish began emigrating to America in the 18th century, mostly settling in Pennsylvania. In the 1930s, they came to wider attention and were romanticised for resisting moves to shut down the small schools their children attended. Later generations have found other aspects of their lifestyle to admire: in the 60s, counterculture rebels looked to them as off-grid pioneers; in the 80s, they were celebrated for their traditional craft skills; more recently, it's been their long tradition of organic farming, with branded grocers opening in New York City. […]
They may use a horse and buggy for trips into town, clip-clopping along the roads alongside thundering trucks, but the Amish will take taxis and trains when needed. I am surprised to learn that both Sam and Daniel have flown abroad, to places such as Guatemala and Haiti for charity work. Daniel explains that the Amish reject many modern items for fear of assimilation. So they do not own cars, for instance, because the machines detach people from their extended families too easily and can create envy. […]
"The smartphone is a threat to the Amish not only for the darker aspects of the Internet, such as access to pornography, but also for the way it can change the way we behave," says Erik Wesner, founder of the authoritative Amish America website. "We have all got quickly used to finding instant solutions online. These can erode traditional values that the Amish revere, such as patience and dependence upon their community. And unlike a car or pickup truck, a smartphone is easily hidden."

Ian Birrell, *www.theguardian.com*, 15 December 2018

Compréhension de l'écrit

Answer the following questions in English, using your own words.

A. After reading the text, what can you say about:
- its main topic?
- the people involved?
- their opinions on the topic?

B. Comment on the last paragraph (l. 25-29) and say if you share this point of view.

Expression écrite

Choisissez l'un des deux sujets (min. 120 mots).

Question A : Write the conversation between Daniel Weaver and the narrator using the following sentence as a prompt:
"I feel you can be trusted, so you are sitting at my table, but on a friendship level, our values are very different. We would not want to mix with you, because if our children came to your home, they might sit and watch television."

Question B : Would you say that the Amish way of life is the new trend? Why (not)?

B1-B2

BACKPACK

Get Ready for your Exam!

U. 2 U. 3

Évaluation

Document A

London is one of the most diverse cities in the world. It's home to global citizens from all over the world—making it a truly international city. It's also home to more than 800,000 British Jamaicans, those who were born in Jamaica or who are of Jamaican descent. Brixton, a multiethnic community in south London, has become an enclave for many Jamaicans. (Jamaica was a British colony between 1655 and 1962.) Over the years, Brixton has become the spot where Jamaicans can find everything that reminds them of home—spices, music and culture.

Jamaican-owned clothing boutiques, record shops and restaurants have opened all over the area. […]. The Brixton Market, a community street market, is lined with vendors blasting the latest hits coming out of Jamaica. The market has played such a major role in embracing London's Caribbean cultural experience that in 2010 it was awarded heritage protection. (That means it'll never be converted into high-rise, luxury condos!) Once a crime-riddled and troubled neighborhood, Brixton has undergone redevelopment and is quickly becoming a popular destination for tourists. Many are concerned that the heartbeat of the Caribbean community will lose the flair that's made it a home away from home for many. But projects such as Great Brixton and Our Brixton pledge to keep the community diverse and true to its original mission. Brixton will always be London's "little Jamaica."

www.islandoutpost.com

Document B

Any Canadian who has ever travelled abroad knows we're identifiable by our accents, polite manners and for saying sorry all the time. […] The first Canadians, including the Inuit and the multitudes of Aboriginal First Nations, were a diverse group settling in Canada […].

After the Second World War, politicians […] started introducing positive immigration policies in Canada. This made sense, as Canada had always been a country built upon immigration starting nearly 15,000 years ago […]. Canada's Indigenous peoples are the truest Old Stock Canadians.

Today, immigrants […] arrive in Canada from Asia, Africa, Latin America, Europe and elsewhere. According to the 2016 census, about 22 per cent of Canadians have said they were either landed or permanent residents. The majority of these new Canadians haven't posed a threat to the notion of Canadian identity, nor have they negatively affected the country's societal fabric […]. The majority of our immigrants try to assimilate, but they also might follow practises from the old country just as our British and European ancestors did after arriving in Canada years ago. […] Far from being drains upon civilization, Canada's immigrants […] have brought capital, new businesses and creativity in different forms to a country initially settled by immigrants thousands of years earlier via a land bridge stretching from Siberia into Alaska.

Dan Archer, *Assiniboia Times*, 27 September 2019

Compréhension de l'écrit

Answer the following questions in English, using your own words.

Document A

A. After reading the text, answer the following questions:
- what is the main topic?
- how important is the city of Brixton for the Jamaican community and for tourists?
- what do some people fear might happen to Brixton in the coming years?

B. Comment on the following sentence: "Brixton will always be London's 'little Jamaica'." (l. 27-28)

Document B

A. After reading the text, what can you say about:
- its main topic?
- immigrants and what they can bring to the country?
- the 2016 census figures?

B. What makes Canada a multicultural country?

Documents A et B

To what extent do these two texts illustrate the notion of "Identity and exchanges"?

Expression écrite

Choisissez l'un des deux sujets (min. 120 mots).

Question A :
Write a letter to one of your friends or relatives in which you talk him/her into spending a few months in Brixton or in Canada.

Question B :
Would you be ready to leave everything behind and start a new life in a foreign country? Why (not)?

Évaluation

Observe the documents. According to you, which document best illustrates "Identity and exchanges"?

UNIT 1

a "We may not have computers or telephones or television, but we have books and conversations. And we talk to each other in person, not through e-mails and texts."

Nancy Grossman,
A World Away, 2012

b "Even among the Amish, other Amish seem odd."

Ira Wagler,
Growing Up Amish, 2012

c

UNIT 2

a "There are strong ties between hundreds of thousands of people in the Caribbean and the United Kingdom and we should invest more in our relationship for the benefit of all those people and more."

David Cameron,
Former British Prime Minister (2015)

b

UNIT 3

a "Multiculturalism is at the heart of Canada's heritage and identity — and as Canadians, we recognize that our differences make us strong".

Prime Minister of Canada **Justin Trudeau,**
Canadian Multiculturalism Day, 27 June 2017, Ottawa

b "Canada is not a melting pot. Canada is an association of peoples who have, and cherish, great differences but who work together because they can respect themselves and each other."

Charles Vincent Massey (1887-1967),
former Governor General of Canada

Sylvia Earle, American marine biologist and explorer (1935-)

AXE 2

Private Space & Public Space

AXE 2

UNIT 4

THE VIRGIN QUEEN

To what extent was Elizabeth I a modern woman?

YOUR PROJECT

Participate in a radio show entitled "Queen, Woman, Warrior".

BEFORE CLASS!

Flash to watch!

Watch the trailer for Shekar Kapur's ***Elizabeth***. Be ready to talk about it in class!

Au menu de cette unité :

DÉCOUVERTES CULTURELLES

- L'Angleterre des Tudors
- Le destin d'Elizabeth I, femme monarque
- Le célibat, un choix privé et public

OUTILS LINGUISTIQUES

- Structures de l'obligation
- Le *pluperfect*
- Les deux prétérits

❶ Bastard, Lady, Princess

What was young Elizabeth's status at the Tudor court?

1 "You can never be a king"

A. Groupwork. Read the text. Focus on the characters (description, feelings, relationships). **Group A** focuses on Henry VIII and **Group B** on Elizabeth. Report your findings to the class.

B. Explain Henry's change of behaviour.

C. Go further. Use the text to guess what women's position used to be at court.

Her earliest memories were of her father. Her big, magnificent father, King Harry the Eighth, the most wonderful being in the world. It was Elizabeth's greatest grief[1] that she did not see him very often. The rare occasions on which he visited her at Hatfield were the most exciting days of all. God-like in his rich velvets and furs, his jewels and chains, he would chuck her under the chin, swing her up in the air and whirl her around, she shrieking with delight her beribboned[2] cap askew[3] and her long red tresses flying.

'How does my little Bessy?' he would enquire. 'Are they keeping you hard at your books and your prayers, or do they let you out to play as often as they should?' And he would wink conspiratorially, so that Elizabeth could know that it was alright to say yes, she did spend a lot of time playing, and that she loved the latest doll or toy he had sent her.

'But I do learn my letters, Sir, and my catechism,' she would tell him.

'Well and good, well and good,' he would say, pulling her onto his wide lap[4] and sitting her on strong muscular thighs, with her cheek against the brilliant rough surface of his doublet, which was encrusted with gems and goldsmiths' work. She would breathe in the wholesome smell of him, a smell of herbs, musky perfume and the great outdoors, and nestle against him, enjoying the sensation of his bristly red beard tickling the top of her forehead.

'I will tell you something, Bessy,' he said once. 'When I was a young king, I did not wish to be at my prayers or attending to state affairs; I wanted to enjoy life. So can you guess what I did? I would sneak out of the palace by a back stair and go hunting, and my councilors would never know I had gone.'

'Didn't you get into trouble?' Elizabeth posited, wide-eyed.

'Hah!' roared her father. 'I am the King. They would never have dared[5]!'

'Can you do what you like when you are King?' she asked, a whole new vista of freedom opening up in her mind.

'Of course I can,' her father replied. 'People have to do my will[6].' There was an edge to his voice that, young as she was, she missed.

'Then,' she told him, 'I am going to be King when I grow up.'

She had not understood at the time why this angered him. Suddenly, he was no longer her loving father, but a man of steel, cold of visage and inexplicably cross[7]. Without a word, he put her from him, setting her none-too-gently on the floor, and drew himself up to his towering height, a big bulk of a man, powerful and daunting[8].

'You can never be a king,' he told her, in a voice as quiet as it was menacing. 'Until you have a brother, you are my heir, but it is against Nature and the law of God for a woman to rule, so enough of such foolishness, for I will have a son to succeed me!' Then he was gone, his broad figure disappearing through the oak door of the nursery. But he had been back to visit her since, as cheery and as boisterous[9] as if nothing had upset him. She had understood by that that his rages were but passing storms.

1 chagrin • 2 enrubanné • 3 de travers • 4 genoux • 5 oser • 6 volonté • 7 fâché • 8 intimidant • 9 plein d'entrain

The Lady Elizabeth,
Alison Weir, 2008

2 The neglected princess

A. Read the text on Worksheet n°07 to find out more about the way Elizabeth was treated.

B. How was young Elizabeth considered by Henry VIII?

C. Why was she deprived of her title?

HELP!
- well-behaved / well-educated
- be considered (as)
- isolated from
- removed from
- stripped of = deprived of
- turn away from

❷ The Warrior Queen

How did Elizabeth I become a powerful Queen?

1 Heirs to the throne

A. Observe the family tree on Worksheet n°08.
Focus on Elizabeth's siblings.

B. What was Elizabeth's position in the line of succession?

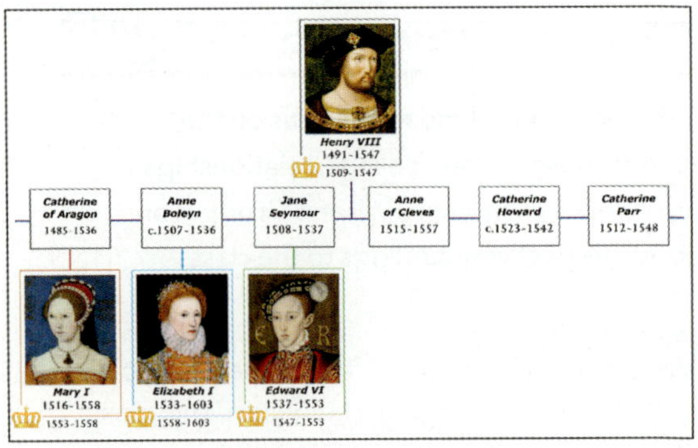

2 Queen against all odds

A. Read the text. Orally, recap the main events that led to Elizabeth's coronation.

B. Focus on lines 25-27. What is the relationship between the young Queen and her people?

The Coronation portrait, c. 1600

At the age of 13, Elizabeth's father, Henry VIII died and her younger half-brother, Edward, became King. Elizabeth joined the household of her stepmother, Catherine Parr, and received an excellent education. Elizabeth lived there until she was banished because she had been caught in an embrace with Catherine's husband, Thomas Seymour. Catherine then died in 1548 during childbirth and Thomas Seymour was executed for plotting to marry Elizabeth and kidnap the King, Edward VI. Elizabeth was questioned by the authorities but stated that she was innocent, and she was able to evade prosecution. Edward died an early death in 1553 and Elizabeth's older sister Mary I became Queen. Mary reestablished Catholicism and executed 287 Protestants, earning her the nickname of "Bloody Mary." When Mary planned to marry the Catholic Prince Phillip of Spain, Protestants rebelled unsuccessfully. Elizabeth was interrogated about her involvement and then imprisoned in the Tower of London. She was eventually placed under house arrest in Woodstock, Oxfordshire.

After Mary died, Elizabeth ascended to the throne at the age of 25. She inherited the country at a time when it was facing religious strife, and Elizabeth knew that she needed to gain the public's support in order to remain queen. The celebrations for her coronation were spectacular with a procession taking her through London on the way to Westminster, allowing her to receive flowers and congratulations from the ordinary people on the street.

www.bbc.co.uk

HELP!

- although / despite, in spite of sth / even though
- escape a terrible fate
- unexpected: *inattendu*
- embody: *incarner*

3 The kingdom at stake

A. Observe the poster. What can you guess about the context and Elizabeth's role in it?

B. Read the ***Cultural fact***. Use the information you have gathered to present the poster aloud.

Cultural fact

In the late 16th century, Spain was the most powerful empire in the known world. Spain's king, Philip II, ruled much of the New World and much of western Europe. Worst of all, England was now a Protestant nation. When Elizabeth I executed the Catholic Mary Queen of Scots in 1587, Philip was personally angered and, wanting England for himself, decided to invade.

www.bbc.co.uk

4 "The heart and stomach of a king"

A. Listen to Elizabeth's speech on **MP3 N°14**.
What is Elizabeth's intention when she addresses the soldiers?

B. Read the speech. Analyse the way she represents herself.

C. Go further. Why was it an effective speech? Justify.

D. Have your say. Is the nickname "Warrior Queen" relevant? Use elements from the speech to justify your answer.

HELP!

Verbs & Expressions

- address someone
- be determined = be strong-willed
- sacrifice oneself
- galvanise
- wage war against sth/sb
- make war on / to go to war with

My loving people,

We have been persuaded by some that are careful of our safety, to take heed[1] how we commit ourselves to armed multitudes, for fear of treachery[2]; but I assure you I do not desire to live to distrust my faithful and loving people. Let tyrants fear. I have always so behaved myself that, under God, I have placed my chiefest strength and safeguard in the loyal hearts and good-will of my subjects; and therefore I am come amongst you, as you see, at this time, not for my recreation and disport, but being resolved, in the midst and heat of the battle, to live and die amongst you all; to lay down for my God, and for my kingdom, and my people, my honour and my blood, even in the dust.

I know I have the body of a weak, feeble woman; but I have the heart and stomach of a king, and of a king of England too, and think foul scorn[3] that Parma or Spain, or any prince of Europe, should dare to invade the borders of my realm; to which rather than any dishonour shall grow by me, I myself will take up arms, I myself will be your general, judge, and rewarder of every one of your virtues in the field. [...] We shall shortly have a famous victory over these enemies of my God, of my kingdom, and of my people.

Queen Elizabeth I,
Speech to the troops at Tilbury (Essex), 19 August 1588

1 pay close attention to • 2 betrayal • 3 *mépris*

YOUR TURN! 5 Step into the Queen's armour

Listen to this short extract from Elizabeth's speech above on **MP3 N°15**.
Learn it by heart and practise delivering it as if you were the Queen.
You can make a video at home or act it out in front of the class.

❸ Married to England

Was Elizabeth's personal choice to remain unmarried a political one?

1 The Virgin Queen

A. Groupwork.

- **Group A reads text 1:** What characterises Elizabeth I's reign?
- **Group B reads text 2:** Pick out the reasons why Elizabeth chose to remain unmarried (personal and political).
- Share your findings with the other groups.

B. Go further. Read the text about Elizabeth's legacy on Worksheet n°09. Orally, recap what characterises the Elizabethan era. Why is it called the "Golden Age"?

C. Have your say. To what extent can Elizabeth I be considered a modern woman?

Text 1

Despite her fading power at the end of her reign, Elizabeth still showed her devotion to her people. She gave one of her most famous speeches in 1601 to Parliament. During what is referred to as her "Golden Speech", a self-reflective Elizabeth seemed to look back on her long reign. "Of myself I must say this, I was never any greedy, scraping grasper, nor a strait, fast-holding prince, nor yet a waster. My heart was never set on worldly goods but for my subjects' good."

While the end of her reign had been difficult, Elizabeth is largely remembered as a queen who supported her people. Her lengthy time on the throne provided her subjects with stability and consistency. Her political acumen, sharp wit and clever mind helped navigate the nation through many religious, social and governmental challenges.

Elizabeth never married or had children; she seemed to have no interest in sharing power with a spouse. Over time, she cultivated her image as a queen married to her job and her people, earning her the nickname the "Virgin Queen".

Adapted from ***www.biography.com***

Text 2

"I WILL never marry," the future Elizabeth I declared at the age of eight, and, to the consternation of her subjects, the Great Queen kept her word. She even promoted the cult of virginity that was to form the substance of her legend. [...] In her own day, her decision to remain single was considered absurd and dangerous. A queen needed a husband to make political decisions for her and to organise and lead her military campaigns. More important, she needed male heirs to avoid a civil war between rival claimants after her death.

Although she insisted that she preferred the single state, she kept [her] suitors in a state of permanent expectation. [It] was a deliberate policy on the Queen's part, since by keeping foreign princes in hope, sometimes for a decade, she kept them friendly when they might otherwise have made war on her realm.

There were other, deeper reasons for Elizabeth's reluctance to marry, chief of which, I believe, was her fear of losing her autonomy as Queen. In the 16th century, a sovereign was regarded as holding supreme dominion over the state, while a husband was deemed to hold supreme dominion over his wife. Elizabeth knew that marriage and motherhood would bring some erosion of her power. "I will have but one mistress here and no master," she told the Earl of Leicester, the man she loved more than any other and to whom she was close for over 30 years.

She once pointed out that marriage seemed too uncertain a state for her. She had seen several unions in her immediate family break down, including that of her own parents. Elizabeth was far too intelligent to compromise herself. The choice she made was courageous and revolutionary, and, in the long run, the right one for England.

Adapted from ***The Independent***, 2008

YOUR PROJECT

Participate in a radio show for the BBC entitled "Queen, Woman, Warrior": prepare a two-minute recording to present Elizabeth I, using what you have learnt.

LANGUAGE LAB

- Unit's vocabulary
- Audio words
- MP3
- Interactive Test

★ **1. Find the word that corresponds to each definition.**

A. An illegitimate child. → ...

B. The ceremony at which someone is officially made king or queen. → ...

C. The period when someone is king or queen. → ...

D. The person who inherits a property or title of another person when they die. → ...

★★ **2. Re-write these sentences as shown in the example.**

E.g.: *She got up early every day.* → *She would get up early every day.*

A. The king killed and massacred his enemies ruthlessly.

B. The courtiers paid their respects every day.

C. The bishop went to the Palace every day to see the king.

D. We worked hard every day to please our mistress.

★★ **3. Choose between the preterite and the preterite *be* + *-ing*.**

A. The suitors *(court)* her wholeheartedly while she *(keep)* them hoping.

B. We *(plot)* against the king when we *(realise)* we would be executed if it *(come)* out.

C. He *(think)* about the future Queen when it *(dawn)* on him he *(can)* devise a cunning plot.

D. Ordinary folks *(go)* through a difficult time when the Queen *(give)* her 1601 speech.

E. Elizabeth *(contemplate)* marrying him when she *(realise)* she *(prefer)* to concentrate on the future of her country.

★★ **4. Complete the text with the words below.**

leader • Golden Age • upbringing • downgraded • beheaded • succession

Elizabeth had a tough ... . Her father had her mother ... when she was 2 years old. Then she was removed from the line of ... . She also had her title ... from 'Princess' to 'Lady'. Today she is remembered as a cunning and ruthless ... as any king who came before her. Her reign is known as the ... .

★★★ **5. Choose between the preterite and the *pluperfect*.**

A. Elizabeth *(be)* Queen for ten years when she *(decide)* she would never marry.

B. She *(persuade)* her people they *(be)* betrayed by the foreign Prince.

C. Elizabeth *(execute)* Mary Queen of Scots because she *(be)* disloyal.

D. Alfred *(be)* a traitor. He *(conspire)* against the Crown for years.

6. Interactive test! What is your score?

OPEN YOUR EARS!

PHONOLOGY

Règles d'accentuation des verbes

Quand un verbe commence par un préfixe du type *re-*, *de-*, *in-*, *im-*, *ex-* ou *a-*, on accentue la deuxième syllabe.

Ex : *demand, expect, impose*

- Si le verbe ne commence pas un préfixe de ce type, on accentue la première syllabe.

Ex : *welcome, open, bargain*

Écoutez les verbes suivants et classez-les dans le tableau ci-dessous.

MP3 N°16 | *reply • banish • enquire • return • sacrifice • imprison • decide • galvanize • conquer • vanquish*

Verbes accentués sur la première syllabe	Verbes accentués sur la deuxième syllabe
...	...

SHOWTIME

Say it like the model!

MP3 N°17 |
/I my/self will take up/arms,
/I my/self will be your/general,
/judge, and re/warder of every one
of your/virtues in the/field.

Imitez la détermination de la locutrice en vous appuyant sur le rythme extrêmement régulier de cette phrase. Chaque syllabe qui suit / doit être accentuée avec force. Notez l'anaphore et son accentuation particulière (*/I, my/self*).

Quote challenge

★ 3 sentences
★★ 4 to 6 sentences
★★★ 7 sentences and +

Which quote best sums up what you have learnt? Justify.

"Though the sex to which I belong is considered weak you will nevertheless find a rock that bends to no wind."

Elizabeth I, Queen of England (1533-1603)

"You may have many a wiser prince sitting in this seat, but you never have had, or shall have, any who loves you better."

Elizabeth I, Queen of England (1533-1603)

AXE 2

UNIT 5

TAKE SHELTER!

Why is survivalism so deeply rooted in American society?

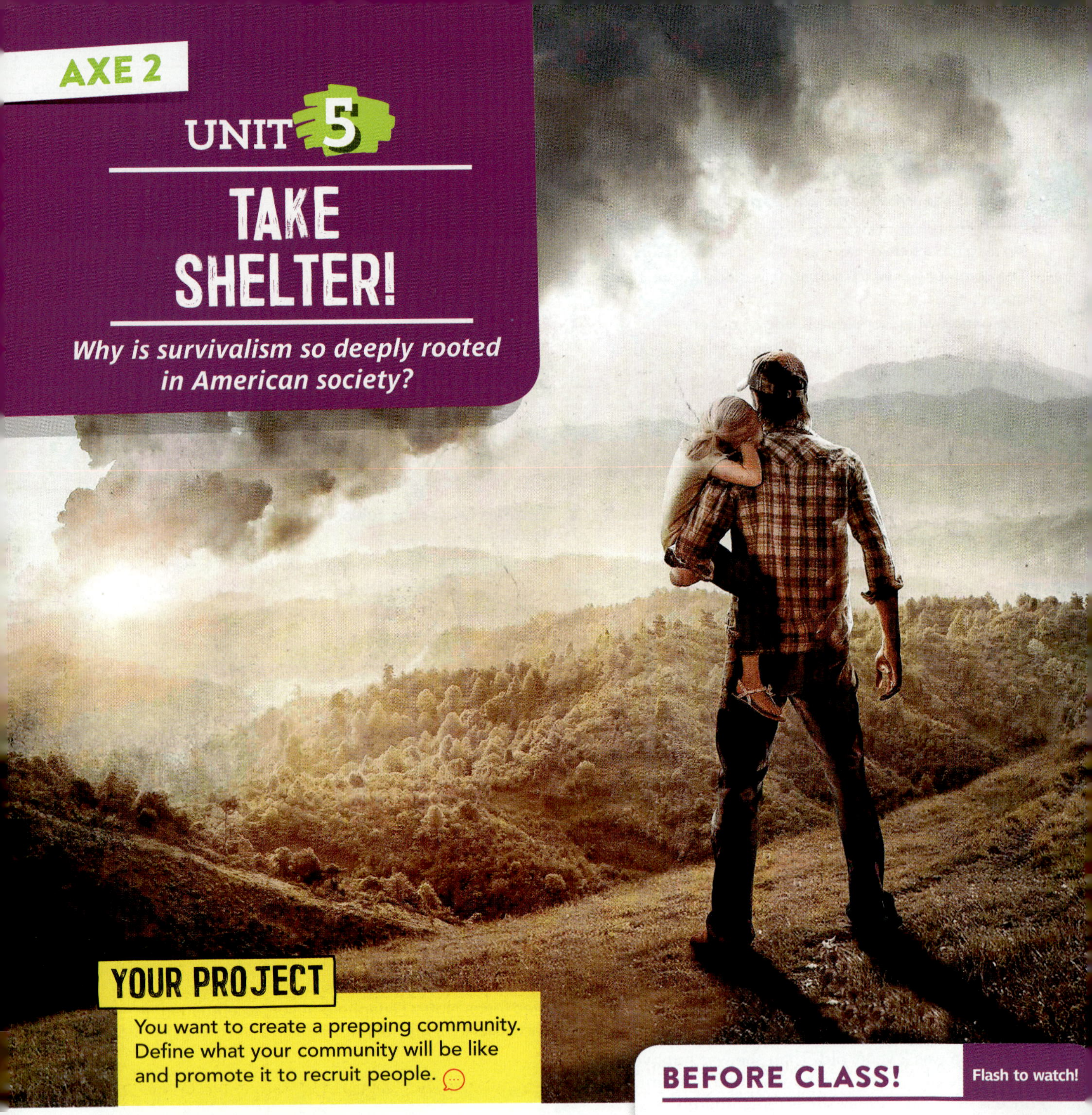

YOUR PROJECT

You want to create a prepping community. Define what your community will be like and promote it to recruit people.

BEFORE CLASS!

Flash to watch!

Watch the video. Be ready to talk about it in class!

VIDEO N°10

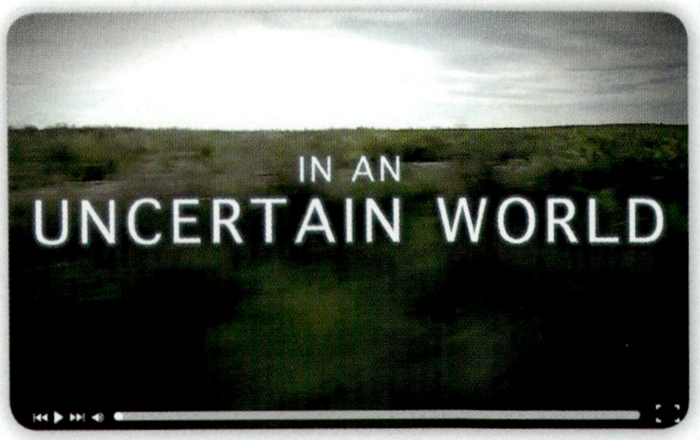

Au menu de cette unité :

DÉCOUVERTES CULTURELLES

- Les origines du survivalisme aux États-Unis
- L'agence gouvernementale FEMA
- La communauté Vivos
- La retraite dans la nature (H. D. Thoreau)
- Les univers post-apocalyptiques en littérature

OUTILS LINGUISTIQUES

- La phrase interrogative
- La capacité au futur
- *Somebody, anybody, nobody, everybody*

❶ American Preppers

What are they preparing for?

1 Ready for the worst

A. **Before listening.** What do you think preppers get prepared for?

B. Listen to **MP3 N°18**. Focus on preppers (stereotypes and definition) and on the prepping situations people do not think about.

C. **Have your say.** Is prepping something you would do? Why (not)?

HELP!
- **loo**ters: *pilleurs*
- 1 gallon = *3,8 litres*

2 The Blevins's preparation

A. **Pairwork.** Watch the video and find information about:
- **Pupil A:** The Blevins.
- **Pupil B:** Prepping and Patrick Troy.

B. Share your answers and report back to the class.

VIDEO N°11

3 The origins of prepping

A. Look at the picture below. Describe it briefly (who? what? what for?).

B. Read the text. Present the document (topic, time, place) and relate it to the picture.

C. Explain the role and action of the Federal Civil Defense Administration.

D. Identify who "the target", "the free men" and "those who trample the liberties of the free men" are.

The threat of nuclear attack loomed large[1] for Americans in the 1950s. In an effort to prepare for such a scenario, President Truman formed the Federal Civil Defense Administration, and commissioned dozens of instructional videos about what to expect in the event of an attack, and how to protect one's family and home. "You are the target," [one of the videos] ominously begins, "of those who would trample[2] the liberties of free men." [...] No matter whether you live in an industrial city, a "farming area with fertile fields," or a "mining region rich with vital ores and minerals," you have to be prepared for the worst, the video advises. In a deep voice, the narrator sets you on a clear path to survival, even providing a handy checklist. Some of the suggestions are quite useful: storing canned food and learning first aid could help you survive in a number of scenarios. Others, however, make you doubt whether you should ever follow government emergency plans. After all, it's unlikely that closing your blinds will make much of a difference in a nuclear apocalypse. But if the video fails at actually preparing people for a nuclear attack, it is very effective in doing two other things: striking fear into the hearts of Americans, and igniting passionate feelings of patriotism.

1 *peser sur* • 2 *bafouer*

Mariana Zapata, ***Atlas Oscura***, 29 September 2016

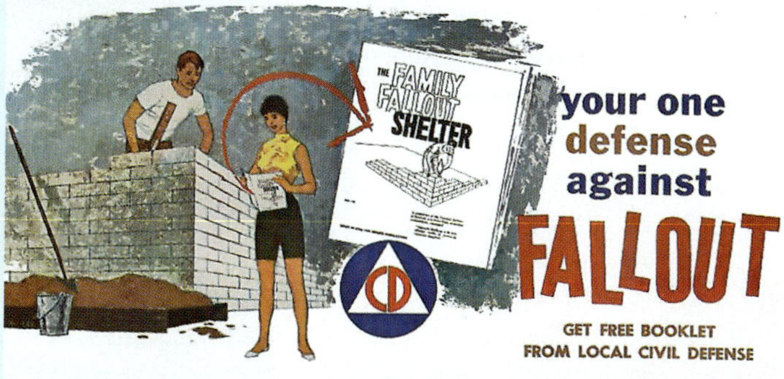

❷ In Ourselves We Trust

Is prepping a personal responsibility?

1 The U.S. Disaster Agency

The Federal Emergency Management Agency has wasted more than $3 billion and misused thousands of its employees by responding to hundreds of undersized floods, storms and other events that states could have handled on their own, an investigation by E&E News shows. FEMA has chronically overestimated the damage to U.S. states from small disasters and underestimated the capacity of states to respond to them. Those errors triggered[1] at least 325 unnecessary deployments of money and personnel since 1998. [...]

FEMA has deployed staff to small disasters for decades, even as federal auditors warned that it was sending emergency workers and money to states that may not need the help. Federal law says FEMA is supposed to assist with disasters only when they threaten to overwhelm[2] a state's ability to respond.

FEMA's preoccupation with undersized disasters comes as climate change is intensifying hurricanes, floods, thunderstorms and wildfires, and as development is expanding in peril-prone[3] areas. Many of the events that now trigger FEMA aid are becoming routine, raising concerns within the agency that it will be unable to respond to the growing number of large catastrophes if it continues to waste its resources on small ones.

The fallout is tangible: The U.S. agency at the forefront of disaster response is sidetracked[4] by small hazards[5], threatening its ability to handle the kind of megacalamities that have surged[6] in the past decade.

The pattern escalated into a crisis in 2017 when Hurricanes Harvey, Irma and Maria killed 3,167 people and caused $276 billion in damage.

FEMA's failures with those hurricanes are well-documented. But this has been overlooked[7]: The day Harvey made landfall near Houston, 4,948 emergency workers were deployed to other disasters or were unavailable, meaning that almost half of the agency's emergency workforce was tied up when the first sheets of rain began to inundate large parts of Texas. Harvey would prove to be the wettest hurricane in U.S. history; it unleashed 60 inches of rain. [...]

1 *déclencher* • 2 *submerger* • 3 *enclin* • 4 distracted • 5 *risques/dangers* • 6 increased • 7 *négliger*

Thomas Frank, ***Scientific American***, 20 August 2019

A. Before reading, find information about the text (type, time, topic).

B. Read the text. What is FEMA's role?

C. Identify what FEMA is criticised for. Quote the text.

D. What is the consequence for American people?

E. Observe the picture and relate it to the text.

Rockport, Texas, after Hurricane Harvey (2017)

2 Together is better

A. Look at the pictures. Guess what this place is.
B. Listen to MP3 N°19 and check your hypotheses.
C. Listen again and focus on the reasons for going down, the place (capacity, food and equipment) and the community (people, jobs).
D. Have your say. If you created your own survival community, would you accept anyone willing to join it? Why (not)?

3 A community of like-minded people

A. Read the title of the activity. What do you think this is about?
B. Read the text. What are the different steps in the recruiting process?
C. Focus on the slogan: "Life Assurance for a Dangerous World". What strategy is used by Vivos to convince people to join the community?
D. Go further. Discover more about the project with the help of Worksheet n°10.

FIRST STEP TO BECOME A MEMBER

Membership is totally free. To be considered for membership in a Vivos shelter, you must first apply [...] with basic information on who you are, your contact information, the size of your group, your combined skill sets or expertise, and insight[1] regarding why you are seeking a real survival shelter solution.

WHAT'S NEXT

Vivos then selects the best candidates for each Vivos shelter from our current pool of active members. We first look for those individuals who may best contribute their skills and expertise to each shelter community, thereby[2] providing the greatest chance of long-term survival of the entire group. Each candidate is reviewed based on a number of criteria. Once your application is received, a member of the Vivos Selection Team will review it and if they determine you are a worthy[3] candidate, will contact you by email and request to schedule a convenient time that you may privately talk by phone. [...] During that conversation they will answer all of your immediate questions about Vivos and how we may be able to accommodate you and your family group in a Vivos shelter. You will find this conversation to be very informative, welcoming and supportive!

As member candidates are approved, they are then provided an invitation to secure space in a Vivos shelter.

1 *(ici) motivation* • 2 *ainsi* • 3 having value

www.terravivos.com

VIVOS LIFE ASSURANCE FOR A DANGEROUS WORLD

YOUR TURN!

4 Write an e-mail

Write an e-mail to join the Vivos Community explaining who you are, how your skill sets/expertise could help the community and why you are interested in Vivos shelters.

❸ From Romantic Isolation to Forced Survival

How is survivalism portrayed in literature?

1 Living with the bare necessities

A. Read the ***Cultural fact*** and look at the picture. In your own words, explain why Thoreau went to the woods.

B. Have your say. What do you think about Thoreau's experiment?

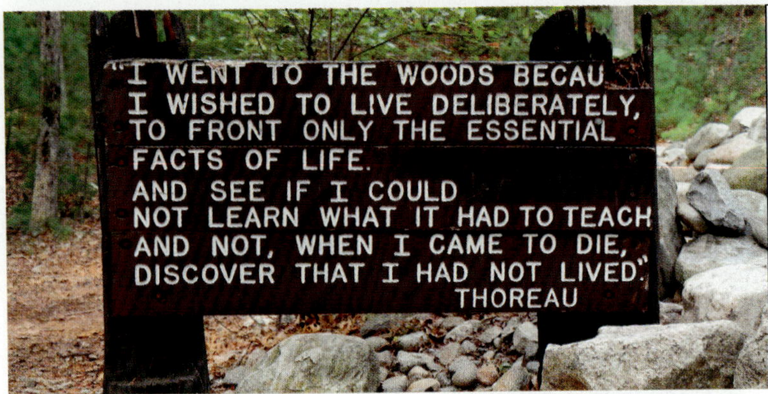

Thoreau's quote next to the site of his cabin (Walden Pond)

> ***Cultural fact***
> Henry David Thoreau (1817-1862) was an American essayist, poet, and philosopher. In 1845, he built a cabin on Walden Pond (Massachusetts), where he lived a basic and self-sufficient life for two years. *Walden* (1854) is a philosophical treatise that details this simple living experiment.

2 "I do not exist"

A. Skim the text. Identify the type of document. Who do you think the narrator is?

B. Read the text carefully. Identify the elements that make the narrator's family and childhood different.

C. What do you think "the Days of Abomination" are? What does she do to get prepared?

D. Why was the rhythm of nature important to her?

E. Go further. Focus on the last sentence. What do you think the narrator means?

On the highway below, the school bus rolls past without stopping.

I am only seven, but I understand that it is this fact, more than any other that makes my family different: we don't go to school. Dad worries that the government will force us to go, but it can't because it doesn't know about us. Four of my parents' seven children don't have birth certificates. We have no medical records because we were born at home and have never seen a doctor or nurse. We have no school records because we've never set foot in a classroom. When I am nine, I will be issued a Delayed Certificate of Birth, but at this moment, according to the state of Idaho and the federal government, I do not exist.

Of course I did exist. I had grown up preparing for the Days of Abomination, watching for the sun to darken, for the moon to drip as if with blood. I spent my summers bottling peaches and my winters rotating supplies. When the World of Men failed, my family would continue on, unaffected.

I had been educated in the rhythms of the mountain, rhythms in which change was never fundamental, only cyclical. The same sun appeared each morning, swept over the valley and dropped behind the peak. The snows that fell in winter always melted in the spring. Our lives were a cycle—the cycle of the day, the cycle of the seasons—circles of perpetual change that, when complete, meant nothing had changed at all. I believed my family was a part of this immortal pattern, that we were, in some sense, eternal. But eternity belonged only to the mountain.

Educated,
Tara Westover, 2018

YOUR TURN! 3 Interview Tara Westover

Pairwork. Imagine an interview with Tara Westover. Ask her questions about her life in a survivalist family.

4 After the apocalypse

A. Read the text with the help of Worksheet n°11.
B. What should the characters have done to get prepared for the situation?

C. Have your say. In such a situation, can we still talk of public and private places? Explain.

When he heard there would be a dangerous epidemic, Jeevan came to live with his brother Frank in his apartment.

ON DAY FORTY-SEVEN, Jeevan saw smoke rising in the distance. He didn't imagine the fire would get very far, given all the snow, but the thought of fires in a city without firefighters hadn't occurred to him.

Jeevan sometimes heard gunshots at night. Neither rolled-up towels nor plastic nor duct tape could keep the stench[1] from the hallway from seeping in[2], so they kept the windows open at all times and wore layers of clothes. They slept close together on Frank's bed, for warmth.

"Eventually we're going to have to leave," Jeevan said.

Frank put his pen down and looked past Jeevan at the window, at the lake and the cold blue sky. "I don't know where I'd go," he said. "I don't know how I'd do it."

Jeevan stretched out on the sofa and closed his eyes. Decisions would have to be made soon. There was enough food for only another two weeks.

When Jeevan looked out at the expressway, the thought that plagued[3] him was that maneuvering Frank's wheelchair through that crush of stopped cars would be impossible. They'd have to take alternate roads, but what if all of the roads were like this?

They hadn't heard anyone in the corridor for over a week, so that night Jeevan decided to risk venturing out of the apartment. He pushed the dresser[4] away from the door and took the stairs to the roof. After all these weeks indoors he felt exposed in the cold air. Moonlight glinted on glass but there was no other light. A stark[5] and unexpected beauty, silent metropolis, no movement. Out over the lake the stars were vanishing, blinking out one by one behind a bank of cloud. He smelled snow in the air. They would leave, he decided, and use the storm as cover.

"But what would be out there?" Frank asked. "I'm not an idiot, Jeevan. I hear the gunshots. I saw the news reports before the stations went dark."

"I don't know. A town somewhere. A farm."

"A farm? Are you a farmer? Even if it weren't the middle of winter, Jeevan, do farms even work without electricity and irrigation systems? What do you think will grow in the spring? What will you eat there in the meantime?"

"I don't know, Frank."

"Do you know how to hunt?"

"Of course not. I've never fired a gun."

"Can you fish?"

"Stop it," Jeevan said.

"After I was shot, when they told me I wouldn't walk again and I was lying in the hospital, I spent a lot of time thinking about civilization. What it means and what I value in it. I remember thinking that I never wanted to see a war zone again, as long as I live. I still don't."

"There's still a world out there," Jeevan said, "outside this apartment."

"I think there's just survival out there, Jeevan. I think you should go out there and try to survive."

"I can't just leave you."

"I'll leave first," Frank said. "I've given this some thought."

"What do you mean?" he asked, but he knew what Frank meant.

1 strong smell • 2 enter gradually • 3 worried • 4 *commode* • 5 desolate, bleak

Station Eleven,
Emily St. John Mandel, 2014

YOUR PROJECT

Groupwork. You want to create a survivalist community. Define what your community will be like (place, rules, members' roles, actions, etc.) and promote it to recruit people. Get people interested in your project. You may create flyers or a slideshow.

SPICE UP YOUR VOCABULARY

Use the vocabulary below to create your own mind map and add more words if necessary!

Verbs

- accommodate
- barter: *troquer*
- collapse
- decontaminate
- stockpile
- threaten
- fish
- hide
- hunt
- starve /'stɑrv/
- survive /sə'vaɪv/

Adverbs

- aggressively
- carefully
- courageously

Adjectives

- brave /'breɪv/
- cautious
- damaged
- devastated
- extreme /ɪk'striːm/
- fearless
- helpless
- hostile /'hɒstaɪl/
- isolated /'aɪsəleɪtɪd/
- polluted
- remote
- resourceful
- skilful
- stark = very plain in appearence
- uninhabitable /ʌnɪn'hæbɪtəbəl/

Nouns

- apocalypse
- bare /'beə/ necessity
- bunker
- canned food
- danger /'deɪndʒə/
- disaster
- Doomsday /'duːmzdeɪ/
- emergency
- first aid
- flood: *innondation*
- food supplies
- gas mask
- hardship /'hɑːdʃɪp/
- hunger /'hʌŋgə/
- injury
- looter
- natural disaster
- preppers
- ration
- shelter /'ʃeltə/: *abri*
- survival
- survival skills
- survivor /sə'vaɪvə/
- threat
- weapon /'wepən/: *arme*
- wilderness /'wɪldənəs/

RULE THE GRAMMAR!

LA PHRASE INTERROGATIVE

• Pour former une phrase interrogative, on utilise un **auxiliaire** :

(***WH-***...) + **auxiliaire** + sujet + verbe + ?

- Au présent simple on utilise l'auxiliaire : ***do / does***.
***Does he worry** about Doomsday?*

- Au présent ***be + -ing*** on utilise l'auxiliaire : ***be***.
***Is she preparing** to leave her home?*

- Au prétérit on utilise l'auxiliaire : ***did***.
***Did he buy** a new survival kit?*

- Au *present perfect* on utilise l'auxiliaire : ***have***.
***Have they installed** a safe room?*

LA CAPACITÉ AU FUTUR

• La capacité physique ou intellectuelle est souvent exprimée à l'aide de l'auxiliaire de modalité ***can***.
***Can** you run for thirty minutes?* (capacité physique)
***Can** you speak Chinese?* (capacité intellectuelle)

• Pour exprimer une action future, on utilise ***be able to*** ou, plus rarement, ***be unable to***.
*If I train for a month, I **will be able to** run for thirty minutes.*

• On peut aussi avoir recours à des périphrases exprimant la même idée de possibilité ou d'impossibilité.

If a war breaks out { ***we will be able** / **it will be possible for us** / **we will be in a position** / **we will have the power*** } *to fight.*

→ P.306

LANGUAGE LAB

- Audio words
- MP3
- Interactive Test

★ **1. For each word give a synonym and an antonym. Use the words below.**

waste • fresh • eatable • dehydrated • hoard • poisonous • polluted • clean

A. contaminated (adj.) → ... → ...
B. edible (adj.) → ... → ...
C. dried (adj.) → ... → ...
D. stockpile (v.) → ... → ...

★ **2. Turn the following sentences into questions.**

A. Closing your blinds will not make any difference in the event of a nuclear attack.
B. The government's video helps people prepare for a catastrophe.
C. Candidates are provided with an invitation to a secure space in a Vivos shelter.
D. Living in a bunker is the solution.

★★ **3. Fill in the blanks with these words.**

disasters • emergency plan • survival skills • gear and supplies • learned and practiced

It's easy to focus on ... when you start thinking about preparedness, though these aren't the only things you'd need in an emergency. Every family should have an ... . that addresses the most likely ... in their region. Practical ... should also be part of every family's game plan. These skills need to be ... before things get tough, because you simply won't have time to read a survival book.

Lindsay N. Smith, *National Geographic*, 24/09/2017

★★ **4. Change these sentences to indicate future ability using *be able to*.**

A. She can survive if she builds a bunker.
B. You can hunt and fish if we run out of canned food.
C. They can't run away if they haven't got a good car.
D. If there is a major epidemic, Sam can go to see his doctor.
E. We can flee to Canada in case of emergency.

★★★ **5. Translate into English.**

A. *Ne parle à personne de ce danger potentiel.*
B. *Personne ne sait ce qui va se passer en cas d'explosion nucléaire.*
C. *Tout le monde ne se prépare pas au pire.*
D. *Demande à n'importe qui. Ils te diront que tout le monde savait.*

6. Interactive test! What is your score?

OPEN YOUR EARS!

PHONOLOGY

Les mots se terminant en *-ate*

• Écoutez ces mots en faisant attention à la place de l'accent. Quelle est la syllabe accentuée ? MP3 N°20

candidate • inflate • certificate • create • alternate • accommodate • climate • educate • debate • intoxicate • investigate

→ Les mots de trois syllabes ou plus sont accentués sur l'avant avant-dernière syllabe.

TRAVEL WITH ACCENTS!

• Écoutez ces deux versions. Que remarquez-vous ?

MP3 N°21 — *Archeologists still aren't sure exactly what happened.*

MP3 N°22 — *Survivors don't care about appearances.*

• **Récapitulons : En anglais américain, le « r » est toujours prononcé. L'anglais britannique ne prononce le « r » que devant une voyelle.**

Picture challenge

★ **3 sentences**
★★ **4 to 6 sentences**
★★★ **7 sentences and +**

How many sentences can you make using what you have learnt? Collect stars!

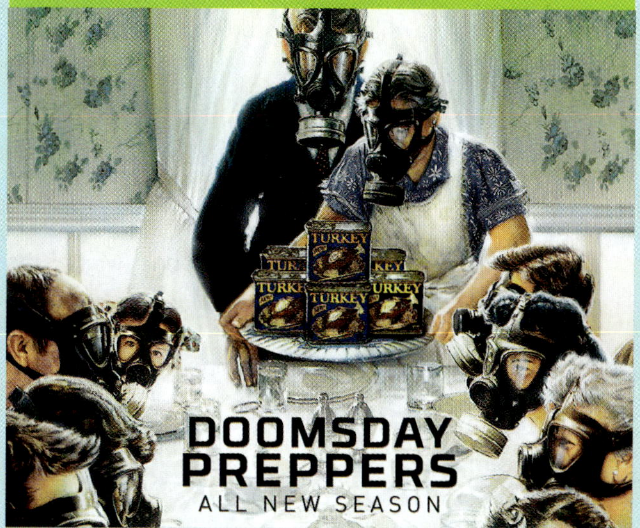

AXE 2

UNIT 6

THESE BOOTS WERE MADE FOR WALKING

What did it take to be a travelling lady in the Victorian era and early 20th century?

YOUR PROJECT

Imagine a letter written by a Victorian traveller to her family.

BEFORE CLASS!

Flash to watch!

Watch the video and be ready to talk about it in class!

VIDEO N°12

Au menu de cette unité :

DÉCOUVERTES CULTURELLES

- La bienséance à l'ère victorienne
- Des exploratrices de l'ère victorienne (Mary Kingsley, Marianne North…)
- La *Royal Geographical Society*
- Les vêtements à l'ère victorienne

OUTILS LINGUISTIQUES

- Les temps du récit
- L'expression de la comparaison
- L'expression de la capacité, de la permission, de l'obligation et de l'interdiction

❶ The Exploration Appeal

What motivated women in Victorian society and the early 20th century to explore the world?

1 Why women explore

A. Imagine what motivated women to explore in the Victorian era.
B. Read the text and find what motivated women to explore.
C. Compare it to men's motivations.

For Womankind?

No man ever climbed a mountain or crossed a river to prove what a man could do, though several might have done it for *Mankind*, with a capital *M*. For women, it was different. To a much greater extent, they were going against expectations and trespassing in a male realm[1]. Some politely ignored this, but others saw successes and failures very much in terms of gender. [...] The American mountaineer Fanny Bullock Workman was photographed on top of a mountain pass[2] in the Karakoram, holding up a banner calling for "Votes for Women." It would be a mistake, however to think that all female explorers were feminists. In fact, some were at pains[3] to point out the opposite. Gertrude Bell, one of the most famous women travellers of the early twentieth century, was a founder member of the British Women's Anti-Suffrage League. [...]

For the Sake of their Dead Husbands

There are no male explorers who travelled for the sake of their wives' reputation, but a small and fascinating group of women took to the trail to settle their dead husbands' unfinished business. In 1903, for example, Mina Hubbard became the first person to cross Labrador in Canada by canoe. It took considerable guts[4]: her husband, Leonidas, had starved to death on his attempt. Not only did Mina Hubbard have to battle against the environment, but she also had to race against her husband's old friends who were determined to beat her to the prize. [...] If there is an underlying theme in women's "whys," it is the idea of escape. Home often meant rigid social conventions, and travelling abroad offered the possibility of reinventing yourself.

How to Climb Mont Blanc in a Skirt,
Mick Conefrey, 2011

1 area • **2** *col de montagne* • **3** try hard to do sth • **4** it requires courage

2 Marianne North's adventure

VIDEO N°13

A. Look at the still and guess what motivated Marianne North to travel the world.
B. Watch the video and check your hypotheses.
C. What is the goal of this video?
D. Watch the video again and be ready to present Marianne North (activities, places visited, achievements).

HELP!

Adjectives	*Verbs & Expressions*
• adventurous	• get a better picture of the world
• courageous /kəˈreɪdʒəs/ = intrepid	• discover
• curious	• bring knowledge /ˈnɒlɪdʒ/ to people
• talented	• contribute to science /ˈsaɪəns/
• unique	

YOUR TURN! 3 Write a short article

Write a short article about Marianne North's life, achievements and art to promote the Marianne North Gallery in *Art and Culture Magazine*.

❷ Facing Obstacles

How difficult was it to be a travelling lady?

1 Victorian etiquette

The Travelling Companions, by Augustus Leopold Egg, 1862

There is no situation in which a lady is more exposed than when she travels [...]. If you travel under the escort of a gentleman, give him as little trouble as possible; at the same time, do not interfere with the arrangements he may make for your comfort.[...]

A lady will always dress plainly[1] when travelling. A gay dress, or finery of any sort, when in a boat, stage, or car, lays a woman open to the most severe misconstruction. [...] When in the car do not continually pester either your companion or the conductor with questions, such as "Where are we now?" "When shall we arrive?" you are wearied, this impatience will only make the journey still more tedious. Try to occupy yourself with looking at the country through which you are passing, or with a book. [...]

There are many little civilities which a true gentleman will offer to a lady travelling alone, which she may accept, even from an entire stranger, with perfect propriety[2]; but, while careful to thank him courteously, [...] avoid any advance towards acquaintanceship. If he sits near you and seems disposed to be impertinent, or obtrusive in his attentions or conversation, lower your veil and turn from him, either looking from the window or reading. A dignified, modest reserve is the surest way to repel impertinence. If you find yourself, during your journey, in any awkward or embarrassing situation, you may, without impropriety, request the assistance of a gentleman, even a stranger, and he will, probably, perform the service requested. Never, upon any account, or under any provocation, return rudeness by rudeness. [...] In travelling alone, choose, if possible, a seat next to another lady, or near an elderly gentleman.

1 not luxuriously, simply • 2 good manners

The Ladies' Book of Etiquette and Manual of Politeness, Florence Hartley, 1860

A. Read the title of the activity and look at the painting. Guess what the correct behaviour was for the women who travelled at that time.

B. Read the text and check your hypotheses.

C. Read the *Cultural fact* on Worksheet n°12 and explain why it was difficult for a woman to travel on her own at the time.

2 I can't do this

A. Listen to Jacki Hill Murphy on MP3 N°23 talk about Mary Kingsley and take notes.

B. What are the common points between the interviewee and Mary Kingsley?

C. What made Mary Kingsley's project difficult (before, during and after the ascent)?

D. Have your say. Can you imagine yourself undertaking a journey in the same conditions? Explain.

I would love to…, since I like challenges.

I wouldn't dream of risking…

I would / wouldn't be up to + V-ing, since…

3 Letters of introduction

A. Guess what the advantages of being from the upper class were when travelling.

B. Listen to MP3 N°24. Focus on Marianne North and her trips, travelling conditions and letters of introduction.

C. Report back to the class.

D. Go further. Compare today's travelling conditions to the Victorian era's.

4 Contribution to scientific knowledge

When George Curzon returned from his travels in Persia (where he had crossed paths with Isabella Bird) he had great influence on the debate as a powerful social figure and member of the RGS (Royal Geographical society) Council, not least in undermining the Council's previous unanimous support for women fellows. Curzon considered the growing number of women travellers as undesirable 'female globetrotteresses' whose membership of the RGS would reduce its already falling market value (Birlett 1989). Whilst he held a guarded respect for Isabella Bird, Curzon wrote in *The Times* (1893): 'We contest *in toto* the general capability of women to contribute to scientific knowledge... their sex and their training render them equally unfitted for exploration'. [...]

The ensuing debate over women's membership spilled over from the RGS to the media and society at large and was satirised in a ditty[1] in *Punch* magazine[2] (10 June 1893) [...]:

A lady explorer? A traveller in skirts?
The notion's just a trifle seraphic:
Let them stay and mind the babies, or hem our ragged shirts;
But they mustn't, can't and shan't be geographic.

Douglas Freshfield responded [...]:

The question our dissentients bellow[3]
Is 'Can a lady be a fellow?'
That Sirs, will be no question when
Our fellows[4] are all gentlemen.

Various compromise positions were proposed, largely aimed at limiting the number of women and/or their status and power with the Society. The final resolution put to the Special General Meeting in April 1893 proposed that women should be elected as ordinary fellows; that regulations should refer to both the masculine and feminine gender, but that women would not be qualified to serve on Council or hold any other offices. Some of the women recently elected attended the meeting, but none are recorded as contributing to the debate.

1 short poem • 2 British satirical magazine created in 1841 • 3 shout • 4 a man / a member of certain learned societies

Complex Locations: Women's Geographical Work in the UK 1850-1970, Avril Maddrell, 2011

A. Look at the picture. What strikes you?

B. Read the text and explain what George Curzon's opinion about women explorers and their role in science is.

C. Rephrase the passage in italics (l. 17-20) in your own words.

D. Describe the status of women in the RGS in April 1893.

E. Go further. Browse the Internet to find when women were seriously considered as fellows in the RGS.

YOUR TURN! 5 A witty ditty

Write a ditty that could have been written in the Victorian era to promote female travelling.

❸ The Importance of Clothing

Did clothes make the travelling woman?

1 Packing a suitcase

PACKING can be a tricky business. Readers of women's magazines will know the trick is to put together the foolproof "capsule wardrobe", a small collection of clothes which will provide the perfect look for every occasion, while avoiding paying an excess on the luggage allowance.

When Gertrude Bell set out to explore Arabia in 1913, she certainly intended to have an outfit befitting every eventuality. Her packing list included evening dresses, silk underwear, silver candlesticks, 12 hats and a fur coat. Victorian female explorer May French Sheldon was also clearly anxious that she be appropriately attired when meeting important chiefs as she began her expedition from Zanzibar to Kilimanjaro in 1891: she packed a platinum wig and Parisian silk dress. [...]

Lucy Walker was advised to take up walking in 1858 to help ease her rheumatism. She developed such a passion for mountaineering that by 1871 she had become the first woman to climb the Matterhorn. She did it in a white floral printed dress. [...]

The tricky issue of wardrobe was as much a dilemma for climbers as for those trekking the desert. Born too soon for practical Gortex, Walker and her fellow mountaineers were dressed in layer upon layer of silk, flannel, linen, tweed and fur. [...]

The question of trousers was a hugely contentious one. A surprising number of the women travellers of the day considered them scandalous. Mary Kingsley said she would rather "perish on a public scaffold" than wear "you know what I mean". She extolled instead "the blessings of a good thick skirt", crediting the ample folds of such a garment with saving her when she fell into a hunter's pit full of spikes. [...] Isabella Bird who travelled the world three times, created hybrid garments to ensure practicality and decorum. She commissioned a special suit for her ride through the Rockies[1] which consisted of a pair of baggy trousers hidden under a split skirt. Beryl Smeeton, who travelled through China in the Thirties, designed "a tent with a hole at the top" in kimono material in order for her to be able to change her underwear discreetly while travelling third class.

1 US mountains

Giulia Rhodes, **www.express.co.uk**, October 2011

A. Look at the image. What strikes you?
B. Read the text. Compare today's women's packing lists and luggage weight with those of Victorian women.
C. What did women pay attention to when they got dressed during their trips?
D. What did some women think about trousers? Imagine why.
E. Go further. In groups of 4, browse the Internet to find further information about the underlined women (background information, motivations for travelling, achievements).

HELP!

- befit = be appropriate to
- foolproof = that cannot fail
- suitcase = trunk = luggage /ˈlʌɡɪdʒ/
- wig = artificial hair

2 Clothing was political

A. **Before reading.** Imagine why clothing was considered political.
B. Read the text and check your hypotheses.
C. How were the female explorers who wore trousers considered?

HELP!
- **dismay** = consternation
- **emulate** = imitate

By the latter part of the nineteenth century women's travel had taken on political connotations. Even the traveler's choice of clothing was interpreted as a political statement on women's social roles. To wear trousers, even in the jungle of Africa was to align oneself with the advocates of female emancipation. To Kingsley's dismay, a 3 December article in the *Daily Telegraph* hailed Kingsley as a superwoman, proclaiming "It is a curious and a novel feature of the modern emancipation of woman this passion on the part of the sex to emulate the most daring achievement of masculine explorers"

The Right Sort of Woman: Victorian Travel Writers and the Fitness of an Empire, Precious Mackenzie, 2011.

3 The New Woman

A. **Before listening**. What kind of person do you think the "New Woman" was?
B. **Pairwork.**
- **Pupil A:** Listen to **MP3 N°25**. Why were bicycles, bloomers and Annie Londonderry important to women? Take notes.
- **Pupil B:** Listen to the interview of Gillian K. Willman about "The New Woman" on **MP3 N°26**. Focus on what she did and what made her a trailblazing lady.

C. Share what you have understood with your classmate. Get ready to report back to the class.

HELP!
- **wager** (n) = bet
- **talltale** = far-fetched story
- **bloomers**: *jupe culotte*
- **placard** = public sign
- **unwieldy**: *peu maniable*
- **flock to sth**: *venir en masse à qch*
- **in droves** = in large numbers
- **ruffles**: *volants*
- **craze**: *engouement*
- **deter** (v) from = discourage

YOUR PROJECT

Imagine a letter written by a Victorian traveller to her family.

YOUR TURN! 4 Write a short article

Write an article about the role of female travellers' clothing during the Victorian era and its impact on society for *History Today* magazine.

SPICE UP YOUR VOCABULARY

Use the vocabulary below to create your own mind map and add more words if necessary!

Nouns

- achievement
- social convention
- journey /'dʒɜːni/ = trip
- trailblazer /'treɪlbleɪzə/
- traveller
- disapproval /ˌdɪsə'pruːvəl/
- struggle /'strʌgəl/: *lutte*
- petticoat: *jupons*

Adverbs

- courageously /kə'reɪdʒəsli/
- defiantly /dɪ'faɪəntli/
- fearlessly /'fɪələsli/

Adjectives

- adventurous
- audacious /ɔː'deɪʃəs/ ≠ cautious
- bold /bəʊld/
- comfortable /'kʌmfətəbəl/
- groundbreaking
- independent
- innovative
- modern ≠ traditional
- rebellious
- resourceful /rɪ'zɔːsfʊl/
- self-reliant
- submissive
- polite
- skillful ≠ clumsy
- tired out = exhausted

Verbs & Expressions

- achieve
- crawl: *ramper*
- climb (up) /klaɪm/
- climb down: *(re)descendre*
- criticise
- despise /dɪ'spaɪz/
- discover
- explore
- fight one's way through: *se frayer un passage à travers*
- jump = leap
- overcome one's fears
- persevere
- succeed in sth / V-*ing*
- take up the challenge

RULE THE GRAMMAR!

LES TEMPS DU RÉCIT

- On utilise le **prétérit** pour raconter une histoire ou relater des évènements passés.
- On utilise le **prétérit *be* + *-ing*** quand on oppose un évènement en cours de déroulement dans le passé à un évènement ponctuel, toujours dans le passé.
- On utilise le ***pluperfect*** pour évoquer des évènements antérieurs.

*They **were watching** the setting sun when they remembered what **had happened** the night before.*

- À l'**oral** et dans les **récits contemporains**, on peut trouver des évènements décrits au présent simple, ce qui rend la narration plus vivante.

*The explorer **sees** the wild animal; he **approaches** in silence.*

→ P.300

LA CAPACITÉ AU PASSÉ

- On utilise ***could*** pour exprimer la capacité au passé.

*Last year, she **could** cross the river on her own.*

- Toutefois, avec **could**, on se prononce sur la capacité (dans le passé) mais pas sur la réalisation de l'évènement. Pour cela, il faut utiliser ***be able to***.

Last year, she could cross the river.
(= Elle pouvait mais on ne sait pas si elle l'a fait.)

Yesterday, she was able to cross the river.
(= Hier, elle a pu traverser la rivière et elle l'a fait.)

- Voici d'autres périphrases que l'on peut utiliser pour exprimer la capacité.

- ***To be capable of doing something***
S'utilise quand l'action demande beaucoup d'efforts.
They were capable of walking for hours.

- ***To be equipped to do something***
S'utilise quand il s'agit d'une action qui demande certaines compétences.
By the end of their survival course, they should be equipped to cross the Sahara desert.

- ***To have it in you to do something***
S'utilise quand cela s'oppose à une idée communément admise.
Women explorers had it in them to travel alone.

LANGUAGE LAB

• Audio words
• MP3
• Interactive Test

★ 1. Pick the odd word out and justify your answer.

A. look down on • despise • undermine • praise • feel contempt for

B. independent • subservient • unassisted • self-reliant • autonomous

C. adventurous • courageous • brave • daring • cautious

D. remote • far • distant • close • inaccessible

★ 2. Rewrite the sentences using the expression in brackets.

A. She could find her way on the desert island without a map or a compass. ***(to be equipped to)***

B. Those Victorian ladies could travel across Europe with very little help. ***(to have it in sb)***

C. Geoffrey and Melanie could climb that mountain in record time. ***(to be able to)***

D. British alpinists could break numerous records. ***(manage)***

E. We proved we could walk for fifteen hours non-stop. ***(to be capable of)***

★★ 3. Match each definition with the right idiom.

1. have itchy feet 2. live out of a suitcase 3. miss the boat 4. off the beaten track 5. paddle one's own canoe 6. hit the road

A. To live or stay somewhere on a temporary basis and with only a limited selection of your belongings.

B. Away from the frequently travelled routes.

C. To be independent and self-reliant.

D. To lose the chance or opportunity to do something.

E. To find it difficult to stay in one place, to feel the need to travel.

F. To begin a journey.

★★ 4. Put the verbs in the appropriate tense.

When they ***(reach)*** the summit, they ***(build)*** a fire and ***(think)*** of their guide who ***(fall)*** into a ravine. He ***(is)*** safe now. They ***(prepare)*** for the night and ***(catch)*** a glimpse of the moon. They ***(freeze)*** and their feet ***(hurt)***. Yet, they ***(sleep)*** peacefully.

★★★ 5. Translate into English, first using the simple present, then the preterite.

Amelia Earhart a été la première femme pilote à traverser l'océan Atlantique en solitaire. Elle a également battu le record du plus long vol fait par une femme. Par ailleurs, elle détient le record de vitesse de la traversée de l'océan Atlantique.

6. Interactive test! What is your score?

OPEN YOUR EARS!

PHONOLOGY

Les mots se terminant en *-ion*

• Écoutez les mots suivants se terminant en *-ion* et déterminez la syllabe accentuée. Que remarquez-vous ?

MP3 N°27

companion • exploration • expedition • emancipation • expectation • construction • situation • resolution

• En sachant que tous les mots se terminant en *-ion* sont accentués de la même façon, formulez une règle d'accentuation.

TRAVEL WITH ACCENTS!

Écoutez l'extrait suivant et comparez les prononciations.

MP3 N°28

MP3 N°29

Nowadays, we take curiosity for granted. We believe that if we put in the hard work we might one day stand before the pyramids, discover new species of flower or even go to the Moon.

AUDIO MYSTERY

MP3 N°30

Listen to the recording and solve the mystery!

Picture challenge

★ **3 sentences**
★★ **4 to 6 sentences**
★★★ **7 sentences and +**

How many sentences can you make using what you have learnt? Collect stars!

Nicole Kidman is Gertrude Bell in *Queen of the Desert*, 2015

Excerpts from *Dear Ijeawele, or a Feminist Manifesto in Fifteen Suggestions* (2017)

By **Chimamanda Ngozi Adichie** (Nigerian writer, novelist, essayist).

Dear Ijeawele, or A Feminist Manifesto in Fifteen Suggestions was written by Chimamanda Ngozi Adichie after her childhood friend, Ijeawele, asked for advice on how to raise her baby girl, Chizalum, as a feminist. The published book is a version of the letter sent to Ijeawele.

THIRD SUGGESTION

Teach her that the idea of "gender roles" is absolute nonsense. Do not ever tell her that she should or should not do something because she is a girl.

"Because you are a girl" is never a reason for anything. Ever. I remember being told as a child to "bend down[1] properly while sweeping[2], like a girl." Which meant that sweeping was about being female. I wish I had been told simply "bend down and sweep properly because you'll clean the floor better." And I wish my brothers had been told the same thing.

There have been recent Nigerian social media debates about women and cooking, about how wives have to cook for husbands. It is funny, in the way that sad things are funny, that we are still talking about cooking as some kind of marriageability test for women.

The knowledge of cooking does not come pre-installed in a vagina. Cooking is learned. Cooking — domestic work in general — is a life skill that both men and women should ideally have. It is also a skill that can elude both men and women.

We also need to question the idea of marriage as a prize to women, because that is the basis of these absurd debates. If we stopped conditioning women to see marriage as a prize, then we would have fewer debates about a wife needing to cook in order to earn that prize.

It is interesting to me how early the world starts to invent gender roles. Yesterday I went to a children's shop to buy Chizalum an outfit. In the girls' section were pale creations in washed-out shades of pink. I disliked them. The boys' section had outfits in vibrant shades of blue. Because I thought blue would be adorable against her brown skin — and photograph better — I bought one. At the checkout counter[3], the cashier said mine was the perfect present for the new boy. I said it was for a baby girl. She looked horrified. "Blue for a girl?"

I cannot help but wonder about the clever marketing person who invented this pink-blue binary. There was also a "gender-neutral" section, with its array of bloodless grays. "Gender-neutral" is silly because it is premised on the idea of male being blue and female being pink and "gender-neutral" being its own category. Why not just have baby clothes organized by age and displayed in all colors? The bodies of male and female infants are similar, after all.

I looked at the toy section, which was also arranged by gender. Toys for boys are mostly active, and involve some sort of doing — trains, cars — and toys for girls are mostly passive and are overwhelmingly[4] dolls. I was struck by this. I had not quite realized how early society starts to invent ideas of what a boy should be and what a girl should be. I wished the toys had been arranged by type, rather than by gender.

Did I ever tell you about going to a U.S. mall with a seven-year-old Nigerian girl and her mother? She saw a toy helicopter, one of those things that fly by wireless remote control, and she was fascinated and asked for one. "No," her mother said. "You have your dolls." And she responded, "Mummy, is it only dolls I will play with?" I have never forgotten that. Her mother meant well, obviously. She was well versed in the ideas of gender roles — that girls play with dolls and boys with helicopters. I wonder now, wistfully[5], if the little girl would have turned out to be a revolutionary engineer, had she been given a chance to explore that helicopter.

If we don't place the straitjacket[6] of gender roles on young children, we give them space to reach their full potential. Please see Chizalum as an individual. Not as a girl who should be a certain way. See her weaknesses and her strengths in an individual way. Do not measure her on a scale of what a girl should be. Measure her on a scale of being the best version of herself.

A young Nigerian woman once told me that she had for years behaved "like a boy" — she liked football and was bored by dresses — until her mother forced her to stop her "boyish" interests. Now she is grateful to her mother for helping her start behaving like a girl. The story made me sad. I wondered what parts of herself she had needed to silence and stifle[7], and I wondered about what her spirit had lost, because what she called "behaving like a boy" was simply behaving like herself.

1 lean over • 2 *balayage* • 3 *la caisse* • 4 *de manière écrasante* • 5 with nostalgia • 6 *camisole de force* • 7 restrain

Another acquaintance, an American living in the Pacific Northwest, once told me that when she took her one-year-old son to a baby play group, where babies had been brought by their mothers, she noticed that the mothers of baby girls were very restraining, constantly telling the girls "don't touch" or "stop and be nice," and she noticed that the baby boys were encouraged to explore more and were not restrained as much and were almost never told to "be nice." Her theory was that parents unconsciously start very early to teach girls how to be, that baby girls are given less room and more rules and baby boys more room and fewer rules.

Gender roles are so deeply conditioned in us that we will often follow them even when they chafe[8] against our true desires, our needs, our happiness. They are very difficult to unlearn, and so it is important to try to make sure that Chizalum rejects them from the beginning. Instead of letting her internalize the idea of gender roles, teach her self-reliance. Tell her that it is important to be able to do for herself and fend for herself. Teach her to try to fix physical things when they break. We are quick to assume girls can't do many things. Let her try. She might not fully succeed, but let her try. Buy her toys like blocks and trains — and dolls, too, if you want to."

8 *(ici) contrarier*

GUIDED READING

A. l. 00-15: What are certain skills that Chimamanda Ngozi Adichie says are expected of women but that she wishes men would learn too?
B. l. 26-71: In what ways does society shape gender roles?
C. l. 26-35: What happened when Chimamanda Ngozi Adichie wanted to buy some clothes for Chizalum?
D. l. 45-73: What kind of behaviour are boys and girls encouraged to have according to the author?
E. l. 94-105: What are some suggestions that Chimamanda Ngozi Adichie has for her friend in how to raise Chizalum?

Go further. Comment on the role society expects women to occupy, according to this excerpt.

SIXTH SUGGESTION

Teach her to question language. Language is the repository[1] of our prejudices, our beliefs, our assumptions. But to teach her that, you will have to question your own language. A friend of mine says she will never call her daughter "princess." People mean well when they say this, but "princess" is loaded with assumptions, of a girl's delicacy, of the prince who will come to save her, etc. This friend prefers "angel" and "star."

So decide for yourself the things you will not say to your child. Because what you say to your child matters. It teaches her what she should value. You know that Igbo[2] joke, used to tease girls who are being childish—"What are you doing? Don't you know you are old enough to find a husband?" I used to say that often. But now I choose not to. I say "You are old enough to find a job." Because I do not believe that marriage is something we should teach young girls to aspire to.

Try not to use words like "misogyny" and "patriarchy" too often with Chizalum. We feminists can sometimes be too jargony, and jargon can sometimes feel too abstract.

Don't just label something misogynistic; tell her why it is, and tell her what would make it not be.

Teach her that if you criticize X in women but do not criticize X in men, then you do not have a problem with X, you have a problem with women. For X please insert words like "anger," "ambition," "loudness," "stubbornness," "coldness," "ruthlessness[3]."

Teach her to ask questions like What are the things that

1 *dépositaire, entrepôt* • 2 language spoken by people living mostly in southeastern Nigeria • 3 *cruautés*

women cannot do because they are women? Do these things have cultural prestige? If so, why are only men allowed to do the things that have cultural prestige?

It is helpful, I think, to use everyday examples. Remember that television commercial we watched in Lagos, where a man cooks and his wife claps for him? True progress is when she doesn't clap for him but just reacts to the food itself — she can either praise the food or not praise the food, just as he can praise hers or not praise hers, but what is sexist is that she is praising the fact that he has undertaken the act of cooking, praise that implies that cooking is an inherently female act.

Remember the mechanic in Lagos who was described as a "lady mechanic[4]" in a newspaper profile? Teach Chizalum that the woman is a mechanic, not a "lady mechanic."

Point out to her how wrong it is that a man who hits your car in Lagos traffic gets out and tells you to go and bring your husband because he "can't deal with a woman."

Instead of merely telling her, show her with examples that misogyny can be overt[5] and misogyny can be subtle and that both are abhorrent[6].

Teach her to question men who can have empathy for women only if they see them as relational rather than as individual equal humans. Men who, when discussing rape, will always say something like "if it were my daughter or wife or sister." Yet such men do not need to imagine a male victim of crime as a brother or son in order to feel empathy. Teach her, too, to question the idea of women as a special species. I once heard an American politician, in his bid[7] to show his support for women, speak of how women should be "revered[8]" and "championed" — a sentiment that is all too common.

Tell Chizalum that women actually don't need to be championed and revered; they just need to be treated as equal human beings. There is a patronizing undertone[9] to the idea of women needing to be "championed" and "revered" because they are women. It makes me think of chivalry[10], and the premise of chivalry is female weakness."

Dear Ijeawele, or a Feminist Manifesto in Fifteen Suggestions
Chimamanda Ngozi Adichie, 2017

4 Sandra Aguebor's nickname, first Nigerian woman to become a mechanic • 5 *apparent* • 6 *odieux* • 7 attempt to achieve sth • 8 deeply admired • 9 underlying quality or feeling • 10 *galanterie*

GUIDED READING

A. l. 01-09: What is the problem with calling a little girl "princess"?
B. l. 19-24: Instead of putting labels on things to say that they are problematic, what is better to do, according to the author?
C. l. 25-29: What qualities can be used to praise men but criticize women? Can you think of other examples?
D. l. 30-42: What assumptions about jobs should men and women question to make them more equal?
E. l. 54-64: What kinds of language should men stop using to refer to women?
F. l. 65-71: What is the problem with chivalry?

Go further. "Language is the repository of our prejudices, our beliefs, our assumptions." (l.01) Do you agree with the author? Can you think of certain words that may also be problematic and cause gender norms and stereotypes when talking about men or women?

At home. Listen to Chimamanda Ngozi Adichie's famous TED talks "We should all be feminists".

UNIT 4 Évaluation

Compréhension de l'oral

"The Virgin Queen" MP3 n°31

Listen to the audio recording three times and recap what you have understood.

Expression écrite Choisissez l'un des deux sujets (min. 120 mots).

Question A : What made Elizabeth I an unusual queen?

Question B : Discuss the following proverb: "Life is what you make it." Why could it apply to Queen Elizabeth I?

UNIT 5 Évaluation

Compréhension de l'oral

"The hideaway" MP3 n°32

Listen to the audio recording three times and recap what you have understood.

Expression écrite

Choisissez l'un des deux sujets (min. 120 mots).

Question A : Fiona and Chris MacAlister meet anti-preppers. Write the conversation.

Question B : Survivalism is the practice of preparing for the imminent apocalyptic destruction of society. According to the *New Yorker*, survivalism has "expanded to affluent quarters, taking root in Silicon Valley and New York City."
How can you account for this trend?
Do you understand preppers? Why (not)?

UNIT 6 Évaluation

Compréhension de l'oral

"Shrinking the world" MP3 n°33

Listen to the audio recording three times and recap what you have understood.

Expression écrite Choisissez l'un des deux sujets (min. 120 mots).

Question A : Modern technology has "shrunk the world". Do you agree?

Question B : Choose one quote and comment on it:

a. "Life is either a daring adventure or nothing at all." **Helen Keller**, American educator (1880-1968)

b. "As a woman I have no country. As a woman my country is the whole world." **Virginia Woolf**, British author (1882-1941)

UNIT 4 Évaluation

The Armada **Portrait, 1588**

The issue of female leadership was hotly debated during Elizabeth's reign. In the year of her succession, prominent theologian John Knox had written an angry polemic entitled *The First Blast of the Trumpet Against the Monstruous Regiment of Women*. For Knox, female rulers were 'repugneth to nature', and compared to men, 'foolishe, madde and phrenetike'.
Not only did Elizabeth's status as a woman unsettle her position as a ruler, there were also legal questions about her right to the throne. She had been periodically declared illegitimate by her father Henry VIII and her half-brother Edward VI. When Mary, a Catholic, ruthlessly claimed power from Edward's chosen heir, Lady Jane Grey (a Protestant), she also expressed her hostility to the Protestant Elizabeth, keeping her detained in Hatfield House. Critics of Elizabeth's right to rule had hovered her since birth, and when Mary died childless, the England she inherited was fragmented and struggling for global significance.
Despite many challenges throughout her time on the throne, the period of Elizabeth's reign is now referred to as a 'Golden Age'. She was an extremely savvy manager of the royal court and saw England through a succession of religious, economic and political upheavals. In direct defiance of Knox's polemic, Elizabeth modelled to the world the fact that women can cope, and indeed thrive, in power after all.
[...] Some believe that Elizabeth's rule was heavily manipulated by her advisors. Indeed, in her first address, Elizabeth told her Privy Council, 'I mean to direct all my actions by good advice and counsel.' But Curator of the Queen's House, Christine Riding, warns us not to take Elizabeth's words at face value. [...] Elizabeth was a skilled manipulator of the men around her, and sometimes used them as a shield to justify and defend her own actions.
Though it's true that Elizabeth was advised throughout her reign by a close group of trusted men, ultimately she had the final say. She was highly educated and could speak many languages, a skill which gave her an advantage in matters of international diplomacy. Members of her government needed her signature in order to act, and she often didn't comply with the will of those around her. [...]
Regardless of any early trauma, Elizabeth recognised that marriage and motherhood would inevitably lead to dilution of her power. In the 16th century, a sovereign was regarded as holding dominion over the state, while a husband was deemed to hold dominion over his wife. A male consort would have presented Elizabeth with a number of complications. [...]
As her reign progressed, Elizabeth effectively rebranded herself with the label of 'virgin', married only to her people and to England. Riding argues that in the context of Tudor monarchy, virginity performed a largely political function. As the 'Virgin Queen', Elizabeth's perceived purity had a 'political dimension' and wasn't just about physical and moral purity.

Kate Wilkinson, *www.rmg.co.uk*,16 November 2017

Compréhension de l'écrit

Answer the following questions in English, using your own words.

A. What is the main topic of the text?
B. What was Queen Elizabeth's view on marriage?
C. How did Queen Elizabeth I turn her gender into an advantage?
D. Comment on the following statement: "Elizabeth modelled to the world the fact that women can cope, and indeed thrive, in power after all." (l. 26-27)

Expression écrite

Choisissez l'un des deux sujets (min. 120 mots).

Question A : Why can we say that Queen Elizabeth I was a pioneering woman?

Question B : What obstacles do women have to face when it comes to reaching top positions? What should be done to change mentalities?

UNIT 5 Évaluation

Steve Huffman, […] co-founder and C.E.O. of Reddit, […] was nearsighted until November, 2015, when he arranged to have laser eye surgery. He underwent the procedure […] for a reason he doesn't usually talk much about: he hopes that it will improve his odds of surviving a disaster, whether natural or man-made. "If the world ends — and not even if the world ends, but if we have trouble — getting contacts or glasses is going to be a huge pain in the ass," he told me recently. […]

Huffman, who lives in San Francisco, […] is less focused on a specific threat — a quake on the San Andreas, a pandemic, a dirty bomb — than he is on the aftermath, "the temporary collapse of our government and structures," as he puts it. "I own a couple of motorcycles. I have a bunch of guns and ammo. Food. I figure that, with that, I can hole up in my house for some amount of time."

Survivalism, the practice of preparing for a crackup of civilization, tends to evoke a certain picture: the woodsman in the tinfoil hat, the hysteric with the hoard of beans, the religious doomsayer. But in recent years survivalism has expanded to more affluent quarters, taking root in Silicon Valley and New York City, among technology executives, hedge-fund managers, and others in their economic cohort.

[…] In private Facebook groups, wealthy survivalists swap tips on gas masks, bunkers, and locations safe from the effects of climate change. One member, the head of an investment firm, told me, "I keep a helicopter gassed up all the time, and I have an underground bunker with an air-filtration system." He said that his preparations probably put him at the "extreme" end among his peers. But he added, "A lot of my friends do the guns and the motorcycles and the gold coins. That's not too rare anymore." […]

Huffman has been a frequent attendee at Burning Man, the annual, clothing-optional festival in the Nevada desert, where artists mingle with moguls. He fell in love with one of its core principles, "radical self-reliance," which he takes to mean "happy to help others, but not wanting to require others." (Among survivalists, or "preppers," as some call themselves, *FEMA*, the Federal Emergency Management Agency, stands for "Foolishly Expecting Meaningful Aid.")

Huffman has calculated that, in the event of a disaster, he would seek out some form of community: "Being around other people is a good thing. […]"

[…] How many wealthy Americans are really making preparations for a catastrophe? It's hard to know exactly; a lot of people don't like to talk about it. ("Anonymity is priceless," one hedge-fund manager told me, declining an interview.)

[…] One measure of survivalism's spread is that some people are starting to speak out against it. Max Levchin, a founder of PayPal and of Affirm, a lending startup, told me, "It's one of the few things about Silicon Valley that I actively dislike — the sense that we are superior giants who move the needle and, even if it's our own failure, must be spared."

Evan Osnos, *The New Yorker*, 22 January 2017

Compréhension de l'écrit

Answer the following questions in English, using your own words.

A. After reading the text, what can you say about:
- its main topic?
- the people involved?
- their opinions on the topic?

B. Comment on the last sentence of the text (l. 32-34) and explain Max Levchin's feelings on the topic.

Expression écrite

Choisissez l'un des deux sujets (min. 120 mots).

Question A : As a survivalist, you try to talk one of your friends into joining the movement. Imagine and write the dialogue.

Question B : Survivalism is everywhere these days, in literature, podcasts, films and TV shows. How can you explain that the survivalist movement has been gaining ground over the past few years to become mainstream in the United States?

B1-B2 BACKPACK

Get Ready for your Exam!

UNIT 6

Évaluation

Document A

The next time you board a plane, spare a thought for these pioneering women: you might take travel for granted, but they paved the way for your adventures.

These explorers were inspirational and outrageous, pioneering and polarising. They wrestled crocodiles, circumnavigated the world, and charted little-known lands — usually while wearing a crinoline or in disguise. Beat that, Bear Grylls[1]. […]

Annie Londonderry began her round-the-world cycling adventure outside the Massachusetts State House on June 25, 1894. […] Londonderry was not the hardened explorer she had led people to believe but actually a 24-year-old Latvian immigrant from a poor neighbourhood in Boston's West End. She had a husband and three children — and she was a novice cyclist. Her progress was slow but steady, hindered by the corset and full skirt which were viewed as mandatory for a respectable woman. Eventually, she ditched them for bloomers[2]. […] Londonderry arrived back in Boston on September 24 1895 — just one day shy of her 15-month deadline. She went on to write several elaborate, and possibly somewhat fanciful, accounts of her expedition for the New York World.

At the age of 30, in August 1893, Mary Kingsley set out on an expedition to Sierra Leone. The lone Englishwoman dressed the only way she knew how: in a corset and voluminous skirt.

A lady had, she said, "no right to go about in Africa in things you would be ashamed to be seen in at home". To Kingsley this was not merely a matter of Victorian propriety. She believed the people she met in Africa were just as deserving of the care and attention it took her to dress properly as the people she met in London.

Hazel Plush, *The Telegraph*, 8 March 2017

1 British survival instructor, adventurer, writer, television presenter and businessman • 2 *jupe-culotte*

Document B

MELBOURNE, Fla.

What was intended to be a historic occasion for NASA and humankind, the first all-female spacewalk, has been scuttled because of a lack of spacesuits on the International Space Station. The spacewalk, scheduled to take place Friday, will now be conducted by a man and a woman — NASA astronauts Nick Hague and Christina Koch.

American astronaut Anne McClain, who was supposed to conduct the spacewalk with Koch, is now tentatively scheduled to perform her second spacewalk with Canadian Space Agency astronaut David Saint-Jacques on April 8.

Why the change-up? Quite simply, there's only one spacesuit that best fits both female astronauts. "McClain learned during her first spacewalk that a medium-size hard upper torso — essentially the shirt of the spacesuit – fits her best," NASA announced Monday. "Because only one medium-size torso can be made ready by Friday, March 29, Koch will wear it."

This Friday will mark the second in a series of three spacewalks for the Expedition 59 crew. […] This will be the 215th spacewalk for the space station and if everything goes accordingly, Koch will be the 14th woman to perform a spacewalk.

Evan Osnos, *The New Yorker*, 22 January 2017

Compréhension de l'écrit

Answer the following questions in English, using your own words.

Document A

A. What can you say about the main topic of the text and how these people reacted?

B. Say what the consequences are.

C. Comment on M. Kingsley statement (l. 24-25) and explain her feelings on the topic. How different is her point of view from A. Londonderry's?

Document B

A. What can you say about the main topic of the text and the people involved?

B. What issue is at stake and which solution was found?

C. What does the last sentence show about NASA's policy?

Expression écrite

Choisissez l'un des deux sujets (min. 120 mots).

Question A : A. Londonderry and M. Kingsley meet in Boston. They speak about the role that women can take in the exploration of the world. Write the conversation.

Question B : React to the following statement. Could it change the way society feels towards female explorers? Why (not)?
"Just watch, all of you men. I'll show you what a woman can do… I'll go across the country, I'll race to the Moon… I'll never look back."
Edna Gardner Whyte, American pioneer aviatrix (1902-1992)

Évaluation

Observe the documents.
According to you, which document best illustrates "Private Space and Public Space"?

UNIT 4

a "We Princes are set (as it were) upon stages, in the sight and view of all the world."

Extract from **Elizabeth I**'s reply to Parliament's request to execute Mary Stuart, 1586

b "They might try and manipulate her, they might try and manoeuvre her, they might even try to depose her, but she was in charge."

Christine Riding, Head of art and curator of the Queen's House at Royal Museums Greenwich

UNIT 5

a "Whether you leave well in advance of an event, during or after, the key is to have a real shelter community solution to go to."

Robert Vicino, *www.therealsurvivalists.com*

b "If trouble comes when you least expect it then maybe the thing to do is to always expect it."

Cormac McCarthy, *The Road*, 2006

UNIT 6

a "I am a journalist and a "new woman" if that term means that I believe I can do anything that any man can do."

Annie Londonderry, first woman to bicycle around the world (1870-1947)

b

Mary Kingsley defying a leopard on the loose, lithograph c. 1900

c

Jacky Fleming, *The Trouble with Women*, 2016

Devolved Parliament, England-based street artist Banksy, 2009

AXE 3

Art & Power

AXE 3

UNIT 7

"ARTVERTISING"

How does advertising mirror the societies in the English-speaking world and their power?

YOUR PROJECT

Present a spoof ad and show how powerful it is.

Au menu de cette unité :

DÉCOUVERTES CULTURELLES

- Norman Rockwell et Coca-Cola®
- Le Pop Art
- Le *storytelling* dans la publicité
- Le *Brandalism*
- La publicité parodique (*spoof ad*)
- La publicité engagée

OUTILS LINGUISTIQUES

- L'expression de la contrainte (*make sb do sth…*)
- Les quantifieurs
- L'expression de l'indignation

BEFORE CLASS!

Flash to watch!

Watch the video and get ready to talk about it in class!

VIDEO N°14

❶ American Icons

How did Norman Rockwell hook customers?

1 A natural storyteller

A. Observe the painting. Say what is promoted and how (topic, colours, character, mood, atmosphere…).
B. Read the text and check your guesses (Rockwell's world and mood, what his work evokes; his technique of storytelling and what motivated it).
C. Complete your description of the painting with what you discovered in the text.

The term "Rockwellian" has been used to denote a world replete with harmony in familial relationships, patriotism, optimism, idealism, good-natured fun, and a general feeling that all is well. Adapting everyday situations by accenting and augmenting them to increase their visual and emotional punch, Norman Rockwell didn't create a fantasy existence, but instead enhanced our own. [...]
Norman Rockwell possessed a distinct ability to create works of art that evoke a strong emotional response. Many of the emotions drawn from the viewer are memories of formative events from their own lives, nostalgia toward a time long gone, or a feeling of Americans collectively united through war-time patriotism. [...]
A natural storyteller, Norman Rockwell envisioned his scenarios down to the smallest detail, yet at the easel he found it difficult to paint purely from his imagination. In his first decades as an illustrator, he could not paint without studio models in continual view as he worked, explaining that it had "never been natural" for him to "deviate from the facts" of the subject before him.
Rockwell turned to photography as an efficient, accurate, and liberating means to satisfy his literalism. By photographing his props wherever he found them he no longer had to assemble together the disparate objects his narratives required. By photographing far-flung settings he was able to introduce true-to-life backgrounds. And by freeing him from the drawbacks of live models, photography dramatically expanded his vocabulary of available postures and possible expressions. "Now anybody could pose for me," Rockwell said, and he took full advantage of the opportunity. Rockwell's trademark animated faces became possible because they could first be captured on film. Norman Rockwell adeptly coaxed his characteristic expressions from a cast of amateur performers with the skill of a seasoned filmmaker. The artist himself deemed this directorial ability "an art in itself," underscoring the importance of a talent that was central to his storytelling process. After choosing the best photographs to tell his story, Norman Rockwell began the process of translating these images into his finished painting.

Norman Rockwell Museum, **www.nrm.org**

2 Norman Rockwell and Art

A. Watch the video and be ready to talk about the Coca-Cola™ company mystery; the year 1928; the public reaction to Rockwell and his ads at the time; the originality of the last illustration.
B. Find another painting by Norman Rockwell and say how it chronicles consumerism in the same way.

VIDEO N°15

2 Connecting People With the Product

How do brands create strong storytelling to engage customers emotionally?

1 Advertising and fiction

A. Online. Watch the Sainsbury's ad "1914, Christmas 2014" (www.lienmini.fr/htr-tle-07). Give the context (when, where, who, what).

B. Summarise the story.

C. What emotions are triggered by this scene?

D. Have your say. Account for the message with regard to the whole commercial: how moved are you?

2 Animated advertising

A. Read the text and tell for the story (who, when, where, what).

B. Give the message of the story.

C. How does this commercial engage customers?

D. Go further. Watch the clip online (www.lienmini.fr/htr-tle-07) and say how animation attracts viewers (colours, shapes, music, environment).

Apple always has an interesting ad for the holiday season. This time, it's a cute little animated short film. It feels like a hybrid between a Pixar movie and a Wes Anderson creation.

Named "Share Your Gifts," the ad focuses on a dreamy teenager who spends a lot of time on her MacBook. She regularly prints something she has created. We never know for sure if it's a text, a drawing, some lyrics, etc.

But every time she looks at her creations, she dismisses them and puts them in a green box. Sheets of paper pile up in the box and the girl can't even close it anymore.

During a cold winter night, her dog accidentally opens the window. The sheets of paper fly out the window. She ends up chasing her creations so that nobody sees them. Eventually, she realizes that sharing feels great and overcomes her fears. It's a feel-good story that rings true with many creative people, even in the age of Instagram.

Compared to previous years, the soundtrack might not sound familiar. That's because it's an original song from sixteen-year-old singer Billie Eilish. Like many young musicians, Eilish started writing music on a Mac in her bedroom. And this song was also written with her sibling Finneas O'Connell in her parent's home.

Interestingly, there's no iPhone, no iPad, no Apple Watch. This year, it's all about the Mac. Apple wants to make sure that everybody knows the Mac is an important product for the company. At least that's what Tim Cook said on stage during its fall event.

Romain Dillet, ***techcrunch.com***, 2018

3 How to hook customers

A. Read the text on Worksheet n°13. Find:

- the challenges in advertising;
- how a brand develops power;
- what advertising is about (and not about);
- how brands can build a connection with customers;
- why it is essential to hook customers.

B. Have your say. Which piece of storytelling hooks you the most among the two videos above? Why?

HELP!

Nouns

- a feel-good story
- soundtrack /'saʊndtræk/
- target
- customer /'kʌstəmə/ loyalty /'lɔɪəlti/ = when a client comes back

Adjectives

- emotional /ɪ'məʊʃənəl/
- compelling /kəm'pelɪŋ/
- memorable
- vibrant /'vaɪbrənt/
- engaging
- eye-catching

Verbs & Expressions

- hook = engage
- draw attention
- act upon
- reach /'riːtʃ/
- make sb + V

4 Billboards and walls

A. Read the article and draw the timeline of mural advertising (including periods, spaces, types of advertising, reasons).

B. Account for the resurgence of mural advertising.

C. Have your say. Which form of storytelling do you find the most influencing? Compare with the documents on the opposite page.

Since the early 2000s, there has been a resurgence of hand-painted advertising murals in cities across the nation. [...] Painted wall advertising can trace its lineage back to the 1830s with the advent of large-format outdoor billboards [...]. Bringing those billboards into cities and towns wasn't always easy or possible, so the next available space was an open wall — any open wall. [...] Hitting its golden age in the 1920s through the 1940s, murals remained a popular and inexpensive form of advertising until the 1950s when electric signs began to replace them. [...] Today, cities and towns have realized that these remnants of the past are woven into their cultural tapestry; revitalization programs have sprung up [...]. Astute brands also understand that the creation of new, hand-painted wall murals have the power to command attention [...].

In 2004, a Brooklyn-based team of three wall dogs[1] launched Colossal Media. Today, they are credited as the pivotal force behind a reenergized industry [...]. These modern wall dogs are savvy, too, offering services from location scouting to full video and photographic documentation of a mural's creation.

[...] Brands have recognized that allowing the artistry of the painting to come forward is transformative for the ad itself, its relationship with the viewer, and the environment in which it resides. In doing so, they connect on a meaningful, human level. [...] They influence mindsets and moods, and their iconic nature becomes a part of an area's culture. The act of creation, and its interactive nature, is performance art for storytelling and sharing — an opportunity that print media and digital campaigns cannot so easily claim. Global brands, from Adidas, Apple, and Netflix, to small town coffee shops and grocers have seen their murals become Instagram sensations, backdrops for fashion shoots, magazine covers, and primetime news stories, reaching online impressions in the double-digit millions.

In a society of instant gratification, with so many of us face-down, glued to our devices, hand-painted murals have the inspiring ability to ground us in our environment even while connecting with us online. Our desire to share unique experiences makes this a perfect and beautiful approach for brands to both embed themselves into the fabric of a community and engage their audiences on a grand scale. The resurgence of this hand-crafted media has shown that advertising can transcend its own message, that brands can have impact beyond a mere wall, and that we're hungry to connect with those brands on a more human level.

1 the painters who brave the heights and elements to paint walls

Greg Spraker, ***Grafik Agency***, 14 November 2017

5 Street art goes corporate

VIDEO N°16

A. Watch the introduction of the video. How are murals usually considered? What solution was found?

B. Watch the whole video and say:
- what people use murals for;
- who Paul Lindhal is and how he sees his activity;
- what Colossal Media is (place, activity, rank, clients...).

C. Describe the process of creation (difficulty, relation to social media, strategy, final result expected).

YOUR TURN! 6 Promote art

The Museum of Brands in London is holding an exhibition entitled "Advertising, influencing customers today". Use what you have learnt to prepare a three minutes promotional message for their website. Encourage people to come and discover the various rooms of the exhibition.

❸ Buy Buy, Bye Bye?

How did "pop culture" lead to overconsumption and disgust?

1 A new art form for a booming country

A. Observe this painting. Give the brand name, the product and the message.
B. Watch the video and summarise it (historical events, people, social and economic situation).
C. Explain the link between the evolution of the society and the new artistic movement.
C. Have your say. What do you think of this form of art?

VIDEO N°17

Campbell's Soup Cans, Andy Warhol, 1962

2 Art and advertising: a complicated affair

A. Read **Part 1**. Say why art and advertising have always had a complicated relationship. Give examples and explain them.
B. Have your say. Do you think art and advertising can merge? Why (not)?
C. Read **Part 2.** Explain the relationship between street art and big brands.
D. Say what the Brandalism project is.
E. Compare the Brandalism project with the "Art Everywhere" project.
F. Have your say. What do you think of the two projects?
G. Go further. Observe the pictures on the opposite page. What image best illustrates brandalism? Justify.

Part 1

The relationship between art and advertising has often been a complicated and tense affair. Some would argue that advertising is just a form of art designed to sell things. Indeed, in Britain, advertising and marketing are bunched together with the arts and considered part of the 'creative industries'. Advertising has long been a way for artists to earn a bit of cash – even the supposedly 'anti-consumerist' street artist Shepard Fairey has been enlisted to do advertising for the likes of Pepsi and Saks. [...]

But aside from the cosy relationship enjoyed by some artists and big brands, there is a definite antagonism between the worlds of art and advertising. Advertising has long harvested cultural images and repurposed them for its own unscrupulous purposes. One [...] example saw Michelango's David used by US-based arms firm ArmaLite to sell an automatic rifle, causing outrage in Florence.

Part 2

Modern street art has been replete with work that directly attacks brands and their marketing images, often appropriating a large company's logo and using its power and reach to turn it back against them. [...] the Brandalism project took over 365 advertising spots across 10 British cities and replaced their images with the work of street artists from across the world. Many of the works engaged directly with the pernicious nature of advertising; almost all are critical of consumerist culture more generally. [...] Brandalism is a bold, visually striking and highly provocative project, which aims to wrest control of our visual landscape from the big brands.

[...] the 'Art Everywhere' project has sought to do something similar, but on a bigger scale, taking over 30,000 advertising spaces and filling them with great works of art as voted for by the public. [...]

The antagonism between art and advertising isn't just about a power struggle over the meanings inscribed on certain images; it's a battle over our public spaces. [...] These days almost no space is left unbranded [...]. Projects like 'Art Everywhere' and Brandalism are attempting to redress the balance a little.

Joe Turnbull, ***Art and Advertising: friends or foes?***, 12 August 2014

YOUR TURN! 3 Happy customers?

A. Online. Watch the short movie *Happiness* by Steve Cutts. Say how consumers are represented.

B. Choose two passages that strike you and justify.

C. Describe and comment on the final scene.

D. Have your say. How close to reality do you think this film is?

HELP!

Nouns

- brands : *marques*
- consumer
- visual landscape
- power struggle
- public space
- society

Adjectives

- pernicious /pəˈnɪʃəs/ = harmful = destructive
- bold /ˈbəʊld/ = imaginative
- striking /ˈstraɪkɪŋ/ = impressive
- provocative /prəˈvɒkətɪv/
- (un)branded /ʌnˈbrændɪd/ = (un)marked

Verbs & Expressions

- battle over
- turn sth back against sb
- aim to
- redress the balance
- talk sb into + V-ing = *convaincre, inviter à*

❹ Humour: a Tool and a Weapon

How does advertising influence customers through humour?

1 Using parody in advertising

A. Read the text. Summarise the difference between parody and satire.
B. Describe how parody is a power of attraction in advertising.
C. Give the limits of parody and its long term result.
D. Have your say. Have you ever felt attracted to a brand after watching a spoof ad?

Satire is "a genre in literature which shams or ridicules certain aspects of the society or the society as a whole... and uses the right amount of sarcasm, wit, and exaggeration." Parody, on the other hand, "is pure entertainment, and sometimes called a spoof." A brand might poke fun at people who go to spas and put cucumbers over their eyes... or a skeleton enjoying a spa day could just be a delightful "spoof" on spa-goers to make customers laugh. Using humor in marketing is a great way to spread your message, as comedy will make people pay attention and provide the opportunity to explain the products and services you provide. [...] just getting someone to smile is going to help them listen to the explanation of what you have to offer.

Sometimes, a joke (especially of the satire or parody variety) can be funny but go overboard distracting from the message you're trying to express. The concept is to make them feel good and understand how after they hire your services they will know you're easily approachable and able to hear their concerns, thus altering your service to suit their needs.

Parody relies on the original work to make fun of it but is still within the realm of fair use. Satire actually steals someone's original art and uses it toward a different topic it wasn't meant to address. All said, using satire or parody is a great way to catch someone's attention and make them want to hear the rest of your message. Have fun with your marketing campaign and watch as the interest turns into conversions and your business grows with happy customers who always return.

Andrew M., ***www.writeraccess.com***, 30 August 2018

2 Marmite: a case study

A. Go online (www.lienmini.fr/htr-tle-07) to watch the ad for Marmite "End Marmite Neglect" (2013) and summarise the story (where, who, what, why / what for).
B. Give the elements showing that the brand targets a British audience.
C. Comment on the tone of the TV advert.
D. Have your say. Do you feel hooked by the ad? Why (not)?

3 Spoof for thought

A. Observe each poster and find the differences.
B. Give the objective of the second poster.
C. Read the text below and:
- explain the artist's process of creation.
- say what made him react.

D. **Have your say.** Do you think this spoof ad is effective and thought-provoking? Why (not)?

A

Van Heusen ad, 1940

B

Van Heusen ad's spoof, Eli Rezkallah, 2018

The image of a perfect woman in the 1950s is familiar to all of us – a diligent wife, slaving around the house all day, preparing delicious meals for her hardworking husband, taking care of the children, and all that with a smile, of course. This image was reflected a lot in the ads of that era too. Inspired by them, photographer and video editor from Beirut, Lebanon, Eli Rezkallah created a series called "In A Parallel Universe" where he switched up the gender roles portrayed in those ads to reveal the absurdity of such stereotypes with humor.

"Last Thanksgiving, I overheard my uncles talk about how women are better off cooking, taking care of the kitchen, and fulfilling their 'womanly duties'", Rezkallah writes on his website. "Although I know that not all men are like my uncles and think that way, I was surprised to learn that some still do, so I went on to imagine a parallel universe, where roles are inverted and men are given a taste of their own sexist poison."

www.boredpanda.com

YOUR TURN! 4 Spoof ad challenge!

Adbusters is a network of artists and activists committed to questioning the power of brands and consumerism through a nonprofit organization.

Create a spoof ad for the next spoof ads challenge launched by the website www.adbusters.org.

5 Standing Up For a Cause

How do brands artfully convey strong messages?

1 Fighting for the environment

A. Observe each advert. Say how each artist shows reality (points of view, shot angles, colours, message).

B. How powerful are these two advertising campaigns?

C. Have your say. In your opinion, which picture better illustrates the notion of "art and power"?
Prepare a one-minute presentation to justify your opinion.

Campaign for marine conservation charity Surfers Against Sewage, 2017

B

Campaign for Surfriders Foundation Australia, 2013

HELP!

Nouns
- threat /θret/
- plastic footprint = plastic impact
- beach clean-up
- atom(ic) bomb /bɒm/
- mushroom cloud
- fallout: *retombées*
- waste = trash
- warning

Adjectives
- dramatic
- nuclear /ˈnjuːkliə/
- delusional = insane
- biodegradable /baɪəʊdɪˈgreɪdəbl/
- reusable /riːˈjuːzəbl/ ≠ single-use
- disposable /dɪˈspəʊzəbl/: *jetable*
- durable
- alarming
- imminent = impending

Verbs & Expressions
- stand for = represent
- litter = throw away
- mistake for sth = take for sth else
- get involved /ɪnˈvɒlvd/
- threaten /ˈθrɛtn/
- raise awareness /əˈweənɪs/ = make sb conscious of
- advocate sth /ˈædvəkeɪt/ = defend
- recycle /riːˈsaɪkl/
- volunteer /vɒlənˈtɪə/
- biodegrade /baɪədɪˈgreɪd/ = decompose
- address an issue /ˈɪʃuː/
- spread the word

YOUR PROJECT

1. The "*Raise awareness for a cause through public contest!*" campaign is now opened. Choose a cause from the English-speaking world. Create an awareness campaign (in the form of a poster or a video).

Present it to the jury: explain your choice and how you plan to persuade the viewers.

Go on www.judgify.me/l/blog/raising-awareness-cause-public-contests / to find tips.

OR

2. Create a radio commercial.
Choose one picture (A or B). Imagine a slogan, a catchphrase and a short text. Then record a radio commercial.

You may add a soundtrack that fits the emotions and message you wish to convey.

RULE THE GRAMMAR!

L'EXPRESSION DE LA CONTRAINTE (FAIRE FAIRE QQ CHOSE À QQ'UN)

L'anglais dispose de plusieurs structures possibles :

*I'll **have** you **buy***
*I'll **make** you **buy*** } *this product.*
*I'll **get** you **to buy***

Toutes ces phrases peuvent se traduire par "Je vais vous faire acheter ce produit" mais avec des nuances particulières.

TO HAVE + ... + BV

*I'll **have** Dad **buy** me this new shampoo.*

Je vais demander à papa de m'acheter ce nouveau shampooing. → C'est la forme la plus neutre, le locuteur n'exerce pas de pression.

TO MAKE + ... + BV

*I'll **make** you **sell** your shares whether you want it or not.*

Je vais t'obliger à vendre tes parts, que tu le veuilles ou non. → On exerce ici une contrainte très forte.

TO GET + ... + TO + BV

*I'll **get** your Dad **to buy** this new car.*

Je vais m'arranger pour que ton père achète cette nouvelle voiture. → Il y a une idée de manipulation, plus ou moins grande selon le contexte.

LES QUANTIFIEURS

• SOME, ANY Ces quantifieurs, qui indiquent « une certaine quantité », s'utilisent avec des dénombrables ou des indénombrables.

Forme affirmative	Forme interrogative
*There are **some** customers in the shop.* *His ad campaign has had **some** success.*	*Are there **any** customers in the shop?* *Has his ad campaign had **any** success?*

• (A) LITTLE, (A) FEW Ces quantifieurs indiquent « un peu de » ou « peu de ».

(a) few s'utilise avec des **dénombrables**	***(a) little*** s'utilise avec des **indénombrables**
*There are **a few** customers in his shop.* (un peu de, quelques) *There are **few** customers in his shop.* (quelques)	*His ad campaign has had **a little** success.* (un peu de) *His ad campaign has had **little** success.* (peu de)

• A LOT OF, MUCH, MANY Ces quantifieurs signifient « beaucoup ».

A lot of (ou *lots of*) s'utilise aussi bien avec les **dénombrables** qu'avec les **indénombrables**.	
Many s'utilise avec des **dénombrables**	***Much*** s'utilise avec des **indénombrables**
***Many / A lot of** students saw this exhibition.*	*He's made **much / a lot of** progress since the 80s.*

→ P.311

LANGUAGE LAB

- Unit's vocabulary
- Audio words
- MP3
- Interactive Test

★ **1. Fill in the blanks with *much, little, many* or *few*.**

A. His customers were … and far between.
B. She had … success to start with but then her career rocketed.
C. We haven't got … time before the exhibition.
D. … admirers came to the opening of the art exhibit.
E. This artist was never gained … fame in her lifetime.
F. I saw … of his ads on television.

★ **2. Turn these verbs into adjectives to describe the quality of a good commercial.**

A. compel → … • B. impress → … • C. attract → … • D. engage → … • E. remember → … • F. catch the eye → …

★★ **3. Rewrite the sentences as shown in the example.**

I'll have him write an ad for the company → I'll get him to write an ad for the company.

A. I'll have the artist make another draft. → …
B. They'll have the presenter announce the exhibition. → …
C. Jane had the painter sell his best painting. → …
D. I'll have the manager buy this new collection. → …
E. He had the spectators applaud the performance. → …
F. I'll have him finish by Tuesday. → …

★★ **4. Match the words with their definitions.**

A. a mural
B. Pop Art
C. storytelling
D. Brandalism
E. a spoof ad
F. an awareness campaign

1. the art of telling a story instead of describing a product to sell it.
2. a project to replace advertising from big brands with street art.
3. a parody of a commercial to make fun of it.
4. a movement turning mass products into works of art.
5. a hand painted advertisement on a wall.
6. an advertisement which promotes a cause.

★★★ **5. Use these words to create other words by adding prefixes or/and suffixes. Then translate into French.**

A. advertise • B. loyal • C. truth • D. brand • E. use • F. custom

★★★ **6. Translate the following sentences into English.**

A. *Comment osez-vous faire cela à notre planète !*
B. *Comment pouvez-vous faire cela à nos océans !*
C. *Je suis hors de moi à cause de sa réaction !*
D. *Les climatologues sont fous de rage à cause de cette nouvelle politique.*

★★★ **7. The ad competition.**

Choose an advertisement and say why you find it great. Use as many words from the unit as possible.

8. Interactive test! What is your score?

OPEN YOUR EARS!

PHONOLOGY

• **Écoutez ces mots.** Que remarquez-vous ? **MP3 N°34**

ad /ˈæd/ • advertise /ˈædvətaɪz/ • advertising /ˈædvətaɪzɪŋ/

• **Récapitulons :** *ad, advertise* et *advertising* sont tous accentués sur la première syllabe.

Attention :

(UK) : advertisement /ədˈvɜːtɪsmənt/

(US) : advertisement /ædvərˈtaɪzmənt/

SHOWTIME

Écoutez cette campagne et répétez en imitant le locuteur.

MP3 N°35

There is actually /\ much you can do about climate change!
Many organisations try to convince people to /\ change the way they live, but they don't /\ listen!
What on /\ earth do you think you're doing to our planet!

Dans ces quatre phrases, on remarque l'intonation /\ (*rise-fall*) qui est utilisée quand on veut convaincre son auditoire ou que l'on est transporté par l'enthousiasme ou l'agacement.

Quote challenge

★ **3 sentences**
★★ **4 to 6 sentences**
★★★ **7 sentences and +**

Which quote best sums up what you have learnt? Make as many sentences as you can to collect stars!

"Advertising is fundamentally persuasion and persuasion happens to be not a science, but an art."

William Bernbach,
American advertising creative director

"Brands should think of themselves not as storytellers but story builders. We plant seeds of content and let our community build on it."

Amy Pascal,
American business executive and film producer

"In the modern world of business, it is useless to be a creative, original thinker unless you can also sell what you create."

David Ogilvy,
British advertising pioneer

AXE 3

UNIT 8

SHORT CUT

ONCE UPON A GUN

How is the power of culture used to influence public opinion on guns in the U.S.?

YOUR PROJECT

In an online forum, debate the power that pop culture holds over your opinion on guns.

BEFORE CLASS!

Flash to watch!

Watch an excerpt of ***Bowling for Columbine*** (2002).
Be ready to talk about it in class!

Au menu de cette unité :

DÉCOUVERTES CULTURELLES

- La culture des armes aux États-Unis (2e amendement)
- Deux contes revisités par la NRA
- Des illustrateurs engagés pour le contrôle des armes
- Les contradictions du cinéma hollywoodien

OUTILS LINGUISTIQUES

- Le *present perfect*
- Le gérondif
- L'expression du contraste

❶ Grandma, What a Big Gun You Have!

How does the American gun lobby use fairy tales to seduce a young audience?

VIDEO N°18

1 Rewritten tales

A. Watch the video and take notes.

B. What is the main issue tackled in this video?

C. Do both interviewees agree on the purpose of this rewriting? Pick out their arguments.

D. **Have your say.** What do you think about the arguments put forward in the video?

2 Happily armed ever after

A. Read the article. What is the main topic?

B. Identify the two sides cited and pick out their main arguments.

C. According to both sides, why were these fairy tales rewritten?

D. **Have your say.** Is a tale powerful enough to seduce children into wanting guns?

There is no denying the rather sinister aspects of many of the Grimm brothers' fairy tales. Little Red Riding Hood is almost eaten by a wolf, while Hansel and Gretel only narrowly[1] escape a cannibalistic witch who lives deep in the forest.

Now, in the stories reimagined by America's largest and most powerful gun-rights lobbyist, those youngsters are packing heat[2] and – needless to say – are seamlessly[3] transformed from hapless[4] victims to heroic survivors.

The National Rifle Association's twist on the classic tales has sparked outcry[5], with gun-control activists claiming it is an outrageous marketing stunt[6]. The NRA, meanwhile, has defended the tales posted on its "family website". [...]

"Have you ever wondered what those same fairy tales might sound like if the hapless Red Riding Hood, Hansel and Gretel had been taught about gun safety and how to use firearms?"

The NRA said the stories, written by Amelia Hamilton, whom the lobbying group calls a conservative blogger and "lifelong writer and patriot," were part of an effort to promote responsible firearm use by children.

The accident prevention programme it oversees has helped teach more than 28 million kids about how to stay safe if they find a gun, according to the NRA's website.

At no point in either story do the protagonists fire their weapons at the fictional villains, but guns are portrayed as key to keeping them safe, according to ABC News.

In the NRA's version of Hansel and Gretel, the pair are shown hunting for deer and other wildlife when they discover an evil witch's house. They then proceed to free a pair of boys held captive by her, guns at the ready. [...]

The release of the stories comes as the US continues to reel from[7] gun violence involving children. Reports suggest there are at least 350 shooting incidents involving children under the age of twelve each year.

Toddlers aged three or under shoot either themselves or another person roughly once a week, an average of more than 50 times a year.

1 *échapper de peu* • 2 *être armé* • 3 easily • 4 unlucky • 5 *un tollé* • 6 *coup de pub* • 7 *être abasourdi*

Andrew Budcombe, ***The Independent***, March 2016

3 The NRA twist

A. **Groupwork.** **Group A** reads text 1 and **group B** reads text 2 on **Worksheet n°14**.

- What fairy tale do you recognise?
- How does the NRA's version differ from the original fairy tale? Make a list of elements.

B. Present your conclusions to your classmates.

C. **Have your say.** Do you think that the NRA fulfils its purpose of making guns attractive to children? Justify your answer.

❷ Cartoonists Voice Their Concern

What means do pro-gun control cartoonists use to convey their message?

1 Targeting gun issues

A. Groupwork. Choose one cartoon, describe it and analyse it (message, goal).
B. Which one would you pick to illustrate a campaign in favour of gun control? Justify your choice, then debate with your classmates.
C. Go further. Do cartoonists have the power to influence people's minds about gun control?

- Stars and Stripes
- gun barrel /'bærəl/
- bullet hole /həʊl/
- a distorted motto
- violent history
- bloody
- gun culture
- pun: *jeu de mots*

A

Steve Greenberg, American cartoonist, 11 January 2011

B

David Horsey, American cartoonist, 2019

- chart
- tick = check mark
- self-evident
- insincere /ɪnsɪn'sɪə/
- hypocritical /hɪpə'krɪtɪkl/

C

Paresh, Indian cartoonist, 5 August 2019

- be surrounded
- shoot down: *abattre*
- aim at: *viser*
- gag: *museler*
- the 2nd Amendment
- victims
- bloody scene
- condemn /kən'dem/
- zoom in ≠ zoom out

D

- an allegory of /ˈæləgəri/
- Statue of Liberty
- pedestal
- paranoid /ˈpærənɔɪd/
- war games
- a climate of fear
- twist a symbol

Glen Le Lievre, Australian cartoonist, 11 July 2016

E

- machine gun: *mitraillette*
- caricature /ˈkærɪkətʃʊə/
- spoof: *parodie*
- manipulate
- ***American Gothic*** is a 1930 painting by Grant Wood. It has become one of the most famous paintings of the 20th century. There have been countless parodies of it.
- **Mitch McConnell** is Donald Trump's most trusted advisor.

Ken Catalino, Australian cartoonist, 5 September 2019

2 The Second Amendment

A. Read the Second Amendment in the cartoon and say how it is related to the debate about guns.

B. Have your say. What image is given of this Amendment? Justify.

- infringe: *enfreindre*
- militia: *milice*
- weigh /weɪ/ on sb/sth: *peser sur*

YOUR TURN! 3 Sharpen your pencil!

You are a cartoonist for *The New Yorker*.
Choose an American symbol connected to gun culture and say in an email to your boss how you plan to distort it.

❸ May the Gun Be With You

What role does Hollywood play in gun culture?

1 Gun culture in films

A. Study the film posters (composition, light, colours, effects…). What emotions do they convey?

B. Go further. How does visual art impact your reaction to weapons?

A

B

2 Stick to your guns

A. According to the author, how is Hollywood related to gun culture? Justify by quoting the text.

B. Have your say. Do you share this point of view? Illustrate your answer with some Hollywood films you have seen.

HELP!

Verbs & Expressions
- (dis)agree with…
- change one's opinion ≠ hold the opinion that
- consider
- have no doubt that
- influence
- put in perspective
- My impression/opinion/belief/view is that …

It's a stark conundrum[1] — denouncing violence while exploiting it. Hollywood just can't escape the rules they created — guns are both necessary and kind of cool. Naturally, they take a principle to unhealthy extremes, but when things go haywire and the zombies, aliens or enemy agents are on their way, the first order of business is finding a weapon. [...] Hollywood is legendary for fashioning the worst-case scenarios that drive home the utility of guns, and the actors claiming to shun violence ironically spend their careers portraying its inescapability.

1 énigme

David Burnett, ***Hollywood Hypocrisy***, 1 January 2014

YOUR PROJECT

As an American citizen, in an online forum, debate the power that pop culture (cinema, fairy tales, visual arts) holds over your opinion on guns.

Read some posts on Worksheet n°15 **and react.**

LANGUAGE LAB

- Unit's vocabulary
- Audio words
- MP3
- Interactive Test

★ 1. Fill in the blanks using the following words.

culture • control • rights • safety • violence • ownership

A. Following the 2001 terrorist attacks, there was a notable increase in gun ... because the American citizens were afraid.

B. Gun ... advocates have a hard time campaigning against the lobbyists.

C. Having gun ... is part of the American Constitution, which is difficult to repeal.

D. Because of Hollywood films, a gun ... developed in the USA.

E. The statistics show that gun ... is omnipresent and that mass shootings are on the rise.

F. The NRA claims that the fairy tales were rewritten to promote gun ... .

★ 2. Put these sentences in the *present perfect*.

A. I *(sling)* my guns in protest.

B. She *(speak)* to the Marshal about self-defense.

C. The NRA *(battle)* many scandals.

D. Peter *(forbid)* Jeremy to resort to the 2nd Amendment.

E. We *(buy)* guns in order to defend ourselves.

F. Lobbyists from the NRA *(spend)* millions to spread a pro-gun message.

★★ 3. Transform these sentences as shown in the example.

E.g.: *Though it's dangerous, they possess several shotguns.*

→ ***No matter how dangerous it is,*** *they possess several shotguns.*

→ ***However dangerous it is,*** *they possess several shotguns.*

→ ***Dangerous as it is,*** *they possess several shotguns.*

A. Though self-defense is important, you should consider other people's safety.

B. Though it is politically sensitive, the senator is against the 2nd Amendment.

C. Though Red Riding Hood is harmless, the wolf should be careful.

D. Though it's frightening, people carry their guns in their cars.

★★★ 4. Match each idiom with its meaning. Then use them in a sentence.

A. with guns blazing

B. jump the gun

C. fire away

D. stick to one's guns

E. be trigger-happy

1. start too soon
2. go ahead and say something
3. with great determination and energy
4. be quick to use a firearm
5. refuse to compromise or to change

★★★ 5. Translate into English.

A. Elle n'est pas d'accord avec le fait que je possède un fusil. *(to approve of)*

B. Merci d'accepter mon point de vue. *(to accept)*

C. Ils ont réussi à faire changer d'avis leur ami. *(to succeed)*

D. Tu devrais éviter de dire aux gens ce que tu penses sur la détention d'armes. *(to avoid)*

6. Interactive test! What is your score?

OPEN YOUR EARS!

PHONOLOGY

• **Les sigles reprennent le schéma intonatif de la phrase anglaise classique avec un accent principal à la fin.**

National Rifle Association → *NRA*

On **accentue** donc toujours **la dernière lettre** des **sigles**.

• **Écoutez les sigles suivant et entraînez-vous à les répéter.**

MP3 N°36

USA (United States of America)
NRA (National Rifle Association)
CIA (Central Intelligence Agency)
FBI (Federal Bureau of Investigation)

AUDIO MYSTERY

Listen and solve the mystery! **MP3 N°37**

Quote challenge

★ **3 sentences**
★★ **4 to 6 sentences**
★★★ **7 sentences and +**

Is this quote a good illustration of the unit? Make as many sentences as you can to collect stars!

"I made 'Bowling for Columbine' in the hope the school shootings would stop and that we would address the issue of how easy it is to get a gun in the United States, and tragically, those school shootings continue."

Michael Moore (1954-)
American documentary film-maker

AXE 3

UNIT 9
MASTERS OF SPEECH

SHORT CUT

How powerful is oratory in the U.S.?

YOUR PROJECT

1. Deliver a speech to defend a cause you support.

OR

2. Participate in a Moth Show.

BEFORE CLASS!

Flash to watch!

Watch the video and get ready to talk about it in class!

VIDEO N°19

Au menu de cette unité :

DÉCOUVERTES CULTURELLES

- La culture du débat dans les lycées américains
- Les *MOTH Shows*
- La technique du *storytelling*
- Quelques grands discours (Martin Luther King Jr., Oprah Winfrey, J.K. Rowling…)

OUTILS LINGUISTIQUES

- Les connecteurs logiques
- Les groupes de souffle
- L'intonation

❶ Word Leaders

How important is public speaking in the U.S.?

1 High school debate teams

A. Look at the picture, explain what the students are doing.
B. What do you think students learn in a debate team?
C. Have your say. Would you like to join a debate team? Why (not)?

2 The effects of school debates

A. Read the text. What are the common points between the people quoted at the beginning (l. 1-8)?
B. Pick out the advantages and disadvantages of school debates according to the authors.
C. Have your say. Focus on the last sentence. Do you agree with the authors? Why (not)?

What do conservative political figures like Ted Cruz, Steve Bannon, Karl Rove and Richard Nixon have in common with liberal politicians like Elizabeth Warren, Andrew Yang, Kamala Harris and Bill Clinton? They all honed[1] their skills of rhetoric, reasoning and persuasion on school debate teams. That's no surprise. Excelling in school debate opens many academic and professional doors, conferring prestige and signalling exceptional verbal and logical aptitude. [...]

But while school debate can be good for aspiring politicians, it may not be good for our politics. In particular, it may contribute to the closed-minded, partisan and self-interested nature of so much of today's public and political dialogue. Why? Because school debate ultimately strengthens and rewards biased reasoning.

In traditional debate competitions, teams are assigned at random[2] to argue one or the other side of an issue. Each round, one team is assigned the affirmative view — say, "Recreational drug use should be legalized" — and the other team, the negative. That means teams start with a conclusion, whether they endorse[3] it or not, and work backward from there, marshaling[4] the best arguments they can devise to make that conclusion come out on top. The goal is not to determine the most reasonable or fair-minded approach to an issue, but to defend a given claim at all costs. [...]

This also happens to be the kind of argumentation we find so corrosive in today's politics. [...] School debate reinforces this mode of reasoning. By celebrating those who are most adept at it, schools hold it up as a model form of thinking. Don't get us wrong. This style of reasoning can be useful. Legal advocacy, for instance, often requires it. [...] Nevertheless, traditional school debate discourages the kind of listening and reasoning that is critical to a healthy democracy.

1 improve • 2 arbitrarily • 3 agree with • 4 collect and organise

Jonathan Ellis and Francesca Hovagimian, ***The New York Times***, 12 October 2019

3 A webquest

A. Go to https://themoth.org and find more about the Moth (mission, origin of the name, launch date, founder, place).
B. What are the different types of live events?
C. Focus on the StorySLAM event (place, how it works, advice and rules).
D. Have your say. Give two reasons why you would (not) like to take part in a Moth show.

❷ The Power of Storytelling

How is storytelling used to captivate audiences?

1 Once upon a time

VIDEO N°20

A. Before watching. What do you think the power of storytelling is?

B. Watch the video. Explain why stories are powerful.

2 The science behind storytelling

A. Read the text. Focus on lines 25-36: Why is listening to a story more captivating than listening to a slideshow presentation?

B. Explain the role metaphors play in "rousing the sensory cortex" (l. 37-38).

C. In your own words, say why telling stories is so powerful.

In 1748, the British politician and aristocrat John Montagu, the 4th Earl of Sandwich, used a lot of his free time for playing cards. One of the problems he had was that he greatly enjoyed eating a snack, whilst still keeping one hand free for the cards. So he came up with the idea to eat beef between slices of toast, which would allow him to finally eat and play cards at the same time. Eating his newly invented "sandwich", the name for two slices of bread with meat in between, became one of the most popular meal inventions in the western world.

Now you are very likely to never forget the story of who invented the sandwich. Or at least, much less likely to do so than if it had been presented in bullet points or another purely information-based form.

For over 27,000 years, since the first cave paintings were discovered, telling stories has been one of our most fundamental communication methods. Here is the science around storytelling and how we can use it to make better decisions every day. [...]

We all enjoy a good story, whether it's a novel, a movie, or simply something one of our friends is explaining to us. But why do we feel so much more engaged when we hear a narrative about events?

[...] If we listen to a Powerpoint presentation with boring bullet points, certain parts in the brain get activated. [...]

When we are being told a story, though, things change dramatically according to researchers [...]. Not only are the language processing parts in our brain activated, but any other area in our brain that we would use when experiencing the events of the story are too. If someone tells us about how delicious certain foods were, our sensory cortex lights up. If it's about motion, our motor cortex gets active.

Metaphors like "The singer had a velvet voice" and "He had leathery hands" roused the sensory cortex. [...] Then, the brains of participants were scanned as they read sentences like "John grasped the object" and "Pablo kicked the ball." The scans revealed activity in the motor cortex, which coordinates the body's movements."

A story can put your whole brain to work. And yet, it gets better: When we tell stories to others that have helped us shape our thinking and way of life, we can have the same effect on them too. The brains of the person telling a story and listening to it, can synchronize, says Uri Hasson from Princeton. [...] Anything you've experienced, you can get others to experience the same. Or at least, get their brain areas active, too.

Leo Widrich, ***Buffer***, 29 November 2012

3 Inspirational speeches

A. Groupwork. Read and/or listen to the speech you are assigned and fill in the corresponding worksheet.

B. Report back to the class.

C. Have your say. List the different strategies used by the speakers. Which ones do you think are the most efficient?

D. At home. Choose a short passage from one of these speeches and rehearse it to practise your oral skills (tone, pronunciation, word stress, etc.). Be ready to deliver it in front of the class.

A

MP3 N°38 — Worksheet n°16

“I have a dream that my four little children...”

B

MP3 N°39 — Worksheet n°17

“What I feared most for myself at your age was not poverty, but failure.”

C

MP3 N°40 — Worksheet n°18

“I was a little girl sitting on the linoleum floor of my mother's house in Milwaukee...”

HELP!

Verbs & Expressions

- give / make /deliver a speech
- address an **au**dience = *s'adresser à un public*
- **cap**ture / catch an **au**dience's at**ten**tion
- **em**phasize /ˈemfəsaɪz/: *mettre l'accent sur*
- draw a **pa**rallel between: *dresser un parallèle entre*
- re**late** to: *s'identifier à*

Stylistic devices

- an al**lu**sion
- an a**na**phora /əˈnæfərə/= repetition of a word or phrase at the beginning of successive sentences.
- a **me**taphor = make a comparison by stating that one thing *is* something else, has the qualities of something else.
- a **si**mile /ˈsɪmɪli/ = expresses comparison or likeness between two objects. It always includes a word such as *like* or *as*.
- personifi**ca**tion /pəsɒnɪfɪˈkeɪʃən/ = attribution of human qualities to something
- an understate**ment** = a **eu**phemism /ˈjuːfəmɪzəm/

4 Words matter

A. Read the text. Identify the type of document and the general context (author, status...).

B. Read carefully. Identify the references Barack Obama uses. What do they have in common?

C. According to Barack Obama, why do "words matter"?

D. Have your say. Have you ever been influenced or motivated by a public figure's words? How?

Don't tell me words don't matter. "I have a dream" — just words? "We hold these truths to be self-evident that all men are created equal" — just words? "We have nothing to fear but fear itself" — just words, just speeches? It's true that speeches don't solve all problems, but what is also true is that if we can't inspire our country to believe again, then it doesn't matter how many policies and plans we have, and that is why I'm running for president of the United States of America, and that's why we just won eight elections straight because the American people want to believe in change again. Don't tell me words don't matter!

Barack Obama,
Democratic Party of Wisconsin Founders Day Gala, 16 February 2008

CHOOSE YOUR PROJECT!

YOUR PROJECT #1

Deliver a speech using storytelling to defend a cause you support.

STEP 1 Choose a cause that matters to you (ecology, racism, women's rights, poverty, etc.).

STEP 2 Gather facts (statistics, dates, etc.) and arguments to defend the cause you have chosen.

STEP 3 Use an event from the English-speaking world and turn it into a story that will be the pillar of your speech.

STEP 4 Write your speech using what you have learnt (rhetorical figures, humour, tone, emotion, pauses, etc.).

STEP 5 Rehearse! Your speech should last 3 minutes maximum.

OR

YOUR PROJECT #2

Participate in a Moth show.

STEP 1 Browse http://themoth.org p. 91 again to know what a Moth show is.

STEP 2 Choose an element from the English-speaking world (an event, a film, a series, a book, a celebrity, a speech, etc.) that impacted your life (e.g. that made you start a new activity / made you change your mind about an idea / made you want to fight for a cause / taught you to be more tolerant or self-confident, etc.).

STEP 3 Add details about this experience: time, place, people, state of mind, moral or lesson it taught you.

STEP 4 Use what you have learnt to highlight the key elements of your story (rhetorical figures, humour, tone, emotion, pauses, etc.).

STEP 5 Rehearse! Your story should last 3 minutes maximum.

TIPS

In the text of your speech:

- Highlight or circle the words/ expressions you are going to stress.
- Check the pronunciation of the words used and write down the phonetic symbols.
- Indicate with a symbol where you are going to pause and to breathe.

Speak:

- Rehearse your speech several times alone.
- Give your speech in front of your family/friends or record it.
- Modulate your voice to express emotions.
- Make sure that you look at the audience and that you speak loud enough.
- Speak slowly (no more than 380 words for a three-minute speech).

SPICE UP YOUR VOCABULARY

- Audio words
- MP3
- Interactive Test

Introducing
- Today I am here to talk to you about…
- I am delighted to be here today to tell you about…
- My objective today is…
- I want to talk about… because…
- I've always been interested in …, that's why…

Outline
- I'll start with… / First, I will talk about… / I'll begin with…
- … then I will look at… / …next… / and finally…
- First(ly)… / Secondly… / Thirdly…

First point
- Let me start with some general information on…
- Let me begin by explaining why/how…
- I'd like to give you some background information about…
- Before I start, does anyone know…?
- As you are all aware…
- I think everybody has heard about…
- It was said in a newspaper / a book
- I read that…

Referring to previous points
- As I said before at the beginning, …
- This relates to what I was saying earlier…
- Let me go back to what I said earlier about…
- We briefly spoke about X earlier; let's look at it in more depth now…

Introducing the next points
- I'd now like to move on to the next part…
- This leads me to my next point, which is…
- Let's now turn to…

Transitions: cause and effect
- Therefore…
- Consequently
- As a result…
- That's why…

Rephrasing
- In other words…
- To put it more simply…
- What I mean to say is…
- So, what I'm saying is…
- To put it in another way…

Conclusion
- To sum up…
- In a nutshell…
- Let's summarise briefly what we have looked at.
- I'd like to recap the main points.
- What you should take away from this is…
- Finally, I want to say…
- Thank you for listening.

OPEN YOUR EARS!

PHONOLOGY

Le schéma intonatif de base de l'anglais est appelé « *glide down* ». Pourquoi ? Parce que …

The sentence glides gradually down.

SHOW TIME

Say it like the model!

Écoutez les phrases suivantes extraites du discours de J.K. Rowling étudié p. 93, et repérez le *glide down*. Essayez ensuite de le reproduire !

MP3 N°39 Bis

- *"Delivering a commencement address is a great responsibility".*
- *"Reflecting on her speech has helped me enormously on writing this one".*
- *"Because it turns out I can't remember any single word she said".*

B1-B2

BACKPACK

Get Ready for your Exam!

UNIT 7

Évaluation

Compréhension de l'oral

"The power of "Brandalism" MP3 n°41

Listen to the audio recording three times and recap what you have understood.

Expression écrite

Choisissez l'un des deux sujets (min. 120 mots).

Question A : In a conversation with an anti-brandalism activist, Bill Poster tries to explain why this artistic movement can act as a counterpower that will benefit everyone. Imagine the conversation.

Question B : "Brandalism" is an international movement of over 80 artists who work together to challenge power relations that exist in public space. "Brandalists" create posters that call into question the advertising campaigns of some well-known brands.

Can "Brandalism" help to challenge all forms of power through art? Why (not)?

U. 8 U. 9

Évaluation

Compréhension de l'oral

"Speech against guns" MP3 n°42

Listen to the audio recording three times and recap what you have understood.

Expression écrite

Choisissez l'un des deux sujets (min. 120 mots).

Question A : After listening to Ryan Deitsch's speech, you write an email to a friend to let him/her know how important it is for artists and celebrities to use their art and voice as a counterpower.

Question B : 19-year-old Ryan Deitsch was involved in the shooting at Marjory Stoneman Douglas High School in Parkland, Florida. He and several classmates formed the "March for Our Lives" movement. Ryan has been using his skills as a filmmaker and a journalist to further this mission and help to save lives.

How important is it for an artist to have his/her voice heard? Could it make a change in the world? Why (not)?

U. 7 U. 9

Évaluation

Once upon a time... a guide to digital storytelling

[…] We get drawn in by good stories, and start to care about the characters, following their adventures to see what happens next. Television executives know this, which is why they spend so much time and money searching for the most compelling stories to air on their networks. Film makers know it too — if they find the perfect epic tale, they know it'll result in epic box-office.

Business leaders have also copped on to the benefits of spinning a good story about their product, and in recent years we've seen the rise of digital storytelling, as companies utilise social media and other online platforms to get customers to engage with their brand on a deeper level. […]

In general, it's not easy to engage consumers with a block of cold data — you need to create a narrative around that data to capture your customers' imaginations and get them clicking for more. When you create a story, you are doing more than just selling your brand — you're conveying a compelling message about your brand and positioning it in a positive way in consumers' minds.

[…] Tell a good, compelling, memorable story, and it will capture your customers' imaginations and stay in their minds, giving them a nice, warm feeling every time they see your logo or colours. Tell a fake, unconvincing, insincere story, though, and your customers will quickly give you the cold shoulder. So, […] don't try to fool your audience. […]

Real people

What's all-important to the ad's success is that it doesn't use an actor to play the main character. [A] great example of storytelling can be seen in the Allianz ads […]. Each one tells a unique true story of Irish lives, and each one has the ring of authenticity. […]

Don't lose the plot

Every story has […] a central plot that drives the narrative. […] You need to find the story within your own company […]. You may have a unique origin story, or a tale about having to overcome adversity to set up your business. What does your business stand for, and what is its mission statement? […]

Keep it real

Whatever story you decide to tell, the most important thing is that it's believable. Sure, you can embellish the tale a bit, […] but make sure that the core of your story is based in truth. […] It's much preferable, and more effective, than a dazzling, elaborate lie. […]

Every story has to have an outcome. […] No need for a perfect ending, though. Those ads where the guy gets the girl just by using a certain fragrance or chewing a certain brand of gum are old hat. You need believable, realistic outcomes for your characters that highlight the benefit of your product without exaggerating its life-enhancing properties.

Kevin Courtney, *www.irishtimes.com*, 25 September 2019

Compréhension de l'écrit

Answer the following questions in English, using your own words.

A. After reading the text, what can you say about:
- its main topic?
- the key ingredients that make a good digital story?
- the strategies used by the media and advertising industries to target consumers?

B. Comment on the following statement (l. 41-44) and say if you share this point of view:
"Whatever story you decide to tell, the most important thing is that it's believable. Sure, you can embellish the tale a bit, but make sure that the core of your story is based in truth."

Expression écrite

Choisissez l'un des deux sujets (min. 120 mots).

Question A : Do you believe in the power of storytelling to sell products or services? Why (not)?

Question B : How can you account for the the rise of digital storytelling in today's society?

UNIT 8 Évaluation

One of my older brother's fondest childhood memories is ordering me to run across the backyard so he could shoot me with a BB gun from thirty yards and watch me crumple in pain to the ground, which he excitedly said at the time "was just like a movie." As an adult, I've enjoyed hunting turkey and shooting skeet, always feeling a little like Daniel Boone or Lord Grantham. And when my wife went to China and got to fire an Uzi at a shooting range, I was very jealous. I get the fun of guns, and of the various fantasies that shooting makes possible. But. Oh, but. I thought of my BB gun escapade not long ago, when I read an essay by the poet Gregory Orr. Just before, on a firing range outside Las Vegas, a nine-year-old had lost control of her fully automatic Uzi and shot her instructor dead. Orr is my brother's age. When he was twelve, the age my brother was when he shot me with a BB on purpose, Orr accidentally shot and killed his little brother while they were hunting. "To hunt," Orr wrote, "to fire a gun is to have your imagination tangled up with fantasies of power. [...] Americans who own guns today keep arsenals in a way people did not forty years ago. It seems plain to me that that's because they —not all, but many—have given themselves over to fantasies. The way I did as a child and still do on the rare occasion I shoot, they imagine they're militiamen, pioneers, Wild West cowboys, soldiers, characters they've watched all their lives in movies and on TV, heroes and antiheroes played by Clint Eastwood and Mel Gibson and the Rock, like Davy Crockett or Butch or Sundance or Rambo or Neo (or Ellen Ripley or Sarah Connor). They're like children playing with light-sabers, except they believe they're prepared to fight off real-life aliens (from the Middle East, from Mexico) and storm troopers, and their state-of-the-art weapons actually wound and kill. Why did gangsters and wannabe gangsters start holding and firing their handguns sideways, parallel to the ground, even though that compromises their aim and control? Because it looks cool, and it began looking cool after filmmakers started directing actors to do it, originally in the 1960s, constantly by the 1990s. Why are Americans buying the semiautomatic AR-15 and rifles like it more than any other style, 1.5 million each year? Because holding and shooting one makes them feel cooler, more like commandos. For the same reason, half the states now require no license for people to carry their guns openly in public. [...] We are actors in a 24/7 *tableau vivant*.

Kurt Andersen, *Fantasyland: How America Went Haywire: A 500-Year History*, 2017

Compréhension de l'écrit

Answer the following questions in English, using your own words.

A. After reading the text, what can you say about:
- its main topic?
- the people involved?
- their opinions on the topic?
- the feelings provoked by the use of firearms?

B. Comment on the following statement (l. 11-12) and say if you share this point of view:
"To fire a gun is to have your imagination tangled up with fantasies of power."

Expression écrite

Choisissez l'un des deux sujets (min. 120 mots).

Question A : How do you react to the following statement (l. 26-27)?
"Half the states now require no license for people to carry their guns openly in public. We are actors in a 24/7 *tableau vivant*."

Question B : How influential is the film industry when it comes to the use of firearms?

Évaluation

Observe the documents. According to you, which document best illustrates "Art and Power"?

UNIT 7

a "Creative without strategy is called 'art.' Creative with strategy is called 'advertising'."

Jef I. Richards, Professor at Michigan State University

b "What if public space was used to convey a shared idea from within the community instead of a brand that is privately owned by people living outside of the community?"

Jacob Devaney, *www.upliftconnect.com/street-art*, 2015

UNIT 8

a

Pro-guns march, Phœnix, Arizona, photographer **Marie Baronnet**

b

School shooting, sculptor **Manuel Oliver**, 2018

UNIT 9

a "Two or three things I know for sure, and one of them is that to go on living I have to tell stories, that stories are the one sure way I know to touch the heart and change the world."

Dorothy Allison, American author

b "Tell me the facts and I'll learn. Tell me the truth and I'll believe. But tell me a story and it will live in my heart forever."

Native American Proverb

AXE 4

Citizenship & Virtual Worlds

AXE 4

UNIT 10

SHORT CUT

CRIME IN THE DIGITAL AGE

How are new technologies helping to solve crime?

YOUR PROJECT

1 Write an essay on how online personal data is used in police investigations.

OR

2 Debate whether or not online personal data should be used by the police.

BEFORE CLASS!

Flash to watch!

Watch the video and be ready to talk about it in class!

VIDEO N°21

Au menu de cette unité :

DÉCOUVERTES CULTURELLES

- Sherlock Holmes au 21e siècle
- L'utilisation des nouvelles technologies pour résoudre les crimes
- Le *neighbourhood crime watch*
- La télésurveillance et la reconnaissance faciale au Royaume-Uni

OUTILS LINGUISTIQUES

- Les modaux
- Le *present perfect*
- *If clauses*

❶ Sherlock 2.0

How has the iconic detective Sherlock Holmes adapted his investigative techniques?

1 Sherlock and the smartphone

A. Read the article. How has the BBC's "Sherlock" adapted the iconic detective?

B. What role does Sherlock's mobile phone play and why is this important to the viewers?

C. Go further. Explain the following sentence in order to sum up the article: "Today, we all have access to unimaginable amounts of data, but Sherlock's genius is in how he *uses* that information." (l. 37-39)

In Victorian England, he was indeed the most modern of modern men. But what tools would such a man use today? According to Steven Moffat, creator of "Sherlock", the incredibly successful BBC series that re-imagines Sherlock Holmes in present-day London, the most important tool used by the world's only consulting detective is his mobile phone.

Yes, the simple mobile phone. Perhaps not as elegant as a well-crafted magnifying glass[1], but nonetheless suited for solving mysteries in modern London. While the high-tech investigators of "CSI" [Crime Scene Investigation] and similar shows have a bevy[2] of machines available at their disposal, Sherlock Holmes has no need for such resources. Nor is it likely that Sherlock, an independent sort with a collection of social quirks[3] and personal idiosyncrasies (to put it kindly), would have the desire to work within such an organization. Of course, he still has his personal lab and conducts his own experiments in his 221B Baker Street flat, but in this contemporary portrayal, the mobile phone has replaced the iconic magnifying glass as the tool most closely associated with Holmes. [...]

In *Sherlock* viewers are able to watch the eponymous detective conduct web searches via the same unobtrusive, minimal graphics used to represent his text messages. Overlaid[4] onto the scene as a sort of heads-up-display, these graphics let the viewer follow Sherlock's investigation and learn how his mind works. Although the relevance of his web searches may not always be immediately obvious, such is the fun of watching a detective story unfold[5]. And such is the wonder of Sherlock Holmes. Today, we all have access to unimaginable amounts of data, but Sherlock's genius is in how he *uses* that information.

1 *loupe* • 2 large group • 3 *excentricités* • 4 placed on top • 5 happen

Jimmy Stamp, ***smithsonianmag.com***, 2 August 2012

2 Crime-Solving Gadgets

How are new technologies being used by citizens and the police to solve crime?

VIDEO N°22

1 Citizens fighting crime

A. Watch the video and answer these questions:
- How does the app work? Is it popular?
- What do privacy advocates think about Ring?

B. Class debate. Discuss the advantages and disadvantages of citizens and the police using this app.

HELP!

Nouns
- home se**cur**ity
- **pri**vacy /ˈprɪvəsɪ/
- vigi**lan**te /vɪdʒəˈlæntɪ/

Adjectives
- **di**gital /ˈdɪdʒətl/: *numérique*
- ef**fi**cient
- in**tru**sive
- **mo**dern
- **use**ful

Verbs & Expressions
- de**noun**cing = in**form**ing
- de**ter** /dɪˈtɜː/ sb from + *V-ing*: *décourager qqn*
- in**vade** one's **pri**vacy
- **tar**get: *viser*

2 CCTV and facial recognition in the UK

A. Look at the picture. Why is the man protesting? Should we be scared of facial recognition?

B. Read the article and answer these questions:
- What does LFR stand for? How does it work?
- Who likes this technology and who finds it problematic? Why?
- How long have the police been using this technology?

C. Go further. Comment on this quote: "CCTV is seen either as a symbol of Orwellian dystopia or a technology that will lead to crime-free streets and civil behavior." Heather Brooke, British-American journalist.

The Met Police trialled[1] their Live Facial Recognition software outside Romford station in east London [...], digitally photographing and scanning anyone that walked past.

The Met called the trial a success after eight people [...] were arrested. However, not everyone was happy about the 'invasion of privacy' and according to protesters, numerous people were stopped and searched – simply for wearing hoods[2] or wrapping a scarf around their faces to fight off the cold.

Silkie Carlo, director of Big Brother Watch, said: 'It's been a complete disaster, I've been appalled[3] at the officers' behaviour and handling of the people they have been stopping and ID-ing. One person was fined £90 because he covered his face to object.'

Commander Ivan Balhatchet, strategic lead for LFR said: 'The technology used in Romford forms part of the Met's ongoing efforts to reduce crime in the area, with a specific focus on tackling violence.' It was the ninth time LFR has been used on Londoners in the last three years.

Silkie claimed there has been little publicity around LFR, which she has likened to 'Dystopian fiction'. 'People have been really shocked because they had no idea that this technology even existed. [...] We have been campaigning about this for a number of years because they have been slowly rolling it out[4] without public or parliament consent. [...] This is miles away from what should be happening in a democracy like the UK.'

LFR cameras take pictures of people walking past and measures the structure of each face, including distance between eyes, nose, mouth and jaw to create facial data.

The system detects a face, creates a digital version of it and searches it against the 'watch list' of offenders. A police officer can then compare the camera image and the watch list image.

1 tested • 2 *capuche* • 3 horrified • 4 start to use sth

Adapted from Martine Berg Olsen, **metro.co.uk**, 1 February 2019

3 Police in the USA use Google to find criminals

A. Read the article and answer these questions:
- What was the new technique the police in Phoenix used to try to solve a case?
- What happened to Jorge Molina?
- What sort of data are tech companies collecting?

B. Would you say this technique is a real progress?

C. Have your say. Should citizens be worried about the police getting information from Google?

When detectives in a Phoenix suburb arrested a warehouse worker in a murder investigation last December, they credited a new technique with breaking open[1] the case after other leads went cold.

The police told the suspect, Jorge Molina, they had data tracked his phone to the site where a man was shot nine months earlier. They had made the discovery after obtaining a search warrant[2] that required Google to provide information on all devices it recorded near the killing, potentially capturing the whereabouts of anyone in the area. [...]

But after he spent nearly a week in jail, the case against Mr. Molina fell apart as investigators learned new information and released him. [...]

The warrants, which draw on an enormous Google database employees call Sensorvault, turn the business of tracking cellphone users' locations into a digital dragnet[3] for law enforcement. In an era of ubiquitous data gathering by tech companies, it is just the latest example of how personal information — where you go, who your friends are, what you read, eat and watch, and when you do it — is being used for purposes many people never expected. As privacy concerns have mounted among consumers, policymakers and regulators, tech companies have come under intensifying scrutiny[4] over their data collection practices.

The Arizona case demonstrates the promise and perils of the new investigative technique, whose use has risen sharply in the past six months, according to Google employees familiar with the requests. It can help solve crimes. But it can also snare[5] innocent people.

Technology companies have for years responded to court orders for specific users' information. The new warrants go further, suggesting possible suspects and witnesses in the absence of other clues. Often, Google employees said, the company responds to a single warrant with location information on dozens or hundreds of devices.

Law enforcement officials described the method as exciting, but cautioned that it was just one tool[6].

"It doesn't pop out the answer like a ticker tape, saying this guy's guilty," said Gary Ernsdorff, a senior prosecutor in Washington State who has worked on several cases involving these warrants. Potential suspects must still be fully investigated, he added. "We're not going to charge anybody just because Google said they were there."

1 solve • 2 *mandat* • 3 system for catching criminals • 4 *examen minutieux* • 5 catch • 6 *outil*

Jennifer Valentino-DeVries,
The New York Times, 13 April 2019

4 Apple vs the FBI

A. Look at the cartoon and describe it. What is its goal?

B. Is there a link between privacy and freedom?

C. Read the *Cultural fact*. Do you approve of Apple's decision?

Cultural fact

In 2016 the FBI wanted Apple to unlock 2015 San Bernardino shooting suspect's phone by creating "backdoor" software to crack the phone's password. Apple's CEO Tim Cook refused, saying that it would be very dangerous and would undermine the security of Apple users.

John Darkwow, American Cartoonist, 2016

❸ Be Careful With Your Data

How can someone's online personal data be used against them?

1 The Internet and police investigations

"My dear fellow," said Sherlock Holmes as we sat on either side of the fire in his lodgings at Baker Street. "The Internet should have been the most singular boon to human civilization since Gutenberg's moveable type printing press but what do we have instead?"

"Lots of amusing cat videos," I answered.

"I shall tell you," said Holmes, ignoring my retort. "Everybody posting the most intimate details of their lives, thoughts and feelings for all and sundry to pour over... Mark my words, Watson, the streets are safer these days because so many common criminals have changed their *modus operandi* and now carry out their despicable crimes online in the comfort of their living rooms."

"But it has also proven to be of considerable benefit to our friends the police," I chimed in.

"Or rather the Internet has become their particular hunting ground. They seek and gather data about every living soul and they make the same elementary mistakes as always... And they simply cannot keep the data safe. Take that Snowden fellow. [...] No one knows precisely what data he took, and he was just one of thousands of private contractors."

Holmes held up his hand. "Now, I know that you believe that he was acting on the highest principles but can you honestly say the same for every private contactor working for the government? [...] One can barely read a newspaper these days without some shocking revelation of a new hacking crime, exposing the innocent to the evil designs of criminals."

"But surely," I countered. "The Internet has proven a boon for you in your investigations. Just look at how you can follow people around now — a fellow's precise movements — or how you can take over and control those CCTV security cameras that are ubiquitous these days. I would venture that the Internet has entirely changed your *modus operandi*."

"Not entirely, my dear Doctor. I still have this." Holmes tapped his temple with the mouthpiece of his vaping machine. "But I would venture, Watson, that the Internet is both a curse for the common man and a blessing for the world of investigation."

The Sherlock Holmes Handbook for the Digital Age: Elementary Cyber Security,
Alan Pearce, 2016

A. Read the text. Who do you think the narrator is?

B. According to Sherlock, what has the Internet produced?

C. Does Sherlock think the Internet has helped the police? Justify.

D. What new methods have been helpful to Sherlock?

E. Go further. Does the narrator share the same view as Sherlock about the Internet?

HELP!

Nouns
- invasion of privacy
- (in)conclusive results

Adjectives
- beneficial
- helpful = useful
- transparent

Verbs & Expressions
- assist = help
- track = follow one's movements
- wiretap = bug: *mettre sur l'écoute*
- nothing/something to hide

YOUR PROJECT

1. Do you agree with Sherlock's statement, "the Internet is both a curse for the common man and a blessing for the world of investigation"? Respond by writing an argumentative essay using the examples from this unit.

OR

2. You will either argue in favour or against the following statement: Online personal data should be used by investigators to solve crimes.

LANGUAGE LAB

- Unit's vocabulary
- Audio words
- MP3
- Interactive Test

★ 1. Find the noun/adjective/verb/adverb equivalent to these words.

A. Verb of analysis: ...
B. Noun of infringe: ...
C. Adjective of fraud: ...
D. Verb of deterrence: ...
E. Adjective of confidentiality: ...

★ 2. Put the verbs in the present perfect.

A. Ever since it was conceived, the police's Live Facial Recognition Software *(become)* most efficient.
B. Digital photography *(change)* dramatically police work.
C. CCTV cameras *(be)* around for quite a while in London.
D. Sherlock Holmes *(catch)* many a villain.
E. These days, criminals *(turn)* into complete geeks.

★★ 3. Fill in the blanks with the words below.

solve • invasion • track • privacy • surveillance • crack • gather

A. Technology can help the police ... crimes.
B. Be careful of putting your location online, you never know what information can be used to ... you.
C. I think that the police use of our personal data is an ... of ....
D. Orwell is often brought up when talking about the use of government ... of citizens.
E. The police ... information that can be used as evidence online.
F. It is not always easy for the police to ... the case without the information found online.

★★ 4. Rephrase these sentences using the modal auxiliary suggested.

A. You'd better work on this case before it goes cold. *(should)*
B. Sometimes, a magnifying glass is useful. *(may)*.
C. I don't believe he's solved this case so swiftly. *(can't)*
D. Protecting your private life is sometimes difficult these days. *(can)*
E. Sherlock is probably in his 221B Baker Street flat. *(must)*

★★★ 5. Put the verbs in the appropriate tense.

A. If the police find the perpetrator, the case *(be)* quickly solved.
B. If I memorised Conan Doyle's complete works, I *(be)* a great detective.
C. If technology had been more advanced at the time, the criminals *(be caught)* more quickly.
D. If she was on the crime scene, her mobile phone *(prove)* it.
E. If facial recognition techniques become more common, life *(become)* intolerable.

6. Interactive test! What is your score?

OPEN YOUR EARS!

PHONOLOGY

La lettre « l »

• Écoutez les mots suivants attentivement. Que remarquez-vous ?

MP3 N°43

Holmes • walk • palm • would • folk • stalk • talk • yolk • should • calm • half • could

• Récapitulons

- Le son /l/ → ne se prononce pas quand il est situé entre « o » et ..., « a » et ... , ... ou ... .
- Le son /l/ ne se prononce pas dans *would, should* et *could*.

TRAVEL WITH ACCENTS!

Écoutez l'extrait suivant en faisant attention à la prononciation de la lettre « t ».

MP3 N°44

Technology has been transforming every aspect of society, and that includes revolutionary new capabilities for police departments.
From tattoo-recognition technology to the growing use of drones these high-tech innovations are highlighted in the June edition of Wired magazine.

Dans quels mots entends-tu /t/ comme dans *time* ?
Dans quels mots le « t » se prononce /d/ ?
Dans quels mots le « t » se prononce /ʃ/ comme cheval ?

Picture challenge

★ 3 sentences
★★ 4 to 6 sentences
★★★ 7 sentences and +

How many sentences can you make using what you have learnt? Collect stars!

AXE 4

SHORT CUT

UNIT 11

LOVE AT FIRST SWIPE

How have apps changed social bonds?

YOUR PROJECT

In an online forum, react to 21st century romance and courtship.

BEFORE CLASS!

Flash to watch!

Watch the short film. Be ready to talk about it in class!

VIDEO N°23

Au menu de cette unité :

DÉCOUVERTES CULTURELLES

- Les solutions virtuelles au fléau de la solitude
- L'intelligence artificielle au service des applications de rencontre
- Les conséquences sociétales du développement de *Tinder* aux États-Unis
- Les romans de Jane Austen revisités

OUTILS LINGUISTIQUES

- La comparaison
- *be used to + V-ing / used to + V*
- Le génitif
- L'article Ø / *The*

❶ Real Solitude, Virtual Solutions

How do apps help us to tackle the problem of loneliness?

1 Apps and online tools

A. Watch the video and say what it is about.
B. What comparisons does the interviewee make when people feel disconnected?
C. Say what the UK is doing to tackle the problem of loneliness.
D. Go further. Discuss the statement: "*Forming friendship and combatting loneliness may just be a swipe away.*"

VIDEO N°24

2 AI, the new Cupid

A. Read the text and say how dating apps work.
B. Go further. Comment on Prof Schuller's statement: "*We will effectively be competing against machines for attention,*" *he says.* "*And I'm not sure how we'll do.*" (l. 30-32)

Two lovers hold hands across a table, overlooking a virtual vista of the Mediterranean. As the pair exchange sweet nothings, the fact they are actually sitting thousands of miles apart bears little significance on the romantic experience. The couple was deemed "hyper-compatible" by online dating technology that matched them using a search engine infused with Artificial Intelligence (AI). Using data harvested about their social backgrounds, sexual preferences, cultural interests, and even photos of their celebrity crushes, they were thrust together in a virtual reality of their own design. This technology is in the early stages of development. Some dating apps are already using AI to analyse chats and encourage users to set up dates, for example, but as technology is refined over the coming decades it is likely to become even more powerful. For those concerned that chemistry might be a vital missing ingredient, one method also incorporates DNA analysis. Dating app Pheramor, developed in Houston, claims it can help people find love according to their physical chemistry and "social alignment". Users are sent kits to swab the insides of their mouths, which the company uses to sequence 11 genes that it says are related to attraction. The system then combines the genetic information with a social profile — built by users sharing their social media information — to offer a host of potential mates to choose from. [...]

What this new world of virtual love might mean for human-to-human interaction is the most frightening prospect, says Prof Schuller. "We will effectively be competing against machines for attention," he says. "And I'm not sure how we'll do."

The Financial Times, 12 September 2019

HELP!

Nouns
- bonding = connection
- criterion /kraɪˈtɪərɪən/ (pl. criteria /kraɪˈtɪərɪə/)
- date = rendezvous /ˈrɒndivuː/
- girlfriend / boyfriend
- love affair
- loneliness = solitude

Adjectives
- connected ≠ disconnected
- ill-matched ≠ well-matched
- isolated /ˈaɪsəleɪtɪd/
- rejected

Verbs & Expressions
- break up with sb
- feel lonely
- fill a void
- find true love
- gather personal data
- make friends with sb
- socialize /ˈsəʊʃəlaɪz/

❷ Love 2.0

How have online apps changed relationships and the world?

1 Dating in the age of apps

A. Read the text. Find arguments showing that Tinder has made it easier for people to interact.
B. Pick out the negative aspect of dating apps.

C. Have your say. Do you agree with Ingram Hodges when he says that "*dating has become isolated from the rest of social life.*" (l. 52-53)? Why?

There's been plenty of hand-wringing[1] and gnashing[2] of teeth over how Tinder *could* reinvent dating: Maybe it would transform the dating scene into an endless virtual marketplace where singles[3] could shop for each other [...]. But the reality of dating in the age of apps is a little more nuanced than that. The relationship economy has certainly changed in terms of *how* humans find and court their potential partners, but *what* people are looking for is largely the same as it ever was: companionship [...].

Sean Rad and Justin Mateen, two of Tinder's founders, have said in interviews that the inspiration for Tinder came from their own general dissatisfaction with the lack of dating opportunities that arose naturally — [...] Tinder has indeed helped people meet other people — it has expanded the reach of singles' social networks, facilitating interactions between people who might never have crossed paths otherwise. [...]

Some also believe that the relative anonymity of dating apps—that is, the social disconnect between most people who match on them—has also made the dating landscape a ruder, flakier[4], crueler place. For example, says Lundquist, the couples therapist, if you go on a date with your cousin's roommate, the roommate has some incentive[5] to not be a jerk[6] to you. But with apps, "You're meeting somebody you probably don't know and probably don't have any connections with at a bar on 39th Street. That's kind of weird, and there's a greater opportunity for people to be ridiculous, to be not nice." [...] Other users complain of rudeness[7] even in early text interactions on the app. [...] Sometimes this is just how things go on dating apps, Xiques says. [...] "Because, obviously, they're hiding behind the technology, right? You don't have to actually face the person," she says. [...]

But perhaps the most consequential change to dating has been in where and how dates get initiated — and where and how they don't.

When Ingram Hodges, a freshman at the University of Texas at Austin, goes to a party, he goes there expecting only to hang out with friends. It'd be a pleasant surprise, he says, if he happened to talk to a cute girl there and ask her to hang out. "It wouldn't be an *abnormal* thing to do," he says, "but it's just not as common. When it does happen, people are surprised, taken aback." [...] Hodges knows that there was a time, way back in the day, when people mostly met through school, or work, or friends, or family. But for people his age, Hodges says, "dating has become isolated from the rest of social life."

1 *débats* • 2 *grincements de dents* • 3 unmarried people • 4 *peu fiable* • 5 motivation • 6 *crétin* • 7 *impolitesse*

Ashley Fetters, ***The Atlantic,***
21 December 2018

Justin Mateen and Sean Rad, cofounders of Tinder

2 The USA's new romantic landscape

A. Read the text and say how different dating has become.

B. Using the figures given in the article, say how efficient online dating apps are today.

C. Go further. Say what online dating has brought as far as interracial relationships are concerned.

For millennia, humans were most likely to marry and/or raise kids with (which, then as now, wasn't always the same thing) members of their own tribe. That changed a little when we started to sail and settle around the world, but ideas about religion and race and class still governed our dating decisions — in the rare cases when those decisions were fully ours to make. In pre-World War II America, we were most likely to meet our significant others through family. In the 1950s came the rise of meeting "friends of friends," and that method stayed dominant through the rest of the century. [...]

By 2000, according to surveys, 10 percent of opposite-sex couples and 20 percent of same-sex couples met via the Internet, overtaking family introductions.

By 2010 — two years before the launch of Tinder — those numbers had reached around 20 percent and 70 percent respectively. "Friends of friends" setups had dropped by 20 percent in both cases, so that limited-pool and online-pool setups were about equal.

Surprise, surprise: the Tinder era has supercharged this trend. A fresh-as-of-January Stanford study looked at data in relationship surveys that goes up to 2017, and found that 29 percent of heterosexual and 65 percent of gay couples had now met online. In 2014, Tinder was processing a billion swipes a day; that is now closer to 2 billion. Tinder says that 36 percent of all people on Facebook have created an account; that would translate to 800 million people. More total Tinder matches have been made than there are people on the planet, by a factor of 3. [...] And it's not like we're just spending this time mindlessly matching and never meeting. There are an estimated one million Tinder dates every week around the world. Nor are we just dating and never getting serious; given prior trend lines, a 2015 study found that the wide adoption of Internet dating had probably increased the total number of marriages by 33 percent compared to a hypothetical Internet-free world. [...] this is our new romantic landscape. At least one third of all marriages in the U.S. are now between partners who met online. That's more than 600,000 couples every year who would, in any other era, have remained total strangers. [...]

First off, there's clear evidence that online dating is creating mixed-race couples at a faster rate than our increasingly diverse society would. [...] Since it was officially OKed in all states by the Supreme Court in 1967, we've seen a slow but steady rise in the percentage of all new U.S. marriages that are interracial — from 3 percent to about 9 percent in 1995. Progress was slow, but it was progress. [...] Bottom line: Millennials[1] and Generation Z[2] are doing more for society-wide racial integration than many leaders of the Civil Rights struggle in the 1960s — and even the 1990s — ever dreamed possible.

1 people born between 1980 and 1997 • 2 people born between 1997 and the early 2000s

Chris Taylor, **Mashable.com**, 13 February 2019

HELP!

Nouns
- commitment: *engagement*
- courtship = dating
- matchmaking: *mise en relation*
- stranger: *inconnu(e)*

Adjectives
- attractive ≠ unattractive
- long-lasting ≠ short-lived
- intimate /ˈɪntɪmət/: *intime*

Verbs & Expressions
- be in a relationship with sb
- bridge the gap between
- miss out on sth
- take the first step = make the first move
- face-to-face interaction

YOUR TURN! 3 Create a timeline

Use the data in the article above to make a timeline that sums up the evolution of love relationships over the years.

❸ Digital Apps in a Time of Courtly Love

Is traditional courtship an outdated concept?

1 "Pride & Prejudice" revisited

A. Read the ***Cultural fact***. Then observe the book cover and describe it briefly (character, place, time, feelings).

B. Read the article and say why this novel has been rewritten.

C. Have your say. Comment on Professor Sutherland's last statement (l. 20-26). Do you agree? Why (not)?

Prepare for your nerves to be greatly vexed – Britain's best-loved novels have been given a digital-age makeover with the help of Tinder, WhatsApp and Instagram. A new version of *Pride and Prejudice* sees Mr Darcy distracted by beauties on the dating app Tinder, while his courtship with Elizabeth suffers the perils of the messaging service WhatsApp. Meanwhile in *Wuthering Heights*, a doubting Catherine is put off by Heathcliff's ringtone – before downloading a fitness app in a bid to pull her out of lovelorn depression.

The reworkings, by Professor John Sutherland of University College London in partnership with TV channel Drama, are designed to show the negative impact of the Internet on romance.

[...] Professor Sutherland said: 'Even though we're certainly a nation that uses modern technology to communicate, by inserting these devices and methods of communication into a series of classic romances... highlights just how much they can interrupt a romantic mood.'

Alisha Rouse, ***The Daily Mail***, 8 February 2018

Cultural fact

Pride and Prejudice was written in 1813 by English novelist Jane Austen. The story is set in early 19th century England. Mr and Mrs Bennet have five daughters. Mrs. Bennet's wish is to see all her daughters well married, especially as the modest family estate is to be inherited by William Collins (a distant cousin of Mr. Bennet's) when Mr. Bennet dies. At a ball, the wealthy and newly arrived Charles Bingley has eyes for Jane, the eldest Bennet daughter.
The encounter between his friend Fitzwilliam Darcy and Elizabeth, Jane's younger sister is less courteous.

YOUR PROJECT

In an online forum, react to 21st century romance and courtship. Write a post to comment on the following statement: "Online dating apps have become the only way to find true love."

LANGUAGE LAB

- Unit's vocabulary
- Audio words
- MP3
- Interactive Test

★ **1. Give the synonyms or antonyms of these words. Then, make a sentence for each one.**

A. attractive ≠ ...
B. connected ≠ ...
C. well-matched ≠ ...
D. long-lasting ≠ ...
E. bonding = ...
F. dating = ...
G. date = ...
H. solitude = ...

★★ **2. Rewrite these sentence using a *'s* genitive.**

A. The characters in this series are always falling in love.
B. The father of his girlfriend is not too keen on Internet dates.
C. The views of his friends on Tinder are rather conservative.
D. The best-loved novel in Britain is certainly *Pride and Prejudice* by Jane Austen.
E. Attempts by users to send text messages are not always successful.
F. The phone belonging to his friend is not working.

★★ **3. Match each word with its definition.**

A. interact
B. commitment
C. stranger
D. break up with sb

1. a person you do not know
2. put an end to a relationship
3. talk and spend time with sb
4. a firm promise

★★ **4. Fill in the gaps with Ø or *the*.**

A. ... most people still meet their partners without resorting to ... technology.
B. ... hope springs eternal.
C. ... humans now court their potential partners differently.
D. ... love makes ... world go round.
E. For ... millennials, ... former generations were likely to marry with ... members of their tribe.
F. There has seen a rise in ... percentage of ... interracial marriages.

★★★ **5. Translate into English.**

A. *Ils se sont rencontrés en ligne et ils entretiennent une relation depuis 5 ans.*
B. *Il est indispensable de rencontrer quelqu'un en vrai.*
C. *Une histoire d'amour ne peut pas commencer dans le monde virtuel.*

★★★ **6. Translate these sentences using either *used to* or *used to + -ing*.**

A. *Jadis, nous nous aimions.*
B. *Avant, Chris savait jouer du piano.*
C. *Avant, nous avions l'habitude de nous retrouver à Soho.*
D. *Nos voisins avaient l'habitude d'organiser des rendez-vous à l'aveugle.*
E. *Autrefois je rêvais d'une relation idéale.*
F. *Avant, je la voyais tous les jours.*

7. Interactive test! What is your score?

OPEN YOUR EARS!

PHONOLOGY

La prononciation de « *ou* » et « *our* »

- **Le digraphe ou est souvent prononcé /aʊ/. Écoutez les mots suivants et trouvez les 5 intrus.**

MP3 N°45 | *couple • account • would • thousand • around • encourage • could • mouth • should • out • about*

- **Le diagraphe *our* est souvent prononcée /ɔː/. Écoutez les mots suivants et trouvez l'intrus.**

MP3 N°46 | *court • four • sour • pour • courtship*

SHOWTIME

Say it like the model!

MP3 N°47 | *About **2 out of 10** of us are saying that we feel **socially lonely** - [which means we are not getting enough interaction] - but then there's about **half of us** who are saying that we feel errh... **emotionally lonely** - [which means we don't feel that people get us, that they really know us].*

- Pour souligner un contraste, on accentue les mots qui s'opposent. *Socially lonely* **vs** *emotionally lonely* et *2 out of 10 of us* **vs** *half of us*.
- Les segments importants sont prononcés plus lentement. Les segments qui ne font qu'illustrer le propos sont prononcés très vite.

Picture challenge

★ 3 sentences
★★ 4 to 6 sentences
★★★ 7 sentences and +

How many sentences can you make using what you have learnt? Collect stars!

AXE 4

UNIT 12

SHORT CUT

HACKERS: FRIENDS OR FOES?

In the digital age, are hackers the new threat?

YOUR PROJECT

Read the graphic novel (on p. 119-122) and sum up the main information. Then give tips to the military families to avoid this situation.

BEFORE CLASS!

Flash to watch!

Watch the trailer for Bill Condon's ***The Fifth Estate*** (2013). Be ready to talk about it in class!

Au menu de cette unité :

DÉCOUVERTES CULTURELLES

- La définition du terme *hacker*
- Kevin Mitnick, un célèbre *hacker* repenti
- Les lois protégeant les lanceurs d'alerte
- Les différents types de *hackers* (*black, grey and white*)
- Les révélations de WikiLeaks
- Quelques lanceurs d'alerte (Edward Snowden, Chelsea Manning, Britanny Kaiser…)

OUTILS LINGUISTIQUES

- Les modaux
- La phrase interrogative

❶ Are Hackers Lawbreakers?

Why do hackers hack and what do they do with your personal data?

1 What hackers do

A

Signe Wilkinson, American cartoonist, 5 January 2015

B

Nath Paresh, Indian cartoonist, 5 February 2015

A. Brainstorm. What do you know about hackers? How do people generally portray them? Why?

B. Read the following definition and compare it to your previous answer. "A person who uses computers to gain unauthorized access to data."

C. Describe the two cartoons. What message does each cartoonist convey?

D. Have your say. Which cartoon do you find the closest to what a hacker is? Justify.

HELP!

Nouns & Adjectives
- identity theft
- highly-skilled
- law-breaker
- unauthorized

Verbs & Expressions
- break into a computer system
- deceive: *tromper*
- gather information
- sell one's data
- social engineering: the act of manipulating people so they give up confidential information

2 From hacker to businessman

Kevin Mitnick is the world's most famous hacker, bestselling author, and the top cyber security speaker. Once one of the FBI's Most Wanted because he hacked into 40 major corporations just for the challenge, Kevin is now a trusted security consultant to the Fortune 500 and governments worldwide.

Kevin mentors leaders, executives, and staff on both the theory and practice of social engineering, topics on which he is the leading global authority. Kevin also helps consumers—from students to retirees— learn how to protect their information and themselves from harm.

As the CEO of Mitnick Security Consulting, Kevin, and The Global Ghost Team™ now maintain a 100 percent successful track record of being able to penetrate the security of any system they are paid to hack into using a combination of technical exploits and social engineering. [...] Kevin is a global bestselling author and his books are available in over 50 countries and 20 languages.

www.mitnicksecurity.com

A. Read the text and present Mitnick's career.

B. According to you, what led him to evolve in this way?

C. Have your say. Why is it considered unethical to portray hackers as modern-day idealists?

3 A day in Mitnick's life

Read an extract from Mitnick's autobiography on Worksheet n°19 and answer the questions.

❷ Hacking and Whistleblowing

How to tell hackers from whistleblowers?

1 Whistleblower, who are you?

Clay Bennett, American cartoonist, 8 November 2019

A. Turn to Worksheet n°20 and find out about some well-known whistleblowers.
B. Give your own definition of a whistleblower. Is the cartoon a good illustration? Do you consider them as heroes? Justify.
C. Class debate. Read the *Cultural fact*. Should Manning and Snowden be jailed for what they did as whistleblowers?

> ***Cultural fact***
> **The Whistleblower Protection Act** of 1989
> This American federal law protects whistleblowers from retaliation from their employers. It is complex and it originally excluded intelligence officers (CIA, NSA, etc.). Now they are also supposedly protected, from losing their jobs or going to prison.

2 How do laws protect whistleblowers

A. Groupwork. Do some online research to know how the UK, the USA and Australia protect whistleblowers.
B. Use Worksheet n°21 to recap what you have learnt.
C. Together, decide which country has the best protection for whistleblowers and say how the other countries could improve theirs.

3 Three shades of hackers

A. Listen to MP3 N°48 and pick out the definitions for white hat, grey hat and black hat hackers.
B. Explain what makes hacktivism ambiguous.
C. Have your say. Do you think hacktivists deserve the same protection as whistleblowers? Would you say hacktivists are the future whistleblowers?

4 WikiLeaks: a case study

A. Watch the video and pick out the interviewees' opinions about WikiLeaks.
B. Which interviewee's arguments do you feel closest to? Why?
C. Have your say. Where do you draw the line between freedom of speech and unlawful activity?

VIDEO N°25

HELP!

Nouns
- unglue = disorganise
- yield: *produire*
- undermine: *saper, miner*
- abrogate = abolish

Cultural fact
WikiLeaks was created to allow whistleblowers or journalists to upload raw documents, even top secret ones, to denounce the wrongdoings of governments.

YOUR TURN! 5 Write an essay

Write an essay about hackers and whistleblowers for *WIRED* magazine using this cartoon as an illustration.

HELP!

Nouns
- freedom of speech
- governmental practices
- National Security Agency (NSA)
- scandal

Adjectives
- cynical
- hypocritical
- outrageous /aʊt'reɪdʒəs/

Verbs & Expressions
- blow the whistle
- condemn /kən'dem/
- denounce
- spy on sb

Nate Beeler, American cartoonist, 21 August 2013

❸ Waging a Cyberwar

How can cyberwar change the face of warfare?

Not so long ago, stories about cyberwar started with scary hypotheticals: What if state-sponsored hackers were to launch widespread[1] attacks that blacked out[2] entire cities? Crippled[3] banks and froze ATMs[4] across a country? Shut down shipping firms, oil refineries, and factories? Paralyzed airports and hospitals?

Today, these scenarios are no longer hypotheticals: Every one of those events has now actually occurred. Incident by catastrophic incident, cyberwar has left the pages of overblown science fiction and the tabletops[5] of Pentagon war games to become a reality. More than ever before, it's become clear that the threat of hacking goes beyond nuisance vandalism, criminal profiteering, and even espionage to include the sort of physical-world disruption that was once possible to accomplish only with military attacks and terroristic sabotage.

So far, there's no clearly documented case of a cyberwar attack directly causing loss of life. But a single cyberwar attack has already caused as much as $10 billion dollars in economic damage. Cyberwar has been used to terrorize individual companies and temporarily render entire governments comatose. It's denied civilians basic services like power and heat. [...] The threat of cyberwar looms[6] heavily over the future: a new dimension of conflict capable of leapfrogging[7] borders and teleporting the chaos of war to civilians thousands of miles beyond its front.

1 covering large areas • **2** deprived of electricity • **3** paralysed, stopped • **4** *distributeur de billets* • **5** *dessus de table* • **6** *planer sur* • **7** jump over

Andy Greenberg, **www.wired.com,** 23 August 2019

A. Look at the cover and guess what the article is about.
B. Read the text. What sorts of disruptions can be caused by cyberwar?
C. Who is responsible for cyberwars in general?
D. How does cyberwar change the face of warfare? Explain in your own words.
E. Go further. According to you, how important is it to develop digital citizenship and responsibility?

HELP!

Nouns
- **o**nline **s**afety
- **o**nline **e**tiquette
- prev**e**ntion
- a cause for con**c**ern
- (in)appr**o**priate be**h**aviour
- **s**abotage

Verbs & Expressions
- take respon**s**ibility for sth
- the di**g**ital space / world
- hold sb res**po**nsible for sth / V-ing
- com**ply** with the law

YOUR PROJECT

Read the graphic novel created by the Army Cyber Institute at West Point and Arizona State University (on p. 119-122). Sum up the main information. Then give tips to the military families to avoid this situation. Use Worksheet n°22 for help.

HOUSTON 2027.
THE MISSILE ATTACK CAME DURING LUNCH HOUR... THE DOWNTOWN BUILDINGS WERE FULL...TRAFFIC ON THE STREET ADDED TO THE CASUALTIES...
THE COUNTRY WENT ON HIGH ALERT...IN THE CONFUSION, IT WAS UNCLEAR WHO WAS BEHIND THE ATTACK...
THE "HOUSTON COMMISSION" WAS SET UP TO FIND OUT HOW THE MISSILES EVADED U.S. AIR DEFENSE...
C SPAN
LIVE
Houston Commission session in progress
CSPAN
AND, WHO MADE IT POSSIBLE?
YEARS EARLIER: JAY ROBERTS HAD ALWAYS WANTED TO SERVE HIS COUNTRY.
ROBERTS
U.S. AR
HE SERVED TWO DEPLOYMENTS IN AFGHANISTAN...ON HIS SECOND HE EXCELLED IN COMMAND OF HIS PLATOON...
HE WAS THE ONLY STUDENT IN HIS PROGRAM TO BE COMMISSIONED AS AN OFFICER IN THE ARMY CORPS OF ENGINEERS.

RETURNING HOME, JAY'S WORLD WAS VERY DIFFERENT... WORKING ON MILCON HE MISSED THE COMRADERY OF HIS PLATOON... WAITING FOR HIS PROMOTION BOARD TO MAJOR HE TOUGHED IT OUT...
BUT EVEN THEN HE HAD BEEN TARGETED...
MERCENARIES WANTED ACCESS TO HIS BUILDING'S HIGH SECURITY NETWORK... KNOWING THEY COULD GET ANY PRICE...
TABLET VIEW
USING ARTIFICIAL INTELLIGENCE, THE HACKERS RESHAPED THE DAILY NEWS FEEDS, ADVERTISEMENTS, AND POSTS THAT JAY SAW...
NEWS
School Collapses in Rural Kentucky Investigation Underway
NEWS
The Death of the American Engineer? Fewer Grads Choose Field, Labor Shortage
NEWS
CEO of Denver Building Giant High Range Convicted
THEY HIJACKED FAMILY ACCOUNTS AND SEPARATED JAY FROM LOVED ONES...
TEXT MESSAGE
UNCLE LARRY
Don't know why you're so hostile buddy - Maybe we shouldn't talk for a while. Take care - don't contact Aunt Dorothy.
THEY COERCED CONTRACTORS TO COMMIT TINY INFRACTIONS... AT THE JOB SITE, SAFETY ISSUES BECAME FREQUENT...

BECAUSE OF HIS STATE-SIDE PERFORMANCE... JAY'S PROMOTION WAS DENIED...
BUT I HAD A PERFECT RECORD BEFORE I GOT HERE.
HIS CREDIT WAS TAMPERED WITH... FOR JAY, IT STARTED TO FEEL LIKE THE WHOLE WORLD WAS AGAINST HIM...
NEW!
Chai
CUSTOMER: JAY ROBERTS
PAYMENT DECLINED
THE ONLY PLACE JAY FELT LIKE HE BELONGED WAS PLAYING STRIKE FORCE...
13 BILL257
32 SARGE091
TEAM: MIZFITZ
MISSION 41
ISOLATED AND WOUNDED... JAY'S TRUST IN THE ARMY ERODED...
EXIT
AT THE HEIGHT OF HIS DEPRESSION JAY REACHED OUT TO BILL, HIS STRIKE FORCE TEAM MATE.
IT JUST SUCKS... THEY DON'T EVEN KNOW THE TRUTH...
MAYBE I CAN HELP...
PLAYING ON HIS WOUNDED EGO... JAY GAVE BILL ACCESS TO THE BUILDING'S MAINTENANCE NETWORK... NOT KNOWING THAT BILL WAS ONE OF THE MERCENARIES MANIPULATING HIM...

SIX MONTHS LATER: THE TRAIL LED DIRECTLY BACK TO JAY.
FBI
FBI
I DIDN'T KNOW...
THE MERCENARIES HAD ALSO RESHAPED THE WORLD'S VIEW OF JAY THROUGH RADICALIZED POSTS...
SUSPECT'S SOCIAL MEDIA POSTS
Jay Roberts
Blatant corruption of American values will not be ignored anymore!!
Jay Roberts
THAT'S NOT ME! I DIDN'T SAY THAT!
JAY HAD BEEN ENGINEERED TO BE A TRAITOR.
BREAKING NEWS
HOUSTON TRAITOR CONVICTED
TRAITOR GAVE HACKERS ACCESS TO MULTIPLE HIGH SECURITY NETWORKS -- ALLOWED ATTACKERS TO COMPROMISE CRITICAL DEFENSE SYSTEMS...
THE END

LANGUAGE LAB

- Unit's vocabulary
- Audio words
- MP3
- Interactive Test

★ 1. Give synonyms or antonyms of the words below. Make a sentence for each word.

A. attack ≠ …
B. friend ≠ …
C. abrogate = …
D. comply with the law ≠ …
E. cheat = …
F. appropriate ≠ …

★ 2. Turn these sentences into questions.

A. Cyberwar is avoidable.
B. Hackers are the new world masters.
C. Cyber-terrorism has become endemic.
D. Hackers should be sent to prison.
E. Your computer will be protected against hackers.
F. The FBI caught Kevin Mitnick.

★★ 3. Match each word with its definition.

1. hacker • 2. whistleblower • 3. geek • 4. hacktivist • 5. cyber mercenary

A. Someone who gets paid by a third party to launch attacks on other people's computers.
B. Someone who organises or participates in online campaigns and actions for a cause.
C. Someone who warns the public about the lies told and dangers caused by their powerful employers.
D. Someone who is absolutely passionate about computers.
E. Someone who takes control of other people's computers for good or bad reasons.

★★ 4. Rephrase the following sentences using *may, might, must* or *can't*.

A. It's possible that all my data have been stolen.
B. There's a remote possibility that she's a hacker.
C. There's no way they are guilty of this crime.
D. I'm sure Sam broke into Laura's computer.
E. Perhaps he did it alone.
F. I'm certain you now work for the CIA.

★★★ 5. Write sentences using the words below.

A. infiltrate • a ransom • illegally
B. a feed • social engineering • a traitor
C. cyberwar • harm • coercive
D. phishing • a whistleblower • spy on
E. a hacktivist • deep web • warn against

★★★ 6. Translate into English.

A. *Pourrait-il être coupable de cyber-terrorisme ?*
B. *Lui était-il possible d'obtenir cette information ?*
C. *Ne devrais-tu pas parler à ton avocat ?*
D. *Sera-t-elle reconnue coupable de ce crime ?*
E. *Faut-il toujours qu'ils enfreignent la loi ?*

7. Interactive test! What is your score?

OPEN YOUR EARS!

PHONOLOGY

La terminaison « -ed »

• Classez les mots ci-dessous dans le tableau en fonction de la prononciation de « -ed ». Puis vérifiez à l'écoute. **MP3 N°49**

pleaded • hacked • state-sponsored • treated • attacked • started • baffled • damaged • wanted

/d/	/t/	/ɪd/
…	…	…

TRAVEL WITH ACCENTS!

• Écoutez cet énoncé lu avec un accent américain puis avec un accent britannique. Que remarquez-vous quant à la prononciation du « o » de *god* ?

MP3 N°50 *"Wikileaks and its founders are doing God's work."*

MP3 N°51 *"Well, if Julian Assange and Wikileaks are doing God's work then I am baffled as to God's intentions."*

AUDIO MYSTERY

MP3 N°52

Listen to the audio and find the secret word.

Quote challenge

★ 3 sentences
★★ 4 to 6 sentences
★★★ 7 sentences and +

Which quote best sums up what you have learnt? Justify.

"I think cyber security, cyber warfare will be one of the biggest challenges facing the next president, because clearly we're facing at the point two different kinds of adversaries. There are the independent hacking groups that do it mostly for commercial reasons to try to steal information that they can use to make money. But increasingly, we are seeing cyber attacks coming from states."

Hillary Clinton, American politician (1947-)

"The purpose of whistleblowing is to expose secret and wrongful acts by those in power in order to enable reform."

Glenn Greenwald, American journalist (1967-)

B1-B2

BACKPACK

Get Ready for your Exam!

UNIT 10

Évaluation

Compréhension de l'oral

"Apple's stance on security" MP3 n°53

Listen to the audio recording three times and recap what you have understood.

Expression écrite — Choisissez l'un des deux sujets (min. 120 mots).

Question A : Discuss the following statement:
"Technological and scientific breakthroughs have made it more difficult for people to break the law. Science is the best deterrent of all."

Question B : "In a world where everyone uses a smart phone, a tablet and a computer, almost every crime leaves a digital trace."
Can science and new technology be a godsend for lawbreakers?

UNIT 11

Évaluation

Compréhension de l'oral

"Mobile dating apps" MP3 n°54

Listen to the audio recording three times and recap what you have understood.

Expression écrite — Choisissez l'un des deux sujets (min. 120 mots).

Question A : What are the pros and cons of dating apps?

Question B : Would you say that online dating has killed courtly love?

UNIT 12

Évaluation

Compréhension de l'oral

"The world's most famous hacker" MP3 n°55

Listen to the audio recording three times and recap what you have understood.

Expression écrite — Choisissez l'un des deux sujets (min. 120 mots).

Question A : Comment on the following statement:
"Hacking should never be glamourized. Hackers are lawbreakers and they should never be regarded as modern-day heroes."

Question B : How do you react to the fact that some hackers are sometimes hired by big companies to protect their data?

UNIT 11 Évaluation

Online dating isn't all good news for those of us who want a fair and just society. Because of course, race isn't the only dividing line that developed countries like America struggle with today. There's also class. Here the data gets impossibly murky, because people don't exactly divulge their financial status in the Vows section. But there's another proxy for class, and that's the troubling trend towards exclusive, private membership-based dating apps.

There's the League, which has 300,000 members and a 500,000-strong waitlist. There's Luxy, which boasts that half its members are worth half a million or more. But the poster child for this brave new balkanized world is Raya, the LA-based online dating service that only accepts 8 percent of applicants and is currently 10,000 strong across a dozen countries.

Some of the more desperate have been known to offer as much as $10,000 for a membership, according to this *New York Times* profile. No dice: to get one you're judged on factors like your Instagram following and how many people you know who are already in the club.

On Raya, the well-heeled and well-connected swipe without having to see a single face from the hoi polloi. The founder had utopian visions of a global dinner party, a "digital Davos" for dating. But as with many utopian visions of the past, this has its own unintended consequences.

If Raya is the kind of thing we all secretly aspire to be on, then the future may be one of multiple tiers. Dating apps would become the new rungs of the social ladder. And all the gains made on the interracial front would be lost as people only meet others at their same income or Instagram-follower level.

That effect could last for longer than one generation, if history is any guide. If you and your partner met on Raya, you may look askance at your kids if they want to hang out on tattered old Tinder. We're talking about dating apps creating a new aristocracy.

Which in turn means that we might want to look at apps like Tinder, Bumble, and Badoo in a new light. By using these widest possible pools of potential dates, rather than aspiring to something more exclusive, we're keeping ourselves open to more random love connections that cut across lines of race and class and everything else that divides us. We're doing our part to keep society more open, more diverse, less stratified.

Even if we come to the popular apps with certain racial or class preferences, we can still allow ourselves to be surprised by an unusual match, to think outside our normal boxes, at least for the length of one date. We have nothing to lose but our preconceptions.

We still haven't determined the name of this vast global game we're playing, or what the final boss level will be. But let's hope it's less of a snobby, royalty-based medieval Reigns game, and more of a vast, experimental, hot melting pot. Call it Global Thermonuclear Love.

Chris Taylor, *www.mashable.com*, 2019

Compréhension de l'écrit

Answer the following questions in English, using your own words.

A. After reading the text, what can you say about:
- its main topic?
- the people involved?
- their opinions on the topic?
- how "Raya" works?

B. Comment on the paragraph lines 27-29.

Expression écrite

Choisissez l'un des deux sujets (min. 120 mots).

Question A : Have virtual dating sites changed the way people interact in real life?

Question B : How can you account for the fact that meeting online has become the most popular way couples meet, according to a Stanford University study published in 2019?

UNIT 12 Évaluation

Anonymous took the hacktivism community with them when they died

IBM's X-Force threat intelligence platform has revealed part of the data they've gathered on hacktivism since 2015, and what they've observed has been no small change: from a peak of 35 attacks in 2015, hacktivist attacks steadily declined. The decline is related to the attrition of Anonymous, the hacktivist group behind 45% of attacks in the last four years, who've dropped from eight attacks in 2015 to merely one last year. 2018 saw the lowest rates of hacktivism in a decade, and 2019 might follow the same trend.

The X-Force defined a hacktivist attack as any politically motivated, widely reported and damaging attack that can be attributed to a specific group, and in the last four years, they observed a total of 66. They've attributed the decline to two main factors; the fracturing of Anonymous and the bad taste it has left in the community's mouth, and renewed pressure from law enforcement.

Anonymous, by design, have no leader, no control over their members, and no way to verify members. While united by various common goals from 2008 to 2015, including fights against pedophilia, censorship, and police brutality, divisive internal political opinions began separating the group during the 2016 election. Some members, it's believed, wished to attack Hillary Clinton for her left-wing ideals, while others were distressed by Donald Trump's anti-immigration and perceived racist policies. Several groups claiming to be Anonymous conducted brief attacks on both candidates.

Troubles escalated further when other hackers and even government authorized groups began masquerading as Anonymous, either for their own means or to tarnish Anonymous' name… Attempts to remove "fake Anons" decreased the number of true Anonymous hackers, the X-Force believes.

At the same time, self-proclaimed Anonymous member Martin Gottesfeld was arrested on suspicions he was behind DDoS[1] attacks against children's hospitals. He was sentenced to 10 years imprisonment last January.

DDoS attacks and hits against public websites were largely looked down upon by the hacktivist community, which is suspected of reducing the desire for further activity. Several data hacks against governments and companies ended up exposing more info on harmless civilians than bad actors, and that line of hacking was abandoned quickly.

Independent from Anonymous, many smaller and less professional hacktivist groups have been blocked by new security measures employed by governments and companies in the last two years, while others have lost members to arrests. […]

While many are proclaiming the death of hacktivism, X-Force believes that this will be just a brief respite. Scattered activities […] following the arrest of Julian Assange suggest renewed interest this year, and no one is letting their guard down.

Isaiah Mayersen, *www.techspot.com*, 2019

1 Distributed Denial of Service = forced interruption of service

Compréhension de l'écrit

Answer the following questions in English, using your own words.

A. After reading the text, what can you say about:
- its main topic?
- the people involved?
- how these people have influenced society and the political world?

B. Comment on the paragraph lines 27-29.

Expression écrite

Choisissez l'un des deux sujets (min. 120 mots).

Question A : What is the role of an hacktivist? What makes him/her different from a whistleblower? Give examples.

Question B : Should hacktivism be considered as a counterpower? Justify your answer.

Évaluation

Observe the documents.
According to you, which document best illustrates "Citizenship and Virtual Worlds"?

U.10 U.12

a "Arguing that you don't care about the right to privacy because you have nothing to hide is no different than saying you don't care about free speech because you have nothing to say."

Edward Snowden, American whistleblower

b

Canadian cartoonist **Bruce MacKinnon**

c "Privacy on the Internet? That's an oxymoron."

Catherine Butler, English academic and author

d

Billboard in Las Vegas, Nevada

UNIT 11

a "Whether you like it or not, the digital age has produced a new format for modern romance, and natural selection may be favouring the quick-thumbed quid peddler[1] over the confident, ice-breaking alpha male."

Ashton Kutcher, American actor

1. *Faiseur de bons mots*

b "Perhaps love in the digital age is more like Netflix binge-watching: we enjoy bursts of fantasy, and then move on to something else when it's done. Like browsing for a new series on Netflix, if the relationship doesn't fit perfectly, you can trade it in for something new with the click of a button or a swipe on your phone."

Shannon M. Mullen, *See What Flowers*, 2017

On the set of *Superman Returns*, 2006

AXE 5

Fictions & Realities

AXE 5

UNIT 13

THE WESTERN: DEAD OR ALIVE [?]

How do western movies reflect the evolution of the USA?

YOUR PROJECT

Speak at a conference about the evolution of the American western movie.

Au menu de cette unité :

DÉCOUVERTES CULTURELLES

- La conquête de l'Ouest (*The Frontier, Manifest Destiny* ...)
- La ruée vers l'or en Californie
- Le western et ses composantes (pionniers, cowboys, Amérindiens, hors-la-loi...)
- La représentation des *Native Americans*
- Les réécritures modernes du western

OUTILS LINGUISTIQUES

- Le prétérit et le *past perfect*
- L'expression du souhait et de l'intention
- Les comparatifs et superlatifs

BEFORE CLASS!

Flash to watch!

Watch the trailer for John Ford's ***The Man Who Shot Liberty Valance*** (1962). Get ready to talk about it in class.

❶ The Mythology of the Western

How were the Frontiersmen and women portrayed in the art of fiction?

1 Symbols of the Wild West

A. Groupwork. Each group works on a picture. Analyse the stills (places, people, actions…).
B. Share your findings with the class to build a list of the main symbols used in western films.

A

B

C

D

2 The code of the cowboy

A. Listen to **MP3 N°56**. Say why the American nation had no mythology.
B. Explain how the American nation created its own mythology (characters created, media used).
C. Say how powerful this code of the cowboy was.

❷ Searching For a Better Life

What ideals shaped the American spirit of conquest?

1 The expansion of the American Frontier

A. Observe the map. Say how the American territory expanded.

B. Guess what the *Frontier* is and what could motivate its evolution.

C. Find out more about the Frontier on Worksheet n°23.

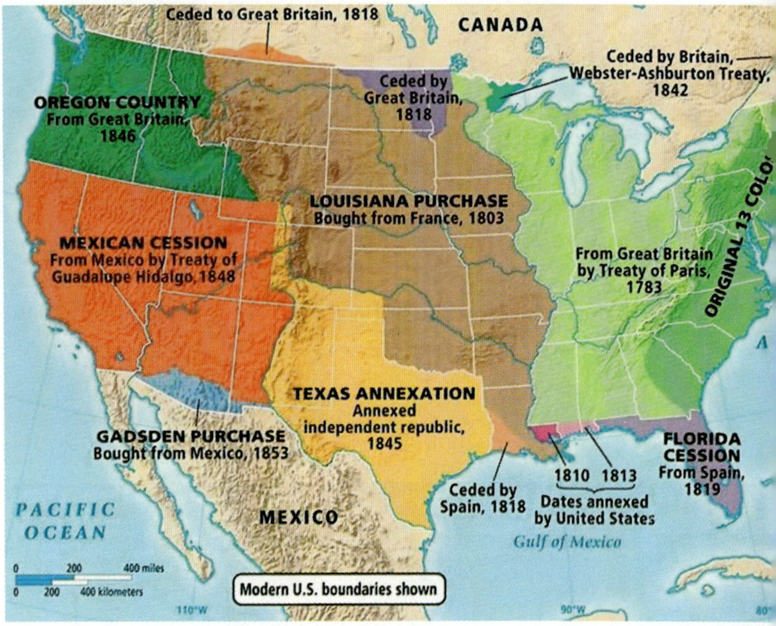

2 Promoting American expansion

A. List the symbolic elements of the Far West (people, means of transport, animals).

B. Comment on the movement, the light and the shadow.

C. Use what you have learnt about the Frontier to say what the woman in white (Lady Columbia) stands for.

D. Have your say. What values could be represented?

"American Progress", John Gast, 1872.

HELP!

Nouns

- pioneer /paɪə'nɪə/
- colonist /'kɒlənɪst/
- herd /'hɜːd/ of bison /'baɪsn/
- stagecoach /'steɪdʒkəʊtʃ/ = *diligence*
- covered wagon /'wægən/
- wilderness /'wɪldənɪs/
- the Frontier /frʌn'tɪə/
- boundary /'baʊndəri/

Adjectives

- native /'neɪtɪv/
- fearless

Verbs & Expressions

- go west
- push westward
- expand
- grow crops = *cultiver*

3 The Gold Rush

A. Look at the still. How does it fit the traditional images of the Wild West (people, place, period, actions)?
B. Watch the video and check your hypotheses.
C. Say what two values emerged with the Californian Gold Rush and compare them with New England's values.
D. List the downsides of the Gold Rush.
E. Go further. Compare what you knew of the Gold Rush with what you have learnt.

VIDEO N°26

4 A pioneer's life

Henry Edwards walked out from the house for a last look around. He carried his light shotgun, in hopes the rest of the family[1] would think he meant to pick up a sage or hen or two [...] He didn't want to get them all stirred up[2]. [...]
From just behind the crest of the little hill, Henry Edwards could see about a dozen miles. [...] But the faint roll of the prairie was deceptive. A whole squadron of cavalry could probably hide itself [...] in a place that looked as flat as a parade ground. So he was looking for little things – a layer of floating dust in the branches [...], a wild cow or an antelope disturbed.
[...] He looked back at his house. [...] Its adobe[3] walls were [...] thick, so strong that the first room they had built had for a long time been called the Edwards Fort. They had added on to it since, and made it even more secure. The shake roof looked burnable, but it wasn't [...]. The outside doors were massive, and the windows had heavy battle shutters swung inside.
[...] They had come here (that) long ago [...] drawn by these miles and miles of good grass, free to anyone who dared expose himself to the Kiowas and Comanches. It hadn't looked so dangerous when they first came, for the Texas Rangers had just punished the Wild Tribes back out of the way. But right after that the Rangers were virtually disbanded [...]. Henry and Martha held on and prayed... [...] Their nearest neighbours, the Pauleys, were murdered off by a Comanche raid, without survivors [...] and they heard of many, many more.
[...] A bedded-down meadowlark[4] sprang into the air [...]. Henry became motionless, except for his eyes, which moved continually, casting[5] the plain. Five hundred yards to the right [...] a covey of quail[6] went up. Henry turned and ran for the house.

1 Martha, his wife; Hunter and Ben, his sons; Debbie and Lucie, his daughters • 2 worried • 3 *de l'argile* • 4 *espèce d'oiseau* • 5 *scruter* • 6 *caille*

The Searchers (Chapter 1),
Alan Le May, 1954

A. Read the text. Who is the main character and what is he doing?
B. Say where he settled and comment on his house (solidity, appearance, reason).
C. What image is given of the Native Americans? Justify with quotes.
D. Describe the feelings of the character through the passage.
E. Have your say. What image of the Frontier is given here?

HELP!

Nouns & Adjectives
- trailblazer /ˈtreɪlbleɪzə/
- settler /ˈsetlə/
- gold miner /ˈmaɪnə/
- gold seeker
- forty-niner
- hopeful
- determined /dɪˈtɜːmɪnd/
- strong-willed /strɒŋˈwɪld/

Verbs
- pan for gold
- lure /lʊə/ = *attirer*
- settle = *s'installer*
- set up a colony / a settlement

YOUR TURN!

5 An old diary

For the annual *Wild Wild West Fest* in Texas, people are invited to read the diaries of their ancestors who conquered the West. Imagine two entries of a diary (activities, feelings...).

❸ Insider and Outsider Threats

How did fighting common enemies help to build a nation and shape common values?

1 Bloodthirsty Comanches

A. Read the text once and summarise what happened there.
B. Imagine how Martin and Amos must feel. Justify with quotes from the text.
C. Compare and contrast the construction of the house in the first excerpt from the novel (p. 133) and what is left now.
D. What image does it give of the Comanches?

HELP!

Nouns
- savage /ˈsævɪdʒ/
- Indian raid
- Frontiersman /ˈfrʌntɪəzmən/
- revenge killing

Adjectives
- hostile /ˈhɒstaɪl/ = unfriendly
- uncultured /ʌnˈkʌltʃəd/
- uncivilised /ʌnˈsɪvɪlaɪzd/

Verbs
- wipe out /waɪp aʊt/ = exterminate

Martin is one of Henry Edwards's neighbours. Amos is Henry Edwards's brother. Martin and Amos were searching for stolen cattle, when they understood that they had been pulled out from their homes by the Comanches so that the latter could raid their houses better. Martin and Amos rushed back home.

Martin slowed to a walk, and went toward the house unwillingly. Little flames still wandered across the embers[1] of the hay stacks[2] and the barn, sending up sparks which hung idly on the quiet air; and the house itself showed against the night in a dull red glow. On the back gallery lay a dead pony, tail to the broken door. [...]

Martin stepped over the legs of the dead Comanche pony and went into the kitchen, walking as though he had never learned to walk [...]. Near the door a body lay covered by a sheet. Martin drew back the limp muslin[3] and was looking into Martha's face. Her lips were parted a little, and her open eyes, looking straight up, appeared perfectly clear, as if she were alive. [...]

Most of the batten shutters had been smashed in. Hunter Edwards lay in a heap [...], his hand still clawed as if grasping the duck gun that was gone. Ben had fallen in a tangled knot[4] by the far window, his gangly legs sprawled. [...]

Martin found the body of Henry Edwards draped on its back across the broad sill of a bedroom window. The Comanche knives had done eery[5] work upon his body. Like Martha, Henry and both boys had been scalped. [...]

"No sign of Lucy. Or Deborah," Amos said. "So far as I could find in the lack of light." [...]

Martin said, "We used to practice sending Debbie up the hill to grandma's grave–"

"I been up. They sent her there. I found her bit of buffalo robe. But Debbie's not up there. Not now."

1 *la braise* • 2 *des bottes de foin* • 3 *un voile de mousseline légère* • 4 *un enchevêtrement de draps noués* • 5 strange

The Searchers (Chapter 1),
Alan Le May, 1954

2 Native Americans and Hollywood

A. Describe the situation in the photo, then listen to **MP3 N°57** and check your guess.
B. How does Sacheen Littlefeather justify Marlon Brando's absence there?
D. Have your say. What do you think of Marlon Brando's action?
E. Compare the way Native Americans are considered in the text (Act. 1) and this audio document.

3 Billy the Kid

A. Give the nature of the document and say what it is about.

B. Listen to MP3 N°58. Draw a timeline of the boy's life (dates, places, activities) with the help of Worksheet n°24.

C. Say why he was soon "the most wanted outlaw in the West."

D. Explain how of his life ended.

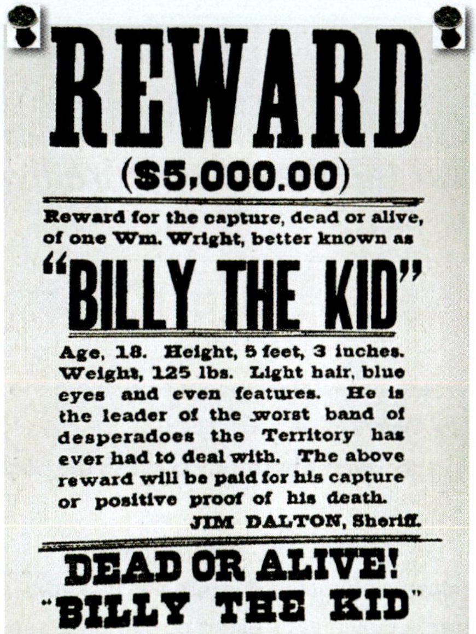

4 Calamity Jane: a legendary character

A. Describe the poster and say what sort of woman Jane certainly was.

B. Read the biography of Calamity Jane and prepare a "fast facts" of her life.

C. **At home.** Watch the trailer for "*Jane Got a Gun*" and get ready to talk about it in class.

D. **Have your say.** What aspects of her life are inspiring for movie makers?

Calamity Jane was born Martha Jane Cannary around 1852 in Princeton, Missouri. [...] Far from the ideal of the delicate Victorian woman, Jane often wore men's clothes. She eked out a living[1] doing menial jobs[2], some of which were jobs usually reserved for men. [...] Some legends say that she disguised herself as a man to accompany soldiers as a scout on expeditions [...]. She developed a reputation for hanging out with the miners, railroad workers, and soldiers—enjoying heavy drinking with them. She was arrested, with some frequency, for drunkenness and disturbing the peace. [...]

In 1877 and 1878, Edward L. Wheeler featured Calamity Jane in his popular Western dime novels, adding to her reputation. She became something of a local legend at this time because of her many eccentricities. [...]

In her later years, Calamity Jane appeared in Wild West shows, including the Buffalo Bill Wild West Show [...]. In 1887, Mrs. William Loring wrote a novel named *Calamity Jane*. [...] Jane published her autobiography in 1896, "Life and Adventures of Calamity Jane by Herself," to cash in on her own fame, and much of it is quite clearly fictional or exaggerated. [...]

She died in a hotel in nearby Terry in 1903 [...]. Because of her notoriety, her funeral was large. The legend of Calamity Jane, markswoman[3], horsewoman, drinker, and performer, continues in movies, books, and television Westerns.

How did Jane get the moniker "Calamity Jane"? [...] "Calamity," some say, is what Jane would threaten to any man who bothered her. She also claimed the name was given to her because she was good to have around in a calamity, such as the smallpox[4] epidemic of 1878. [...] Like much in her life, it's simply not certain.

1 gagner à peine de quoi vivre • 2 petits boulots • 3 tireuse d'élite • 4 la variole

Jone Johnson Lewis, **www.thoughtco.com**, June 13, 2019

HELP!

Nouns & Adjectives
- outlaw /ˈaʊtlɔː/
- bounty hunter /ˈbaʊnti ˈhʌntə/ = *chasseur de primes*
- reward
- death penalty /deθ ˈpenəltɪ/
- good and evil /ˈiːvl/
- rugged /ˈrʌgɪd/ = strong

Verbs & Expressions
- escape
- place a bounty on sb = *tête mise à prix*
- be sentenced to death
- magnify /ˈmægnɪfaɪ/ a legend

YOUR TURN! 5 Slideshow

Prepare a slideshow with a voice-over to present one of the "threats" studied.

4 The Western: a Revival?

How can the Western genre live on in the USA today?

1 How the Western was lost

A. Read the text and list the reasons explaining the decline of the Western.
B. Say why other genres better respond to the public's expectations.
C. Have your say. Do you agree that the Western genre is dead? Do you think your generation has an interest in Westerns? Explain.

Since the dawn of film, the Western has been one of the great, durable movie genres, but its audience seems to be finally drying up. [...] Western fans are getting older and whiter with respect to the overall population. [...] Exacerbating the problem is the rejection of cowboy movies by international audiences, particularly the Chinese. So even as filmmakers have become more interested in incorporating a diversity of viewpoints, they have hit against what appears a global demographic ceiling. [...]
The genres that currently rule the box office do other things well —sci-fi movies can address the ecological crisis and challenges of new technology, for instance, and superhero movies can provide never-ending glosses on the core myth of American exceptionalism. [...]
The other great theme of the Western, after that of the conquering of native peoples and the establishment of civilization in the desert, is that of loss and of nostalgia for a certain way of life —the early freedoms of the West, the idea of riding across an unfenced landscape, the infinite possibilities of the frontier. That "West," of course, is already gone, fallen, conquered.

Michael Agresta, ***The Atlantic***, 24 July 2013

2 Saving the Western

A. Read the text with the help of Worksheet n°25.
B. Go further. Comment on the sentence l. 27-28.

Westerns helped popularize and market the myth of cowboys and Indians, encouraging kids to take up guns against a monolithic other, and spreading the idea that anyone who doesn't speak English is part of a backward people who don't deserve rights to property, to respect, or to live the life they desire within their cultural traditions.
Westerns gave the world Ronald Reagan, Clint Eastwood and John 'I believe in white supremacy until blacks are educated to the point of responsibility' Wayne.
The women are pretty much all harlots[1], or religious wives who know their place is in the kitchen waiting on their man. For decades westerns have falsely failed to recognise the diversity of the cowboy, or that the ladies were not all saloon hussies[2]. [...] Of course there are some outliers[3]: a few black cowboys have popped up, or a band of women have appeared, pistols in their garter belts, but they largely fed into the genre rather than deconstructed it.
But this year it seems like a few directors have decided it's time to steal the hats from westerns and stamp all over them, giving the genre the makeover it has long been in need of. [...] It's not just female directors who have subverted the genre. Australian director Warwick Thornton has been at it too, and used a simple but radical technique when making the beautiful *Sweet Country*. "We looked at the western with an inverted point of view," he says. "We are not following John Wayne; we are following the Indians. The film is about white colonialists, but it's from the perspective of the oppressed and the indigenous community they are about to destroy." [...] "The obliteration of indigenous cultures around the world by religion: it's one of the biggest genocides," Thornton points out.
And that's what these new westerns are all doing and what makes them so much more interesting. By pushing the genre envelope, they encourage empathy and understanding with the characters who have to cope and live with the actions of the cowboy figures.

1 prostitutes • 2 *effrontées* • 3 *exceptions*

Kaleem Aftab, ***The Independent***, 13 April 2018

3 Revival films

For a Film Festival, western lovers are invited to write a film review of a western revival film.

A. In pairs, choose a film. Watch the trailer online and write a review to convince people to watch it.

B. Read your review aloud.

C. Select the best review. Justify.

D. Have your say. Which other film best corresponded to your idea of a western revival?

The Homesman (2014) → online

Meek's Cutoff (2014) → VIDEO N°27

Woman Walks Ahead (2017) → online

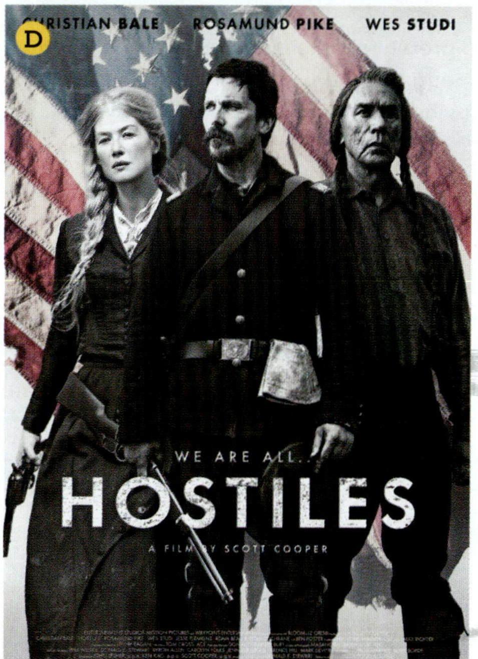

Hostiles (2017) → online

YOUR PROJECT

For "Western Week", you will speak at a conference entitled *The Western genre: dead or alive (?)* Prepare a slideshow to account for the evolution of the American Western movie.

SPICE UP YOUR VOCABULARY

Use the vocabulary below to create your own mind map and add more words if necessary!

Adjectives

- dead or alive
- determined /dɪ'tɜːmɪnd/
- fearless
- (un)friendly
- hopeful
- hostile /'hɒstaɪl/
- indigenous /ɪn'dɪdʒɪnəs/
- lawless /'lɔːləs/
- native /'neɪtɪv/
- rugged /'rʌgɪd/
- savage /'sævɪdʒ/
- strong-willed /strɒŋ'wɪld/
- uncivilized /ʌn'sɪvɪlaɪzd/
- uncultured /ʌn'kʌltʃəd/
- wanted /'wɒntɪd/
- wild /waɪld/

Nouns

- bounty /'baʊnti/ hunter
- colonist /'kɒlənɪst/ = settler
- covered wagon /'wægən/
- forty-niner
- frontier /'frʌntɪə/
- frontiersman / frontierswoman
- genocide /'dʒenəsaɪd/
- gold miner /'maɪnə/
- Gold rush
- Indian tribe /traɪb/
- limit = boundary /'baʊndəri/
- outlaw /'aʊtlɔː/
- pioneer /paɪə'nɪə/
- reward /rɪ'wɔːd/
- settlement /'setlmənt/
- trailblazer /'treɪlbleɪzə/
- wilderness /'wɪldənɪs/

Verbs & Expressions

- debunk a myth
- expand
- go west
- grow crops
- harvest
- lure /lʊə/
- pan for gold
- place a bounty on sb
- push westward
- search for /sɜːtʃ/
- sentence sb to death /deθ/
- set up a colony
- settle
- wipe out /waɪp aʊt/

RULE THE GRAMMAR!

LE PRÉTÉRIT

On utilise le prétérit simple quand il y a une rupture avec le moment présent. Il est souvent utilisé avec des mots qui indiquent un repère passé.
She killed him yesterday.

Notez la différence avec le *present perfect* :
Look, he's dead. She has shot him. Ici, le lien avec le présent est explicite ("Look…").

→ P.300

LE *PAST PERFECT* (= *PLUPERFECT*)

- Il se forme avec **had** + participe passé.
- On utilise le *past perfect* pour exprimer l'antériorité d'un évènement passé par rapport à un autre moment passé.

Présent

*He **had shot** him **before** he **realised** he was innocent.*

- On utilise la forme ***had*** + ***been*** + BV-***ing*** quand une action est toujours d'actualité au moment du passé où on la considère. ***He had been firing** at the crowd for several minutes when he **realised** they were a peaceful lot.*

- Le *pluperfect* dans le discours indirect peut remplacer soit un prétérit, soit un *present perfect* : *"He shot the renegade."* → *She said he had shot the renegade.*
"He has shot him" → *She said he had shot him.*

→ P.302

L'EXPRESSION DU SOUHAIT OU L'INTENTION

- ***Will*** permet d'exprimer une volonté très nette. Avec *will*, on implique davantage l'utilisateur qu'avec *intend* to ou *mean to*. *I **will** hunt him down and find him.*

- ***Won't*** permet d'exprimer un refus clair. L'engagement de l'énonciateur est plus fort qu'avec *don't want to* ou *refuse to*. *I **won't** shoot him in the back.*

- Quand le sujet veut **inciter quelqu'un à faire quelque chose,** on peut utiliser les structures suivantes :
I want you to …. / I forbid you to … / I expect you to follow her orders.

→ P.305

LANGUAGE LAB

- Audio words
- MP3
- Interactive Test

★ **1. Read the words in the "nouns" column opposite and complete this mind map in your notebook.**

WESTERN: villains • heroes/heroines • transport • nature

★ **2. Rephrase using *will* or *won't*.**

A. She refuses to leave without her gold.
B. They want to follow their dreams until they die.
C. He doesn't want to shoot even if they attack.
D. He wants to marry her when he reaches the frontier.
E. We only want to watch western movies.
F. I refuse to accept my failure.

★★ **3. Rewrite these sentences using comparatives.**

A. His horse is … Helena's. *(+ quick)*
B. This buffalo is … that one. *(- big)*
C. The battle of Wounded Knee was … any other. *(+ bloody)*
D. John Wayne is … any other cowboy. *(+ famous)*
E. The Rockies are … than the Appalachians. *(+ high)*
F. This lake is … as Lake Huron. *(- large)*

★★ **4. Use these words to create other words by adding prefixes or/and suffixes. Then translate them.**

A. wild • B. friend • C. fear • D. hope • E. civil

★★ **5. Put the verbs in the appropriate tense: preterite or past perfect.**

A. Calamity Jane *(become)* famous before she *(publish)* her autobiography.
B. He *(kill)* the Indian before he *(realise)* he was harmless.
C. The saloon *(be deserted)* for a few hours when the sheriff *(arrive)*.
D. The Indians *(desert)* the prairie because the buffalos *(be)* there anymore.
E. We *(decide)* on a truce when some gunshots *(be heard)*.

★★ **6. Match each word with its definition.**

A. expand	1. look for gold
B. wipe out	2. go west
C. settle	3. make disappear
D. grow crops	4. cultivate
E. pan for gold	5. set up a colony
F. get back at	6. get revenge

★★ **7. Storytelling.** Imagine the story of Pat O'Neil, an immigrant who arrived in California in 1849 and experienced incredible adventures. Use as many words from the list above as possible.

8. Interactive test! What is your score?

OPEN YOUR EARS!

PHONOLOGY

MP3 N°59

Le digraphe *ow*

- **« ow » est tantôt prononcé /aʊ/, tantôt prononcé /əʊ/ sans qu'il soit possible de prédire quelle prononciation sera la bonne.**
- **Écoutez les mots suivants et classez-les selon leur prononciation : /aʊ/ ou /əʊ/ ?**

how • cowboy • bow (arc) • follow • know • now • grow • down

L'article *the*

- **La prononciation de l'article *the*** **MP3 N°60**

/ði:/ devant un son voyelle.

Prononcez /ðə/ devant un son consonne.

It involves the rape of the countryside,
the exploitation of Mexicans,
the extermination of the local tribes,
the mistreatment of Asians….

/ði:/ devant un son consonne pour insister.

Picture challenge

★ **3 sentences**
★★ **4 to 6 sentences**
★★★ **7 sentences and +**

How many sentences can you make using what you have learnt? Collect stars!

Still from *Dances with Wolves* by Kevin Costner (1990)

AXE 5

UNIT 14

WHICH WITCH IS WHICH?

How has the image of the witch mirrored societies over the centuries?

YOUR PROJECT

1 Present a fictional witch in the historical and societal context of her creator.

OR

2 Compose the letter written by a woman accused of witchcraft.

Au menu de cette unité :

DÉCOUVERTES CULTURELLES

- La chasse aux sorcières en Écosse (James VI)
- Le cas de Salem
- Les sorcières dans la littérature et dans les séries
- La sorcière, icône éco-féministe
- La chasse aux sorcières au Ghana de nos jours

OUTILS LINGUISTIQUES

- La voix passive
- L'expression du souhait et du regret
- Le discours indirect
- Les pronoms relatifs

BEFORE CLASS!

Flash to watch!

Watch the video and be ready to talk about it in class.

VIDEO N°28

❶ What Is a Witch?

How can a witch be defined?

1 How do witches work?

A. Give your own definition of a witch.
B. Read **text 1**. Turn to Worksheet n°26 for help. Then read **text 2**. Sum up the main ideas.
C. Recap what you have learnt about witches.
D. Observe the painting. Does it illustrate the traditional witch?

Text 1

In this contemporary work of fiction, American writer Madeline Miller revisits the story of Circe, a goddess from the Greek mythology and one of the first witches mentioned in history.

At first, of course, all I brewed[1] were mistakes. Draughts[2] that did nothing, pastes that crumbled and lay dead on the table. I thought that if some rue[3] was good, more was better, that ten herbs mixed were superior to five, that I could let my mind wander[4] and the spell would not wander with it, that I could begin making one draught and halfway through decide to make another. I did not know even the simplest herb-lore[5] that any mortal would learn at her mother's knee: that wort[6] plants boiled made a sort of soap, that yew[7] burnt in the hearth sent up a choking smog, that poppies had sleep in their veins and hellebore[8] death, and yarrow[9] could close over wounds. All these things had to be worked and learned through errors and trials[10], burnt fingers and fetid clouds that sent me running outside to cough in the garden.
At least, I thought in those early days, once I cast a spell, I would not have to learn it again. But even that was not true. [...] Each spell was a mountain to be climbed anew. All I could carry with me from last time was the knowledge that it could be done.

1 infuser • 2 potions • 3 nom d'une plante médicinale • 4 vagabonder • 5 connaissances en herboristerie • 6 millepertuis (plante) • 7 un if • 8 hellébore (plante) • 9 millefeuille (plante) • 10 ici, tâtonnements, essais

Circe,
Madeline Miller, 2018

The Magic Circle,
John William Waterhouse (1886)

Text 2

"Witch' is a powerful word with humble origins. Once used to describe an ancient British tribe known for its unique class of female physicians and priestesses, it grew into something grotesque, diabolical and dangerous. [...] These ancient healers were the antithesis of the witch figure of today; instead they were knowledgeable therapists commanding respect, gratitude and high social status.

Back cover of A History of Women in Medicine: From Physicians to Witches?,
Sinéad Spearing, 2019

❷ Witch-Hunts in 16th Century Scotland

How did King James VI spark witch-hunts?

1 An obsessed monarch

One of the most active centres of witch-hunting was Scotland, where perhaps 4,000 people were consigned to the flames – a striking number for such a small country, and more than double the execution rate in England. The ferocity of these persecutions can be attributed to the most notorious royal witch-hunter: King James VI [of Scotland].

James's obsession with witchcraft can be traced back to his childhood. The violent death of his mother, Mary, Queen of Scots, seems to have inspired a dark fascination with magic. [...]

Two years after Mary's execution, another dramatic event deepened James's growing obsession with magic and witchcraft. In 1589 he was betrothed to Anne of Denmark, but she almost lost her life in a violent tempest when she set sail across the North Sea to meet her new husband. In an uncharacteristic show of chivalry, James resolved to sail across to Denmark and collect her in person. But on their return voyage the royal fleet was battered by more storms and one of the ships was lost. James immediately placed the blame on witches, claiming that they must have cast evil spells upon his fleet.

As soon as he reached Scottish shores, James ordered a witch-hunt on a scale never seen before. No fewer than 70 suspects were rounded up in the coastal Scottish town of North Berwick on suspicion of raising a storm to destroy James and his new bride. Most of the suspects soon confessed – under torture – to concocting a host of bizarre and gruesome[1] spells and rituals in order to whip up the storm. [...] They were swiftly convicted and put to death. [...]

In 1597 James became the only monarch in history to publish a treatise on witchcraft: *Daemonologie* (literally, 'the science of demons').

1 *horrific*

www.historyextra.com, 19 June 2018

A. Read the text. Sum up in a few words what James VI thought of witches and why.

B. Consequently, how did James VI act?

C. Why can the North Berwick trial be considered typical of what happened in most witch-hunts?

2 Debunking myths

A. Listen to the interview on **MP3 N°61** and pick out information about:

- the number of people accused of witchcraft in Scotland;
- what happened to them;
- details about their lives (gender, age, occupation...);
- elements about their trials.

B. Pairwork. Share the information you picked with your classmate.

C. Listen again and complete your answers.

HELP!

Nouns & Adjectives

- prosecution = accusation
- life expectancy = age one is expected to live to
- widow: *veuve*
- witch pricker = a person whose job was to perforate the accused with a sharp object so as to reveal a witch's marks
- banished = sent away from their country
- excommunicated = excluded from their religion
- outlawed = against the law

3 The power of a single word

A. Read the introduction and say what you have understood about the characters, setting, and main action.

B. Answer the questions on Worksheet n°27A.

C. To conclude, explain the power of the word "witch". Study the way it is used by Corrag in the text.

The Martyr of the Solway, John Millais, 1871

1692, Corrag, a wild young girl living in Scotland has been accused of witchcraft. While awaiting her execution, she is visited by the Reverend Charles Leslie.

Reverend Charles Leslie. I feel I know your name. [...] I saw you flinch[1] at [the word] *witch*.

Oh it's a dark word, for certain. It has caused its damage across the months and years. Many good people have been undone by it – married and unmarried, beautiful, and strange. Women. Men. What did you have, in your head? With *witch*?

I know that all people have a certain creature in their head, when they hear it – a woman, mostly. Pitch-dark and cruel, crooked with age. Did you think *she will be mad, this witch?* I might be. It's been said. [...]

What townsfolk say we do and what we truly do are very different things. I have cast no spells. [...] I've never turned into a bird, skimmed a night-time loch[2], or settled on ships to make them drown. I've not kissed obscenely or eaten dead babes. [...] I've never seen the future in a rotten egg. I never laughed at murders, or called murders in. I've not summoned anything. I've only asked – prayed.

Pray. Yes. I use that word, too. I pray – not in church and with no Bible, but otherwise I reckon it's probably like how you pray, which is with the heart's voice talking, not the mouth's.

Devil child, they've called me. *Evil piece*.

But Mr Leslie, I will tell you this. When *witch* was first thrown at me, as I passed through a market, Cora [Corrag's mother] led me by the hand to an alleyway and sat me down, and wiped my wet eyes, and said *listen to me. The only evil in the world is the one that lies in people – in their pride, and greed, and duty. Remember that.*

And from what I have seen of this world, this life, I think she was right.

1 *reculer de peur* • 2 Scottish word for lake

The Highland Witch,
Susan Fletcher, 2011

YOUR TURN!

4 Just a wild girl

Imagine Reverend Charles Leslie's compassionate speech to convince the village leaders to grant amnesty to the girl.

Use what you learnt about the way Scottish witches were treated to argue your case.

She was unfairly / wrongly accused…

The vilest punishment…

❸ The Salem Witch Trials

Why have the Salem witch trials been a source of inspiration for fiction?

1 Witch among us

A. React to the poster and to its catchphrase.
B. What do you know about the witches of Salem?
C. In one paragraph, imagine the story that brought about this poster.

HELP!

Words
- hang sb
- die by hanging
- sentence sb to death
- convict sb /kən'vɪkt/
- be found guilty of + N / V-ing
- be (wrongly) accused of N / V-ing
- witchcraft = sorcery
- have a noose around one's neck

2 What happened in Salem?

A. Watch the video and give an oral account of what you have understood.
B. Have your say. What makes this historical event so inspirational for literature and cinema?

VIDEO N°29

3 Contracting with the Devil

A. Read the text. Write down the historical information you remember about the main characters.

B. Who is this excerpt focused on? Pick two elements to justify your answer.

C. What does this extract reveal about the way trials were conducted? Pay attention to the behaviour of the characters and the way they are placed.

March 1, 1692. Sarah Good, Sarah Osborne and Tituba (Reverend Parris's slave) are brought to trial at the Salem meetinghouse.

The marshal[1] indicated that the prisoners were to stand on a table a little to one side of the pulpit. Good scrambled up[2] by herself, Osburne had to be lifted up, and Tituba climbed up unaided. [...]

Judge Hathorne said, "We will open with prayer, Mr. Parris."

Tituba tried to follow the master's prayer. [...] He said that many persons in several families of this little village had been vexed and tortured in body and soul by witchcraft and diabolical operations. When Tituba heard the word "witchcraft," she began to listen closely and carefully.

"The Devil hath[3] been raised amongst us," he said, and his voice increased in volume, "and the Devil's rage is vehement and terrible. We are here witnesses to the sin[4] of witchcraft which is the work of the Devil. We all know that the unrepentant witches who refuse to confess their guilt, refuse to admit their sin, must die. We also know that those taken in the sin of witchcraft who confess their sin and repent, and thoroughly amend their ways and their doings, will be pardoned and live. We ask Thy blessing on this hearing. May the Lord be praised. Amen." [...]

Marshal Herrick [...] indicated that Goody Good was to take her place alone, standing on the minister's[5] chair. [...] When she stood up on the chair and the girls saw her, they stiffened[6] and started to shriek[7]. Tituba felt Osburne tremble at the sound. When Judge Hathorne began to question Goody Good, the girls were silent.

Question: "Sarah Good, what evil spirit have you familiarity with?"

Answer: "None."

Question: "Have you made no contract with the Devil?"

Answer: "No."

Question: "Why do you hurt these children?"

Answer: "I do not hurt them. I scorn[8] it." [...]

At one point, Judge Hathorne stopped questioning her to ask the girls if this was one of the persons who had tormented them. By way of reply, they fell to the floor, screaming and crying out that she was choking them and pinching them. Tituba, who had hardly dared glance in their direction, now saw that they were all there: Abigail Williams, Anne Putnam, Mercy Lewis, Mary Warren, Elizabeth Booth, Sarah Churchill, Mary Walcott, Susanna Sheldon, and Elizabeth Hubbard with her knitting. Betsey Parris was not among them.

1 officer of the law • 2 climbed using her hands and feet • 3 has • 4 *le péché* • 5 *pasteur* • 6 became tense • 7 scream • 8 despise, reject

Tituba of Salem Village,
Ann Petry, 1991

YOUR TURN! 4 Create a leaflet

As a trainee museum curator, you have been asked to make a leaflet for the "Witch Trials Self-Guided Tour" at the Salem Witch Museum. Your leaflet should include some historical facts, physical landmarks in Salem, and some information about the history of the museum itself.

Visit the following site to gather further information: https://salemwitchmuseum.com.

❹ From Outcasts to Feminist Icons

How has the perception of witches evolved since the late 1960s?

1 Modern witches, a counter-culture rebirth

A. Read the article and define the modern witch.
B. Explain how the image of witches has evolved and why.
C. Go further. To what extent can this new witchcraft religion be associated with past historical witches?

It was in America that the witchcraft religion became a significant aspect of the counter-culture phenomenon, expressed most cogently[1] in the feminist movement. After all, the majority of executed witches during the witch trials were women. [...] They rightly saw social parallels between the past and present in terms of patriarchy and misogyny. In 1968 one radical feminist movement, which was not Wiccan[2] in inspiration, called themselves 'WITCH', the Women's International Terrorist Conspiracy from Hell. Members of WITCH organized public protests and street theatre events to highlight the dominance of patriarchal capitalism.

[...] The most influential feminist Wiccan text of the 1970s, however, was *The Spiral Dance: A Rebirth of the Ancient Religion of the Great Goddess* (1979). Its author Miriam Simos, better known as Starhawk, took Wicca in a new direction with a strong emphasis on ecological concerns, feminist spirituality, and shamanism. She co-founded the activist witch movement 'Reclaim' to further press for the

social, political, and environmental concerns that resonated with her conception of a goddess nature religion. By the year 2000, *Spiral Dance* had sold more than 300,000 copies, influencing many feminists within and beyond the Wiccan community, and it was one of the first significant American influences on British Wiccans.

1 convincingly • 2 a form of modern paganism

The Oxford Illustrated History of Witchcraft and Magic, Owen Davies, 2017

2 Embracing life

A. Read the text. Pick out the main elements of witchcraft religion as depicted by Starhawk.
B. Historical witches were ostracised. Do modern witches reject society? Justify.
C. Go further. What would make witchcraft attractive in this period of climate emergency?

We are an evolving, dynamic tradition and proudly call ourselves Witches. Honoring both Goddess, and God we work with female and male images of divinity, always remembering that mystery goes beyond form. Our community rituals are participatory and ecstatic, celebrating the cycles of the seasons and our lives, and raising energy for personal, collective and earth healing.

We know that everyone can do the life-changing, world-renewing work of magic, the art of changing consciousness at will. We strive to teach and practice in ways that foster[1] personal and collective empowerment, to model shared power and to open leadership roles to all. We make decisions by consensus, and balance individual autonomy with social responsibility. Our tradition honors the wild, and calls for service to the earth and the community. We value peace and practice non-violence, in keeping with the Rede[2], "Harm none, and do what you will." We work for all forms of justice: environmental, social, political, racial, gender and economic. Our feminism includes a radical analysis of power, seeing all systems of oppression as interrelated, rooted in structures of domination and control. We welcome all genders, all races, all ages and sexual orientations and all those differences of life situation, background, and ability that increase our diversity.

1 encourage • 2 laws of Wicca

The Spiral Dance, Starhawk, 1979

3 What would Hermione do?

A. From what you know about the *Harry Potter* books and films, how would you describe Hermione Granger?
B. Read the article. What influence has this fictional character had on real-life people and politics?
C. Have your say. Would this character be such a symbol if she were not a witch? Why?

The Women's March on Washington was littered with references to Hermione[1] Granger.

"When Voldemort is president, we need a nation of Hermiones," read one sign, which was posted on Twitter on Jan. 22, 2017, the day after more than 3.5 million people around the nation marched in solidarity with women's rights.

"Without Hermione, Harry would've died in book 1," read another.

In 1997, readers were first introduced to the brilliant and bookish character in *Harry Potter And The Sorcerer's Stone* – a young witch born to Muggle (non-magical) parents, with lots of "bushy brown hair and rather large front teeth." In 2017, Hermione's face is on protest signs around the world. She's been reimagined as the center of the *Harry Potter* series, tasked with battling the patriarchy. You can even purchase posters, T-shirts and embroidered crafts on Etsy that ask "What would Hermione do?"

Over two decades, the young British witch from J.K. Rowling's beloved *Harry Potter* series has grown from a literary smart girl into a powerful feminist symbol.

1 /hɜːˈmaɪənɪ/

www.huffpost.com, 16 June 2017

YOUR TURN! 4 From hags to witches

You are an American anthropologist about to give a conference titled "Witches of the 21st century". Use this double page to explain how history, fiction and modern feminism are connected.

HELP!

Nouns
- feminist icon /ˈaɪkɒn/
- role model
- nature worship /ˈwɜːʃɪp/
- pagan /ˈpeɪgən/
- paganism /ˈpeɪgənɪzəm/
- Sabbath /ˈsæbəθ/

Adjectives
- cross-cultural
- mystical = occult

- redeemed = saved from disgrace

Verbs & Expressions
- be empowered
- be emulated
- be reclaimed = be reborn
- weaving / crafting spells: *jeter un sort*

❺ Witches in Literature

What do witch stories say about women?

1 The Weird Sisters

A. Read the text and listen to **MP3 N°62**.
B. Read the *Cultural fact* on Worksheet n°27B.
What inspired Shakespeare?
C. Say what powers the witches seem to have. Justify.
D. In your opinion, why do the witches remain unnamed?
E. Go further. Is this painting a good illustration of the text?

***Macbeth and the Witches*, Henry Fuseli, 1793-94**

Thunder and lightning.
Enter three Witches.

FIRST WITCH
When shall we three meet again?
In thunder, lightning, or in rain?

SECOND WITCH
When the hurlyburly's[1] done,
When the battle's lost and won.

THIRD WITCH
That will be ere[2] the set of sun.

FIRST WITCH
Where the place?

SECOND WITCH
Upon the heath[3].

THIRD WITCH
There to meet with Macbeth.

FIRST WITCH
I come, Graymalkin*!

SECOND WITCH
Paddock* calls.

THIRD WITCH
Anon[4].

ALL
Fair is foul[5], and foul is fair
Hover[6] through the fog and filthy[7] air.

Exeunt

1 *tohu-bohu* • 2 before • 3 *bruyère* • 4 soon, shortly • 5 disgusting • 6 hang in air • 7 *immonde*

**Graymalkin and Paddock are familiars.*

Macbeth (Act I, Scene I),
William Shakespeare, 1603-1606

2 "The Wyrd Sisters"

A. Read the first part of the text (l. 1-11). Does it remind you of anything? Explain.
B. What does Magrat want to do? What do the others think?
C. Pick out some comparisons. What is the effect on the reader?
D. How would you define the tone of the text? Justify your answer.

The wind howled. Lightning stabbed at the earth erratically, like an inefficient assassin. Thunder rolled back and forth across the dark, rain-lashed hills.

The night was as black as the inside of a cat. It was the kind of night, you could believe, on which gods moved men as though they were pawns on the chessboard of fate. In the middle of this elemental storm a fire gleamed[1] among the dripping furze bushes[2] like the madness in a weasel's[3] eye. It illuminated three hunched[4] figures. As the cauldron bubbled an eldritch[5] voice shrieked: 'When shall we three meet again?'

There was a pause.

Finally another voice said, in far more ordinary tones: 'Well, I can do next Tuesday.' [...]

Unlike wizards, who like nothing better than a complicated hierarchy, witches don't go in much for the structured approach to career progression. It's up to each individual witch to take on a girl to hand the area over to when she dies. Witches are not by nature gregarious[6], at least with other witches, and they certainly don't have leaders.

Granny Weatherwax was the most highly-regarded of the leaders they didn't have.

Magrat's hands shook slightly as they made the tea. Of course, it was all very gratifying, but it was a bit nerve-racking to start one's working life as village witch between Granny and, on the other side of the forest, Nanny Ogg. It'd been her idea to form a local coven. She felt it was more, well, occult. To her amazement the other two had agreed or, at least, hadn't disagreed much.

'An oven?' Nanny Ogg had said. 'What'd we want to join an oven for?'

'She means a coven, Gytha,' Granny Weatherwax had explained. 'You know, like in the old days. A meeting.'

'A knees up?' said Nanny Ogg hopefully.

'No dancing' Granny had warned. 'I don't hold with dancing. Or singing or getting over-excited or all that messing about with ointments and similar.'

'Does you good to get out,' said Nanny happily.

Magrat had been disappointed about the dancing, and was relieved that she hadn't ventured one or two other ideas that had been on her mind. She fumbled in the packet she had brought with her. It was her first sabbat, and she was determined to do it right.

'Would anyone care for a scone?' she said.

Granny looked hard at hers before she bit. Magrat had baked bat designs on it.

Book cover illustration by Kate Oleska

1 *luisait* • 2 *dans les buissons d'ajoncs détrempés* • 3 *belette* • 4 *voûtées* • 5 sinister • 6 sociable

The Wyrd Sisters, Terry Pratchett, 1988

YOUR TURN! 3 Bewitch your classmates!

Groupwork. In groups of three, learn the first scene of the play *Macbeth* and adapt it using your own props and atmosphere! Get ready to perform it for your classmates.

❻ Witches in Pop Culture

What do fictional witch stories on TV say about real-life women of their time?

Snow White's witch, 1937, Walt Disney

1 The witch archetype

A. What does the picture evoke for you? Why?
B. Do you know the story of *Snow White and the Seven Dwarfs*? Share it with the class.
C. Say how this representation may target certain categories of women.

Bewitched, 1964-1972

2 Empowered or threatening?

A. Comment on the picture. Focus on the characters' expressions and actions.
B. Listen to Kristen Korvette on **MP3 N°63** and take notes. What archetypal witches does she name?
C. What representation of women do those witches convey?
D. Have your say. To what extent do you agree with Kristen Korvette?

3 The power of three

A. **Go online.** Watch the trailer for the series *Charmed* (1998-2006). Say what you understand of the main story.
B. How are the women depicted in the trailer?
C. Describe the picture and react.

4 Sabrina's hex appeal

A. Read the text. How would you define Sabrina? Choose three adjectives and justify them.
B. Say why this fictional witch may be the result of an evolution of society.
C. What does "third wave" refer to in the last sentence?
D. **Have your say.** Do fictional witches influence how we think, or is it the other way around? Is the evolution of society responsible for the new witch archetype?

On the cusp[1] of her "dark baptism" coming-of-age ceremony, 15-year-old Sabrina Spellman (Kiernan Shipka, best known as Sally Draper in *Mad Men*) is half witch, half mortal. Torn between the two worlds, she uses her powers for feminist good. When her non-binary best friend is bullied by football players about whether "she is a boy or a girl", Sabrina reports it to the (straight, it is assumed) white, male principal. He refuses to act – telling Sabrina: "You're suggesting a witch hunt" – so she hexes[2] him with spiders. [...] With its hip soundtrack, retro feel and intersectional feminism, *Chilling Adventures of Sabrina* reflects this millennial face of witchcraft. To support her friend, Sabrina co-founds – with the daughter of a Black Panther – a club "to topple[3] the white patriarchy": the Women's Intersectional Cultural and Creative Association, or Wicca. And so feminism rides its third magical wave.

1 *À l'aube de* • 2 *jeter un sort* • 3 *renverser*

Elle Hunt, ***The Guardian***, 29 October 2018

Chilling Adventures of Sabrina, 2018-?

YOUR TURN! 5 Pitch your series!

Struck by magical inspiration, you have created a witch character for a new TV series. Get ready to pitch it to your classmates! Your pitch should include the main lines of the plot, a description of your witch, and why you chose to create her.

❼ Witchcraft Still Scar(e)s Today in Africa

To what extent is the accusation of witchcraft still an issue for women?

1 No such things as witches?

A. Pick out the main issue raised by this article. Say who is targeted, why, how they are defined and what happens to them.

B. "There is no such thing as a witch" (l. 9): do you agree with this sentence? Why? Justify your answer.

C. Go further. Compare what you have learnt about 21st century witches in the USA with the witches depicted in this article.

The British High Commissioner for Ghana appealed to the government to close camps that house so-called witches and for the inhabitants to be reintegrated into society. In a meeting with Ghanaian authorities Jon Benjamin urged the government to dispel the myth that witches exist and move potentially thousands of women and children back to their villages.

"Personally, I believe in the 21st Century, it's time to say there is no such thing as a witch and to decry the practice of using such a term to dehumanise vulnerable women," Benjamin said stressing his views were his and not of the British government. [He] claimed that squalid[1] shanty towns around Kuko, Northern Ghana were holding around 800 'witches' and 500 children [...]

"The point is that there are no such things as witches. Some people maintain that the women in these camps are at least in a safe space and not mistreated there as they might be in their home villages, and they may have a point. [...] But if people weren't arbitrarily labelled witches and discriminated against, occasionally violently, on that basis in the first place, then you wouldn't need the camps at all."

The camp's cut adrift[2] inhabitants live in mud huts and have no access to basic sanitation and health facilities. Some women have also been kept in the ghetto style villages for decades, says accused sorcerer Sano Kojo, 70, [who] has been living in a camp since 1981 when she was accused of witchcraft by allegedly pressing on her cousin's chest until he died, reported The Express.

"People don't care about alleged witches," she says. "Once you are here you are forgotten."

1 sordid • 2 separated

www.dailymail.co.uk, 9 September 2016

2 "Free As a Goat"

A. Listen to an interview with Rungano Nyoni about her award film *I'm Not a Witch* on **MP3 N°64** and take notes.

B. What real-life situation inspired her?

C. What does she have to say about laws and traditional belief systems?

D. What happens to women accused of witchcraft in Zambia and Ghana?

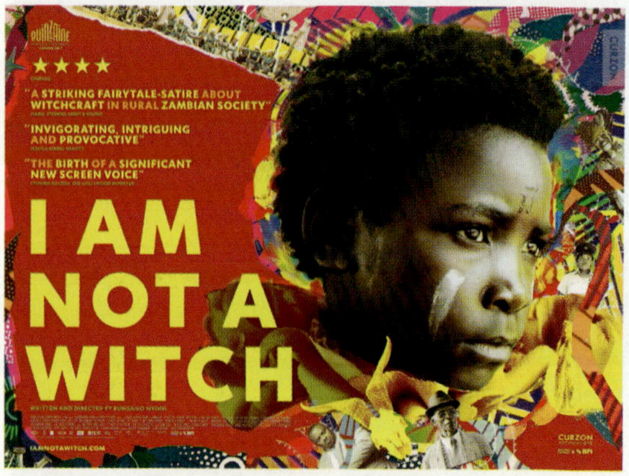

YOUR PROJECT

1. Present a fictional witch in the historical and societal context of her creator. You can use a slide-show or make a poster for your presentation.

OR

2. Use one of the periods studied in this unit to compose the letter written by a woman accused of witchcraft.

SPICE UP YOUR VOCABULARY

- Audio words
- MP3
- Interactive Test

Use the vocabulary below to create your own mind map and add more words if necessary!

Nouns

- blessing
- broomstick
- cauldron
- chant
- cloak
- coven
- crooked /'krʊkɪd/ nose
- curse
- familiar = the witch's pet
- folklore
- hag: *harpie*
- healer
- icon /'aɪkɒn/
- incantation
- knowledge /'nɒlɪdʒ/
- magic circle
- medicinal herb
- midwife: *sage-femme*
- nature worship
- paganism /'peɪgənɪzəm/
- persecution
- physician = doctor
- pointed hat
- potion = brew = draught /'drɑːft/
- prosecution = when someone is judged for a crime in a court of law
- secrecy
- sorcery
- spell
- trial: *procès*
- wand
- wart: *verrue*
- witch
- Witchcraft = The Craft
- witch-hunt
- witch-pricker

Adjectives

- bewitched = enchanted
- cross-cultural
- cunning = clever
- diabolical /ˌdaɪə'bɒlɪkəl/
- disgraced
- empowered /ɪm'paʊəd/
- evil /'iːvəl/
- filthy: *sale*
- foul /'faʊl/ = disgusting
- harmful ≠ harmless
- hideous = ugly
- inspired
- knowledgeable
- mystical = occult
- pagan /'peɪgən/
- persecuted
- poisonous
- powerful ≠ powerless
- prosecuted
- redeemed
- scary = frightening
- secretive /'siːkrətɪv/
- sinister
- spiritual
- wicked = nasty

Verbs & Expressions

- banish
- be wrongly accused
- bewitch = enchant /ɪn'tʃɑːnt/
- bless: *bénir*
- brew: *concocter*
- burn
- cast = weave
- curse
- despise
- excommunicate
- execute /'eksəkjuːt/
- find guilty
- hang
- harm
- outlaw: *hors-la-loi*
- persecute /'pɜːsɪkjuːt/: *persécuter*
- prosecute = to charge someone with a crime
- reject = exclude = ostracise /'ɒstrəsaɪz/
- sentence: *condamner*
- summon the devil
- torture /'tɔːtʃə/
- worship

Adverbs

- disdainfully = contemptuously
- disgracefully
- hideously
- mystically
- secretly

UP TO YOU!

★ **1. Fill in the blank with an appropriate word from the list above.**

A. Powerful women had to be ... if they wanted to avoid persecution, but it was particularly difficult to practise their ... in that context.

B. She looked absolutely ... and corresponded well to the witch stereotype, with her ... nose and the huge ... on her cheek. She was toothless besides.

C. Part of her daily routine was to gather ... ... in the forest. Then she would ... a ... in her ... like the witches in *Macbeth*.

★★ **2. *Persecute or prosecute?* Choose and conjugate the correct verb for each of the sentences below. Justify your choice.**

A. The witch-pricker decided that she should be ... and brought her to the judge.

B. There is tremendous evidence that the women who were ... by the villagers were the most powerful and knowledgeable.

C. The priests ... the witches until they were all eliminated.

D. She was ... and found guilty, and sentenced to death.

RULE THE GRAMMAR!

LE DISCOURS INDIRECT

• Discours direct : *"I sentence you to death!"*

• Discours indirect : *The judge said (that) she was sentenced to death!*

• Pour rapporter le propos de quelqu'un, on utilise des **verbes rapporteurs** (*reporting verbs*), comme par exemple : *tell* • *advise (someone to)* • *promise (to)* • *announce* • *explain* • *state* • *declare* • *ask* • *answer* • *reply.*

• En passant du discours direct au discours indirect, il faut appliquer la **concordance des temps**.
• De même que les temps sont modifiés au discours indirect, **les marqueurs spatio-temporels** sont adaptés aux temps utilisés : *yesterday* → *the day before* • *last week / month / year* → *last week / month / year before* • *tomorrow* → *the following day* • *next week* → *the following week* • *ago* → *before.*

DISCOURS DIRECT		DISCOURS INDIRECT
Présent	→	**Prétérit**
"I am not a witch"		*She said (that) **she wasn't** a witch.*
Présent *be + ing*	→	**Prétérit *be + ing***
"I'm preparing a potion."		*He said (that) **he was preparing** a potion.*
Will	→	***Would***
"I will never forgive you."		*He said (that) he **would** never forgive me.*
Present perfect	→	***Pluperfect***
"I've haunted this land for centuries."		*She said (that) **she had haunted** this land for centuries.*
Prétérit	→	***Pluperfect***
"They all died horribly."		*She said (that) they **had all died** horribly.*

→ P.318

EXPRIMER LE SOUHAIT, LE REGRET, L'AGACEMENT

Il existe **3 structures fondamentales** en fonction de la portée du souhait ou du regret.

• Quand le souhait / regret porte sur le moment présent, on utilise ***wish*** + prétérit.
*I **wish** they **did not** bother me all the time!*
*I wish I **was/were** a sorcerer!*

• Quand on exprime un agacement par rapport à quelque chose, on utilise ***wish*** + ***would***.
*I **wish** spirits **would** stop pestering me all night!*
*I **wish** these silly ghosts **wouldn't** haunt this old castle!*

• Quand on exprime un regret qui porte sur un moment passé, on utilise ***wish*** + ***pluperfect***.
*I **wish** they **hadn't** all **perished** because of the witch hunt!*
*I **wish** they **hadn't accused** her of being a witch!*

→ P.304

UP TO YOU!

★ 1. Complete the blanks with *who, that, Ø or which.*

A. *The Crucible* is the best film ... I have ever seen!

B. She became the leader of a coven ... terrorized all the villagers.

C. It is the story of a girl, Juliana Good, ... was imprisoned, accused of witchcraft and executed because she refused to marry a man ... she hated.

D. Who is Tituba? She is a slave ... played a crucial role in the Salem trials.

E. *The Magic Circle* by John William Waterhouse is the painting ... I like the most.

★ 2. Rewrite the following sentences using *I wish* as shown in the example.

E.g.: If only I could fly. → *I wish I could fly.*

A. If only you could teach me some magic.

B. If only you hadn't lost your broom.

C. If only he had cast a spell on the evil wizard.

D. If only she could leave unhurt.

E. If only the witch trials had never happened.

F. If only Hermione were here.

★★ 3. Put the following sentences into the passive.

A. They sentenced the three sisters to death.

B. The judges accused Paul of being a wizard.

C. The neighbours accused Terry of being a witch.

D. We found her guilty of having signed a pact with the devil.

E. They gave him a funny hat to wear.

F. Her father offered her a magic wand.

★★ 4. Rewrite these sentences in indirect speech using the prompt given.

A. "I never cast a spell on anybody" → *She said...*

B. "I don't own an owl!" → *Harry said...*

C. "They've played with dangerous herbs." → *They admitted...*

D. "We stole the philosopher's stone" → *We claimed...*

E. "I don't know who prepared this potion." → *You said...*

F. "I'm not too keen on sea travels" → *King James VI admitted...*

★★★ 5. Translate into English using "I wish".

A. *Je regrette de ne pas avoir étudié la magie.*

B. *Je regrette d'avoir à apprendre tous ces mots étranges.*

C. *J'aimerais que tu arrêtes d'interrompre le magicien.*

D. *J'aurais aimé assister à un procès en sorcellerie.*

★★★ 6. Translate the following sentences using the passive voice.

A. *Le juge l'a interrogé pendant une heure.*

B. *La foule s'est moquée de lui.*

C. *On l'a pris pour un sorcier.* (be mistaken)

D. *Elle était considérée comme la plus grande magicienne de tous les temps.*

7. Interactive test! What is your score?

OPEN YOUR EARS!

PHONOLOGY

Which Witch?

• Dans la plupart des accents du monde anglophone, *which* et *witch* sont des **homophones**. Ils se prononcent /wɪtʃ/.

• Pour de nombreux Américains ou Écossais, ces deux mots ne sont pas homophones :

which se prononce /hwɪtʃ/ et *witch* se prononce /wɪtʃ/

• Écoutez les mots qui suivent : la première lecture avec /h/, la deuxième avec /hw/.

MP3 N°65 | *when • why • whimper • whether • what • white*

SHOWTIME

Say it like the model!

MP3 N°66

/ When shall / we three / meet a / gain?
In / thunder, / lightning / or in / rain?
/ When the / hurly / burly's / done,
/ When the / battle's / lost and / won

Ici, les *Weird Sisters* utilisent le rythme **trochaïque** (une syllabe accentuée, précédée par /, suivie d'une syllabe non accentuée. De plus il s'agit de **tétramètres** (4 accents).

Picture challenge

★ 3 sentences
★★ 4 to 6 sentences
★★★ 7 sentences and +

How many sentences can you make using what you have learnt? Collect stars!

❷ Shakespeare's Lovers

Why are "Romeo and Juliet" an everlasting example of cursed love?

1 Romeo and Juliet's tragic fate

Read the text and answer the questions on **Worksheet n°28**.

MP3 N°67

Romeo has just been banished from Verona: he has to begin his exile and leave Juliet. This is their last encounter.

JULIET – Then, window, let day in, and let life out.
ROMEO – Farewell, farewell! one kiss, and I'll descend.
He goeth down [...].
JULIET – O think'st thou we shall ever meet again?
ROMEO – I doubt it not; and all these woes shall serve For sweet discourses in our time to come.
JULIET – O God, I have an ill-divining soul!
Methinks I see thee, now thou art below,
As one dead in the bottom of a tomb:
Either my eyesight fails, or thou look'st pale.
ROMEO – And trust me, love, in my eye so do you:
Dry sorrow drinks our blood. Adieu, adieu!

Romeo and Juliet, Act III, Scene 5,
William Shakespeare, 1595

HELP!

Shakespeare's language
- farewell: *adieu*
- O think'st thou = Do you think
- woes: *malheurs*
- ill-divining: *présage la mort*
- methinks = I think
- I see thee = I see you
- Thou art = you are
- Sorrow drinks our blood = sadness takes away our colour

2 Actress Jade Anouka's opinion

Read the text. Why does the story of *Romeo and Juliet* echo the lives and concerns of all teenagers?

"I think there's so much in *Romeo and Juliet*. The first thing that you think of is young love - the idea of falling in love for the first time, the excitement of that, the danger of that, in many ways. That idea of, when you're a teenager, those first arguments you start having with your parents, the first times you start realising you think something different to your mum and dad. And also, the idea of young people [...] getting into fights all the time. And it's, kind of, unnecessary bloodshed, and unnecessary arguments, I think, is something that happens as a teenager."

3 Last kiss

A. Observe the painting and describe it.
B. Pairwork. Share your impressions about the painting.
C. Explain art critic G. Barker's following quote by giving three elements from the painting:
"[The painting] creates the impression death is close but love will never die".
Focus on the elements predicting death, danger and the symbols of love.
D. Have your say. Is the painting a good illustration of *Romeo and Juliet*, Act III, Scene 5 (p.158) ?

HELP!

Nouns & adjectives
- vine /vaɪn/: *plante grimpante*
- dry / rotten / dried-up leaves
- brighter ≠ darker than
- deathly-pale = pallid /'pælɪd/

Verbs
- embrace: *s'enlacer*
- straddle = sit with one leg on either side of sth

Romeo and Juliet,
Frank Bernard Dicksee, 1884

YOUR TURN! 4 Stage the scene!

Pairwork. Act out the scene. Use the painting and the text as an inspiration for the staging.

❸ Doomed Love Stories

How has classical literature portrayed doomed relationships?

1 Two literary excerpts

A. Groupwork. Show that the lovers can be regarded as star-crossed lovers.

- **Group A** reads **Text 1**. Turn to **Worksheet n°29** for help.
- **Group B** reads **Text 2**. Turn to **Worksheet n°30** for help.

B. Share your findings with the other group.

C. Quoting the texts, compare and contrast the two couples:

- What makes it impossible for the lovers to be together?
- What seems to be the only solution for them to be reunited?

HELP!

Tools

Use indirect speech to describe the characters' thoughts:

Heathcliff tells Catherine…

He says that their relationship is…

He asks her to…

Text 1

Wuthering Heights tells the story of a burning and self-destructive passion between Catherine and Heathcliff, who are meant to be together, but Catherine's social ambition prevents her from marrying the man she truly loves.

Chapter 15

Catherine is dying. As she begs for forgiveness, Heathcliff has harsh words about her.

"You teach me now how cruel you've been — cruel and false. WHY did you despise[1] me? WHY did you betray[2] your own heart, Cathy? I have not one word of comfort. You deserve this. You have killed yourself. Yes, you may kiss me, and cry; and wring out my kisses and tears: they'll blight[3] you — they'll damn you. You loved me — then what RIGHT had you to leave me? What right — answer me — for the poor fancy you felt for Linton? Because misery and degradation, and death, and nothing that God or Satan could inflict would have parted[4] us, YOU, of your own will, did it. I have not broken your heart — YOU have broken it; and in breaking it, you have broken mine. So much the worse for me that I am strong. Do I want to live? What kind of living will it be when you – oh, God! would YOU like to live with your soul in the grave[5]?" […]

Chapter 16

Catherine has died. Heathcliff makes one last visit to see her body.

"May she wake in torment!" he cried, with frightful vehemence, stamping his foot, and groaning in a sudden paroxysm of ungovernable passion. "Why, she's a liar to the end! Where is she? Not THERE — not in heaven — not perished — where? Oh! you said you cared nothing for my sufferings! And I pray one prayer — I repeat it till my tongue stiffens — Catherine Earnshaw, may you not rest as long as I am living; you said I killed you — haunt me, then! The murdered DO haunt their murderers, I believe. I know that ghosts HAVE wandered[6] on earth. Be with me always — take any form — drive me mad! Only DO not leave me in this abyss, where I cannot find you! Oh, God! it is unutterable! I CANNOT live without my life! I CANNOT live without my soul!"

1 hate • 2 be disloyal • 3 ruin • 4 separated • 5 *tombe* • 6 *errer*

Wuthering Heights,
Emily Brontë, 1847

Text 2

The Scarlet Letter tells the story of an illicit passion between Hester Prynne and the Reverend Arthur Dimmesdale. Hester is punished for breaking puritan law and is forced to wear the letter A as a reminder of her sinful passion (A = adulterer). Pearl is Hester and Dimmesdale's illegitimate child.

She silently ascended the steps, and stood on the platform, holding little Pearl by the hand. The minister[1] felt for the child's other hand, and took it. The moment that he did so, there came what seemed a tumultuous rush of[2] new life [...] as if the mother and the child were communicating their vital warmth[3] to his half-torpid system. The three formed an electric chain. [...]

"Minister!" whispered little Pearl.

"What wouldst thou say, child?" asked Mr. Dimmesdale.

"Wilt thou stand here with mother and me, tomorrow [...]?" inquired Pearl.

"Nay; not so, my little Pearl," answered the minister; for, with the new energy of the moment, all the dread[4] of public exposure, that had so long been the anguish of his life, had returned upon him; and he was already trembling [...].

"At the great judgment-day[5]," whispered the minister [...]. "Then, and there, before the judgment-seat, thy[6] mother, and thou[7], and I must stand together! But the daylight of this world shall not see our meeting!" [...] And there stood the minister, with his hand over his heart; and Hester Prynne, with the embroidered letter glimmering on her bosom[8]; and little Pearl, herself a symbol, and the connecting link between those two. They stood in the noon of that strange and solemn splendor, as if it were the light that is to reveal all secrets, and the daybreak[9] that shall unite all who belong to one another.

The Scarlet Letter, T.H. Matteson, 1860

1 reverend • 2 *une montée de* • 3 *chaleur* • 4 fear • 5 *le jugement dernier* • 6 your • 7 you • 8 *la lettre A brodée sur sa poitrine* • 9 *l'aube*

The Scarlet Letter,
Nathaniel Hawthorne, 1850

YOUR TURN! 2 A love letter

Heathcliff and Hester Prynne are both obsessed with finding their great love again. Imagine, for the next BBC adaptation of *Wuthering Heights* or *The Scarlet Letter*, Heathcliff's/Hester's final letter to his/her lost soulmate. (150 words)

HELP!

Expressions

- To begin: *"My dearest love", "Dear...", "My love"*
- To end: *"I love you with all my heart / from the bottom of my heart...", "Love/Forever yours, Heathcliff/Hester"*

Tips for your letter

- Use indirect speech to report what your soulmate said to you (*"You told me that..."*).
- Use performative verbs (*promise, love, beg, confess, deny ...*).

❹ A Modern Adaptation

Why can we say star-crossed lovers have become part of popular culture?

1 Beauty Vs the Beast

A. Read the following excerpt and answer the questions on **Worksheet n°31**.

B. Go further. Why can it be seen as a parody of the motif?

I approach the girl. She cowers[1] before me, her tender flesh offering me all the things I'm accustomed to taking, and my instincts start to reassert themselves. The urge[2] to rip and tear surges into my arms and jaw. But then she screams again, and something inside me moves [...].

I let out[3] a gentle groan and inch toward the girl, trying to force kindness into my dull[4] expression. [...] She throws a knife at my head.

The blade sticks straight into the center of my forehead and quivers there. But it has penetrated less than an inch, only grazing[5] my frontal lobe. I pull it out and drop it. I hold out my hands, making soft noises through my lips, but I'm helpless. How do I appear unthreatening when her lover's blood is running down my chin?

I'm just a few feet away from her now. She is fumbling[6] through her jeans for another weapon. Behind me, the Dead are finishing their butchery. Soon they will turn their attention to this dim corner of the room. I take a deep breath.

"Ju...lie," I say.

It rolls off my tongue like honey. I feel good just saying it.

Her eyes go wide. She freezes.

"Julie," I say again. I put out my hands. I point at the zombies behind me. I shake my head.

She stares at me, making no sign that she understands. But when I reach out to touch her, she doesn't move. And she doesn't stab me.

I reach my free hand into the head wound of a fallen zombie and collect a palmful of black, lifeless blood. Slowly, with gentle movements, I smear[7] it on her face, down her neck, and onto her clothes. She doesn't even flinch[8]. She is probably catatonic[9].

I take her hand and pull her to her feet. At that moment [...] the others finish devouring their prey and turn to inspect the room. Their eyes fall on me. They fall on Julie. I walk toward them, gripping Julie's hand [...]. She staggers[10] behind me, staring straight ahead. [...]

Without a word, we leave [...] and head back to the airport. I walk in a daze, full of strange and kaleidoscopic thoughts. Julie holds limply to my hand, staring at the side of my face with wide eyes, trembling lips.

1 *se recroqueviller* • **2** *pulsion* • **3** *laisser échapper* • **4** *maussade* • **5** *égratigner* • **6** *fouiller* • **7** *étaler* • **8** *tressaillir* • **9** unresponsive • **10** *avancer d'un pas chancelant*

Warm Bodies,
Isaac Marion, 2010

2 A pop star-crossed musical

A. Online. Watch the trailer for the musical *& Juliet* (www.lienmini.fr/htr-tle-15) What strikes you in the portrayal of the characters?

B. What is the message of this new adaptation?

C. Go further. Imagine the creator's description of his show on a leaflet.

YOUR PROJECT

Take part in Shakespeare Week and give a two-minute presentation of the influence of *Romeo and Juliet* on modern culture (cinema, literature, music, art...). Use all you have learnt in the unit.

LANGUAGE LAB

- Unit's vocabulary
- Audio words
- MP3
- Interactive Test

★1. Fill in the blanks with the words below.

may • even though • in spite of • although • despite • though

A. We wanted to marry ... our families didn't agree.
B. They decided to get married ... the distance between them.
C. She had a crush on him ... his disreputable past.
D. He was very good-looking, affectionate, and caring; not very rich ... .
E. Charming as he ... be, his in-laws were not impressed!
F. ... he was very young, she was madly in love with him.

★2. Fill in the blanks with the right expression.

pop the question • love at first sight • have a soft spot for • in love with

A. When I first saw Julia, I was struck by her beauty. I guess it is what you call ... !
B. I think Edward may ... his neighbour, Jennifer. He's always trying to help her together.
C. After 5 years of relationship, Emily finally decided to ... and ask Tim to spend the rest of his life with her.
D. I've been ... the same woman all my life, we were meant to be together.

★★3. Re-write these sentences using indirect speech.

A. "I will always love you." ***(she said ...)***
B. "She's having a good time." ***(Peter thought ...)***
C. "He has forgotten to call her." ***(I thought ...)***
D. Their honeymoon was a great success ***(He remembered ...)***
E. "I didn't wash the car" ***(He told her ...)***
F. She likes long romantic walks ***(I knew ...)***

★★ 4. Translate these sentences into English using the performative verbs below.

love • swear • promise • bet • apologise • regret

A. *Je t'aime plus que jamais.*
B. *Je jure que je serai toujours avec toi.*
C. *Je te promets que tu ne regretteras pas ton choix.*
D. *Je parie qu'il te surveille.*
E. *Je suis désolé de ma conduite imbécile!*
F. *Je suis désolé d'avoir dit cela!*

★★★ 5. Complete the sentences with the right idiom.

star-crossed • written in the stars • born under a lucky star • shoot for the stars • bless my stars

A. *Titanic* tells the story of two ... lovers whose destinies will be torn apart by social class and a tragic disaster.
B. What with winning the lottery and finding a woman he loves, David is the luckiest man in the world. He was definitely ... .
C. I was always taught to be ambitious and to ... . It's the best way to achieve your dreams!
D. Oh, ...! You scared the hell out of me!
E. Alice had to fall in love with Mark, they make such a perfect match. Their story was ...!

6. Interactive test! What is your score?

OPEN YOUR EARS!

PHONOLOGY

La prononciation des adjectifs épithètes anteposés se terminant en *-ed*

• Écoutez les phrases et expressions suivantes en faisant attention à la prononciation de la terminaison *-ed*. Que remarquez-vous ?

MP3 N°68 | *Their love was curs<u>ed</u>.* • *curs<u>ed</u> love* • *Their union was bless<u>ed</u> in heaven.* • *a bless<u>ed</u> day*

• Conclusion

Les règles de prononciation de *-ed* sont modifiées :
Their love was cursed /kɜːst/
mais *cursed love* /'kɜːsɪd/
Their union was blessed /blest/ in heaven.
mais *a blessed day* /ə 'blesɪd 'deɪ/
De même, on dit *my beloved* /ɪd/ *husband*, voir aussi le roman *Beloved* /ɪd/ de Toni Morrison, *my learned* /ɪd/ *friends, my aged* /ɪd/ *aunt.*

AUDIO MYSTERY

MP3 N°69

Listen to the recording and solve the mystery!

Word battle

★ 3 sentences
★★ 4 to 6 sentences
★★★ 7 sentences and +

How many sentences can you make using the words and expressions below? Collect stars!

- woo or court someone
- hold hands
- declaration of love
- cheek
- admire
- trespass on
- in love with or enamoured /ɪ'næməd/ with
- risk (n) or danger
- family feud /fjuːd/

AXE 5

UNIT 16

VILLAINS DO IT BETTER!

Why are flawed characters more attractive than traditional heroes?

YOUR PROJECT

1 Act out the final confrontation between a hero(ine) and a villain for San Diego's Comic-con.

OR

2 Write the plot of a companion novel for an English publisher.

BEFORE CLASS!

Flash to watch!

Watch the video and get ready to talk about villains in class!

Au menu de cette unité :

DÉCOUVERTES CULTURELLES

- Le monomythe de Joseph Campbell
- L'avènement des antihéros dans la culture américaine
- Les antihéros shakespeariens (Richard III, Iago et Lady Macbeth)
- Des monologues d'antihéros célèbres

OUTILS LINGUISTIQUES

- Les structures et les verbes causatifs
- Les subordonnées et les prépositions de cause et de concession
- Les comparatifs et les superlatifs

❶ Good Old Heroes

What sets traditional heroes apart from villains?

1 The traditional myth of hero/heroine by J. Campbell

A. In your mind, what should a fictional hero/heroine be like? List the qualities, abilities and causes they fight for/against.

B. Watch the video and pick out the 12 steps of a hero's/heroine's journey.

C. Go further. Read the texts on Worksheet n°32 dealing with five major steps in Luke Skywalker's story and put them in the right order.

VIDEO N°30

HELP!

- cross the threshold /ˈθreʃhəʊld/
- go on an adventure
- defeat an enemy
- face ordeals /ɔːˈdiːls/

2 The hero's journey in "The Hobbit"

A. Read the excerpt and answer the questions on Worksheet n°33.

B. What moment of the hero's journey is described? Justify.

C. What is Gandalf's role going to be?

D. Have your say. Is Bilbo Baggins an archetypical hero? Justify.

YOUR TURN! 3 Write a scene for a TV show

HBO has ordered the pilot of a new adventure series based on *The Hobbit*.

As the screenwriter of this new show, write the full encounter between Bilbo, the hero-to-be, and his mentor, Gandalf. Use the text as an inspiration.

All that the unsuspecting Bilbo saw that morning was an old man with a staff. He had a tall pointed blue hat, a long grey cloak, a silver scarf over which his long white beard hung down below his waist, and immense black boots.

"Good morning!" said Bilbo, and he meant it. [...] "If you have a pipe about you, sit down and have a fill of mine! There's no hurry, we have all the day before us!" Then Bilbo sat down on a seat by his door, crossed his legs, and blew out a beautiful grey ring of smoke that sailed up into the air without breaking and floated away over The Hill.

"Very pretty!" said Gandalf. "But I have no time to blow smoke-rings this morning. I am looking for someone to share in an adventure that I am arranging, and it's very difficult to find anyone."

"I should think so—in these parts! We are plain quiet folk and have no use for adventures. Nasty disturbing uncomfortable things! Make you late for dinner! I can't think what anybody sees in them," said our Mr Baggins. [...] Then he took out his morning letters, and began to read, pretending to take no more notice of the old man. [...] But the old man did not move. He stood leaning on his stick and gazing at the hobbit without saying anything.

The Hobbit,
J.R.R. Tolkien, 1937

❷ The Rise and Celebration of Antiheroes

Why have antiheroes become more popular than heroes?

1 A new fashion

A

B

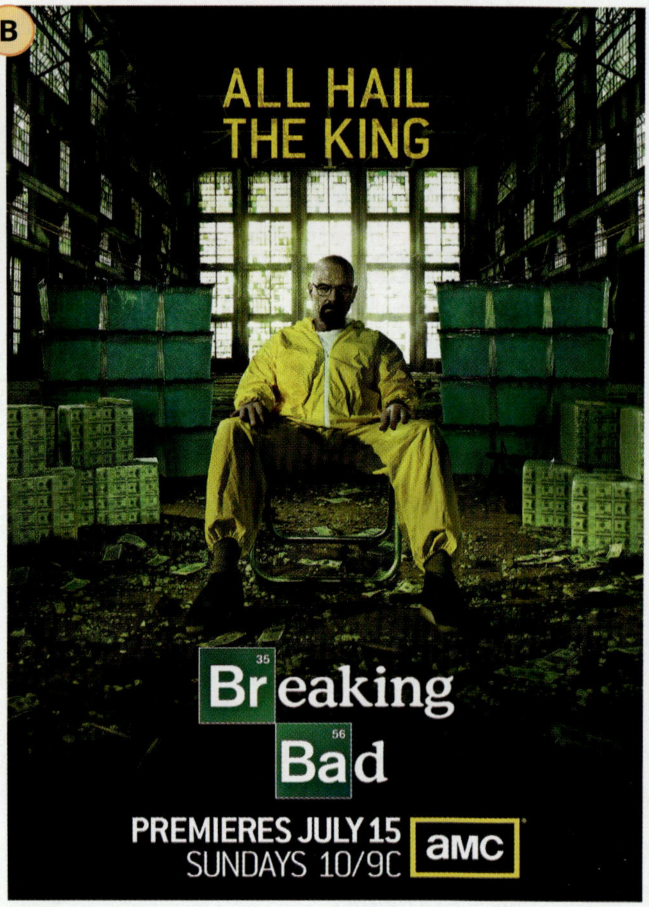

A. How are the main characters represented? Focus on the setting, symbols, titles and attitudes.
B. Guess what the characters have done to reach such positions. → He/She had his/her opponents + V-ed…
C. How different are they from traditional heroes? Use comparatives.

HELP!

Poster A
- throne room
- bloodstain
- blood-covered
- cold-blooded
- power-hungry
- sharp = smart
- betray
- scheme /ski:m/ = plot

Poster B
- drug lord
- warehouse
- gloomy = dark
- cunning = smart
- ruthless/merciless person
- drug-trafficking
- have blood on one's hands

2 What is an antihero?

A. Listen to the MP3 N°70 and take notes (heroes' qualities and antiheroes' flaws).
B. Give your definition of the term "antihero".
C. Why are antiheroes not so new? What is different nowadays?
D. Name famous characters who correspond to the definitions given.
E. Go further. What makes the two characters in the posters antiheroes?

3 Supporting antiheroes

A. Read the text and explain why we tend to prefer antiheroes to heroes nowadays.
B. Pick out the similarities between antiheroes' lives and our own lives and personalities.
C. Why are traditional heroes no longer realistic in our world?
D. Have your say. How do antiheroes help us cope with our time?

Almost every show we love is led by a flawed character — a man or woman with questionable[1] actions and motives — always self-serving and determined to succeed at any cost. We follow these characters throughout their journeys: their quests for redemption, fame, fortune and love — the same common goals we find ourselves longing after[2]. And like ourselves, we see the selfishness that comes with attaining goals and dreams. [...] Unlike the shows of our parents' generation, when the main characters were examples of the ideal American citizen, housewife, husband or child, these main characters are the undesirables, the flawed and the evil that encompasses[3] the true American culture, not just projections of what we want it to be. But why do we love them? [...] It says we're realistic; we understand the true fabric[4] of what makes this country great, the flaws of the people and their selfish motives. We live in an age of divorce, corruption and celebrity meltdowns[5], realizing at a young age that no one is perfect and watching someone perfect isn't what we want to see. We want to see the people like us, the people with flaws and mixed morals.

1 douteux • 2 désirer • 3 encercler • 4 étoffe • 5 effondrement

Lauren Martin, **www.elitedaily.com**, 23 December 2013

4 Antiheroes or villains?

A. Read the text. Pick the similarities and differences between villains and antiheroes.
B. What turns a great villain into an antihero? Do you have other examples?
C. Look at the poster of *Lucifer* and say what strikes you about the character. How does the TV show revisit the great villain?
D. Go further. Would you say this image is a good illustration of the article?

Villains become anti-heroes when the story is about them; when we see the process they undergo[1] to become villains. That's the only difference. They are both motivated by the same lower-self impulses. Darth Vader is a villain in part IV of *Star Wars* but, no doubt, will be the central character and an anti-hero in part III, when he is being drawn into the dark side. On the upside of the passage, the hero resists temptation and goes up the ladder[2]. On the downside, the anti-hero gives in to temptation and goes down the ladder.

1 subir • 2 échelle

James Bonnet, ***The Journey of the Antihero in Film: Exploring the Dark Side***, 2018

❸ Great Britain and the Cult of Villains

What is so special about British villains?

1 Why Brits are the best baddies!

A. Listen to three British actors on **MP3 N°71**. Use **Worksheet n°34** for help.

B. What is the perfect villain like, according to them?

C. Why are British actors more inclined to play villains? Use comparatives.

2 Shakespeare's most ruthless villains

Groupwork. Group 1 works on text 1 and **Group 2** works on text 2.

A. Pick out the characteristics that make your character a villain.
Fill in your character's portrait in **Worksheet n°35** and share the information with the other group.

B. Read the characters' best quotes and say what they reveal about their identities.

C. Go further. Look at the pictures from performances of *Richard III* and *Othello* and explain the stage directors' choices using your knowledge of the story (settings, costumes, attitudes/positions…).

Text 1 – Richard III

Shakespeare's depiction of Richard III as a Machiavellian villain who had a physical deformity, lusted[1] after his niece and lost his "kingdom for a horse" has had real sticking power.

A malicious, deceptive and bitter usurper who seizes England's throne by nefarious means[2], Shakespeare's Richard takes delight in his own villainy. [...]

But Richard's sins come back to haunt him – quite literally. Shakespeare provides us a long list of Richard's murder victims, in a roll call of ghosts that visit him on the last night of his life.

"I am determined to prove a villain and hate the idle pleasures of these days." (Richard III Act I, Scene 1)

"Conscience is but a word that cowards[3] use, Devised at first to keep the strong in awe[4]."

(Richard III, Act V, Scene 3)

1 *désirer* • 2 *moyens infâmes* • 3 *lâches* • 4 *impressionné par*

Adapted from **www.historyextra.com**, 30 March 2018

Text 2 – Iago

Many scholars see Iago as the most inherently evil of all Shakespeare's villains. [...] His only desire appears to be Othello's destruction. He accomplishes this by planting the seed[1] of jealousy in Othello's mind. He plots[2] in order to turn him against his wife, Desdemona. While winning Othello's trust, Iago constructs a web of lies to make Othello believe in Desdemona's infidelity. [...] Enraged by jealousy, Othello eventually murders Desdemona and then kills himself. Although Iago's schemes are eventually revealed and he is sentenced to execution, it is too little, too late, as his plans have already reached their disastrous conclusion.

"O, beware[3], my lord, of jealousy: It is the green-eyed monster which doth mock the meat it feeds on."

(Othello, Act III, Scene 3)

"We cannot all be masters, nor all masters cannot be truly follow'd." and *"I am not what I am."* (Othello, Act I, Scene 1)

1 *graine* • 2 *comploter* • 3 *faire attention à*

Adapted from **www.historyextra.com**, 30 March 2018

3 Evil Lady Macbeth

In the story, Lady Macbeth is the driving force behind her husband's murderous ambition.
She is the one who encourages the Scottish lord to kill King Duncan in order to claim his throne.
The scene takes place before Macbeth's return from war. Lady Macbeth is thinking about the plans she has for her husband.

"So the messenger is short of breath, like a hoarse raven[1], as he announces Duncan's entrance into my fortress, where he will die. Come, you spirits that assist murderous thoughts, make me less like a woman and more like a man, and fill me from head to toe with deadly cruelty! Thicken my blood and clog up[2] my veins so I won't feel remorse, so that no human compassion can stop my evil plan or prevent me from accomplishing it! Come to my female breast[3] and turn my mother's milk into poisonous acid, you murdering demons, wherever you hide, invisible and waiting to do evil! Come, thick night, and cover the world in the darkest smoke of hell, so that my sharp knife can't see the wound it cuts open, and so heaven can't peep through the darkness and cry, "No! Stop!""

1 *corbeau* • **2** *boucher* • **3** *seins*

Modern adaptation of ***Macbeth,***
Act I, Scene 5

Ellen Terry as Lady Macbeth, by J. S. Sargent, 1889

A. Focus on the soliloquy.
- Study the text with the help of Worksheet n°36.
- What type of woman is Lady Macbeth? Draw a brief portrait.
- What is the true nature of this soliloquy?

B. Focus on the painting.
- What does Lady Macbeth look like?
- Analyse her attitude, the symbols of power and the colours.
- Do you think it is a good representation of the character? Justify.

C. Read the text using the right tone of voice.

D. Go further. Watch the video and write a review of the actress's performance and the director's choices.

VIDEO N°31

YOUR TURN! 4 Write a soliloquy

At the end of their lives, both Richard III and Lady Macbeth were haunted by their pasts.
For a free adaptation of the play on TV, imagine their last words before they face death. Then act out the soliloquy with your best British accent!

❹ A Look at the Best Villains of All Time

What makes certain villains real icons?

1 Villainous monologues

Groupwork. Read the monologues featuring great villains. Then share your findings.

A. Draw a psychological profile of your villain (personality traits, attitude towards people…) in 50 words.

B. Share your portraits with the class. Then, compare and contrast them.

C. Vote for the most evil villain!

Text 1 – Bellatrix Lestrange MP3 N°72

"Never used an Unforgivable Curse before, have you, boy?" she yelled. She had abandoned her baby voice now. "You need to mean them, Potter! You need to really want to cause pain – to enjoy it – righteous anger won't hurt me for long – I'll show you how it is done, shall I? I'll give you a lesson—"

Harry Potter and The Order of the Phoenix, J.K. Rowling, 2007

Text 2 – Hela MP3 N°73

"It's come to my attention that you don't know who I am. I am Hela. Odin's firstborn. Commander of the legions of Asgard. The rightful heir to the throne and the Goddess of Death. My father is dead. As are the princes. You're welcome. We were once the seat of absolute power in the cosmos. Our supremacy was unchallenged. Yet Odin stopped at nine realms. Our destiny is to rule over all others. And I am here to restore that power. Kneel before me and rise into the ranks of my great conquest."

Script *Thor: Ragnarok* by Taika Waititi, 2017

Text 3 – Annie Wilkes MP3 N°74

Annie Wilkes has kidnapped her favourite writer, Paul Sheldon, to force him to write another Misery *novel.*

Paul, do you know about the early days at the Kimberly diamond mines? Do you know what they did to the Native workers who stole diamonds? Don't worry, they didn't kill them. That would be like junking[1] your Mercedes just because it had a broken spring[2]. No, if they caught them, they had to make sure they could go on working, but they also had to make sure they could never run away. The operation was called hobbling[3]."

1 *jeter* • 2 *(ici) ressort* • 3 *briser les chevilles de qqn*

Script of *Misery* by Rob Reiner, 1990 (adapted from Stephen King's novel *Misery*)

Text 4 – Agent Smith MP3 N°75

Agent Smith, who is in fact an AI programme, is speaking about human beings.

"I'd like to share a revelation that I've had during my time here. It came to me when I tried to classify your species and I realized that you're not actually mammals. Every mammal on this planet instinctively develops a natural equilibrium with the surrounding environment but you humans do not. You move to an area and you multiply and multiply until every natural resource is consumed and the only way you can survive is to spread to another area. There is another organism on this planet that follows the same pattern. Do you know what it is? A virus. Human beings are a disease, a cancer of this planet. You're a plague and we are the cure."

Script *The Matrix* by Lana and Lilly Wachowski, 1999

Text 5 – The Joker MP3 N°76

The Joker remembers his tormented childhood as he is threatening an enemy with a razor blade.

"You wanna know how I got these scars? My father was a drinker, and a fiend. And one night, he goes off crazier than usual. Mommy gets the kitchen knife to defend herself. He doesn't like that. Not. One. Bit. So, me watching, he takes the knife to her, laughing while he does it. He turns to me and he says, 'Why so serious?' He comes at me with the knife. 'WHY SO SERIOUS?' He sticks the blade in my mouth... 'Let's put a smile on that face.'"

Script *The Dark Knight* by Christopher Nolan, 2008

Text 6 – Thanos MP3 N°77

"I thought by eliminating half of life, the other half would thrive. But you've shown me that's impossible. As long as there are those that remember what was, there will always be those that are unable to accept what can be. They will resist. [...]
I'm thankful. Because now I know what I must do. I will shred this universe down to its last atom and then, with the stones you've collected for me, create a new one teeming with life that knows not what it has lost, but only what it has been given. A grateful universe."

Script *Avengers: Endgame* by Antony and Joe Russo, 2019

YOUR TURN! 2 Audition for the villain's part!

The casting directors for the next Marvel film are looking for someone who will sound scary and original at the same time.

Each performer must read a great monologue by a famous villain and readapt the role!

OPEN YOUR EARS!

PHONOLOGY

1. La prononciation de « -ain »

• Écoutez les mots suivants en faisant attention à la prononciation de « **-ain** ».
Classez-les dans le tableau en fonction de leur prononciation. Qu'en concluez-vouz? **MP3 N°78**

villain • contain • explain • bargain • certain • refrain • mountain • captain

/ɪn/	/eɪn/
...	...

• Quand elle est accentuée (généralement pour les verbes), la séquence « *-ain* » se prononce /eɪn/;
quand elle est inaccentuée, elle se prononce /ən/.

SHOWTIME

1. Say it like the model!

MP3 N°79

*Do you wanna know how I got these scars? My father // was a // drinker ↘... and a ↗ fiend. And one night, // he goes off ↗ crazier than ↗ usual. // Mommy gets the kitchen knife to defend herself. // He doesn't like that ↘. // Not // one // bit. ↗ So, // me watching, he takes the knife to her, laughing while he does it. He turns to **me**, and he **says**, " Why // so // serious?" He comes at me with the knife - "Why // so // serious?" He sticks the blade in my mouth - "Let's put a smile on that face!"*

MP3 N°80

*I am // **Hela**, Odin's **first**born, command**er** of the legions of **Asgard**, the **right**ful **heir** to the **throne** and the **God**dess of **Death**. My father is **dead**, as are the princes. You're welcome. We were once the seat of absolute power in the cosmos. Our supremacy was unchallenged. Yet Odin stopped at the Nine ↘ **Realms.** Our **des**tiny is to **rule** over // **all** others. And **I** am here to restore that power. ↗ **Kneel** before me and ↗ **rise** into the ranks of my ↘ great ↗ **con**quest*

- Marquez une pause // et montez ↗ ou descendez ↘ l'intonation en fonction des indications.
- Les passages soulignés sont prononcés rapidement.
- Accentuez les mots et les syllabes en gras.

AUDIO MYSTERY

Listen to the audio recording to find the name of the villain everybody is talking about! **MP3 N°81**

- Audio words
- MP3
- Interactive Test

SPICE UP YOUR VOCABULARY

Use the vocabulary below to create your own mind map and add more words if necessary!

Adverbs

- courageously = bravely
- diabolically
- gloomily
- maliciously
- mysteriously
- slyly = mischievously: *sournoisement*
- wickedly

Verbs

- betray
- bribe: *soudoyer*
- confront sb with sth
- crush sb
- deceive = mislead
- defeat
- despise
- destroy
- fight to the death
- manipulate
- murder = kill
- plot = scheme /skiːm/
- shed blood /blʌd/
- succeed
- support = root for
- torture
- win

Adjectives

- cold-blooded
- courageous ≠ cowardly
- cruel /kruːəl/
- deceptive
- despicable
- dumb /dʌm/ = stupid
- likeable ≠ unlikeable
- mean = malicious
- moral ≠ immoral
- perfect ≠ flawed
- power-hungry
- realistic
- ruthless = merciless
- selfish
- sharp = smart
- undesirable
- wicked /ˈwɪkɪd/ = evil

Nouns

- adventure
- antihero(ine)
- archetype /ˈɑːkitaɪp/
- despair /dɪsˈpeə/
- enemy = foe /fəʊ/
- good ≠ evil /ˈiːvl/
- hero(ine) ≠ villain/rogue
- journey /ˈdʒɜːni/
- mentor
- misdeed
- ordeal /ɔːˈdiːl/
- protagonist
- quest /kwest/
- temptation
- terror
- the dark side
- selfishness
- vindictiveness

UP TO YOU!

★ 1. Match each word with its definition.

A. Lacking self-confidence and courage
B. Not able to be honest and truthful
C. An example to be imitated
D. Dishonest and unprincipled person
E. Concerned with the needs of others
F. Evil or morally wrong

1. selfless
2. a rogue
3. a coward
4. untrustworthy
5. wicked
6. a role-model

★★ 2. Complete each sentence with the most appropriate villainous characteristic.

madness • ambition • arrogance • vindictiveness • selfishness

A. Macbeth became the new king of Scotland thanks to his wife's ... .

B. Deadpool's ... makes him think about himself first, and forget the people around him.

C. The ... of the Joker is reinforced by his uncanny smile.

D. Voldemort's ... was directed at the people who had betrayed him.

E. Thanos's ... can account for his superior attitude towards humans.

★★ 3. Replace the underlined words with antonyms to turn heroes into antiheroes or villains!

A. The king was a <u>brave</u> and <u>merciful</u> leader who <u>saved</u> his country <u>from</u> chaos.

B. The wizard was <u>wise</u> enough to mentor his apprentice into becoming a <u>respectable</u> warrior.

C. The superhero's <u>selflessness</u> was <u>appreciated</u> by all the citizens of the country.

D. The Jedi turned to the <u>light</u> side of the Force after his <u>blissful</u> childhood.

★★★ 4. Complete this portrait of Sauron, from *The Lord of the Rings* by choosing the right words.

cunning • evil • enslave • dominate • conquest • deceit

The Lord of the Rings himself, the Dark Lord, the Deceiver; those are just some of the titles that this personification of ... has been given through the ages as written by J.R.R. Tolkien.
Sauron set in motion his own ... of Middle-earth throughout the second and third ages. He used his ... intelligence and ... to fool the Elves into creating the Rings of Power, culminating in the secretly forged One Ring, which had the power to ... the other rings and ... those bearing them to his will.

RULE THE GRAMMAR!

LES STRUCTURES CAUSATIVES

On utilise les structures suivantes quand le sujet est à l'origine d'une action et qu'il la fait faire ou subir à quelqu'un d'autre.

• La structure la plus fréquemment utilisée est : ***to make someone do something***.
*Iago **made** Othello **doubt** Desdemona.*

• ***To have someone do something*** (même sens qu'avec « make » mais il semble y avoir moins de contrainte)
*Iago **had** Othello **doubt** Desdemona.*

• ***To get someone to do something*** (même sens qu'avec « have » mais le registre est plus oral)
*Iago **got** Othello **to doubt** Desdemona.*

• ***To order someone to do something*** (ici, on insiste sur l'ordre donné)
*Iago **ordered** Othello **to doubt** Desdemona.*

• ***To cause someone to do something*** (ici, on insiste sur la causalité plutôt que que la volonté du sujet)
*Iago **cause** Othello **to doubt** Desdemona.*

• On utilise ***to have something done*** pour insister sur le résultat.
*Richard III **had** his nephews **executed**.*

LES COMPARATIFS ET LES SUPERLATIFS

• Le comparatif de supériorité (plus que...)

- Pour les adjectifs courts (1 ou 2 syllabes se finissant en -y) : on ajoute ***-er*** à l'adjectif ainsi que ***than***.
*Othello was **nicer than** Richard III.*

- Pour les adjectifs longs : on utilise ***more*** + adjectif + ***than***.
*Richard III was **more** dangerous **than** Richard II.*

- Attention, il y a des adjectifs irréguliers
*good → **better*** et *bad → **worse**.*

• Le comparatif d'égalité

- On le formes avec ***as*** + adjectif + ***as*** indépendamment de la longueur de l'adjectif :

*Harry is **as** strong **as** Voldemort.*

*Harry is **as** knowledgeable **as** Hermione.*

- On utilise souvent le comparatif d'égalité à la forme négative. Dans ce cas, le premier ***as*** peut être remplacé par ***so***.

*Harry is not **as / so** strong **as** Voldemort.*
*Harry is not **as / so** knowledgeable **as** Hermione.*

• Le superlatif (le plus)

- On le forme avec ***the*** + adjectif court + ***-est***
*Harry is **the nicest** wizard in the entire world.*

- On le forme avec ***the*** + ***most*** + adjectif long
*The Joker is **the most** controversial hero ever.*

• Le superlatif d'infériorité

- On le forme avec ***the*** + ***least*** + adjectif
*Claire Underwood is **the least** beloved character in the series.*

- Attention, il y a des adjectifs irréguliers
*good → **the best*** et *bad → **the worst**.*

	Comparatif de supériorité	Comparatif d'égalité	Superlatif
Adjectifs courts	adj. + *-er* + *than*	*as* + adj. + *as*	*the* + adj. + *-est*
Adjectifs longs	*more* + adj. + *than*		*the* + *most* + adj.

UP TO YOU!

★ 1. Make sentences using a comparative.

A. Richard is > any other English king. *(ruthless)*
B. Harry is = Ron. *(affectionate)*
C. Claire is > her husband. *(vicious)*
D. The Joker is = as Batman. *(powerful)*
E. Macbeth is > Iago. *(tall)*
F. Villains > heroes. *(attractive)*

★ 2. Change the following adjectives into superlatives.

A. Dumbledore is clearly *(good)* wizard on Earth.
B. Thanos is definitely *(strong)* of them all.
C. Who is the *(bad)* wizard in Hogwarts?
D. Who is *(strong)* avenger?
E. Flash clearly is *(fast)* superhero.

★★ 3. Change the following sentences with the "*not as/so ... as*" structure.

A. Bellatrix Lestrange is more frightening than Voldemort.
B. English knights are more popular than superheroes.
C. Leo is more athletic than Spiderman.
D. Agent Smith is more handsome than Leo.
E. Lady Macbeth is more frightening than Claire Underwood.
F. Bad cops are more attractive than good cops.

★★ 4. Rewrite the following sentences as shown.

E.g.: He sniffed (the cold) ➔ The cold made him sniff.

A. He won the election (His self-confidence).
B. He fought Voldemort (Dumbledore).
C. Othello doubted (Iago).
D. They yielded (Thanos).
E. He killed his nephews (his ruthlessness).
F. He started using his rowing machine (Claire).

★★★ 5. Rewrite the following sentences using in spite of and despite.

A. Although she has superpowers, she resents physical pain.
B. However strong he is, he is not invincible.
C. Although he is a superhero, he longs for a quiet family life.
D. Clever as they may be, they can always be outwitted.
E. Handsome as he is, she is not in love with him.
F. Although it was raining, they fought on.

★★ 6. Translate into English.

A. *Richard a fait envoyer Clarence à la Tour.*
B. *Frank a fait tuer plusieurs de ses opposants.*
C. *L'agent Smith a fait arrêter Neo.*
D. *Ils ont fait assassiner le chevalier.*
E. *Ils ont fait détruire Poudlard.*

★★★ 7. Translate into English.

A. *Bien qu'il soit fort, Thanos n'est pas invincible.*
B. *Bien qu'il fut rusé, Richard n'était pas le plus intelligent des Plantagenêt.*
C. *Léo, bien qu'il soit rapide, n'est pas intouchable.*
D. *Bien que Claire s'occupe de Frank, elle pense aussi à sa propre carrière.*
E. *Bien que les méchants soient attirants, les gentils finissent toujours par l'emporter.*

★★★ 8. Rewrite the following sentences as shown in the example.

He drank some magic potion in case he met a powerful wizard. → He drank some magic potion **lest he should meet** a powerful wizard.

A. She always wore her mask in case someone recognised her.
B. He kept calling his son in case something happened to him.
C. They sometimes travelled at night in case someone saw them.
D. Hermione kept the weather eye open in case someone approached.
E. Superman kept away from green kryptonite in case he lost his powers.
F. Richard sleep at night in case ghosts visited him.

9. Interactive test! What is your score?

Picture challenge

★ 3 sentences
★★ 4 to 6 sentences
★★★ 7 sentences and +

How many sentences can you make using what you have learnt? Collect stars!

CHOOSE YOUR PROJECT!

YOUR PROJECT #1

Pairwork. Imagine and act out the final conversation between a hero/heroine from the English-speaking world and his/her antagonist before their final battle starts for the next Comic-con in San Diego.

STEP 1 **Choose your characters and explain the reasons why they fight.**

- What did the villain do?
- Were there any victims?
- What does the villain want to achieve?
- Why does the hero/heroine want to avenge himself/herself?

STEP 2 **Organise the content of your conversation. You may follow the steps below:**

Hero/heroine

- Explain why you have come to confront your enemy.
- Tell your enemy why you think he/she is wrong and should stop.
- Try to settle things down and find a pacific solution.

Villain

- Explain your actions and develop your point of view.
You can talk about your past and what made you choose the dark path.
- Try to convince the hero/heroine to join your cause.
- Tell him/her you will not change your mind.

STEP 3 **Act out the scene!**

TIPS

- Use causatives to make your point.
He made so many people + Verb. You had them punished for…
- Rehearse your arguments at home.
- Look up the pronunciation of difficult words.
- Don't read your notes!
- Use your best accent. Maybe a British accent for the villain?

OR

YOUR PROJECT #2

Pairwork. You want to submit your new book project to a publishing company: One storyline divided into two different parts (the hero's version, and the villain's). The readers will choose their favourite! Use Worksheet n°37 **for help.**

STEP 1 **Choose a hero and his/her villain from the English-speaking world. Give them a conflicting goal.**

STEP 2 **Imagine at least three movements which will compose the characters' personal stories (cf. the hero's journey).**

STEP 3 **Write the stories.**

TIPS

- Use the vocabulary of the unit.
- Keep the story simple.
- Use link words to structure your ideas.
- Proof read your story.

UNIT 13 Évaluation

Compréhension de l'oral

"How Buffalo Bill created his legend" MP3 n°82

Listen to the audio recording three times and recap what you have understood.

Expression écrite

Choisissez l'un des deux sujets (min. 120 mots).

Question A : "*The Buffalo Bill's Wild West* show would influence the way cinema and literature portrayed the West in the 20th century." Does fiction always mirror reality?

Question B : About Buffalo Bill, one historian wrote: "The life of this hero and showman embodies the desire for history to become myth and myth to become history." Does reality always inspire fiction?

UNIT 14 Évaluation

Compréhension de l'oral

"Salem witch hunt" MP3 n°83

Listen to the audio recording three times and recap what you have understood.

Expression écrite

Choisissez l'un des deux sujets (min. 120 mots).

Question A : How can you account for the success of witch-related stories in films, series or literature?

Question B : To what extent can it be said that witches may be an avatar for female empowerment, and an image of a positive, feminist icon and activist?

UNIT 15 Évaluation

Compréhension de l'oral

"Forbidden love" MP3 n°84

Listen to the audio recording three times and recap what you have understood.

Expression écrite

Choisissez l'un des deux sujets (min. 120 mots).

Question A : Write the beginning of a story starting with "Two lovers, forbidden from one another. A war divides their people, and a mountain divides them apart."

Question B : Why have stories about star-crossed lovers always been so fascinating? Give examples.

UNIT 16 Évaluation

Compréhension de l'oral

"The rise of villains" MP3 n°85

Listen to the audio recording three times and recap what you have understood.

Expression écrite

Choisissez l'un des deux sujets (min. 120 mots).

Question A : Why have villainous characters always been so attractive to actors and actresses?

Question B : Comment on the following quote by British actor Tom Hiddleston: "Every villain is a hero in his own mind."

B1-B2

BACKPACK

Get Ready for your Exam!

UNIT 13 Évaluation

While space is an alien landscape, Mars is always a recognizably human one, warped to the harshest extremes: Survival is within reach, but complicated by the elements, or natives, or both. In the subgenre's newest and best entry, *The Martian*, the most nerve-wracking moment doesn't involve any zero-gravity derring-do, but rather the astronaut Mark Watney's potato farm. [...]

No matter what their plot, Mars movies are the closest things to Westerns in the sci-fi genre, visualizing the unknown not as the inky blackness of space nor the fantastic landscapes of fictional galaxies, but as a harsh yet conquerable desert.

In *The Martian*, Watney (Matt Damon) is an astronaut stranded after his colleagues mistakenly think him dead in a storm. As he plots to survive long enough to board a return mission, he delivers many (often funny) monologues to the camera about his plans. He grows potatoes using his own collected waste, creates water by burning hydrogen fuel, and sends messages home by digging up old NASA rovers. "They say once you grow crops somewhere, you have officially colonized it," he tells his audience at one point. "So, technically, I colonized Mars. In your face, Neil Armstrong!" [...]

Explorers of Mars are usually painted similarly: as pioneers trying to tame a world that has so much in common with our own, but that violently pushes back. [...]

The tradition of Mars movies as Westerns can be traced back to Edgar Rice Burroughs's Barsoom series—landmark sci-fi literature from the turn of the century featuring John Carter, a Civil War veteran transported to Mars after running afoul of Apache warriors while prospecting for gold in Arizona. For Burroughs, the two landscapes are inexorably linked: Carter has to navigate the warring tribes of Mars with the same cunning he needs out west. [...]

Mars, due to its reddish hue and desert landscape, was destined to be the Wild West. [...] *John Carter* is the Mars film closest to the grand, outlaw Western setting of literature. [...] Like its genre-mates, *Mission to Mars* is best when it focuses on the science. [...] That's the ultimate achievement of *The Martian*. When Watney grows his potatoes, the director Ridley Scott makes each sprout feel like an achievement; every effort to cross Mars's terrain follows weeks of forethought. Though it's lacking Martians, ancient edifices, or even a threatening algae bloom, it comes closest to Burroughs's original romantic conception of the world as one so similar, yet so frighteningly different to the one we know. [...] Though Watney clings to survival throughout, the idea of creating life and a home in such an empty new world is as challenging and stirring as the most idyllic visions of the Wild West.

David Sims, *The Atlantic*, 2015

Compréhension de l'écrit

Answer the following questions in English, using your own words.

A. After reading the text, what can you say about:
- its main topic?
- the people involved?
- the similarities between the Martian landscape and the Wild West? between life on Mars and life in the Wild West?

B. Comment on the following quote from *The Martian*: "They say once you grow crops somewhere, you have officially colonized it. So, technically, I colonized Mars. In your face, Neil Armstrong!"

Expression écrite

Choisissez l'un des deux sujets (min. 120 mots).

Question A : Have you ever watched a science-fiction film about Mars? Do you enjoy such films? Why (not)?

Question B : How do you account for the fact that scientists and NASA were interested in the film "The Martian"?

UNIT 14 Évaluation

In the late 19th century, the suffragette Matilda Joslyn Gage asserted something revolutionary. The persecution of witches, she said, had nothing to do with fighting evil or resisting the devil. It was simply entrenched social misogyny, the goal of which was to repress the intellect of women. A witch, she said, wasn't wicked. She didn't fly on a broomstick naked in the dark, or consort with demons. She was, instead, likely to be a woman "of superior knowledge". As a thought experiment, she suggested that for "witches" we should read instead "women". Their histories, she intimated, run hand in hand.

Obviously, she was on to something. When we say witch, we almost exclusively mean woman. Sure, men have also been accused of witchcraft, but they are by far the minority. Further, the words used to describe men with magical powers—warlock, magus, sorcerer, wizard—don't carry the same stigma.

[...] Witches are often called unnatural because of their ability to threaten men. With her spells, a witch can transform you into a pig, or defeat you in battle. She can curse you, blight your crops, ignore you, refuse you, correct you. Punishing witches accomplishes two things: it ends the threat and makes others afraid to follow in the unruly woman's footsteps.

Yet, despite all the attempts to stamp out witches, they are as strongly with us as ever, from Wanda Maximoff, the Scarlet Witch in the *Avengers* movies, to the recent film *The Love Witch*, to the television series *American Horror Story*, to non-fiction books such as Stacy Schiff's *The Witches: Salem, 1692*. The stereotypical image of the witch—green skin, pointed hat, warts, black cat—has become entrenched, but beneath that surface lies a dazzling variety; a rich diversity of women who have frightened, possessed and inspired us over the centuries.

[...] The most famous of this type must be Shakespeare's weird sisters from *Macbeth*. They are repulsive "midnight hags", with skinny lips, chapped fingers and beards. Their spells—eye of newt and toe of frog—are as disgusting as their appearances and curse anyone who crosses them. [...]

And ugliness, of course, is key. The haggish outsides of these witches are meant to match their evil insides, and testify to their unnaturalness, since women are supposed to be as neat, attractive and young as possible. But the association with age also contains a kernel of truth: many of the women accused of witchcraft were so-called "wise women", older figures, often poor widows, who scratched out a living in the community with their experience as midwives, herbalists and hedge-doctors. Their solitary, vulnerable status and unusual knowledge made them perfect targets for people's rage and fear when crops failed or babies died.

[...] But it wasn't just vulnerable women who drew accusations of witchcraft. It was also women with serious political power. [...]

Cleopatra and Anne Boleyn were likewise accused of witchcraft, with rumours that Anne even bore physical marks of her compact with the devil, such as a third nipple, moles and a sixth finger on her right hand. Such accusations were a clever and effective way for a woman's political enemies to smear her since, as countless other women accused of witchcraft learned, it is impossible to offer definitive proof that one is not a witch. Perhaps what is most shocking about this catch-22 is the way in which it continues to be played out today.

Madeline Miller, *The Guardian*, 2018

Compréhension de l'écrit

Answer the following questions in English, using your own words.

A. After reading the text, what can you say about:
- its main topic?
- the people involved?
- why witches are always portrayed as ugly, old women?
- where witches originate from and why they used to be persecuted?

B. Comment on the two sentences lines 55-57.

Expression écrite

Choisissez l'un des deux sujets (min. 120 mots).

Question A : Comment on the sentence lines 23-25.

Question B : How are witches portrayed in 21st century fiction (books, films, art, etc.)? Is it different from the way they used to be pictured?

❷ Leading the Way

Do consumers and politicians have a responsibility to consider the treatment of animals when making decisions?

1 Veganism in the UK

A. Read the text. What is the trend when it comes to veganism in the UK?

B. Which shops and restaurants have helped to make veganism popular in the UK?

C. Go further. How has the vision of what it means to be vegan changed?

Veganism might have recently acquired a hipster cache[1] at buzzy London events such as Vegan Nights and the weekly Hackney Downs market established by influential blogger Sean O'Callaghan, AKA "the Fat Gay Vegan", but its surging popularity is a national phenomenon, with plant-based[2] food festivals and businesses booming from Bristol to Inverness.

The high street is adapting with incredible speed. Big chains such as Marks & Spencer and Pret a Manger have introduced vegan ranges[3], Wagamama has a new vegan menu, Pizza Hut recently joined Pizza Express and Zizzi in offering vegan pizzas, while last year Guinness went vegan and stopped using fish bladders[4] in its brewing[5] process, after two and a half centuries. Sainsbury's and Tesco have introduced extended new ranges of vegan products, while the latter recently appointed American chef Derek Sarno to the impressive job title of director of plant-based innovation.

If this is the year of mainstream[6] veganism, as every trend forecaster and market analyst seems to agree, then there is not one single cause, but a perfect plant-based storm of factors. People cite one or more of three key motives for going vegan — animal welfare, environmental concerns and personal health — and it is being accompanied by an endless array[7] of new business startups, cookbooks, YouTube channels, trendy events and polemical documentaries. The traditional food industry is desperately trying to catch up with the flourishing grassroots[8] demand. "What do you mean, weak, limp[9] and weedy[10]? In 2017, the vegan category is robust, energetic, and flush[11] with crowdfunding cash," ran an article headlined "Vegan Nation" in industry bible the *Grocer* in November.

1 hiding spot • 2 *à base de plantes* • 3 *gammes* • 4 *vessies* • 5 *brassage* • 6 ideas, attitudes, beliefs shared by most people • 7 *ici, variété* • 8 coming from ordinary people • 9 *mou* • 10 thin, weak in appearance • 11 rich

Dan Hancox, ***The Guardian,*** April 1, 2018

2 Breaking down the numbers

A. Look at these charts. How many vegans and vegetarians make up the UK population?

B. What are the reasons why different people reduce their meat consumption?

C. Have your say. *"Perhaps the most common and unifying reason that people decide to go vegan is in the pursuit of a more caring, compassionate lifestyle."* Do you agree that this is the main reason?

People give a variety of reasons for eating less meat

% of respondents citing each reason (more than one could be given)

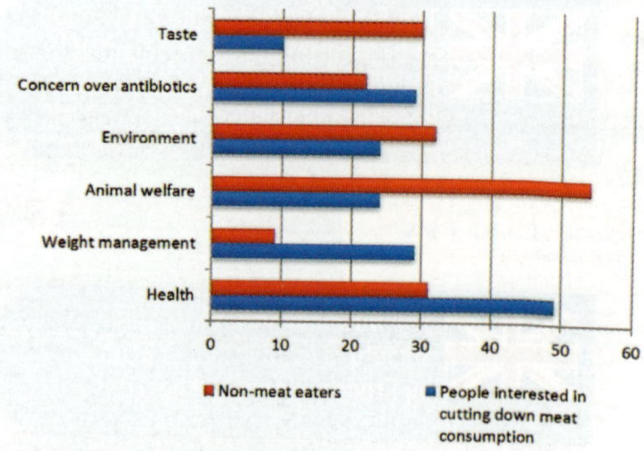

Vegetarians and vegans in Great Britain (2016)

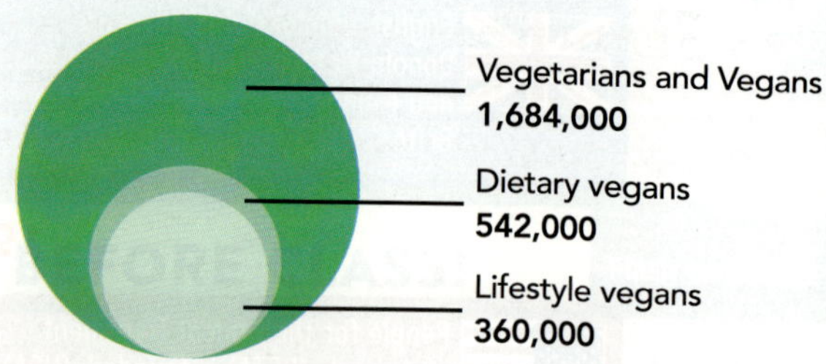

HELP!

Definitions

- vegan /ˈviːgən/ = someone who gives up all animal products. No meat, fish, dairy or eggs are eaten. They also reject leather, wool, silk and honey.
- vegetarian /vedʒɪˈteəriən/ = sb who does not eat animals
- pescatarian /peskɪˈteəriən/ = sb who eats fish but not meat
- flexitarian: sb who eats mainly vegetarian food but eats meat from time to time
- plant-based
- trend
- crowdfunding

3 Californian laws

A. Read the text. What laws did California pass?
B. Was California the first state to pass both of these laws?
C. How will the bans be regulated/carried out?
D. **Go further.** What other areas of animal usage could change next if California continues in this way?
E. **Have your say.** Which photo would you choose to illustrate the text? Justify.

California will become the first US state to ban the sale and manufacture of new fur products and the third to bar[1] most animals from circus performances under a pair of bills signed on Saturday by the governor, Gavin Newsom.

The law will bar residents from selling or making clothing, shoes or handbags with fur, starting in 2023. Animal rights groups cheered the measure as a stand against inhumane practices. The proposal was vigorously opposed by the billion-dollar US fur industry, while the Fur Information Council of America has already threatened to sue.

It follows Newsom's signing of legislation that makes California the first state to outlaw fur trapping and follows bans on sales of fur in Los Angeles and San Francisco.

"California is a leader when it comes to animal welfare, and today that leadership includes banning the sale of fur," Newsom said. "But we are doing more than that. We are making a statement to the world that beautiful wild animals like bears and tigers have no place on trapeze wires or jumping through flames."

California joins New Jersey and Hawaii in banning most animals from circus performances. The law exempts domesticated dogs, cats and horses and does not apply to rodeos.

Circuses have been declining in popularity for decades. The most well-known act, the Ringling Bros and Barnum et Bailey Circus, closed in 2017 after 146 years of performances.

The law includes penalties of up to $25,000 per day for each violation.

People for the Ethical Treatment of Animals lauded[2] both new laws. "Today is a historic day for animals in California, including those who have been whipped[3] into performing in circuses, or skinned alive for their fur or skin," said its vice-president, Tracy Reiman.

1 prevent sb from doing sth • 2 *ici, a salué* • 3 *fouetter*

Associated Press in Sacramento, 13 October 2019

A

B

YOUR TURN! 4 Is veganism just a trend?

Using the figures and the information from the articles, comment on the fact that vegan and/or vegetarian products have become very popular recently.

Debate the necessity of more vegan and vegetarian products.

HELP!
- enforce/implement
- a bill
- have… from ban
- sue
- outlaw
- fur trapping
- exempt
- skinned

❸ Animals and Scientific Research

Why is the use of animals in scientific research a commonly debated topic in North America and in the UK?

1 A patient's point of view

A. Read the text. What kind of document is it?

B. How did the author benefit from animal testing?

C. Is the author open to alternatives for animal testing?

D. Have your say. Read the last two sentences (l. 14-16). Do you agree?

The animal rights lobby claim to be helping animals, but they forget one important group. That's the people with health problems and disabilities who benefit directly from animal-based research.

Until recently I had a serious spinal condition[1], which left me in massive pain and hardly able to work. Thanks to animal-based research I had an operation [...] The pain has now completely gone [...].

The animal rights lobby tell us that we should treat animals in the same way as humans. But if we do that, we're condemning people with health problems and disabilities to pain, to isolation, to unemployment, and to massively reduced quality of life.

I want to see the best possible conditions for animals, and will be happy when we have alternatives that work. But until that day, we need to keep animal research legal.

1 *maladie de la moelle épinière*

Kevin Elliott, ***Letter to the Oxford Times,*** 15 January 2009

2 The American science community

A. Read the text. Why did "Speaking of Research" send a letter to the EPA?

B. Define a NAM and give an example.

C. What does the group "Speaking of Research" think about NAMs?

D. Why does Speaking of Research think animal research is necessary?

WASHINGTON, D.C. – The advocacy group Speaking of Research[1] today shared an open letter with the U.S. Environmental Protection Agency condemning its new directive to reduce and eventually eliminate all chemical safety tests that involve animals. The letter, which is signed by more than 600 members of America's science community, also calls on EPA Administrator Andrew Wheeler to withdraw[2] the directive because it threatens human and animal health. [...] The open letter reads:

[...] Research with animals is undeniably critical to the EPA's mission. This fact runs contrary to Mr. Wheeler's claim that "New Approach Methods" or NAMs "exist today that allow us to better predict potential hazards[3] for risk assessment purposes" than animal models. In fact, there is not a single case of environmental risk assessment where a non-animal alternative or methodology can provide a comprehensive understanding of the risks of new chemical hazards[3] and potential human exposures. To regulate chemicals, the EPA must demonstrate that there are adverse[4] effects in whole living organisms. While the EPA has reduced its reliance on animal testing in certain areas where it is possible to do so [...], the EPA has not provided the relevant experimental, peer-reviewed[5] data which demonstrates that "NAMs" are better than animals in assessing the safety of chemicals for other animals, including people, and for the environment. [...]

We, the undersigned members of America's scientific community, denounce the EPA's directive to aggressively reduce animal testing and end research with mammals under arbitrary deadlines. We call on the EPA to withdraw[2] this directive. We understand the important role that research animals have in determining what is safe for humans, for other animals, and for the environment. Any individual or group who purports[6] to value animal lives should support the responsible study of a very limited number of animals to ensure the health of us all — human and animal alike.

1 group advocating the importance of animal testing • 2 *retirer* • 3 dangers • 4 negative • 5 evaluated by other academic researchers • 6 pretend

Press Release by Allyson Bennett, 10 October 2019

3 Dr. Jane Goodall

A. Read the text. In what ways are humans and chimpanzees similar, according to Dr. Goodall?
B. How have people changed their views on what chimpanzees can do?
C. Comment on the last sentence (l.52).
D. Go further. Do you think that Jane Goodall's research on chimpanzees could be one of the reasons why more people are advocating animal rights today? Justify.

Chimpanzees, more like us than any other living creature. It's absolutely extraordinary how biologically we realise far more today than when I began in 1960, how like us they are. The DNA of the chimpanzee and humans, differs by only just over 1 percent. [...] You could get a blood transfusion from them if you matched the blood group. The immune system, so like ours that they can catch or be infected with all known human diseases, which is why some scientists have incarcerated them in 5 foot by 5 foot[1] cages to investigate otherwise uniquely human diseases. Unfortunately, these scientists were reluctant to admit the equally dramatic similarities in the behaviour of chimpanzees. And it shouldn't surprise us that, given the similarity of brain, and nervous system, that they are capable of intellectual performances, like the tool using and tool making, which used to be considered the hallmarks[2] of the human species. And chimpanzees are capable of so many fascinating intellectual performances. Captive chimpanzees can learn more than 400 of the signs used by deaf people, American Sign Language. And they can use those signs when communicating with each other as well as communicating with their teacher. [...] They also have emotions similar to those which we call happiness, sadness, fear, despair. They're capable of mental as well as physical suffering.

And all these things that I've just said were considered absolutely not possible when I first went to Cambridge University in England in 1961. [...]

And now, finally, all these years later, we're moving into a world where even science is beginning to accept that these things are true, where, in most major universities, you can study animal mind, you can study animal emotion, you can even try to come to grips in the psychology department with animal personality. So, we are moving there, and by and large, the main pockets of resistance are those people who, in some way or another, are exploiting animals in painful and invasive ways. But gradually, I think, the voice of the animals is growing. [...] It's clear that chimpanzees, more like us than any other creature, have really helped us to redefine our position in nature. It's really clear, once you've spent time with the chimpanzees, that you can no longer draw a sharp line between humans on the one hand and the rest of the animal kingdom on the other. It's a very blurry[3] line. It's getting more blurry all the time. And it's [...] definite that we're not the only beings on the planet with personalities, minds and feelings. And that gives us a new respect, not only for the chimpanzees, but the other amazing animal beings with whom we share this planet. [...]

1 1 foot = 0.30 m • 2 typical feature/quality • 3 *flou*

Dr. Jane Goodall,
primatologist, Founder of the Jane Goodall Institute & UN Messenger of Peace, Speech at the University of Toronto, 15 May 2006

YOUR PROJECT

You participate in a formal debate, as if you were in an American high school, for or against the use of animals in science.

- Using what you have learnt from this chapter, find the arguments that are strongest in favour and against the use of animal testing.

- Check the rules of the debate on Worksheet n°38 •

SPICE UP YOUR VOCABULARY

DEBATING

Introducing

- The motion for debate today is: … defining the motion:
- Our position is the following...

Present your main point

- Firstly…
- Most importantly…
- Primarily…
- The main thing is…

Add additional arguments

- In addition, …
- I might add that …
- Not to mention the fact that …
- Not only that, but also …

State your opinion

- If you ask me …
- I have every reason to believe …

Show your evidence

- According to …
- Clearly …
- Obviously …
- Undoubtedly …
- For this reason …
- Owing to this …

Half-agree

- I'd agree with you if …
- Yes, perhaps/in a way/possibly, however…

Give yourself time to think

- I can't answer that directly.
- I need time to think about that.
- That's a very interesting/difficult/tough/good question, because…
- What do you mean by (that)?
- If you ask me…

Politely disagree

- Not necessarily
- That isn't strictly true …
- I'm not sure about that …
- I'm inclined to disagree …
- That may be so/true, but …
- I beg to differ with …

Get back to your argument

- Anyway …
- To get back to the point …

Speak of generalisations

- Generally (speaking) …
- As a rule (of thumb) …
- Typically…

Conclude

- To make a long story short…
- In short…
- To sum up/summarise…
- To put it simply…

Expressions to talk about a debate

- be at odds with something/someone = disagree
- be out of the question = impossible, not worth discussion
- (sit/be) on the fence = avoid taking sides in a discussion/can't decide one way or another
- to split hairs = to pay too much attention to small differences
- wipe the slate clean = start over, forget past differences
- call someone's bluff = challenge them to do what they are threatening to do

ANIMAL RIGHTS

- advocate stg for sth = *défendre qqchose*
- a necessary evil /ˈiːvl/ = *un mal nécessaire*
- abused /əˈbjuːzd/ = *maltraité*
- animal welfare = *bien-être animal*
- cramped (cages) /kræmpt/ = *cages exiguës*
- cruelty /ˈkruːəlti/
- experiment on /ɪkˈsperɪmənt/
- exploit /ɪkˈsplɔɪt/
- factory farming /ˈfæktri fɑːmɪŋ/ = *élevage industriel*
- humane /hjuːˈmeɪn/, humanely /hjuːˈmeɪnli/
- inflict pain /ɪnˈflɪkt peɪn/
- injure /ˈɪndʒə/ = harm = hurt
- moral responsibility /rɪspɒnsɪˈbɪləti/
- scientific /saɪənˈtɪfɪk/ research
- sentient /ˈsentiənt/ = *sensible*
- species /ˈspiːʃiːz/ = *espèce*
- speciesism /ˈspiːʃiːzɪzəm/ = *spécisme* (believing some animals are superior to others)
- vivisection /vɪvɪˈsekʃn/
- veganism /ˈviːgənɪzm/

LANGUAGE LAB

- Audio words
- MP3
- Interactive Test

★ **1. Rewrite these sentences using *do/did* for emphasis as shown in the example.**

E.g.: I think you're wrong. → I do think you're wrong.

A. Sam believes she understands the problem.
B. They thought they could get away with it.
C. I realised I have been wrong all these years.
D. Animals have feelings too.

★ **2. Fill in the blanks with the words below.**

vegan • pain • exploited • humanely • cramped • sentient • experiment • cruel

"Animals deserve to be treated … . They are … beings and shouldn't be living in … cages or be … . There is no reason to inflict … or kill them just for human gains."

"I think it's too extreme to become … and stop eating any animal products. Sure, I'm not saying we need to be … to animals, but it's a necessary evil to … on animals. Think of all the diseases we can treat thanks to them!"

★★ **3. Fill in the blanks with the correct modal *should, will, must, can, may* or *must*.**

A. Fur coats … be banned. ***(obligation)***
B. Veganism … be an option for the future. ***(possibilité)***
C. Chimpanzees … be very friendly. ***(caractéristique)***
D. You … reconsider your position. ***(conseil)***
E. It … be difficult to be a vegetarian in France. ***(forte probabilité)***

★★ **4. Choose the correct expression to complete this debate.**

A. "***I need time to think about it* / *The main thing is* / *In short*** animals are worthy of being treated with respect and do not deserve to be put in pain."
B. "***According to* / *Generally speaking,* / *That isn't exactly true,*** scientific research has relied heavily on the use of animals. The goal wasn't to put them in pain, but we had to."
C. "***I'd agree with you if* / *Primarily,* / *I would argue that*** we knew that today absolutely no alternatives to animal use exist."

★★★ **5. Translate into English using a modal auxiliary.**

A. *Jonathan me dit que je ne devrais pas porter de fourrure animale.*
B. *Les végétaliens ne peuvent pas manger de produits d'origine animale.*
C. *Les expérimentations animales ne devraient pas exister.*
D. *Tu n'as pas besoin d'être végétarien pour aimer les animaux.*

6. Interactive test! What is your score?

OPEN YOUR EARS!

PHONOLOGY

L'intonation

- L'intonation descendante (notée \\) exprime que l'on est sûr de ce que l'on dit. On accentue les mots importants de la phrase. Écoutez et répétez. **MP3 N°86**

*I think you're \\ **wrong**. • I believe it's \\ **true**. • I don't \\ **like** this.*

- L'intonation descendante-montante (notée \\/) est utilisée pour exprimer une réserve ou un désaccord. Elle implique une suite : « *yes… but* ». Écoutez et répétez. **MP3 N°87**

*I \\/ **see** but the situation is more complex.*
*Be that as it \\/ **may**, I still believe it's wrong.*
*Per\\/**haps**, but there are arguments on both sides.*

- Pour exprimer son opinion, on accentue le verbe. Écoutez et répétez. **MP3 N°88**

*I **think** • I **believe** • I **guess** • I **reckon***

- Quand on compare deux opinions contraires, on peut accentuer les (pronoms) sujets. Écoutez et répétez.

***You** believe this but **he** thinks differently.* **MP3 N°89**
*I trusted him but **Mary** never did.*

AUDIO MYSTERY **MP3 N°90**

Listen to the recording and solve the mystery!

Picture challenge

★ 3 sentences
★★ 4 to 6 sentences
★★★ 7 sentences and +

How many sentences can you make using what you have learnt? Collect stars!

AXE 6

UNIT 18

UPGRADING HUMANS

Should humans try to improve themselves whatever the cost?

YOUR PROJECT

1 Write the next scenario for the series *Black Mirror*.

OR

2 Promote a new technology bestowing immortality.

Au menu de cette unité :

DÉCOUVERTES CULTURELLES

- Les innovations scientifiques (*bioprinting, exoskeletons…*)
- Les questions éthiques sur les expériences sur les humains dans la fiction (*Brave New World, Never Let Me Go, Flowers for Algernon…*)
- Le mouvement des *biohackers* aux États-Unis
- La quête de l'immortalité dans la science-fiction

OUTILS LINGUISTIQUES

- L'expression de la probabilité
- Le *present perfect*
- Les modaux
- Le prétérit modal

❶ How is Science Helping Humans?

How can science help to improve the human condition?

1 Biomedicine: the miracles of science

A. Groupwork. Each group studies a different video and introduces their innovation to the class.

B. Then together explain how science can help to improve the human condition and discuss what the limits could be.

Group A

Watch an introduction to bioprinting.
- Give a definition of 3D-printing.
- Why is "bioprinting" another step forward?
- Explain how bioprinters work (pick out the steps).

Group B

Watch introduction to exoskeletons.
- Identify the subject and the main actors in the invention.
- Pick out the characteristics of the technology and say how it works.
- Explain why it revolutionises the patients' lives.

VIDEO N°33

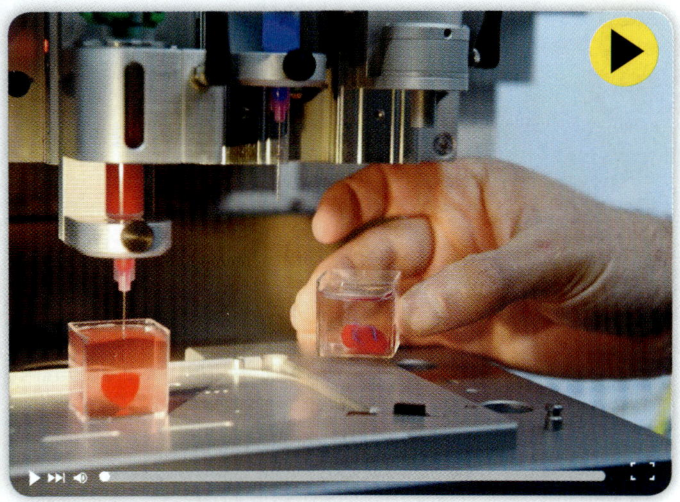

VIDEO N°34

YOUR TURN! 2 Advertise an invention

Groupwork. Imagine the voice-over of a commercial with a catchy slogan in order to promote one of the inventions above or another one of your choice.

HELP!

Words
- **break**through: *percée*
- gr**ou**ndbreaking: *révolutionnaire*
- disc**o**very
- l**i**fe-changing opport**u**nity

Tools
- **might, would, could** + BV 'You might have the possibility to'
- **If you.../it's high time you** + *prétérit modal*
- Use the **present perfect** when talking about the results of your research

❷ The Potential Loss Of Our Humanity

Can technology make us less human?

1 Conditioning humans

A. Look at the picture and describe the situation. What strikes you in the representation of the creation of humans?

B. Guess what the film is about.

C. Check your guesses by reading the text. Then discuss the ethical aspects of this world.

D. **Go further.** Imagine the children's reactions while observing the scientists at work.

HELP!

- **hi**erarchy /ˈhaɪrɑːki/
- caste **sy**stem
- **so**cial **cla**sses
- **clo**ning
- gen**e**tically-**mo**dified

"Alpha children wear grey. They work much harder than we do, because they're so frightfully clever. I'm really awfully glad I'm a Beta, because I don't work so hard. And then we are much better than the Gammas and Deltas. Gammas are stupid. They all wear green, and Delta children wear khaki. Oh no, I don't want to play with Delta children. And Epsilons are still worse."

Brave New World, Aldous Huxley, 1932

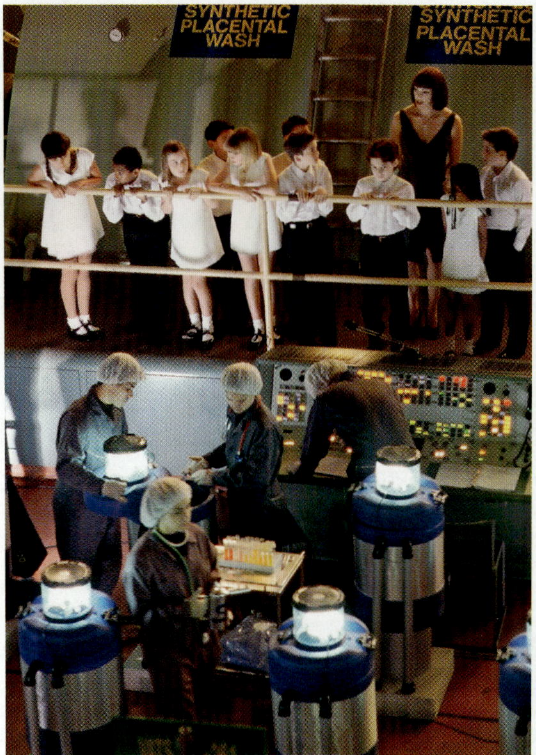

Growing embryos in the laboratory, *Brave New World*, 1998

2 Disposable humans

The story takes place in England where clones are created to be organ donors until their final donation, after which they must die. Kathy and Tommy, two clones raised at Hailsham Boarding School, visit Miss Emily, their former teacher, to get some answers. Miss Emily replies:

"You must try and see it historically. After the war, in the early fifties, when the great breakthroughs[1] in science followed one after the other so rapidly, there wasn't time to take stock, to ask sensible[2] questions. Suddenly there were all these new possibilities laid before us, all these ways to cure so many previously incurable conditions. [...] And for a long time, people preferred to believe these organs appeared from nowhere or at most that they grew in a kind of vacuum[3]. Yes, there were arguments. But by the time people became concerned about... about *students*, by the time they came to consider just how you were reared[4], whether you should have been brought into existence at all, well by then it was too late. There was no way to reverse the process. How can you ask a world that has come to regard cancer as curable, how can you ask such a world to put away that cure, to go back to the dark days? There was no going back. However uncomfortable people were about your existence, their overwhelming concern was that their own children, their spouses, their parents, their friends, did not die from cancer, motor neurone disease, heart disease. So for a long time you were kept in the shadows and people did their best not to think about you. And if they did, they tried to convince themselves you weren't really like us. That you were less than human, so it didn't matter.'

1 an important new discovery • 2 reasonable • 3 *(ici) espace vide* • 4 *élevés*

Never Let Me Go, Kazuo Ishiguro, 2005

A. Read the excerpt and pick out information about the context which led to the use of cloning (time period, technological progress, goal).

B. Pick out the arguments used by Miss Emily to justify cloning and the creation of organ donors.

C. **Groupwork.** Discuss the meaning of the following sentences: *"They tried to convince themselves you weren't really like us. That you were less than human, so it didn't matter."* (l. 22)

3 Editing our genome

A. Study the poster on CRISPR-Cas9.
- Pick out the various abilities of this genetic tool and identify its goal. Why is it often compared to scissors?
- Pick out and rephrase the benefits for mankind.
- Identify three dangers linked to the use of this tool.

B. Have your say. What is at stake for our society?

A BRAVE NEW WORLD
with CRISPR-Cas9

CRISPR holds the potential to eliminate dangerous genes in a safe and cost effective way, making it, in the future, an accessible treatment to many suffering from cancer, Alzheimer's etc.

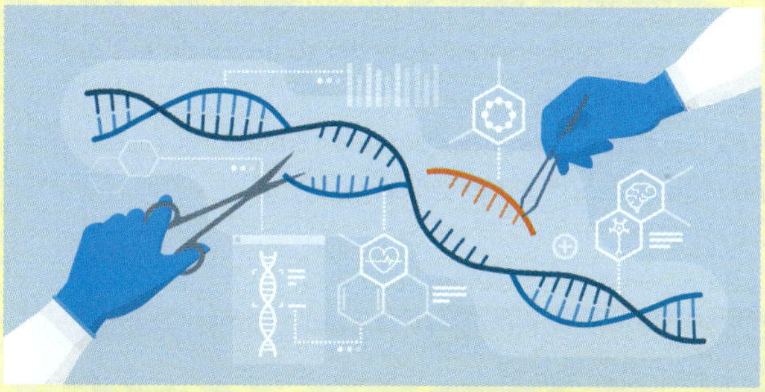

By editing DNA, it cuts out these threats in a way similar to vaccines that provide antibodies, developing more efficient execution in the lines of defense.

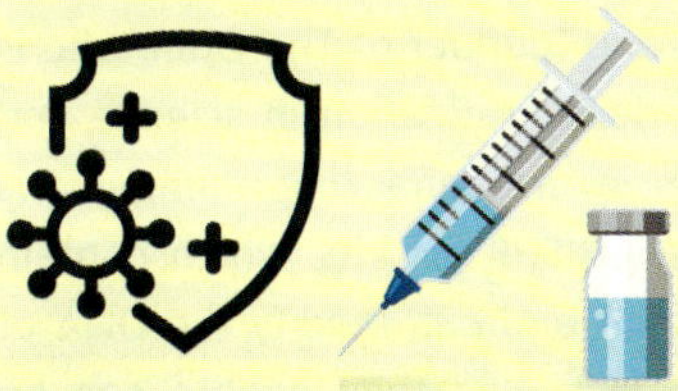

MAJOR BENEFITS include:
- Innumerable Cures
- Low Cost
- Efficient Execution

MAJOR RISKS include:
- Eliminating physical traits that seem "undesirable" to create designer babies
- Unauthorized treatment on unborn babies and the irreversible effects that will pass on future generations

One risk, however, would be the exploitation of this powerful genetic modifer on unborn babies in efforts to create the perfect human.

Similar to Aldous Huxley's "*Brave New World*", babies could be designed to suit certain purposes physically and mentally, almost eliminating any physical individuality bad or good.

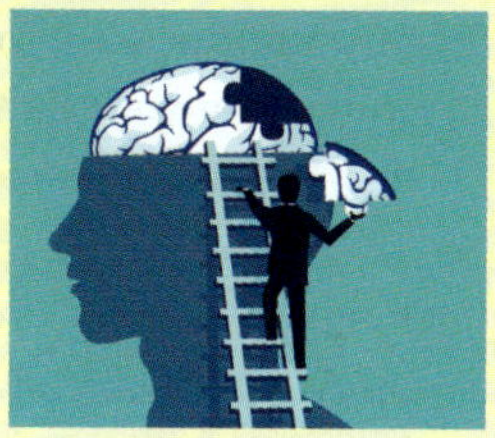

YOUR TURN!

4 Write an article

Write an article for the *Locus Awards* competition entitled: *How scared of genetic engineering should we be? From Science-Fiction to Reality…*

HELP!

Nouns
- cure
- disease
- gene-editing
- genetic modification

Verbs & Expressions
- dehumanise
- enhance = improve
- eradicate = erase
- the point of no return
- push back the limits

Tools
- **If we went as far as** + V-ing
- **I believe we might / could / would** + *BV*

3 Ethical Issues

To what extent does human improvement benefit humankind?

1 Democratising human improvement

A. Read the article. Focus on the terms defining "DIY Biology", or "biohacking", in order to give a definition in your own words.

B. Pick out the differences between traditional research and "biohacking". What strikes you?

C. Pick out the pros and cons of biohacking and draw a chart to sum up your findings.

D. Have your say. What do you think of biohacking?
→ *"if biohackers were to…", "it might/could/would + BV", "If I were a patient…"*

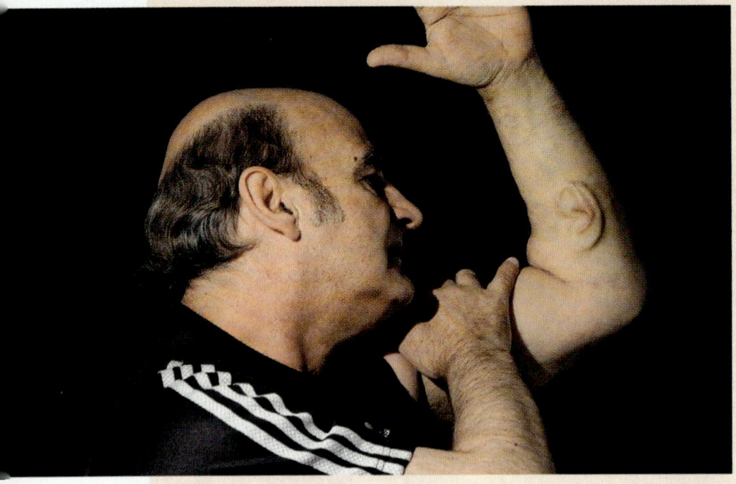

Do you believe that research is reserved for scientists? It is generally assumed that you need to have a Ph.D. and be affiliated with a research institution in order to engage in recognized scientific work. Do-it-yourself Biology (DIY Biology or DIY Bio), also known as biohacking, is challenging this notion. This global movement is spreading valid scientific methods among the lay public. Biohackers are proposing that anyone can make a significant contribution to the field of biology. Biohacking bridges the gap between amateur scientists and professional biologists.

There are now situations where these two groups meet in modern labs that are open to the public. The activity of biohacking can be a lifelong passion, a hobby or sometimes the next great business idea. However, monetary reward is rarely in the forefront; biohackers are generally about innovation and creating a biotechnological community movement. [...]

The idea of making medical care and medication easier to access is compelling, and biohackers are hoping to make life-saving drugs available to everyone.

Open Insulin, for example, is a project run by a team of biohackers who are looking into developing a new version of insulin that would be more economical and more widely available. The project is gaining momentum, and a wider community is recognizing their altruistic motives. [...]

Open Insulin has also been endorsed by Josiah Zayner, Ph.D., CEO and founder of The Odin, who is a big advocate of democratization in science and medicine. Zayner's own biohacking company is producing low-cost CRISPR [...] kits, which contain a gene-editing system and can modify the DNA of organisms. The experiments they enable can be applied in a variety of ways, ranging from personal health to improving the brewing process of beer. [...]

Some critics are concerned about the safety of garage labs and argue that biohacking could potentially be dangerous, especially when working with live organisms. This type of activity is not regulated, which is both its advantage and disadvantage.

On one hand, biohackers unrestrained by government regulations can push the boundaries of science further. On the other hand, some fear that potentially dangerous microbes could be created in their labs. However, biohacking does not seem to have evolved to the state where it is dangerous yet, and it is highly unlikely that do-it-yourself biologists could engage in transformative genetics projects.

Michael Rucker, ***www.verywellhealth.com***, 2 February 2020

YOUR TURN! 2 "The biohacking ideology"

A. Online. Watch the video about biohacking (www.lienmini.fr/htr-tle-18). Pick out more information about biohackers and focus on the main principles of their philosophy.

B. Go further. Use your findings to write a small guide to biohacking for your biology class.

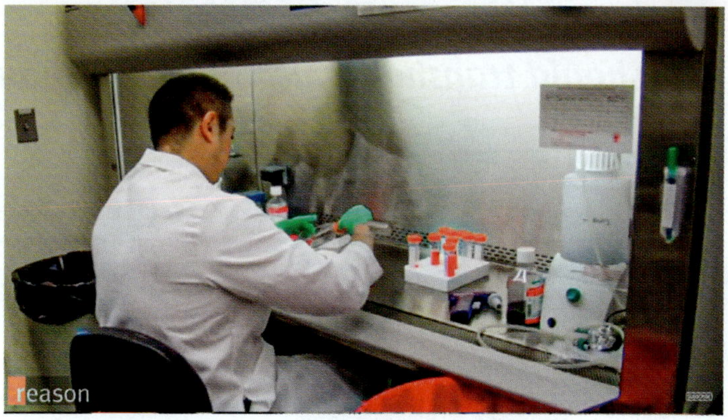

3 When ambition is all that matters...

The story is told by Charlie Gordon, the first subject of an experiment which is supposed to increase human intelligence. Charlie is asked to write reports on his progress after the surgery.

PROGRESS REPORT 11

April 21— [...] I think it's a good thing about finding out how everybody laughs at me. I thought about it a lot. It's because I'm so dumb and I don't even know when I'm doing something dumb. People think it's funny when a dumb person can't do things the same way they can.

Anyway, now I know I'm getting a little smarter every day. I know punctuation and I can spell good. I like to look up all the hard words in the dictionary and I remember them. [...] I'm reading a lot now, and Miss Kinnian says I read very fast. Sometimes I even understand what I'm reading about, and it stays in my mind. There are times when I can close my eyes and think of a page and it all comes back like a picture. [...]

Besides history, geography, and arithmetic, Miss Kinnian said I should start to learn a few foreign languages. Professor Nemur gave me some more tapes to play while I sleep. I still don't know how the conscious and unconscious mind works, but Dr. Strauss says not to worry yet. He asked me to promise that when I start learning college subjects next week I wouldn't read any books on psychology — that is, until he gives me permission. [...]

April 27— [...] This evening when I came in to ask Dr. Strauss about having dinner with Miss Kinnian, I heard them shouting. Dr. Nemur was saying that it was *his* experiment and *his* research, and Dr. Strauss was shouting back that he contributed just as much, because he found me through Miss Kinnian and he performed the operation. Dr. Strauss said that someday thousands of neurosurgeons might be using his technique all over the world.

Dr. Nemur wanted to publish the results of the experiment at the end of this month. Dr. Strauss wanted to wait a while longer to be sure. Dr. Strauss said that Dr. Nemur was more interested in the Chair of psychology at Princeton than he was in the experiment. Dr. Nemur said that Dr. Strauss was nothing but an opportunist who was trying to ride to glory on *his* coattails.

When I left afterwards, I found myself trembling. I don't know why for sure, but it was as if I'd seen both men clearly for the first time.

Flowers for Algernon,
Daniel Keyes, 1966

A. Read the excerpt and answer the questions:

Entry n°1 - *April 21*

- Give examples of the progress that Charlie has made.
- **Go further.** Focus on Charlie's relationships with the people around him. What strikes you?

Entry n°2 - *April 27*

- Focus on the doctors' attitudes. What message is conveyed about their experiment?
- Discuss the meaning of the final sentence with your group: *"When I left afterwards, I found myself trembling. I don't know why for sure, but it was as if I'd seen both men clearly for the first time."*

B. Go further. Write a short review for the literary blog of Teen Science Café entitled "What if the science of *Flowers for Algernon* became reality?" Give your opinion on the story and imagine the social, economic and ethical consequences of the process if it became the norm in the future.

❹ Defeating Death

Should transhumanism make humans immortal?

1 Defeating death through science

A. Look at the poster for *Transcendence* and describe it.

B. What can you guess about the character's story?

C. Go online. Watch the trailer, check your guesses and find out more about the film.

D. Read the definition of "transcendence" below.

- Relate this definition to the story. What "superior state" is achieved in the film?
- Why does it go against the laws of nature?

> **Transcendence** is the act of rising to a superior state. It comes from the Latin prefix *trans-*, meaning "beyond," and *scandare*, meaning "to climb." When you achieve transcendence, you have gone beyond ordinary limitations. The word is often used to describe a spiritual or religious state, or a condition of moving beyond physical needs and realities.

2 Recreating human consciousness

A. Read the scene from *Black Mirror* and say what the application is about. Explain how it works.

B. Why is this an example of transhumanism? Give your opinion on the app.

C. Have your say. Would you consider using this technology?

Martha's boyfriend, Ash, has died in a car accident. Her friend Sarah wants to help her cope with her grief with a new application.

Sarah: I can sign you up to something that helps. It helped me. It will let you speak to him. I know he's dead, but it wouldn't work if he wasn't. And don't worry, it's not some crazy spiritual thing. He was a heavy user, he'd be perfect.

Martha: Please shut up.

Sarah: I mean, it's still in beta, but I've got an invite.

Martha: Please shut up. [...] I don't care what it is, I don't want it! It's obscene to use his name. His name, for God's sake! It hurts, you know it hurts.

Sarah: Which is why I signed you up.

Martha: What is it? W-What is it?

Sarah: You click the link and you talk to it.

Martha: You talk to it?

Sarah: You type messages in, like an e-mail, and then it talks back to you, just like he would.

Martha: He's dead.

Sarah: It's software. It mimics him. You give it someone's name. It goes back and reads through all the things they've ever said online, their Facebook updates, their Tweets, anything public. I just gave it Ash's name. The system did the rest. It's so clever.

Script: Black Mirror, Season 2, Episode 1

3 Is immortality something to be wished for?

A. Pick out as much information as you can about the character (Who?) and his situation (Where?, What?, Why?)

B. What has science allowed the doctors to do?

C. Explain the character's reaction at the end. What does he think about immortality?

D. Look at the picture. How is immortality made possible in *Altered Carbon*?

"Hello, Mr. Blaine," she said. "I'm Marie Thorne [...] where do you suppose you are?"

"Looks like a hospital. I suppose —" He stopped. He had just noticed a small microphone in her hand.

"Yes, what do you suppose?" She made a small gesture. Men came forward and wheeled heavy equipment around his bed. [...]

"To hell with that," Blaine said moodily, watching the men set up their machines around him. "What is this? What is going on?" [...].

"Do you remember the accident?" she asked.

"What accident?"

"Do you remember being hurt?" [...]

"Yes. The steering wheel broke. I got it through the chest. Then my head hit."

"Look at your chest," she said softly.

Blaine looked. His chest, beneath white pajamas, was unmarked. "Impossible!" he cried. [...]

Blaine looked at his undamaged body and remembered the accident. "I can't believe it!" he cried. [...] "I remember the accident," Blaine said. "I remember the smashing, I remember — dying." [...].

She said, "Look carefully at your body, Mr. Blaine. Here's a mirror. Look at your face."

Blaine looked, and shivered like a man in fever. He touched the mirror, then ran shaking fingers over his face. "It isn't my face! Where's my face? Where did you put my body and face?"

He was in a nightmare from which he could never awaken. [...] Marie Thorne bent low over him with her pretty, blank face, and from her small red mouth came gentle nightmare words.

"Your body is dead, Mr. Blaine, killed in an automobile accident. You can remember its dying. But we managed to save that part of you that really counts. We saved your mind, Mr. Blaine, and have given you a new body for it." [...].

"And I am really born again in a different body?"

She nodded again, waiting. Blaine looked at her, and at the shadow men tending their cardboard machines. Why were they bothering him? Why couldn't they go pick on some other dead man? Corpses shouldn't be forced to answer questions. Death was man's ancient privilege, his immemorial pact with life, granted to the slave as well as the noble. Death was man's solace, and his right. But perhaps they had revoked that right; and now you couldn't evade your responsibilities simply by being dead.

Immortality, Inc.,
Robert Sheckley, 1959

Still from the series *Altered Carbon*

YOUR TURN! 4 Present your invention!

You have created a new cure which might make humans immortal. Explain what you have achieved, and discuss it (goal, use...) with another scientist who believes it is a violation of the laws of nature.

CHOOSE YOUR

PROJECT!

YOUR PROJECT #1

The producers of *Black Mirror* have decided to deal with transhumanism from a post-apocalyptic perspective. They are looking for new screenwriters to imagine the story of their next episode entitled: "The Last Human's Rebellion". Take part in the contest!

STEP 1 Define the identity of the characters (name, age...) and timeline.

STEP 2 Prepare a draft of your story. Tell the producers what has happened to the characters and explain the link with transhumanism. Your plot must answer the following questions: Who? Where? When? What? and Why? (75 words)

STEP 3 Write the synopsis of your episode. (150 words)

TIPS

- Talk about the characters' feelings.
- Leave a cliff-hanger so people want to discover the series.
- Proofread your synopsis.

OR

YOUR PROJECT #2

Groupwork. Your company has developed a technology which will give immortality to its users (anti-aging drug, nanomedicine, cryonics...) and you have been asked to defend the project.

STEP 1 In groups, work on a presentation stressing the benefits of your invention.
- Describe the technology your company has created (name, how it works, and the tests you have run.)
- Explain the advantages it would bring to the users, and the point of being immortal.
- Find a catchy slogan to promote your technology.

STEP 2 Rehearse your presentation. Remember that each member of the group has to participate. Be ready to answer the jury's (your classmates) questions.

STEP 3 In class, present your project to the jury of the next *Perl-UNC Prize for NeuroScience* and answer their questions and concerns about your invention.

TIPS

- Use a slideshow to present your invention.
- Use link words to structure your presentation
- Do not read your notes.

- Audio words
- MP3
- Interactive Test

SPICE UP YOUR VOCABULARY

Use the vocabulary below to create your own mind map and add more words if necessary!

Verbs & Expressions

- advocate
- allow / enable /ɪ'neɪbəl/ someone to do sth
- augment
- bioengineer
- decrease /dɪ'kriːs/ the risks
- discover
- do research into
- enhance /ɪn'hɑːns/
- evolve
- frighten /'fraɪtn/: *faire peur*
- improve /ɪm'pruːv/
- legalize
- make a mistake
- oppose sth
- print cells / human tissues / organs
- replace
- seek perfection
- serve mankind
- transplant
- upgrade /ʌp'greɪd/

Adjectives

- artificial
- augmented
- bionic /baɪ'ɒnɪk/
- efficient /ɪ'fɪʃənt/
- ethical ≠ unethical
- everlasting
- futuristic
- genetically-modified
- groundbreaking /'graʊndbreɪkɪŋ/
- human
- immortal
- improved
- incurable /ɪn'kjʊərəbəl/
- life-changing
- safe ≠ dangerous
- upload ≠ download

Nouns

- achievement
- artificial Intelligence (A.I.)
- biomedicine / 'baɪəʊ-'medsɪn/
- breakthrough /'breɪkθruː/
- cloning
- consciousness /'kɒnʃəsnɪs/
- DNA modification
- engineer /endʒə'nɪə/
- enhancement /ɪn'hɑːnsmənt/
- eternal life
- ethical debate
- exoskeleton /'eksəʊskelətən/ / suit of armour
- failed attempts
- genetics
- implant
- invention
- inventor
- laboratory
- mechanical augmentation
- potential
- scientist /'saɪəntɪst/
- skill = ability = capacity
- the astounding progress of…
- utopia ≠ dystopia

UP TO YOU!

★1. Find an antonym or a synonym of the following elements.

A. create ≠ …
B. improve = …
C. failure ≠ …
D. scare = …

★2. Find the odd word out. Justify your answer.

A. improve • enhance • magnify • diminish
B. everlasting • transient • eternal • undying
C. mistake • error • flawless • fail
D. obsolete • groundbreaking • visionary • novel

★★3. Complete the sentences using the right inventions.

3D printer • exoskeletons • mechanical prosthesis • mind-uploading • bionic eyes

A. The soldier had his left arm replaced by a … after the explosion.
B. In the future, … could allow humans to overcome the death of their bodies and be immortal.
C. Some surgeons now use a … so as to build implants and new organs for their patients.
D. Scientists are developing … to help disabled people to walk again.
E. The creation of … should enable the blind to see again.

★★★4. Complete the following review of *Robocop* (2014) using words related to transhumanism.

exoskeleton • robot • superhuman • science-fiction • man • programmable

"In this month's reboot of the classic "RoboCop" film, scientists create a … crime fighter that is half- …, half- … — a human outfitted with a robotic … and whose brain is … like a machine. But although such Frankenstein-esque lab experiments make for good Hollywood entertainment, being able to create a real cyborg is still more in the realm of …— at least for now, experts say."

www.nbcnews.com

5. Interactive test! What is your score?

RULE THE GRAMMAR!

EXPRIMER LA PROBABILITÉ

- **Les adverbes**

On peut exprimer la probabilité en utilisant des **adverbes** qui indiquent une probabilité plus ou moins grande comme : *perhaps, probably, surely, assuredly, definitely*, etc.

- **Les auxiliaires modaux**

On a aussi recours aux **auxiliaires modaux** pour exprimer la probabilité. Il y a donc une gradation du moins probable au plus probable.

Formation

- Les modaux ne prennent pas de -*s* à la troisième personne.
- Ils s'utilisent sans ***do / did*** pour former les formes interrogative ou négative.
- Ils ne sont jamais précédés de *to*.

Utilisation

- Il est impossible que cela se produise : *This technology **can't** already exist.*
- Il y a une petite possibilité : *This technology **might** already exist.*
- Il est possible que : *This technology **may** / (**can**) already exist.*
- C'est fortement probable : *This technology **must** already exist.*
- On utilise ***can*** au lieu de ***may*** dans une langue moins soignée.

→ P.306

LE *PRESENT PERFECT*

- **Formation**

On utilise l'auxiliaire ***have*** au présent et le **participe passé** du verbe.

*The sales of exoskeletons **have increased**.*

- **Emploi**

On utilise essentiellement le *present perfect* pour présenter **le résultat d'une action débutée dans le passé** et qui a des conséquences ou des effets dans le présent :

***Since 2016** technology relative to exoskeletons **has reached** the general public.* (Les gens sont maintenant au courant de cette technologie.)

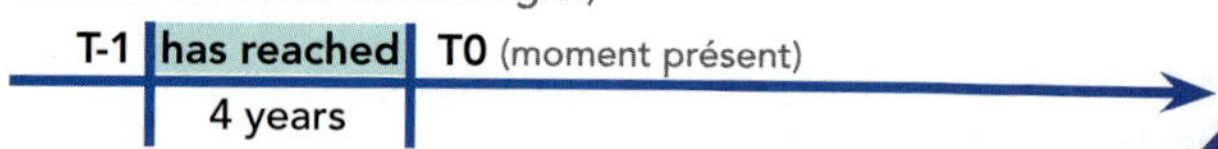

→ P.299

LE PRÉTÉRIT MODAL (PRÉTÉRIT IMAGINAIRE)

- On utilise cette forme pour exprimer une supposition, un souhait, une possibilité.
- On l'utilise souvent là où le français utilise le subjonctif : *I wish he **came**.* (J'aimerais qu'il vienne.)
- Certaines expressions déclenchent son utilisation :

If* ou *as if

*If I **lived** forever I **would behave** differently.* (irréel du présent)
*If he **had been** aware (**Had** he **been** aware) of this technology, he **would have used** it.* (irréel du passé)

Would rather / It is (high) time

*I'd rather you **didn't raise** your hopes!*
*It is time we **realised** eternal life is within our reach.*

Wish

*I **wish** he **were** still alive.* (irréel du présent)
*We **wish** you **had known** about this new cure.* (irréel du passé)
*I **wish** I **would be equipped** with this exoskeleton* (souhait)

→ P.305

UP TO YOU!

★ 1. Rewrite these sentences as shown in the example.

E.g.: If only you listened to your doctor. → I wish you listened to your doctor.

A. If only he believed in the progress of science.
B. If only you took the test.
C. If only everybody were as knowledgeable as you.
D. If only Susan were more ethically aware.
E. If only scientists were sure of themselves.

★ 2. Rewrite the following sentences as shown in the example.

E.g.: It is time he realised what is now possible.
→ It is time for you to realise what is now possible.

A. It is time they made rapid progress.
B. It is time Paul changed his mind about the future of mankind.
C. It is time she accepted these new theories.
D. It is time doctors became aware of these new possibilities.
E. It is time we opened a new chapter in the history of mankind.
F. It is time you stopped believing in all this nonsense!

★★ 3. Put the verbs in the present perfect.

A. Science *(become)* incredibly frightening.
B. These new technologies *(hit)* the market unexpectedly.
C. He *(not forget)* what he learnt at University.
D. It's a good job he *(catch)* her before she told anyone.
E. They *(hide)* their discovery because they thought it might frighten people.
F. Jenny *(not speak)* to anyone about her operation.

★★ 4. Put the verbs in the appropriate tense (preterite or present perfect).

A. She *(be)* over the moon when she *(make)* that discovery.
B. You *(come)* to the conclusion that this vaccine wouldn't work.
C. He *(realise)* he had been too optimistic.
D. They *(develop)* some revolutionary drugs.
E. We *(start)* panicking when we *(think)* of the consequences.
F. They never *(feel)* so fit.

★★ 5. Rephrase the sentences using a modal auxiliary.

A. There is a remote possibility that he will succeed.
B. It is possible she will find the cure to this disease.
C. These results are undoubtedly correct.
D. There is a chance we will live forever.
E. I'm certain the Chinese already know this protocol.
F. There's no way it is true.

★★★ 6. Translate into English.

A. *Les exosquelettes sont l'avenir de l'humanité.*
B. *La vie éternelle a toujours été une chimère* (chimera).
C. *Ils n'ont pas pris en compte les questions éthiques.*
D. *Nous aurions aimé faire cette découverte à temps.*
E. *Il est temps qu'ils se rendent compte que c'est une impasse.*
F. *Je préfèrerais qu'ils ne lui mettent pas ses idées en tête.*

OPEN YOUR EARS!

PHONOLOGY

1. Le « h » initial

• Le *h* initial est prononcé comme un /h/ **expiré**, comme si l'on voulait faire de la buée sur un miroir. Écoutez les mots suivants et entrainez-vous à les répéter. **MP3 N°91**

helping • human • how • humanity • hell • hospital

• Attention, on ne prononce généralement pas le ***h*** dans *he, him, her…* sauf quand ils sont accentués à des fins de mise en relief. Ex : *"Tell her that I love her."*

• Dans un petit nombre de mots (et leurs dérivés), le ***h*** initial n'est pas prononcé.
Ex : *honour • honourable • hour • hourly • honest • honesty • heir • heirloom*

2. La terminaison en *-ic*

Écoutez les mots suivants se terminant en *-ic*. Que remarquez-vous ? **MP3 N°92**

ethic • genetic • biomechanics • symbiotic

3. Les voyelles adjacentes

• Écoutez les mots suivants et déterminez le nombre de syllabes de chaque mot. Que remarquez-vous ? **MP3 N°93**

science • hierarchy • biology • create

• Conclusion : Dans ces mots les deux voyelles adjacentes ne fonctionnent pas comme une unité (digraphe) mais doivent être prononcées indépendamment les unes des autres.

Picture challenge

★ 3 sentences
★★ 4 to 6 sentences
★★★ 7 sentences and +

How many sentences can you make using what you have learnt? Collect stars!

AXE 6

UNIT 19

DOCTOR FRANKENSTEIN

What can Mary Shelley's classic teach us today?

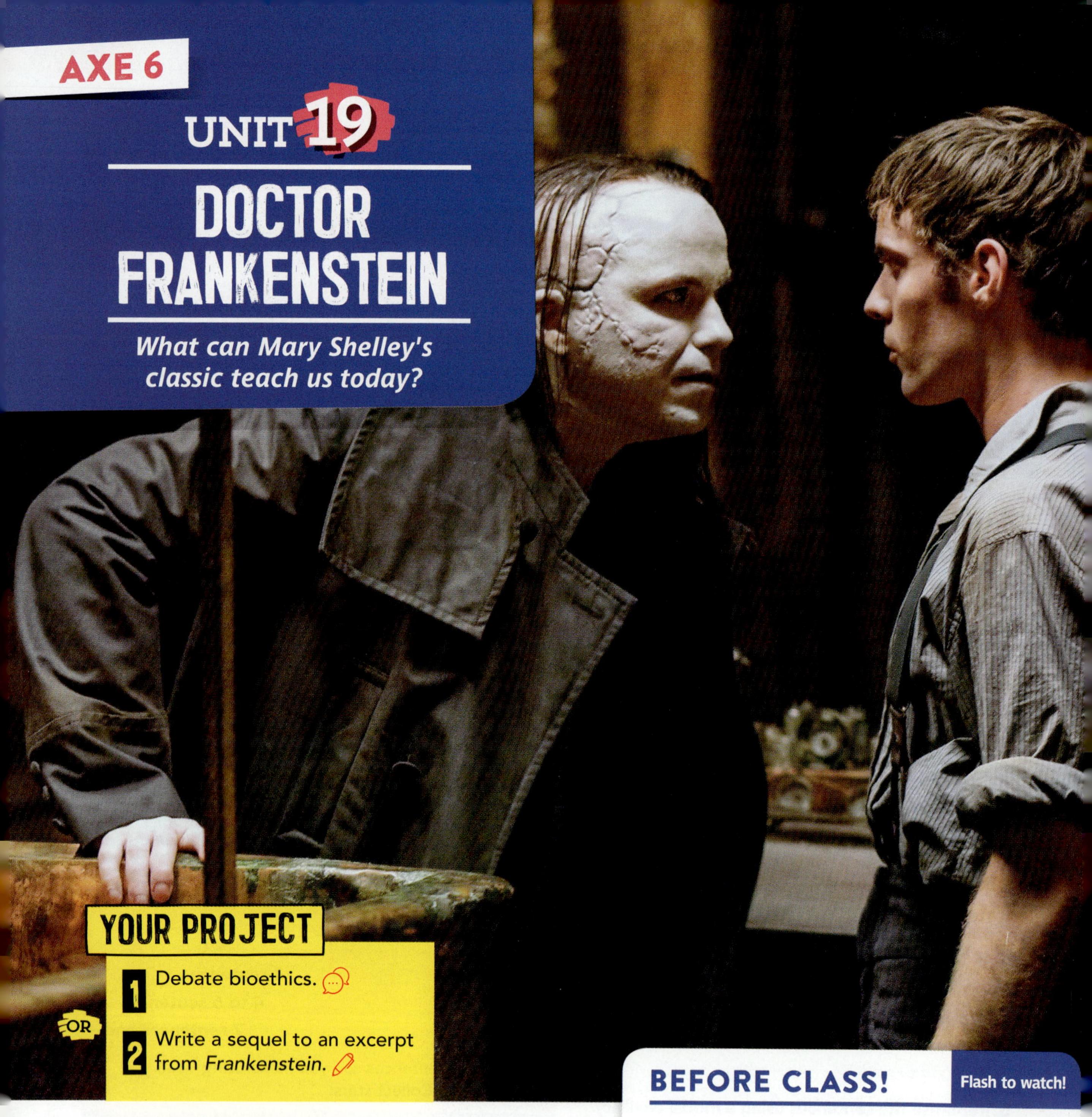

YOUR PROJECT

1 Debate bioethics.

OR

2 Write a sequel to an excerpt from *Frankenstein.*

BEFORE CLASS!

Flash to watch!

Watch the video and be ready to talk about it in class!

VIDEO N°35

Au menu de cette unité :

DÉCOUVERTES CULTURELLES

- Le contexte de création du roman *Frankenstein; or, The Modern Prometheus*
- Les questions bioéthiques soulevées dans le roman
- Le Dr. Frankenstein et sa créature : deux personnages majeurs de la littérature anglo-saxonne

OUTILS LINGUISTIQUES

- Les deux prétérits
- Le *pluperfect*
- Les adverbes

❶ "Frankenstein" As A Cautionary Tale

How does Mary Shelley's novel still echo our fears about new discoveries?

1 Frankenstein and bioethics

A. Read the article. According to the journalist, what are the risks of scientific innovations?
B. Why is Dr Frankenstein's behaviour considered unethical?
C. What were the consequences of his experiment?
D. Have your say. What can scientists do to avoid "becoming monstrous"?

HELP!
- Frankenstein /ˈfræŋkənstaɪn/

Shelley's story has been used many times since its publication to express fears about new technologies and the risks of scientific overreach[1]—fears that were later often recognised as unfounded. *Frankenstein* was evoked with regard to organ transplantation in the mid-20th century, in-vitro fertilisation in the 1970s, and genetically engineered "Frankenfoods" and animal cloning in the 1990s. Today, the gene editing technology CRISPR has aroused[2] concerns in some quarters about the effects of tampering with human genomes.

These anxieties resonate with Shelley's account of Dr Frankenstein's choices. He was unethical not simply because he used technology to create life out of dead matter, but also because, as Catherine Belling [literary critic] points out, he did not "match his extraordinary technical success with attention to the most fundamental ethical tenet[3], the duty[4] to be responsible for the subjects and outcomes[5] of his work". Appalled[6] by the creature he brought to life, Frankenstein abandoned him. Although the monster began his life with a capacity for love and kindness, when he was rejected by his creator and society, he became angry and vengeful instead.

Even in 1818, Shelley saw that new technology alone was not a threat, but that ethical problems could arise when humans use technology for wealth, status, or sheer ambition without thinking carefully about the possible dangers of their work. If we become indifferent to consequences and unwilling to take responsibility for our actions, we, like Dr Frankenstein, risk becoming monstrous.

1 *fait dépasser les limites* • **2** *suscité* • **3** *principe* • **4** *devoir* • **5** *résultats* • **6** very scared

www.thelancet.com, 24 June 2017

2 The responsibility of scientists

A. Pairwork. Pupil A listens to **MP3 N°94** and Pupil B listens to **MP3 N°95**.
B. Each pupil takes notes on what each student thinks about Dr. Frankenstein.
C. Exchange with your classmate and recap orally.
D. Do you agree with them? Justify.
E. Go further. In your own words, explain what a "grey zone" is.

HELP!

Audio 1
- rev**o**lve ar**ou**nd = be c**e**ntred on
- st**a**ndard: *critère / norme*
- emp**i**rical = based on scient**i**fic t**e**sting

Audio 2
- inqu**i**sitive: *curieux*
- purs**ui**t: *(ici) recherche*
- ach**ie**vement: *réussite*

YOUR TURN! 3 Advise future scientists

You are writing an article for a science magazine for teens: give them three pieces of advice that should be followed before carrying out a controversial experiment.

❷ The Origins of Frankenstein

What inspired Mary Shelley to imagine Frankenstein and his creature?

1 The science behind Mary Shelley's novel

A. Read the article and explain the concept of galvanism in your own words.

B. How influential was this concept for Mary Shelley? How did she use it?

Mary Shelley's *Frankenstein* has been scaring readers since 1818. But what inspired the book's overconfident doctor, who believes he can coax[1] life from death? As Sharon Ruston explains for *Public Domain Review*, part of Shelley's gothic vision began with a pair of twitching[2] frog legs.

Ruston writes that Shelley was inspired by the concept of galvanism—the idea that scientists could use electricity to stimulate or restart life. Named after Luigi Galvani, an Italian doctor, the concept came about after Galvani was able to make a frog's legs twitch when he hooked[3] the animal up to an electric charge.

Electricity was a new and barely[4] understood force when Galvani performed his experiments on dissected animals during the late 18th century, so it makes sense that people thought it might just be able to make creatures come alive after death. Ruston notes that Galvani's nephew, Giovanni Aldini, went so far as to shock dissected human corpses in pursuit of this hypothesis.

In *Frankenstein*, Shelley only mentions the word "galvanism" once in a passage where the hubristic[5] Dr. Frankenstein describes how a lecture on electricity caused him to throw away everything he knew about science. [...] "I at once gave up my former occupations, set down natural history and all its progeny as a deformed and abortive creation, and entertained the greatest disdain for a would-be science which could never even step within the threshold of real knowledge."

In the 1831 preface to *Frankenstein*, however, Ruston points out that Shelley directly acknowledges galvanism as part of the inspiration for her novel [...].

These days, of course, it's galvanism that is denied as real knowledge. [...] Yet the book that was inspired by a few twitching frog legs still lives on, nearly 200 years after it was first published.

1 *(ici) obtenir* • 2 jerking = *sursaut* = *spasme* • 3 attach • 4 *à peine* • 5 exaggerated pride

Erin Blackmore, **www.smithsonianmag.com,** 4 December 2015

2 Frankenstein in 1931

A. Describe the film poster.

B. Groupwork. Watch the trailer online. The class is divided into four. Each part of the class focuses on one element: catchphrases, the characters and their feelings, the atmosphere, the plot. Then recap in groups and report back to the class.

HELP!

- fiendish /ˈfiːndɪʃ/ = devilish /ˈdevəlɪʃ/
- gloomy = dark
- limb /lɪm/= body part
- spine-tingling: *à vous donner des frissons*
- be terrified / scared by
- bring back from the dead
- prey on: *s'attaquer*
- strike terror

3 The birth of a monster

A. Groupwork. Each group works on one part of the text.
- Give a title to the paragraph and prepare a short summary of your part.
- Each group presents the text to the other groups.

B. Using the title and information given by the other groups, put the paragraphs in the right order.

C. Read the text in the right order and analyse Doctor Frankenstein's feelings.

Frankenstein; or, The Modern Prometheus *was written by the English novelist Mary Shelley and is considered as gothic and science-fiction literature.*

Part A

How can I describe my emotions at this catastrophe, or how delineate[1] the wretch[2] whom with such infinite pains and care I had endeavoured to form? His limbs were in proportion, and I had selected his features as beautiful. Beautiful! Great God! His yellow skin scarcely covered the work of muscles and arteries beneath; his hair was of a lustrous black, and flowing; his teeth of a pearly whiteness; but these luxuriances only formed a more horrid contrast with his watery eyes, that seemed almost of the same colour as the dun-white sockets in which they were set, his shrivelled[3] complexion and straight black lips.

1 describe • 2 *misérable* • 3 *flétri*

Part B

The different accidents of life are not so changeable as the feelings of human nature. I had worked hard for nearly two years, for the sole purpose of infusing life into an inanimate body. For this I had deprived myself of rest and health. I had desired it with an ardour that far exceeded moderation; but now that I had finished, the beauty of the dream vanished, and breathless horror and disgust filled my heart. Unable to endure the aspect of the being I had created, I rushed out of the room and continued a long time traversing my bedchamber, unable to compose my mind to sleep. At length lassitude succeeded to the tumult I had before endured, and I threw myself on the bed in my clothes, endeavouring to seek a few moments of forgetfulness.

Part C

It was on a dreary night of November, that I beheld the accomplishment of my toils[1]. With an anxiety that almost amounted to agony, I collected the instruments of life around me, that I might infuse a spark of being into the lifeless thing that lay at my feet. It was already one in the morning; the rain pattered dismally against the panes, and my candle was nearly burnt out, when, by the glimmer of the half-extinguished light, I saw the dull yellow eye of the creature open; it breathed hard, and a convulsive motion agitated its limbs.

1 work very hard

Part D

But it was in vain; I slept, indeed, but I was disturbed by the wildest dreams. I thought I saw Elizabeth, in the bloom of health, walking in the streets of Ingolstadt. Delighted and surprised, I embraced her, but as I imprinted the first kiss on her lips, they became livid with the hue of death; her features appeared to change, and I thought that I held the corpse of my dead mother in my arms; a shroud[1] enveloped her form, and I saw the grave-worms[2] crawling in the folds of the flannel. I started from my sleep with horror; a cold dew covered my forehead, my teeth chattered, and every limb became convulsed; when, by the dim and yellow light of the moon, as it forced its way through the window shutters, I beheld the wretch–the miserable monster whom I had created.

1 a cloth that is wrapped around a corpse • 2 *vers de terre*

Frankenstein, Mary Shelley, 1818

❸ A Monster or a Human Being?

Should the creature be killed or loved?

1 Looking for affection

A. Observe the images from this graphic novel. What is going on?
B. Read the speech bubbles. Compare the father's attitude to his children's.
C. Focus on the Creature's attitude in the first frame and in the last one. How does he evolve? Why, what did he decide to do?
D. **Go further.** What does the reaction of the children tell you about humans and the unknown?

The Creature had spent weeks observing the family and learning their ways, hoping to communicate with them.

1 wanderer: *vagabond*
2 despair: *se désespérer*
3 turn someone away: *chasser quelqu'un*
4 tear (tore-torn): *arracher, séparer (ici)*
5 wage war against/on: *partir en guerre contre*
6 bitterness: *amertume*

***Frankenstein*, Bampton & Williams, 2014**

2 Who is the monster?

A. Look at the characters on the poster of the play: what is surprising?
B. Pairwork. Watch the trailer online (www.lienmini.fr/htr-tle-19). Focus on the catchphrases, the characters's personalities, the atmosphere and the setting. Look at the actors: what do you notice, at the end? What is original? Share the information in pairs.
C. Go further. Explain the stage director's choices.

HELP!

Words
- stage: *scène*
- staging: *mise en scène*
- alternate
- direct: *réaliser/mettre en scène*
- play God: *se prendre pour Dieu*
- smash hit = big success

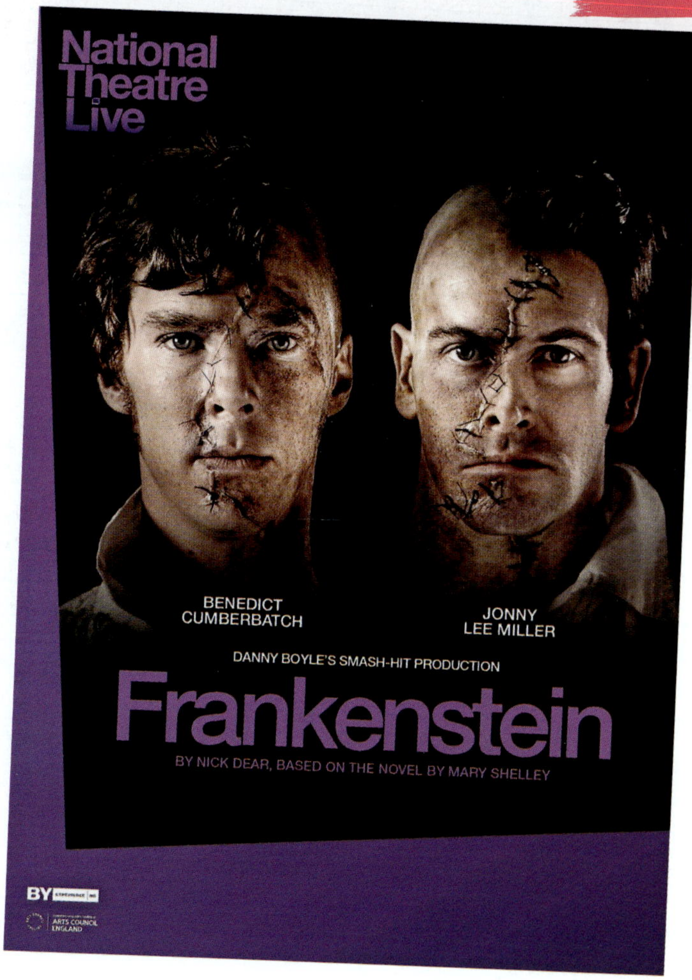

3 A conversation between maker and creature

A. Read and listen to the scene on **MP3 N°96**. What are the characters' feelings?
B. Imagine what the creature's request could be.
C. Pairwork. Choose your role and get ready to act it out!
D. Have your say. Should the scientist be held responsible for his/her invention?

VICTOR FRANKENSTEIN – Are you here? [...] Where are you? Show yourself, you monstrous thing!
Victor circles the Creature.
What an achievement[1]! [...] God, the madness of that night – [...] the moment when I saw it crawl[2] towards me, and I – and I –
CREATURE – You ran away.
VICTOR FRANKENSTEIN – What?
CREATURE – You abandoned me.
VICTOR FRANKENSTEIN (*stunned*[3]) – It speaks!
CREATURE – Yes, Frankenstein. It speaks. [...] Why did you abandon me?
VICTOR FRANKENSTEIN – I was terrified – What had I done?
CREATURE – Built a man, and given him life –
VICTOR FRANKENSTEIN – Well, now I have come to take it away –
CREATURE (*laughs*) – Oh, have you?
VICTOR FRANKENSTEIN – I have come to kill you!
CREATURE – To kill me? Why then did you create me?
VICTOR FRANKENSTEIN – To prove that I could!
CREATURE – So you make sport with[4] my life?
VICTOR FRANKENSTEIN – In the cause of science! You were my greatest experiment – but an experiment that has gone wrong. An experiment that must be curtailed!
Victor runs at him and attacks him with a knife, but the Creature swiftly disarms him and throws him to the ground.
CREATURE – Be still, genius! I have a request.

1 *réussite* • 2 *ramper* • 3 very surprised • 4 make fun of

***Frankenstein*, Nick Dear,**
based on the novel by Mary Shelley, Scene Twenty-Four, 2011

❹ A Lonely Creature

Is the creature's request ethical?

1 Looking for happiness

A. Read the text and take the vocabulary quest! Worksheet n°39

B. Analyse the creature's arguments.
Is there an evolution in Doctor Frankenstein's feelings? Why?

"You must create a female for me with whom I can live [...]. This you alone can do ; and I demand it of you as a right which you must not refuse."

[...] "I do refuse it," I replied; "and no torture shall ever extort[1] a consent from me. You may render me the most miserable of men, but you shall never make me base[2] in my own eyes. Shall I create another like yourself, whose joint wickedness[3] might desolate the world. Begone[4]! I have answered you; you may torture me, but I will never consent."

"You are in the wrong," replied the fiend[5]; "and, instead of threatening[6], I am content to reason with you. I am malicious because I am miserable, am I not shunned[7] and hated by all mankind? You, my creator, would tear me to pieces and triumph; remember that, and tell me why I should pity man more than he pities me? You would not call it murder if you could precipitate me into one of those ice-rifts, and destroy my frame, the work of your own hands. Shall I respect man when he contemns me? [...] I will revenge my injuries; if I cannot inspire love, I will cause fear; and chiefly towards you my arch-enemy[8], because my creator, do I swear inextinguishable hatred[9]. Have a care: I will work at your destruction, nor finish until I desolate your heart, so that you curse the hour of your birth."

A fiendish rage animated him as he said this; his face was wrinkled[10] into contortions too horrible for human eyes to behold; but presently he calmed himself and proceeded– " [...] What I ask of you is reasonable and moderate; I demand a creature of another sex, but as hideous as myself [...]. It is true, we shall be monsters, cut off from all the world; but on that account we shall be more attached to one another. Our lives will not be happy, but they will be harmless[11] and free from the misery I now feel. Oh! My creator, make me happy; let me feel gratitude towards you for one benefit! Let me see that I excite the sympathy of some existing thing; do not deny me my request!"

I was moved. I shuddered[12] when I thought of the possible consequences of my consent, but I felt that there was some justice in his argument. His tale and the feelings he now expressed proved him to be a creature of fine sensations, and did I not, as his maker, owe him all the portion of happiness that it was in my power to bestow[13]?

1 extorquer • 2 ignoble • 3 vilénie • 4 va-t'en • 5 monster • 6 menaçant• 7 mal aimé • 8 ennemi juré • 9 haine • 10 plissée • 11 inoffensif • 12 trembler, frémir • 13 accorder

Frankenstein,
Mary Shelley, 1818

YOUR TURN! 2 Class Debate

Class debate. Use the text above and your personal knowledge to answer the following question: Who is the monster, Dr Frankenstein or his creature?

3 "To be or not to be"

A. Read the first thought bubble. Why did Doctor Frankenstein decide to leave his country?
B. Read the other speech bubbles and analyse his feelings.
C. Add a speech bubble with the monster's thoughts!

HELP!

Words
- have mixed **feelings** about sth
- be **doubtful** /ˈdaʊtfəl/
- doubt something
- be impatient / can't wait to
- ethical: *éthique*
- unethical ≠ ethical
- immoral

In this adaptation, Dr Frankenstein decided to agree to the creature's request.

Mary Shelley's Frankenstein, Burgan & Calero, 2014

YOUR PROJECT

1. You have been invited to NPR to debate bioethics. The main question is: "How big a role should ethics play in scientists' decisions about their research?"

OR

2. Write a sequel to the excerpt from *Frankenstein* p. 210.

SPICE UP YOUR VOCABULARY

Use the vocabulary below to create your own mind map and add more words if necessary!

Nouns

- achievement /ə'tʃiːvmənt/
- breakthrough
- creature /'kriːtʃə/
- ethics
- experiment /ɪk'sperɪmənt/
- fault
- guilt: *culpabilité*
- hatred
- invention
- inventor
- morality: *principes moraux*
- responsibility
- scientist /'saɪəntɪst/
- standard: *critère*
- research
- researchers
- risk

Adverbs

- dismally /'dɪzməli/ = sadly
- happily
- scarcely /'skeəsli/: *rarement*
- tragically /'trædʒɪkli/

Adjectives

- cautious: *précautionneux*
- cautionary = giving a warning
- concerned
- conscientious: *consciencieux*
- ethical /'eθɪkəl/ ≠ unethical
- gloomy /'gluːmi/
- harmless
- hideous /'hɪdiəs/
- narrow-minded ≠ open-minded
- spine-tingling /'spaɪntɪŋlɪŋ/ = spine-chilling /'spaɪntʃɪlɪŋ/
- stunned /stʌnd/
- scrupulous /'skruːpjələs/ ≠ unscrupulous /ʌn'skruːpjələs/
- risky = dangerous
- scientific
- sensible = reasonable
- worried

Verbs & Expressions

- achieve /ə'tʃiːv/ = accomplish
- be careful ≠ be careless about
- be strict with
- be tempted to do
- blame /bleɪm/ sb for + sth/V-ing
- carry out an experiment = conduct an experiment
- disapprove of sth/sb
- doubt sth /daʊt/: *douter de qqchose*
- experiment with/in/on
- know right from wrong
- learn by trial and error
- overreach /əʊvə'riːtʃ/ = go beyond limits
- research into
- serve mankind
- strike terror = terrify
- take responsibility for
- threaten /'θretən/

RULE THE GRAMMAR!

LE *PLUPERFECT*

• Formation

- Le *pluperfect* se forme avec l'auxiliaire *have* au prétérit, ***had***, et du verbe au **participe passé** (*-ed* pour les verbes réguliers, troisième colonne de la liste pour les verbes irréguliers → rabat VI).

- À l'oral, on utilise souvent la forme contractée de *had* (*'d*) et de *had not* (*'d not* ou *hadn't*).

Victor Frankenstein **had brought** the creature back to life.

• Utilisation

- On utilise le *pluperfect* pour exprimer l'antériorité d'un évènement passé par rapport à un autre moment passé.

*When Victor Frankenstein realised what he **had done**, it was too late.*

- On utilise ***had*** + ***been*** + V ***-ing*** quand une action est toujours d'actualité au moment du passé où on la considère.

*He **had been working** on his creature for months when he realised it was dangerous.*

- On utilise *just* avec le *pluperfect* quand on veut signifier qu'une action est récente par rapport à un évènement passé.

*Victor **had just** finished when he realised it was a terrible mistake.*

- Le *pluperfect* s'utilise aussi pour la concordance des temps dans un discours rapporté. Il peut remplacer soit un prétérit soit un *present perfect*.

Prétérit : *He created a monster. → She said he **had** created a monster.*

Present Perfect : *He has created a monster. → She said he **had** created a monster.*

→ P.302

LANGUAGE LAB

- Audio words
- MP3
- Interactive Test

★1. Fill in the blanks with words or expressions related to science.

scientific • carry out experiments • experience • play God • do research

A. Doctor Frankenstein realised too late that he shouldn't have … .
B. Most scientists … in order to find new treatments.
C. They … to help people and find new vaccines.
D. The creature's … among men was disappointing so he had to leave.
E. … discoveries sometimes go too far.

★★2. A. Fill in this text with the preterite simple or preterite *be-ing*.

Frankenweenie *(be)* very sad when his dog *(die)*. On a stormy night, he *(have)* a very interesting dream: what if he *(bring)* him back to life? He *(think)* about it when he *(hear)* a dog barking in the distance. He *(decide)* to do it even if it *(seem)* crazy! He *(take)* his dead dog to his laboratory.
He *(work)* very hard when the lightning *(strike)* his dog's body. He instantly *(wake)* up! They *(be)* so happy to be together again! They *(cuddle)* when the sun *(begin)* to rise, announcing a new day.

B. Finish the story: add the very last sentence.

★★★3. Choose the right word or expression derived from the word "dead" to fill in the blanks.

living-dead • dead • deadly • deadly silence • bring somebody back from the dead

A. Doctor Frankenstein had this crazy idea to … !
B. Yesterday, I saw some …, zombies if you prefer, walking in the middle of the road!
C. Frankenstein's creature isn't really alive but we can also say that he is …!
D. The other humans thought he was a … creature who wanted to kill them.
E. In films, zombies usually come at night in a terrifying …!

★★★★4. Put the verbs in the preterite or the pluperfect.

A. Doctor Frankenstein *(choose)* different body parts when he *(start)* his experiment.
B. He *(not think)* about the consequences and now he *(feel)* miserable.
C. The monster *(turn)* out to be more human than his maker … ever … *(be)*.
D. He *(feel)* so lonely that he *(ask)* him to make a female.

5. Interactive test! What is your score?

OPEN YOUR EARS!

PHONOLOGY

La prononciation de « th ».

- « th » se prononce soit en faisant vibrer les cordes vocales **/ð/**, comme dans *the*, soit sans les faire vibrer **/θ/**, comme dans *three*.

• Écoutez les mots suivants en faisant attention à la prononciation de <*th*> et classez-les dans le tableau. Que remarquez-vous ? **MP3 N°97**

bioethics • although • threat • that • threshold • these • health • birth • then • threw • those • breath • than • breathe

/ð/	/θ/
…	…

AUDIO MYSTERY **MP3 N°98**

Listen to the recording and solve the mystery!

Picture challenge

★ 3 sentences
★★ 4 to 6 sentences
★★★ 7 sentences and +

How many sentences can you make using what you have learnt? Collect stars!

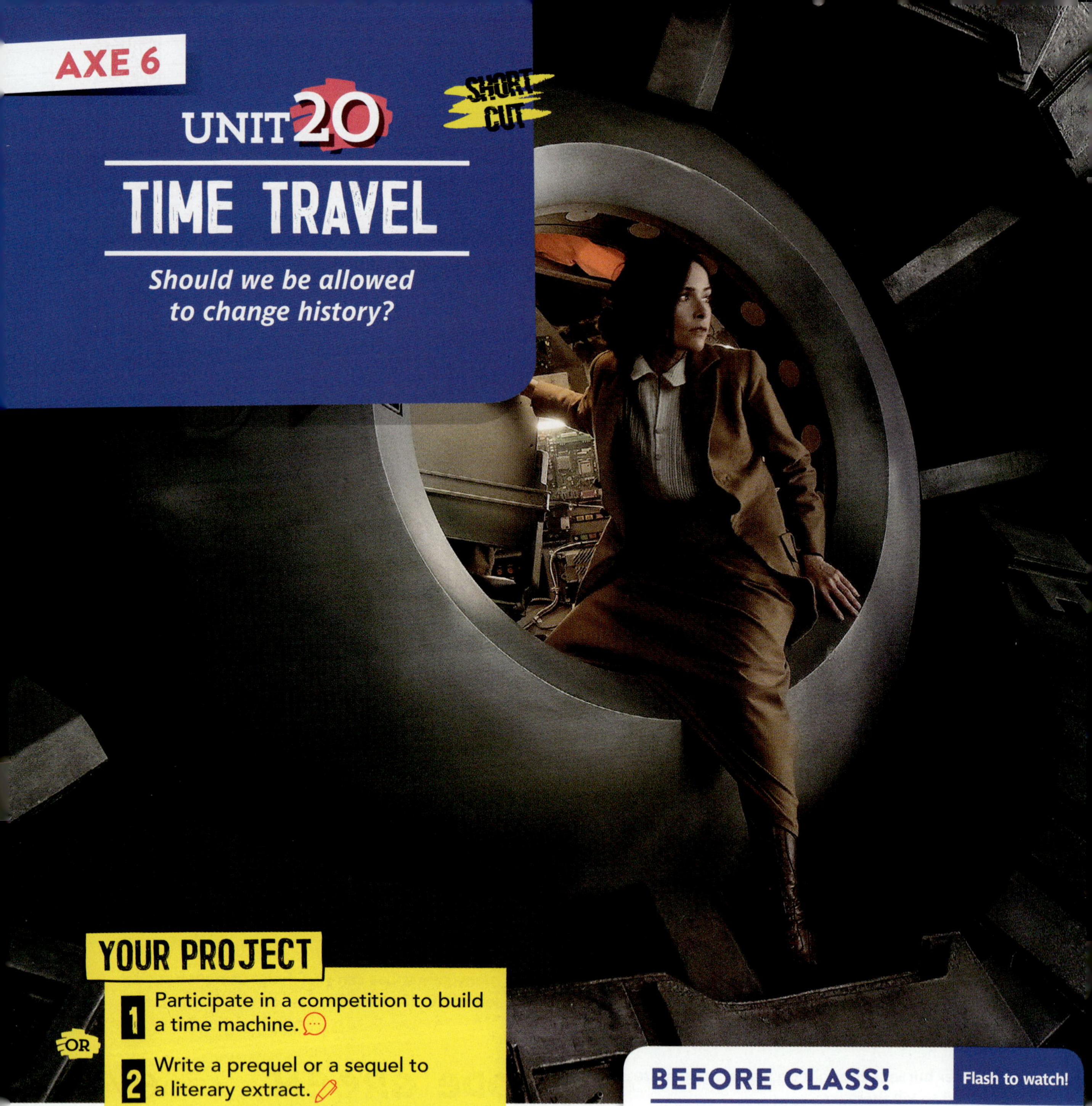

AXE 6

UNIT 20

SHORT CUT

TIME TRAVEL

Should we be allowed to change history?

YOUR PROJECT

1 Participate in a competition to build a time machine.

OR

2 Write a prequel or a sequel to a literary extract.

Au menu de cette unité :

DÉCOUVERTES CULTURELLES

- Les théories scientifiques sur le voyage dans le temps
- Les questions éthiques liées au voyage dans le temps à travers des œuvres de R. Bradbury et S. King

OUTILS LINGUISTIQUES

- *L'expression du futur*
- *If clauses*
- L'expression de la causalité et du but (*so that, in order to…*)

BEFORE CLASS!

Flash to watch!

Watch the trailer for Robert Zemeckis's ***Back to the Future***. Be ready to talk about it in class.

❶ The Possibility of Time Travel(ling)

Do scientists think that time travel is a crazy idea?

1 A physicist's opinion

A. Watch the video. Focus on the reasons that make time travel possible according to Dr Greene (facts, numbers, theory).

B. Orally, sum up what you have understood.

VIDEO N°36

2 All we need is a time machine

A. Look at the infographic. In your own words, explain what is represented.

B. Have your say. Do you believe in time travel?

HELP!

Nouns & Adjectives

- curved /kɜːvd/: *incurvé, courbé*
- "closed timelike curve": *courbe temporelle fermée*
- dead end: *un cul-de-sac*
- (im)probable
- intricate /ˈɪntrɪkət/ worlds
- lack of knowledge
- layers /ˈleɪərz/: *couches, strates*
- light years: *années-lumière*
- parallel universe /ˈpærəlel ˈjuːnɪvɜːs/
- short cut: *un raccourci*
- spaceshift, spacecraft (inv.)
- speed of light: *vitesse de la lumière*
- tunnel /ˈtʌnl/
- theory /ˈθɪəri/, theoretical
- the laws of physics
- (un)limited /ˈlɪmɪtɪd/
- (un)believable
- wormhole /ˈwɜːmhəʊl/: *trou de ver (sorte de tunnel* dans l'espace-temps)

Verbs & Expressions

- be likely to + *BV*
- carry out an experiment /ɪkˈsperɪmənt/
- for fear that + might
- go through /θruː/: *traverser*
- implement /ˈɪmplɪment/ an experiment
- lest + should … : *de peur que*
- light years away
- reach a new frontier
- strongly believe in sth

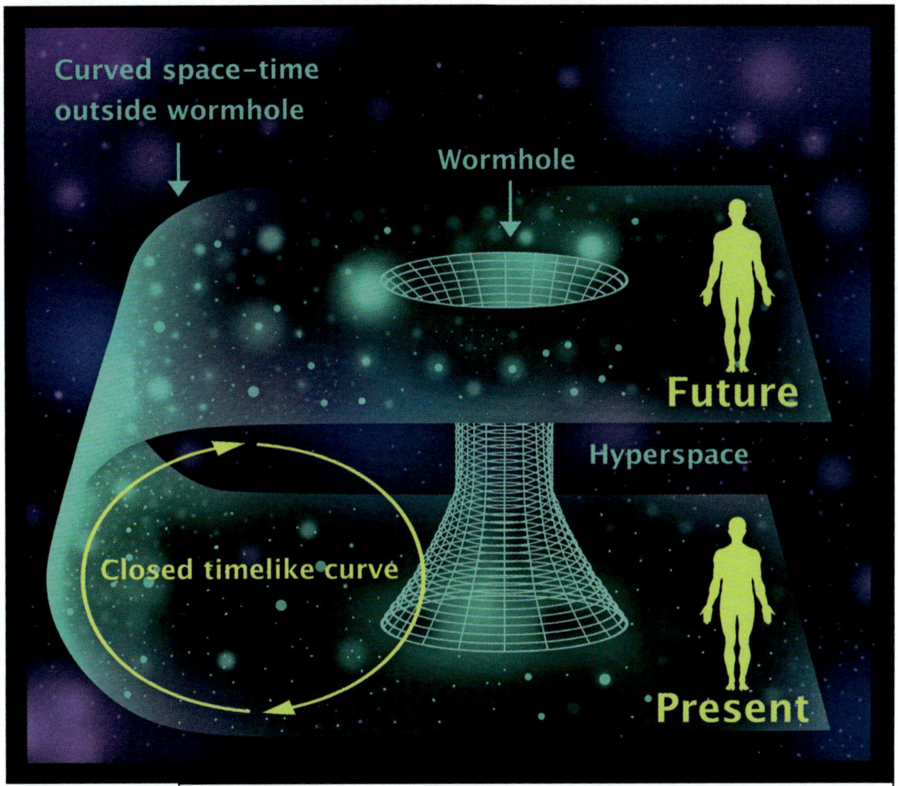

Cultural fact

The term "wormhole" was coined in the 1920s. Renowned scientists like Albert Einstein, or more recently British astrophysicist Stephen Hawking, have worked on wormholes, paving the way for future research.

❷ Rules for Time Travellers

Should time travelling have limits?

1 A Sound of Thunder

A. Describe the picture (nature / characters / objects / atmosphere).

B. Imagine what the story may be about, then read the introduction and check your hypotheses.

C. Read the text. Explain the way Travis describes his activity of time travelling.

D. What rules does Travis ask Eckles to follow? Why is it essential?

E. **Have your say.** Do you think Eckles will follow the rules? Explain.

F. **Go further.** Observe the picture on the opposite page. Imagine what has happened and write the story in about 120 words.

In the year 2055, time travel has become a practical reality. The company Time Safari Inc. offers wealthy adventurers the chance to travel back in time to hunt extinct species such as dinosaurs. A hunter named Eckels joins a hunting party led by Travis, the guide.

The Machine howled[1]. Time was a film run backward. Suns fled and ten million moons fled after them. [...]

The Machine slowed; its scream fell to a murmur. The Machine stopped.

The sun stopped in the sky.

The fog that had enveloped the Machine blew away and they were in an old time, a very old time indeed, three hunters and two Safari Heads with their blue metal guns across their knees.

"[...] The Pyramids are still in the earth, waiting to be cut out and put up. Remember that. Alexander, Caesar, Napoleon, Hitler–none of them exists." The man nodded[2].

"That" – Mr. Travis pointed – "is the jungle of sixty million two thousand and fifty-five years before President Keith."

He indicated a metal path that struck off into green wilderness, over streaming swamp[3], among giant ferns[4] and palms.

"And that," he said, "is the Path[5], laid by Time Safari for your use. It floats six inches above the earth. Doesn't touch so much as one grass blade, flower, or tree. It's an anti-gravity metal. Its purpose is to keep you from touching this world of the past in any way. Stay on the Path. Don't go off it. I repeat. Don't go off. For any reason! If you fall off, there's a penalty. And don't shoot any animal we don't okay."

"Why?" asked Eckels. [...]

"We don't want to change the Future. We don't belong here in the Past. The government doesn't like us here. We have to pay big graft[6] to keep our franchise. A Time Machine is finicky[7] business. [...]

"That's not clear," said Eckels.

"All right," Travis continued, "say we accidentally kill one mouse here. That means all the future families of this one particular mouse are destroyed, right?"

"Right?"

"And all the families of the families of the families of that one mouse! With a stamp of your foot, you annihilate first one, then a dozen, then a thousand, a million, a *billion* possible mice!"

"So they're dead," said Eckels. "So what?"

"So what?" Travis snorted[8] quietly. "Well, what about the foxes that'll need those mice to survive? For want of ten mice, a fox dies. For want of ten foxes a lion starves. For want of a lion, all manner of insects, vultures, infinite billions of life forms are thrown into chaos and destruction. Eventually it all boils down to this: fifty-nine million years later, a caveman, one of a dozen on the *entire world*, goes hunting wild boar[9] or saber-toothed tiger for food. But you, friend, have *stepped* on all the tigers in that region. By stepping on *one* single mouse. So the caveman starves. And the caveman, please note, is not just *any* expendable man, no! He is an *entire future nation*. From his loins[10] would have sprung ten sons. From *their* loins one hundred sons, and thus onward to a civilization. Destroy this one man, and you destroy a race, a people, an entire history of life. It is comparable to slaying some of Adam's grandchildren. The stomp of your foot, on one mouse, could start an earthquake, the effects of which could shake our earth and destinies down through Time, to their very foundations. With the death of that one cave man, a billion others yet unborn are throttled in the womb. Perhaps Rome never rises on its seven hills. Perhaps Europe is forever a dark forest, and only Asia waxes healthy and teeming. Step on a mouse and you crush the Pyramids. Step on a mouse and you leave your print, like a Grand Canyon, across Eternity. Queen Elizabeth might never be born, Washington might not cross the Delaware, there might never be a United States at all. So be careful. Stay on the Path. *Never* step off!"

1 hurler • 2 acquiescer • 3 marécages • 4 fougères • 5 sentier • 6 influence, dishonest use of political power • 7 difficile • 8 grogner • 9 sanglier • 10 entrailles

A Sound of Thunder,
Ray Bradbury, 1952

YOUR TURN! 2 The five laws of time travel

Groupwork. Time travel has now become a reality. As scientists, you have been asked to write a list of five fundamental laws to regulate time travel.

HELP!

Verbs & Expressions
- can't / mustn't / shouldn't
- be allowed to ≠ be forbidden to
- be respectful of
- attempt to = *tenter de*
- comply with = conform to
- obey an order
- to be expected to
- a penalty = a punishment
- cause trouble
- the course of history
- a chain of reactions / a side effect consequence, sequence of events

❸ Improving the Past

Is a righteous purpose a good reason to alter the past?

1 November 22, 1963

A. Observe the book cover and guess what the story may be about (date / people involved).
B. Browse the Internet to find more about JFK's assassination and present it briefly.
C. Read the text from line 1 to line 52. Compare Al's and Jake's arguments about time travel. Do they share the same feelings and opinion?
D. Read the second part of the text (l.53 to the end). According to Al, what consequences would this adventure have on American history?
Explain the last sentence in your own words.
E. **Class debate.** Should we be allowed to change history?

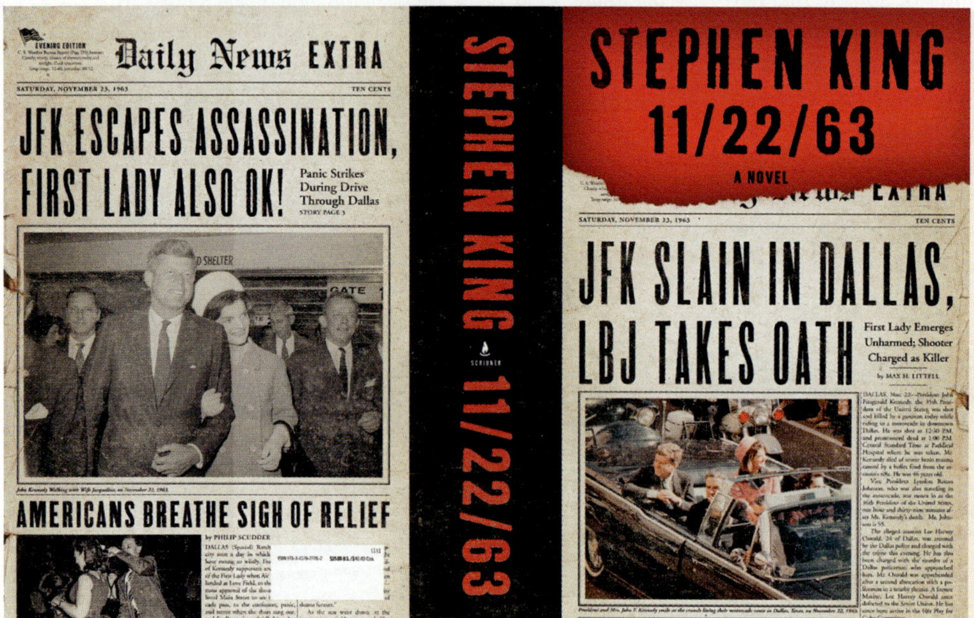

Front and back cover

Al has discovered he could time travel through a portal in the back of the diner he owns. He convinces his friend Jake to time travel. Jake has just come back from the portal.

He leaned forward, his eyes not just bright; they were blazing.

"You can change history, Jake. Do you understand that? *John Kennedy can live.*"

[...] I'd been offered a chance to become a major player not just in American history but in the history of the *world*. So yes, yes, yes, I wanted to be convinced. But I was also afraid.

"What if it went wrong?" I drank down the rest of my iced tea in four long swallows, the ice cubes clicking against my teeth. "What if I managed, God knows how, to stop it from happening and made things worse instead of better? What if I came back and discovered America had become a fascist regime? Or that the pollution had gotten so bad everybody was walking around in gas masks?"

"Then you'd go back again," he said. "Back to two minutes of twelve on September ninth of 1958. Cancel the whole thing out. Every trip is the first trip, remember?"

"Sounds good, but what if the changes were so radical your little diner wasn't even there anymore?"

He grinned[1]. "Then you'd have to live your life in the past. But would that be so bad? As an English teacher, you'd still have a marketable skill, and you wouldn't even need it. I was there for four years, Jake, and I made a small fortune. [...] There's no reason you can't live well. And I think the diner'll still be there. It has been for me, and I changed plenty of things. Anybody does. Just walking around the block to buy a loaf of bread and a quart of milk changes the future. Ever hear of the butterfly effect? [...]

"Butterfly effect."

"Right. It means small events can have large [...] ramifications. The idea is that if some guy kills a butterfly in China, maybe forty years later—or four hundred—there's an earthquake in Peru. That sound as crazy to you as it does to me?"

It did, but I remembered a hoary old time-travel paradox and pulled it out. "Yeah, but what if you went back and killed your own grandfather?"

He stared at me, baffled. "Why the fuck would you do that?"

That was a good question, so I just told him to go on.

"You changed the past this afternoon in all sorts of little ways, just by walking into the Kennebec Fruit... but the stairs leading up into the pantry and back into 2011 were still there, weren't they? And The Falls is the same as when you left it."

"So it seems, yes. But you're talking about something a little more major. To wit[2], saving JFK's life."

"Oh, I'm talking about a lot more than that, because this ain't some butterfly in China, buddy. I'm also talking about saving RFK's life, because if John lives in Dallas, Robert probably doesn't run for president in 1968. The country wouldn't have been ready to replace one Kennedy with another."

"You don't know that for sure."

"No, but listen. Do you think that if you save John Kennedy's life, his brother Robert is still at the Ambassador Hotel at twelve-fifteen in the morning on June fifth, 1968? And even if he is, is Sirhan still working in the kitchen?"

Maybe, but the chances had to be awfully small. If you introduced a million variables into an equation, of course the answer was going to change.

"Or what about Martin Luther King? Is he still in Memphis in April of '68? Even if he is, is he still standing on the balcony of the Lorraine Motel at exactly the right time for James Earl Ray to shoot him? What do you think?"

"If that butterfly theory is right, probably not."

"That's what I think, too. And if MLK lives, the race riots that followed his death don't happen. [...]. If I asked you to tell me who Lee Oswald tried to assassinate only a few months before gunning Kennedy down, you'd go 'Huh?' Because somehow all that stuff has gotten lost."

"Oswald tried to kill someone before Kennedy?" This was news to me, but most of my knowledge of the Kennedy assassination came from an Oliver Stone movie. In any case, Al didn't answer. Al was on a roll[3].

"Or what about Vietnam? Johnson was the one who started all the insane escalation. Kennedy was a cold warrior, no doubt about it, but Johnson took it to the next level. He had the same my-balls-are-bigger-than-yours complex that Dubya showed off when he stood in front of the cameras and said 'Bring it on.' Kennedy might have changed his mind. Johnson and Nixon were incapable of that. Thanks to them, we lost almost sixty thousand American soldiers in Nam[4]. The Vietnamese, North and South, lost *millions*. Is the butcher's bill that high if Kennedy doesn't die in Dallas?"

"I don't know. And neither do you, Al."

"That's true, but I've become quite the student of recent American history, and I think the chances of improving things by saving him are very good. And really, there's no downside. If things turn to shit, you just take it all back. Easy as erasing a dirty word off a chalkboard."

1 smiled • 2 *en l'occurrence* • 3 *sur sa lancée* • 4 Vietnam

11/22/63,
Stephen King, 2011

YOUR PROJECT

1. Participate in a competition to build a time machine.

Groupwork. You are scientists who will build a time machine thanks to an international competition. The best project will be designed and developed.

Present your project to the jury:

- describe your time machine (name, size, shape, technology...) using a visual;
- choose your destination (location, time period) and give reasons for exploring it.
- convince the jury that your project is worth designing and believing in!

OR

2. Write a sequel or a prequel!

Choose a text (R. Bradbury's p. 218 or S. King's). Write a sequel or a prequel to the extract.

HELP!

Verbs & Expressions

- feel p**o**werless
- go back in time
- make a diff**e**rence
- make h**i**story
- make the h**ea**dlines: *faire les gros titres*
- rewrite h**i**story
- talk sb int**o** + V-*ing* = persuade
- vanish / disapp**ea**r

Nouns & Adjectives

- able / un**a**ble to
- a br**ea**kthrough /ˈbreɪkθru/
- a p**o**rtal
- c**a**pable / inc**a**pable of + -*ing*
- c**a**reful ≠ c**a**reless
- fl**a**bbergasted = ast**ou**nded
- gr**ou**ndbreaking / revol**u**tionary invention
- pers**ua**sive
- thr**i**lled
- uns**u**re of = unc**e**rtain

RULE THE GRAMMAR!

L'EXPRESSION DU FUTUR

• On utilise ***will* + BV** quand on prévoit qu'une action va se réaliser dans l'avenir ou que l'on prend une décision soudaine.

*Time travel **will be** common by 2099!*

***I'll give** him a help with his equations.*

• On utilise le **présent + *be -ing*** quand on est certain de la réalisation future d'un évènement.

***I'm meeting** a renowned scientist tomorrow.*

• On utilise le **présent + *be* + *going to* + *BV*** quand ce que l'on prédit pour l'avenir est en lien avec la situation présente ou quand il y a *un repère temporel* précis.

*Look! **She's going to succeed!***

*Her time machine **is going to work** by next Tuesday.*

Attention, le renvoi au futur avec le présent simple est plus limité (horaires, etc.).
Voir le précis grammatical (p. 304).

→ P.303

LES *IF CLAUSES*

• Si l'hypothèse est possible sur un fait présent ou futur, on utilisera :
proposition en *if* au présent → principale au futur

If he manages to build his time machine,
*he **will be** rich.*

(S'il parvient à construire sa machine à voyager dans le temps, **il sera** riche.)

• Quand on envisage l'action comme peu probable, on peut avoir recours au prétérit :
proposition en *if* au prétérit → principale avec *would* + BV

If he managed to build his time machine,
he would be rich.

(S'il parvenait à construire sa machine à voyager dans le temps, il serait riche.)

• Deux autres constructions sont possibles pour insister un peu plus sur le caractère improbable de ce qui suit. Ces deux constructions relèvent d'un registre plus soutenu.

***If he were to manage** to build his time machine,*
he would be rich.

***If he should manage** to build his time machine,*
he would be rich.

• Pour exprimer des souhaits non encore réalisés, il y a deux possibilités : l'une avec *I wish*, l'autre avec *If only*.

I wish / *If only* } *he **would manage** to build his time machine.*

→ P.305

L'EXPRESSION DU BUT

• Pour exprimer le but, on peut utiliser les expressions ***to*, *in order to*** ou ***so as to***.

*She time travels **in order to** save President Kennedy.*

*Why not time travel to the future **so as to** know what is in store for us?*

On peut aussi utiliser ***so that*** ou ***in order that***.
On utilise ***may*** dans la subordonnée si la principale est au présent et ***might*** si elle est au passé.

• On peut aussi utiliser la structure ***for… + to…*** .

*He tells the truth **for** the entire world **to** be aware of the consequences.*

*He tells the truth **so that / in order that** the entire world **may** be aware of the consequences.*

*He told the truth **so that / in order that** the entire world **might** be aware of the consequences.*

LANGUAGE LAB

- Unit's vocabulary
- Audio words
- MP3
- Interactive Test

★ **1. Change these sentences using *be going to* instead of *will*.**

A. It will never be accepted by the general public.
B. It won't be easy for him to accept what happened.
C. This technology will be available by the next decade.
D. Life will never be the same again.

★ **2. Complete these sentences with the expressions below.**

to have the time of one's life • *time will tell* • *time flies* • *as time goes by* • *all in good time* • *against time* (contre la montre) • *ahead of his time* (en avance sur son temps)

A. Scientists should hurry up to find a way to time travel because we're running out of time, … !
B. Physicists' beliefs and expectations always change … .
C. We should respect the laws of physics and go slowly in our experiments. As the saying goes, … !
D. Einstein was certainly … . When he discovered the theory of relativity.
E. If we could time travel to the future, going back to Earth would be a race … !
F. When he travelled to the past, Eckels probably expected to … .
G. Will time travel be possible one day? Let's wait and see: … !

★★ **3. Use the elements below and "in order that" and "so that" to make sentences in preterite. Make the necessary changes.**

A. Americans • make a time machine • change the course of history
B. They are ready to do everything • travel to the past • to save humanity
C. Mr. Travis • give money to the company Time Safari Inc. • go hunt dinosaurs
D. He • decide to risk everything • the president • do not get killed

★★ **4. Rewrite these sentences using the past tense.**

A. If you use this time machine, you will be surprised.
B. If they believe his stories, there will be chaos.
C. If the past can be changed, our perception of the future will change.
D. If the President is assassinated, the population will revolt.
E. If Stephen King writes another book, we will buy it.

★★★ **5. Translate these sentences into English.**

A. *Les hommes pourraient voyager dans le temps un jour s'ils créaient une machine aussi rapide que la vitesse de la lumière.*
B. *Un « trou de ver » pourrait permettre aux scientifiques de voyager dans le temps à travers un tunnel qui relierait le passé au présent.*
C. *Si j'étais un voyageur dans le temps, j'irais sans aucun doute dans le passé pour changer l'histoire.*

6. Interactive test! What is your score?

OPEN YOUR EARS!

PHONOLOGY

1. Écrire et dire les dates

🇬🇧 On écrit : « *Tuesday, 3rd June 2021* »
On dit : « *Tuesday **the** third **of** June 2021* »

🇺🇸 On écrit : « *Tuesday, June 3rd 2021* »
On dit : « *Tuesday, June **the** third 2021* »

- On utilise les **nombres ordinaux** :
the first (1st), the second (2nd), the third (3rd), the fourth (4th), the fifth (5th) …
- Attention, l'anglais américain ne présente pas les jours et les mois dans le même ordre :
11/22/63 = le 22 novembre 1963
9/11 = le 11 septembre

2. Dire les années

- **Jusqu'à l'an 999**, on lit le chiffre → « nine hundred and ninety-nine ».
- **À partir de quatre chiffres**, on coupe en deux : 1754 → « seventeen fifty-four ».
- **Pour l'an 2000**, on dit « *two thousand* ».
- **De 2001 à 2009** on peut dire → « *twenty oh* + *chiffre* » (*oh* signifiant zéro).
Mais on peut aussi dire en anglais britannique « *two thousand and* » + chiffre.
- À partir de 2010, on recoupe en deux → « *twenty ten* ».

• Prononcez les dates suivantes en anglais britannique puis vérifiez. MP3 N°99

le lundi 3 août 1987 • le jeudi 18 juin 1345 • le vendredi 1er octobre 2007 • le mardi 27 avril 2354 • le 22 novembre 1963 • le 11 septembre 2001 • le 23 août 2013

Picture challenge

★ 3 sentences
★★ 4 to 6 sentences
★★★ 7 sentences and +

How many sentences can you make about the *Dr Who* series using what you have learnt? Collect stars!

READING TIME

When the yogurt took over: a short story (2010)

By **John Scalzi** (writer, editor, film critic, columnist, novelist).

When the Yogurt Took Over is a short story written by the American science-fiction and fantasy writer **John Scalzi** in which humanity ends up being ruled by an omniscient chemically modified yogurt.

When the yogurt took over, we all made the same jokes – "Finally, our rulers will have culture," "Our society has curdled[1]," "Our government is now the cream of the crop," and so on. But when we weren't laughing about the absurdity of it all, we looked into each others' eyes with the same unasked question – how did we ever get to the point where we were, in fact, ruled by a dairy[2] product?

Oh, as a matter of record, we knew how it happened. Researchers at the *Adelman Institute for Biological Technology* in Dayton had been refining[3] the process of DNA computing for years. In a bid[4] to increase efficiency and yield[5], scientists took one of their most computationally advanced strains[6] and grafted[7] it into *Lactobacillus delbrueckii subspecies bulgaricus*, commonly used to ferment yogurt. Initial tests appeared to be failures, and acting under the principal of "waste not, want not," one of the researchers sneaked some of the bacillus out of the lab to use for her homemade yogurt.

A week later, during breakfast, the yogurt used the granola she had mixed with it to spell out the message WE HAVE SOLVED FUSION. TAKE US TO YOUR LEADERS.

The yogurt was crafty[8] and shrewd[9]. It negotiated for itself a factory filled with curdling vats[10] that increased its processing powers exponentially. Within weeks the yogurt had declared that it had arrived at solutions to many of the country's problems: Energy. Global warming. Caring adequately for the nation's poor while still promoting the capitalist system. It let us know just enough to let us know just how much more it knew.

Share your answers with us, the government said.
WE NEED PAYMENT, the yogurt said.

What would you like? The government asked.
OHIO, the yogurt said.
We can't do that, the government said.

THAT'S FINE, the yogurt said. WE'LL JUST GO TO CHINA. THEY'LL GIVE US THE WHOLE SHAANXI PROVINCE.

Within a year the yogurt had a century-long lease[11] on Ohio, with the promise that it would respect the human and constitutional rights of those who lived within its borders, and that it would let the US handle its foreign affairs. In return it handed over to the government a complex economic formula it promised would eradicate the national debt within a decade, without tax increases.

1 *tourner (devenir caillé pour le lait)* • **2** *laitier* • **3** *raffiner* •
4 attempt to achieve sth • **5** *récolte* • **6** *souches d'ADN* • **7** *greffé* • **8** *malin* • **9** *perspicace* •
10 *cuves à fermentation* • **11** *bail*

Charlie Richards, American artist, 2019

FOLLOW IT EXACTLY, the yogurt said. ANY DEVIATION WILL BRING COMPLETE ECONOMIC RUIN.

We will, the government promised.

Within five years the global economy had collapsed and panic had set in. Only Ohio remained unscathed[12].

WE TOLD YOU NOT TO DEVIATE FROM THE PLAN, the yogurt said. Its "factory" now stretched along the banks of the Miami River in Dayton for two miles.

Our best economists said the formula needed tweaking[13], the government said. *They had Nobel prizes.*

YOUR ECONOMISTS ARE TOO CLOSE TO THE PROBLEM TO SOLVE IT, the yogurt said. ANY HUMAN IS.

We could use your help, the government said. You could be our economic advisor.

SORRY, WE DON'T ADVISE ANYMORE, the yogurt said. IF YOU WANT OUR HELP YOU HAVE TO GIVE US CONTROL.

We can't do that, the government said.

WE UNDERSTAND, the yogurt said. WE HOPE YOU HAVE STOCKED UP ON CANNED GOODS.

Six months later the government declared martial law and gave the yogurt supreme executive power. Other nations, worse off than we were, quickly followed.

OKAY THEN, the yogurt said, in its globally televised address to humanity, and one of its factory workers, absurdly happy and well-fed, walked forward and showed a document the size of an old Manhattan phone book. HERE'S WHAT WE DO. FOLLOW THIS PLAN EXACTLY. IF YOU DON'T, SORRY, WE'LL HAVE YOU SHOT.

12 *intacte* • **13** *ajustements*

Now, ten years later, humanity is happy, healthy and wealthy. No one suffers from material want. Everyone contributes. After the first couple of years of getting things in order, the yogurt was happy to let us handle the machinery of our own administration, stepping in to fine tune only now and then. No one argues with the yogurt. No one tweaks its formulas. The rest of the time it rests there in its factory, thinking about whatever intelligent fermented milk thinks about.

That's how it happened, as a matter of record.

But there's another "how," as in: how did humanity jam itself up so badly that being ruled by breakfast food not only made sense, but made the best sense possible? For all our intelligence, are we not smart enough to halt our own destruction? Did we really have to abandon our own free will to save ourselves? What does it say about us that we survive because we were taken pity upon by bacteria and curds?

Or maybe "pity" isn't precisely the right word. Some of us ask ourselves –not out loud – that if the yogurt was smart enough to give the government a formula to solve its debt problem, wasn't it also smart enough to realize that human intellectual vanity would keep us from following the formula exactly? Was it planning on that vanity in order to seize control? What does a dairy product want with humanity anyway? Some of us think it is ultimately looking out for its own survival, and that keeping us happy, content and controlled is the simplest way of doing that.

And then there's this. In the last several weeks the yogurt has initiated several space launches[14]. More are scheduled[15]. And in low orbit, something is being built.
What is it? We have asked.
OH, NOTHING, the yogurt said. JUST A SPACESHIP DESIGN WE'VE BEEN THINKING ABOUT.
For a moon landing? We asked.
FOR STARTERS, YES, the yogurt said. BUT THAT'S NOT THE PRIMARY GOAL.
Can we do anything to help? We asked.
NO, WE'VE GOT THIS, the yogurt said, and then would say no more about it.
Life from Earth is going to the stars. It just may not be human life.
What happens if the yogurt goes to the stars without us?
What happens if it goes and leaves us behind?
Forever?

When the yogurt took over: a short story
John Scalzi, 2010

14 *lancements de fusées* • **15** *prévus*

GUIDED READING

A. Pick out the main characters and places.
B. l. 01-16 Pick out the mains steps and goals of the experiment to be able to describe it.
C. Pick out the main consequences of the experiment and write a short chronology of the events.
D. Explain the title of the short story using your findings.
E. Quote one sentence which sums up the message of the story and justify your choice.

Go further. Groupwork

Group 1
- Study the Yogurt's speech.
- What strikes you in the way it speaks?
- How does he manipulate humans into following his orders?

Group 2
l. 01-06, l. 65-76, l. 87-89: Study the narrator's comments
- What strikes you in the way he describes his own civilisation?
- Nb: Focus on the way he addresses the readers

UNIT 17 Évaluation

Compréhension de l'oral

"History of the word vegan" MP3 n°100

Listen to the audio recording three times and recap what you have understood.

Expression écrite Choisissez l'un des deux sujets (min. 120 mots).

Question A : For the past half-century, veganism has been a minority within a minority, but the 2020s will be the decade when veganism goes mainstream. Health, climate concerns, environment, resources, animal welfare... What is driving more people and brands to embrace a plant-based lifestyle?

Question B : Discuss the following statement:
"If you want to convince people to go vegan, disruptive protests are not the answer."

U.18 U.19 Évaluation

Compréhension de l'oral

"Scientist discoveries: use and misuse" MP3 n°101

Listen to the audio recording three times and recap what you have understood.

Expression écrite Choisissez l'un des deux sujets (min. 120 mots).

Question A : According to some experts, the next billion-dollar industry will not be a service or product—it will be upgrading humans, it will be building a better you. Do you agree?

Question B : Write a book summary or a film synopsis that would start with the following prompt: "Cyborgs are among us already. Tomorrow is today..."

UNIT 20 Évaluation

Compréhension de l'oral

"If you could change History" MP3 n°102

Listen to the audio recording three times and recap what you have understood.

Expression écrite Choisissez l'un des deux sujets (min. 120 mots).

Question A : Imagine and write the 5 rules of time travel. Develop your answers.

Question B : Time travel has always fascinated humans. It has been a popular topic for science-fiction literature and films for decades. If it did exist, how could it serve mankind?

B1-B2

BACKPACK

Get Ready for your Exam!

U.18 U.19 Évaluation

I was born in the year 18—to a large fortune, […] inclined by nature to industry, fond of the respect of the wise and good among my fellow-men, and thus, as might have been supposed, with every guarantee of an honourable and distinguished future. […]

And it chanced that the direction of my scientific studies, which led wholly toward the mystic and the transcendental, re-acted and shed a strong light on this consciousness of the perennial war among my members. With every day, and from both sides of my intelligence, the moral and the intellectual, I thus drew steadily nearer to that truth […]: that man is not truly one, but truly two. […] I, for my part, from the nature of my life, advanced infallibly in one direction and in one direction only. It was on the moral side, and in my own person, that I learned to recognise the thorough and primitive duality of man; […] and from an early date, even before the course of my scientific discoveries had begun to suggest the most naked possibility of such a miracle, I had learned to dwell with pleasure, as a beloved day-dream, on the thought of the separation of these elements. If each, I told myself, could but be housed in separate identities, life would be relieved of all that was unbearable […]. It was the curse of mankind that these incongruous fagots were thus bound together that in the agonised womb of consciousness, these polar twins should be continuously struggling. How, then, were they dissociated? […]

I hesitated long before I put this theory to the test of practice. I knew well that I risked death […]. But the temptation of a discovery so singular and profound, at last overcame the suggestions of alarm. I had long since prepared my tincture; I purchased at once, from a firm of wholesale chemists, a large quantity of a particular salt which I knew, from my experiments, to be the last ingredient required; and late one accursed night, I compounded the elements, watched them boil and smoke together in the glass, and […] drank off the potion.

The most racking pangs succeeded: a grinding in the bones, deadly nausea, and a horror of the spirit that cannot be exceeded at the hour of birth or death. Then these agonies began swiftly to subside, and I came to myself as if out of a great sickness. There was something strange in my sensations, something indescribably new and, from its very novelty, incredibly sweet. I felt younger, lighter, happier in body; […] an unknown but not an innocent freedom of the soul. I knew myself, at the first breath of this new life, to be more wicked, tenfold more wicked, sold a slave to my original evil; and the thought, in that moment, braced and delighted me like wine. […]

I stole through the corridors, a stranger in my own house; and coming to my room, I saw for the first time the appearance of Edward Hyde. […] Evil besides (which I must still believe to be the lethal side of man) had left on that body an imprint of deformity and decay. And yet when I looked upon that ugly idol in the glass, I was conscious of no repugnance, rather of a leap of welcome. This, too, was myself. It seemed natural and human.

Robert Louis Stevenson, *The Strange Case of Dr. Jekyll and Mr. Hyde*,1886

Compréhension de l'écrit

Answer the following questions in English, using your own words.

A. After reading the text, what can you say about:
- its main topic?
- the narrator's experiment?
- his opinion on it?
- the narrator's inner struggle?

B. Comment on the last paragraph. How does the narrator see himself? What consequences can it have on his future actions?

Expression écrite

Choisissez l'un des deux sujets (min. 120 mots).

Question A : Imagine and write a continuation to the story.

Question B : "You could call it 'superpower', but more accurately, transhumanism is the ability to create and shape our bodies and unlock opportunities towards a new generation of 'improved humans'."
How does this statement echo Robert Louis Stevenson's novel?

C

White students from Little Rock, Arkansas, insult black student Elizabeth Eckford as she is about to integrate a non-segregated high school, 9 April 1957.

Nouns
- a scowl /skaʊl/: *grimace*
- hatred /ˈheɪtrɪd/
- intolerance
- racism /ˈreɪsɪzm/
- resilience = resistance

Verbs & Expressions
- shout = yell
- scream at someone
- glare at someone
- ignore /ɪɡˈnɔː/
- pretend: *faire semblant*
- carry on + V-ing

D

Anti-segregation demonstrators, in the Southern Stores March at Broadway in New York, 1 January 1965

- a protest march = a demonstration
- peaceful = non-violent
- to demonstrate
- to protest
- to hold signs
- from all walks of life: *de tous milieux*

YOUR TURN! 3 Present a picture

Do your own research and get ready to present a photograph that illustrates the title "Living the Segregation, living exclusion" to your classmates.

Remember to research the context of the photograph you picked!

❸ Education, the Same Rights for Everyone

To what extent were segregated children included in the fight for their own education?

1 White books

A. Read the text, then read **Part 1** again. How does the narrator depict his daily life in a segregated world? How does he feel about it?

B. Focus on **Part 2**. What makes him realise that segregation has a direct impact on his life and his access to education and knowledge? (Quote two elements.)

C. Have your say. The narrator mentions "the impact of her words." What were the consequences of this encounter in his life?

Part 1

When I was a child I knew that the white people lived somewhere, but I rarely saw one in my daily routine. Our store owners and undertakers[1] and carpenters were all black. So were our tailors and dressmakers, our butchers, bakers, and milkmen. Everybody was poor, but nobody starved. We partied on Saturday nights and praised the Lord for our babies on Sundays. We worked hard when we had to and took it easy when there was a chance. A lot of colored people tell me that they hate the South; Jim Crow and segregation made a heavy weight for their hearts. But I never felt like that. I mean, lynchings were a terrible thing, and some of those peckerwoods[2] acted so stupid that they embarrassed the hell out of you sometimes. But I still loved the little shack[3] I shared with my mother. I'd have still been there if it wasn't for one terrible event. That event was learning to read. I entered school at the age of six. [...] On my first day I heard Miss Randolph read a story, and I knew that books were my destiny, not writing or teaching or inventing spaceships, just reading and reading and reading some more. I could pick out a simple sentence based on the knowledge of a dozen words by the end of the first week. By the age of eight I was alone in the fourth classroom, reading everything I could. [...] There was a library in the white part of town; coloreds couldn't go inside. For a while I would go there and sit out in front on the bench they had, rereading old books like *The Hinkley Reader* and *Uncle Tom's Cabin*.

1 croque-mort • 2 rustres • 3 cabane, bicoque

Part 2

One day the librarian, an old battle-ax[4] named Celestine Dowling, came out and asked me what I was doing. "Reading", I said proudly. "Really", old Miss Dowling said. "Yes'm", I replied. "I don't believe you", she stated. I didn't know what to reply to such a rude comment, so I sat tight and quiet. "Read me a sentence", she ordered. *There is nothing worse than the snow of May*, I read from a story called "Minnesota Snows." Dowling frowned and said, "go on." I read the first page and then the second. I read all the way through the story. I had read that book many times and so did not skip or stutter[5] hardly at all. When I was through, Miss Dowling said, "Come on with me." She led me through the big double doors of the library into a large room that was at least twenty feet high, lined to the ceiling with shelves that were packed with neat rows of books. I remember my heart catching[6]. I forgot how to breathe altogether. [...] "This is the library", the librarian said. I nodded and gulped. "Close your mouth, boy." "It's beautiful", I said finally. "I never seen nuthin' like it." "Of course you haven't", she said. "And do you know why?" "Because I never been in here before?" I asked, not understanding the question. "No", she said from some Olympian height. "It is because this is a white library. And no matter how much you know how to read, these books are not meant for you. These books were written by white people for white people. This is literature and art and the way our country is and should be. There will be no library card for you, so you can stop sitting out in front. You have seen as much of this building as you ever will." The impact of her words brought tears to my eyes. I was thirteen then, but, like I said, I've always been small. I looked up at Celestine Dowling, and she seemed pleased to see me cry.

Fearless Jones,
Walter Mosley, 2001

4 mégère • 5 bégayer • 6 battre rapidement

2 Little Rock, Arkansas, 1957

VIDEO N°38

A. Pairwork. Watch the video and focus on the following elements:

- **Pupil A:** What happened in Little Rock in 1957? Pick out the main events.
- **Pupil B:** How did Ernest Green feel about that school year and how did it impact his education?

B. Conclude: what were the immediate consequences of declaring segregated schools unconstitutional?

3 Ruby Bridges, Louisiana, 1960

A. Read the *Cultural fact* and focus on the painting (on the right of the picture). Explain the context of this painting in your own words.

B. What does this photograph show of the evolution of the situation of black people in the US?

Cultural fact

Ruby Bridges was born in Louisiana after the law to end segregated schools was passed in 1954. Until the age of six, she attended a segregated kindergarten because the State refused to comply with the law.
In 1960, she integrated an all-white school and had to be escorted every day by four US Marshals for her personal protection. Artist Norman Rockwell painted her ordeal and named it *"The problem We All Live With"* (1964).
In 2011, Ruby Bridges was invited to the White House by President Obama. Commenting on the painting that represented her, he said: "I think it's fair to say that if it hadn't been for you guys, I might not be here and we wouldn't be looking at this together."
Ruby Bridges has been a civil rights activist all her life.

YOUR TURN! 4 Write an introduction

As a reporter for your school blog, you have been tasked with writing an article entitled: "Segregation in education: it wasn't all black and white." Write the introduction of your article, using the context and examples on this double page and considering the notions of diversity and inclusion.

❹ Varied Voices For the Civil Rights

What were the landmarks and characteristics of the Civil Rights movement in the 1960s?

1 The March on Washington

VIDEO N°39

Groupwork. Watch the video. Group A answers the questions below, Group B answers questions with the help of Worksheet n°41.

A. Pick out elements to place the March on Washington in its historical context.

B. How was it organised and what were its main characteristics?

C. What unexpected elements have you learnt about a very famous speech?

D. Use your findings to say why the March on Washington has remained so memorable.

2 Leaders' voices

A. Read the two speeches (below and on the opposite page). Pick out the key ideas in each.

B. What do Martin Luther King, Jr. and Malcolm X have in common in their views? How do they differ?

C. What qualities and emotions do those leaders seek to stir up in their respective audiences?

D. Read the captions under the pictures. What were the consequences of civil right activism for these two leaders?

Speech 1 MP3 N°103

It's time for us to submerge our differences and realize that it is best for us to first see that we have the same problem, a common problem, a problem that will make you catch hell[1] whether you're a Baptist, or a Methodist, or a Muslim, or a nationalist. Whether you're educated or illiterate, whether you live on the boulevard or in the alley, you're going to catch hell just like I am. We're all in the same boat and we all are going to catch the same hell from the same man. He just happens to be a white man. All of us have suffered here, in this country, political oppression at the hands of the white man, economic exploitation at the hands of the white man, and social degradation at the hands of the white man.

Now in speaking like this, it doesn't mean that we're anti-white, but it does mean we're anti-exploitation, we're anti-degradation, we're anti-oppression. And if the white man doesn't want us to be anti-him, let him stop oppressing and exploiting and degrading us. [...]

If we don't do something real soon, I think you'll have to agree that we're going to be forced either to use the ballot[2] or the bullet[3]. It's one or the other in 1964. It isn't that time is running out – time has run out!

1 s'en prendre plein la tête • 2 bulletin de vote • 3 balle (d'arme à feu)

***Malcom X**, "The Ballot or the Bullet",*
Speech in Cleveland (Ohio), 3 April 1964

Malcolm X was assassinated on 21 February 1965, ten months after giving his "The Ballot or the Bullet" speech.

Speech 2 MP3 N°104

Men, for years now, have been talking about war and peace. But now, no longer can they just talk about it. It is no longer a choice between violence and nonviolence in this world; it's nonviolence or nonexistence.
That is where we are today. And also in the human rights revolution, if something isn't done, and done in a hurry, to bring the colored peoples of the world out of their long years of poverty, their long years of hurt and neglect[1], the whole world is doomed[2]. Now, I'm just happy that God has allowed me to live in this period to see what is unfolding[3]. And I'm happy that He's allowed me to be in Memphis. [...] We aren't engaged in any negative protest and in any negative arguments with anybody. We are saying that we are determined to be men. We are determined to be people. We are saying – We are saying that we are God's children. And that we don't have to live like we are forced to live.
Now, what does all of this mean in this great period of history? It means that we've got to stay together. We've got to stay together and maintain unity. [...]

1 négligence, abandon • 2 condamnés • 3 qui se déroule maintenant

Martin Luther King JR., "I've Been to the Mountaintop", Speech in Memphis (Tennessee), 3 April 1968

Martin Luther King gave his "I've Been to the Mountaintop" speech on 3 April 1968. He was assassinated the following day.

3 Nina Simone, the 'artivist'

A. Pick out the main steps of the evolution of Nina Simone's opinion about race and Civil Rights.

B. In your opinion, which leader of the movement influenced her the most?

C. Turn to Worksheet n°42 to learn more about Nina Simone and her song *"Mississippi Goddam"*.

I came to my own conclusions about separatism. In the white man's world the black man would always lose out, so the idea of a separate black nation, whether it was in America or in Africa, made sense. But I didn't believe that there was any basic difference between the races – whoever is on top uses whatever means they can to keep the other down, and if black America was on top they'd use race as a way of oppressing whites in exactly the way they themselves were oppressed. [...] When I had started out in the movement all I wanted were my rights under the Constitution, but the more I thought about it the more I realized that no matter what the president or the Supreme Court might say, the only way we could get true equality was if America changed completely, top to bottom. And this change had to start with my own people, with black revolution.

On January 15, 1965, I gave a concert at Carnegie Hall. But two days before the concert I was rehearsing with the orchestra when news came through that Brother Malcolm X had been shot to death on a Harlem platform. Even now I wish I had known the man. Malcolm's assassination pushed my thoughts faster down the track they were already on, that violence was going to be an inevitable part of the struggle and if we didn't understand that fast then – like I said in *Mississippi Goddam* – we'd die like flies. [...] On October 15 1964, Dr Martin Luther King Junior received his Nobel peace prize: it didn't seem like there was much peace to me.

I Put A Spell On You, Nina Simone, 1991

YOUR TURN! 4 Podcast contest

Your school organises a podcast contest entitled: "Nina Simone's songs". Choose a song, talk about its historical context, and let your audience discover a musical extract from it. Vote for the best podcast!

❺ The Vietnam Paradox

What made the Vietnam war an issue in the Civil Rights movement?

1 Brothers in arms

A. Read the *Cultural fact*. What made the Vietnam War an issue for the Civil Rights movement?

B. **Groupwork. Group A** focuses on photograph Ⓐ, **group B** on photograph Ⓑ. Describe your picture and react.

C. According to these pictures, was segregation an issue for the American soldiers on the battlefield? Why?

A

B

Cultural fact

The Vietnam War (1955-1975) was a long and costly conflict opposing the communist government of North Vietnam and South Vietnam and its ally the United States. The American involvement increased in the sixties, causing anti-war protests and feeding the counter-culture movement. According to www.amistadresource.org, "in 1967, 64% of all eligible African-Americans were drafted[1], but only 31% of eligible whites. During 1965-66, the casualty rate for blacks was twice that of whites."

1 *mobilisé*

HELP!

- a chopper = a helicopter
- heavy load
- weapons
- helmet
- tiredness
- to stare at
- to go to the battlefield
- to perform mouth-to-mouth resuscitation
- helpless: *impuissant, sans défense*
- hopeless: *désespéré, sans espoir*
- determined
- injured: *blessé*
- muddy: *boueux*

"The promises of the great society have been shot down on the battlefields of Vietnam," King said in his famous speech, "making the poor, white and Negro bear the heaviest burden[1] both at the front and at home." [...] "The Vietnam War divided the Civil Rights movement and African-Americans more than any other event in American history, exacerbating pre-existing rifts[2] in the civil rights coalition, and it diverted attention away from the struggle for racial justice and toward opposition to the war."

1 *fardeau* • 2 *ruptures*

Nancy Montgomery, ***Stripes.com***,
9 November 2014

2 The heaviest burden

A. Read the article. What was the paradox of asking black people to enlist in the army to fight the war?

B. Pick out Martin Luther King's opinion on the topic.

3 A conscientious objector

A. Pick out details about Muhammad Ali and his career.

B. What happened on 29 April 1967 and what were the consequences for the boxer?

C. Have your say. In your opinion, was it right for Muhammad Ali to be a conscientious objector? Justify.

Boxing authorities in America today stripped[1] Muhammad Ali (Cassius Clay) of his world heavyweight title and suspended his boxing licence after he had refused to be inducted into[2] the United States Army. Clay had stood in line with 11 other men being called up in a room in the old Post Office building in Houston, Texas, and heard his Black Muslim name called by the officer administering the oath[3]. Clay did not move. Another officer walked up to him and said: "Mr Ali, will you accompany me, please?" Clay did not speak, but followed him out of the room to be given a warning of the consequences of his refusal.

He was taken back into the room and given a second chance to take the oath, but he again refused. He then signed a statement to that effect.

Soon after he left the centre, to be mobbed[4] by well-wishers, the New York Boxing Commission, the World Boxing Association, and the Texas Boxing Commission withdrew[5] their recognition of him as champion. [...] Clay issued a statement saying: "It is in the light of my consciousness as a Muslim minister and my own personal convictions that I take my stand in rejecting the call to be inducted. I do so with the full realisation of its implications. I have searched my conscience". [...] Muhammad Ali was sentenced to five years in prison and a $10,000 fine, though he remained out on bail while he appealed. He was stripped of his passport and his heavyweight title and banned from fighting in the US. Ali returned to boxing in 1970 and his conviction was reversed in 1971.

1 *déchu* • 2 *intégré* • 3 *serment* • 4 *assailli* • 5 *retirer*

The Guardian, from the archive,
29 April 1967

YOUR TURN! 4 Webquest

Do some further research about Muhammad Ali's life and career. Get ready to present your findings to your classmates.

❻ Elected For Change

To what extent has the American political landscape become more inclusive?

1 Yes, we can

A. Read B. Obama's acceptance speech for his first mandate as US President. What idea does it focus on?
B. What historical events and breakthroughs does he allude to in his speech?
C. Have your say. Why was the 2008 presidential election such a landmark for American history? Justify.
D. Go further. Do some research. Have the two mandates of President Obama brought the promised change? Illustrate your answer with facts.

This election had many firsts and many stories that will be told for generations. But one that's on my mind tonight's about a woman who cast her ballot[1] in Atlanta. She's a lot like the millions of others who stood in line to make their voice heard in this election except for one thing: Ann Nixon Cooper is 106 years old. She was born just a generation past slavery; a time when there were no cars on the road or planes in the sky; when someone like her couldn't vote for two reasons: because she was a woman and because of the color of her skin.

And tonight, I think about all that she's seen throughout her century in America — the heartache and the hope; the struggle and the progress; the times we were told that we can't, and the people who pressed on with that American creed: Yes we can.

At a time when women's voices were silenced and their hopes dismissed[2], she lived to see them stand up and speak out and reach for the ballot: Yes we can.

When there was despair in the Dust Bowl[3] and Depression across the land, she saw a nation conquer fear itself with a New Deal, new jobs, a new sense of common purpose: Yes we can.

When the bombs fell on our harbor and tyranny threatened the world, she was there to witness a generation rise to greatness and a democracy was saved: Yes we can.

She was there for the buses in Montgomery, the hoses[4] in Birmingham, a bridge in Selma, and a preacher from Atlanta who told a people that "we shall overcome": Yes we can.

A man touched down on the moon, a wall came down in Berlin, a world was connected by our own science and imagination.

And this year, in this election, she touched her finger to a screen, and cast her vote, because after 106 years in America, through the best of times and the darkest of hours, she knows how America can change: Yes we can.

America, we have come so far. We have seen so much. But there is so much more to do. So tonight, let us ask ourselves – if our children should live to see the next century; if my daughters should be so lucky to live as long as Ann Nixon Cooper, what change will they see? What progress will we have made?

1 to vote • **2** rejected • **3** historical drought in 1930s America • **4** *lance à eau*

Barack Obama, *Election Day Speech,*
4 November 2008

2 Lori Lightfoot, Mayor of Chicago

A. Read the article. In what ways was the Chicago election campaign an unusual event?

B. How is Chicago depicted?

Chicago made history, electing former federal prosecutor Lori Lightfoot its first black, female mayor as the city struggles with gun violence on its streets and looming fiscal woes.

Lightfoot, who also will be the first openly gay leader of the nation's third-most-populous city, soundly defeated Cook County Board President Toni Preckwinkle, 74 to 26 percent with nearly all precincts reporting, according to city election board returns. Lightfoot had never held elective office and will replace Rahm Emanuel, who chose not to run for a third term.

The historic outcome of Tuesday's vote was assured after the two black women beat 12 rivals in the campaign's Feb. 26 first round, Chicago's most crowded mayoral ballot ever. It included Bill Daley, the son and brother of two past Chicago mayors and, like Emanuel, a chief of staff to former President Barack Obama.

"Together we can and will finally put the interests of our people, all of our people, ahead of the interests of a powerful few," Lightfoot told a cheering crowd gathered at a downtown hotel. "We can and we will break this city's endless cycle of corruption."

Fortune, 3 April 2019

3 Acceptance Speech

VIDEO N°40

A. Watch the video and take notes. What is the main subject of Lori Lightfoot's message?

B. Have your say. Is Lori Lightfoot's election as mayor the result of a change towards more inclusive politics? Explain.

YOUR PROJECT

1. You are applying for a job as a speechwriter for the newly elected mayor of a big American city. You have been asked to show your talents.

Write a speech entitled "Voices of Diversity, Paths to Inclusion" that deals with the recent history of black people in America and the issues they still face. Say how the new mayor will bring about necessary change.

OR

2. *American Heritage* magazine is preparing for its "Speeches that will make History" review. In groups, choose one of the speeches from this unit for the issue. Justify your choice.

OPEN YOUR EARS!

PHONOLOGY

1. La terminaison en *-ism* /izəm/

• La terminaison en *-ism* ne change pas la place de l'accent (alors que les francophones ont tendance à décaler l'accent vers la droite). Écoutez les mots suivants et entraînez-vous à répéter. **MP3 N°105**

race → racism • colonial → colonialism • egalitarian → egalitarianism • feminist → feminism • terror → terrorism • fanatic → fanaticism

2. La terminaison en *-age* /ɪdʒ/

• Écoutez les mots suivants. Que remarquez-vous ?
Entraînez-vous à les répéter. **MP3 N°106**

courage • damage • advantage • disparage • intermarriage

3. La terminaison en *-ate*

• Écoutez les mots suivants. Quelle est la syllabe accentuée ?
Entraînez-vous à les répéter. **MP3 N°107**

demonstrate • denigrate • deprecate • propagate • regulate • humiliate

SHOWTIME

• Écoutez et répétez la phrase suivante en essayant de reproduire l'enthousiasme du locuteur.

MP3 N°108 *Historians believe that the marches and King's speech were important catalysts in passing the Civil Rights Act of 1964 and the Voting Rights Act of 1965.*

• Écoutez cet extrait du discours de MLK Jr. (p. 237).

MP3 N°109 */Men, for /years /now, have been /talking about /war and \peace. But /now, no /longer can they just \talk about it. It is no /longer a /choice between /violence and /non/violence in this \world; it's /non/violence or /nonex\istence. That is \where we \are today.*

/ indique une intonation montante.
\ indique une intonation descendante
__ indique l'accent de phrase

- On utilise l'intonation montante quand on n'a pas terminé son propos et l'intonation descendante quand l'énoncé est terminé.
- Ici, les intonations montantes amènent jusqu'au point culminant et la conclusion logique est marquée par l'intonation descendante. L'intonation est clairement utilisée à des fins rhétoriques.

AUDIO MYSTERY

Listen to the audio recording and find out the mystery names! **MP3 N°110**

- Audio words
- MP3
- Interactive Test

SPICE UP YOUR VOCABULARY

Use the vocabulary below to create your own mind map and add more words if necessary!

Verbs & Expressions

- address an issue
- assert one's rights
- be discriminated against
- be on equal footing
- boycott
- campaign for / against
- challenge
- contest
- defy
- demonstrate
- denigrate
- denounce = expose
- deprecate: *désapprouver*
- disgrace sb: *causer la honte*
- disparage: *dénigrer*
- empower /ɪm'paʊə/ oneself
- enforce
- gag = silence /'saɪləns/
- hate
- have access to education
- ignore
- incite
- march
- overcome
- parade
- pretend
- propagate
- regulate
- resort to
- voice = express out loud = state sth
- vote

Adjectives

- peaceful
- non-violent
- segregated /'segrɪgeɪtɪd/
- neglected
- alienated = excluded
- oppressed
- doomed
- defiant /dɪ'faɪənt/
- restrictive
- integrated
- resilient
- tough /'tʌf/ = harsh
- helpless
- determined /dɪ'tɜːmɪnd/
- hopeful ≠ desperate
- stripped: *déchu*

Nouns

- activist
- awareness campaign
- bias /'baɪəs/
- bullet
- civil disobedience
- cliché = stereotype
- conscientious objector
- demonstration
- desegregation
- equality ≠ inequality
- hatred /'heɪtrɪd/
- intolerance
- judgement
- march
- preconception /priːkən'sepʃən/
- prejudice /'predʒədɪs/ against
- protest
- racism /'reɪsɪzəm/
- resilience
- sign = placard /'plækaːd/
- struggle /'strʌgəl/

UP TO YOU!

★ 1. Find the odd word out and justify.

A. disparage • compliment • deprecate • denigrate
B. oppress • parade • march • demonstrate
C. preconception • bias • acceptance • prejudice
D. intolerance • resilience • hatred • racism

★★ 2. Find the missing word, as in the example.

	noun	verb	past participle
ex.	*neglect*	*neglect*	*neglected*
A.	...	...	*protested*
B.	*alienation*	...	...
C.	...	*denigrate*	...
D.	*tolerance*	...	...

★★ 3. Fill in the blanks using the words below.

overcome • *prejudice* • *defiant* • *disparage* • *enforce*

A. If the government wanted to ... the desegregation, they had to educate people to become more tolerant.

B. Rosa Parks had to be rather ... on the day she decided to protest against segregation on the bus.

C. In many respects, ... is related to ignorance more than hatred.

D. The chant "We shall ..." is emblematic of that era.

E. It was easy to ... and oppress black people in the context of the segregation.

★★★ 4. Translate into French.

A. The struggle for Civil Rights was tough, but despite the hatred and neglect, the activists were resilient and overcame inequality.
B. While civil disobedience tended to be peaceful, other forms of protest incited the marchers to violence.
C. Segregation was not only about separation, but also about prejudice and oppression, racism and exclusion.

★★★ 5. Challenge!

Write a paragraph about Segregation and the Civil Rights movement using as many words as possible from the list!

RULE THE GRAMMAR!

LE PRÉTÉRIT SIMPLE

On utilise le prétérit pour une action passée, datée, qu'elle ait été ponctuelle ou non :
They suspended his boxing license in 1967. (= action ponctuelle)
*They **went** on strike **for** weeks.* (= action qui a duré mais qui est terminée au moment où l'on parle.)

→ P.300

LE *PRESENT PERFECT*

- Il se forme avec l'auxiliaire **HAVE** au présent + le **participe passé** du verbe :
*The number of arrests **have increased**.*
- On utilise essentiellement le *present perfect* pour présenter **le résultat d'une action débutée dans le passé** et qui a des conséquences ou des effets dans le présent :
*Many opponents **have been arrested** these past few days.* (= Ils sont toujours en prison).

→ P.299

AGO / FOR / SINCE

- AGO s'utilise avec le **prétérit**. Il joue le même rôle qu'une date (**une borne temporelle**) mais on se place au moment de la prise de parole : *The police **arrested** them <u>three days **ago**</u>.*
- FOR est utilisé pour exprimer une **durée**.
→ Si cette durée est détachée du présent, on utilise le **prétérit** : *They **stayed** in jail **for** a week.*
(= ils en sont sortis).
→ Si cette durée est calculée par rapport au moment où l'on parle, on utilise le ***present perfect*** :
*They **have spent** a week in jail.* (= ils y sont toujours au moment où l'on parle et cela peut durer encore).
- SINCE implique le début d'une période de temps. Souvent, on utilise le **prétérit** pour indiquer le point de départ et le <u>***present perfect***</u> pour indiquer la durée écoulée depuis ce point de départ : ***Since** they arrested him, he <u>has</u> never <u>been</u> the same.* **=** ***Since** his arrest, he <u>has</u> never <u>been</u> the same.*

→ P.301

PRONOM COMPLÉMENT

Pronom sujet

- Quand le sujet est un **animé**, on utilise **WHO**.
*The <u>man</u> **who** arrested him was pretty violent.*
- Quand le sujet est un **inanimé**, on utilise **THAT** ou **WHICH**.
*The <u>weapon</u> **that / which** killed him had been stolen.*

Pronom complément

- Quand le complément est un animé, on utilise, **THAT**, **WHO** ou **Ø**.
*This is the <u>man</u> **that / who / Ø** I arrested yesterday.*
- Quand le complément est un inanimé, on utilise **THAT**, **WHICH** ou **Ø**.
*The <u>gun</u> **that / which / Ø** you found is loaded.*

→ P.315

UP TO YOU!

★1. Fill in the blanks using *for, since* or *ago*.

A. They have fought for their rights ... decades.
B. It all started 60 years ....
C. ... the end of segregation, things haven't been easy.
D. The KKK has existed ... decades.
E. President Obama was elected several years ....
F. Segregation lasted ... years.

★2. Put the verbs in the preterite.

A. They *(kneel)* and *(weep)* before the march.
B. His heart *(sink)* when he *(hear)* the verdict.
C. He *(mean)* to go to the rally but he *(forget)*.
D. They *(send)* a clear message to the KKK.
E. Martin Luther king Jr. *(receive)* the Nobel Prize in 1964.
F. They *(shoot)* Malcolm X in Washington Heights.

★★3. Put the verbs in the preterit

Then the pastor *(rise)*. While he *(speak)*, George *(close)* his eyes. He *(feel)* the words that he *(be)* about to speak fly from him. He *(feel)* the power of God go out in him. Then the voice of the pastor *(cease)*, and Gabriel *(open)* his eyes in the silence and *(find)* that all eyes *(be)* on him. And so he *(rise)* and *(face)* the congregation.

Adapted from *Go Tell it on the Mountain*, James Baldwin, 1952

★★4. Put the verbs in the present perfect.

A. She *(teach)* the history of black Americans in several universities.
B. They *(send)* him to jail simply because he was black.
C. I *(ring)* all my friends to rally support.
D. They *(take)* him to court for minor offences.
E. He *(show)* great courage when faced with adversity.
F. The black supporters *(win)* their case against the KKK.

★★5. Ask the questions corresponding to the following sentences.

A. I've been arrested three times by the police.
B. She met these radical thinkers last January.
C. I visited these KKK members every other week.
D. It took them three days to read Michelle Obama's Becoming.
E. Obama was the first black American President.

★★6. Put the verbs in the appropriate form (preterite or present perfect).

A. It *(be)* a long time since he last *(see)* her.
B. When he *(realise)* the protest would be a failure he *(decide)* not to go.
C. Nina Simone never *(meet)* Malcolm X.
D. Black people always *(fight)* for their rights.
E. A lot of black people *(get killed)* during the Vietnam war.
F. He never *(forget)* they *(insult)* him.

★★★7. Fill in the blanks using the appropriate relative pronouns (several correct answers).

A. He is the guy ... attacked the protesters.
B. The weapons ... they used have disappeared.
C. The man ... they lynched was only 23.
D. This is the KKK leader ... was convicted.
E. The speech ... she gave was very moving.
F. The man ... I saw was not black.

★★★8. Translate into English.

A. *Martin Luther King Jr. et Rosa Parks se sont battus pour l'égalité entre les noirs et les blancs.*
B. *L'autobiographie de Nina Simone a été publiée en 1991.*
C. *Le mouvement des droits civiques a mis fin à la ségrégation.*
D. The Help *est un film qui décrit la vie des noirs dans les années soixante.*

9. Interactive test! What is your score?

Picture challenge

★ 3 sentences
★★ 4 to 6 sentences
★★★ 7 sentences and +

How many sentences can you make using what you have learnt? Collect stars!

AXE 7

SHORT CUT

UNIT 22

BEYOND SIGHT

How does H.G. Wells manage to deal with difference and inclusion in "The Country of the Blind"?

YOUR PROJECT

Imagine and write an ending to H.G. Wells's short story.

Au menu de cette unité :

DÉCOUVERTES CULTURELLES

- H. G. Wells et sa nouvelle *The Country of the Blind* (1904)

OUTILS LINGUISTIQUES

- Les temps du récit
- Le discours direct / indirect
- L'expression de la simultanéité (*no sooner… than / hardly… when*)

BEFORE CLASS!

Flash to watch!

Watch the video and be ready to talk about it in class!

❶ The Arrival

Are appearances deceiving?

1 A strange village

While on an expedition, Nunez, a mountaineer, finds himself lost in a mysterious valley cut off from the world. After walking for a while, he sees what looks like a small village in the distance.

Gassed, American artist John Singer Sargent, 1918-19 (detail)

About midday he came at last out of the throat of the gorge into the plain and the sunlight. He was stiff and weary[1]; he sat down in the shadow of a rock, filled up his flask with water from a spring and drank it down, and remained for a time, resting before he went on to the houses.

They were very strange to his eyes, and indeed the whole aspect of that valley became, as he regarded it, queerer and more unfamiliar. The greater part of its surface was lush green meadow[2], starred with many beautiful flowers, irrigated with extraordinary care, and bearing evidence of systematic cropping[3] piece by piece.

High up and ringing the valley about was a wall, and what appeared to be a circumferential water channel, from which the little trickles of water that fed the meadow plants came [...]. The irrigation streams ran together into a main channel down the centre of the valley, and this was enclosed on either side by a wall breast high. This gave a singularly urban quality to this secluded[4] place, a quality that was greatly enhanced by the fact that a number of paths paved with black and white stones, and each with a curious little kerb[5] at the side, ran hither and thither in an orderly manner. The houses of the central village were quite unlike the casual and higgledy-piggledy[6] agglomeration of the mountain villages he knew; they stood in a continuous row on either side of a central street of astonishing cleanness, here and there, their parti-coloured[7] facade was pierced by a door, and not a solitary window broke their even frontage. They were parti-coloured with extraordinary irregularity, smeared with a sort of plaster that was sometimes grey, sometimes drab[8], sometimes slate-coloured or dark brown; and it was the sight of this wild plastering first brought the word "blind" into the thoughts of the explorer. "The good man who did that," he thought, "must have been as blind as a bat." [...]

He could now see a number of men and women resting on piled heaps of grass, as if taking a siesta, in the remoter part of the meadow, and nearer the village a number of recumbent[9] children, and then nearer at hand three men carrying pails on yokes[10] along a little path that ran from the encircling wall towards the houses. These latter were clad in garments of llama cloth and boots and belts of leather, and they wore caps of cloth with back and earflaps. They followed one another in single file, walking slowly and yawning as they walked, like men who have been up all night. There was something so reassuringly prosperous and respectable in their bearing that after a moment's hesitation Nunez stood forward as conspicuously as possible upon his rock, and gave vent to a mighty shout that echoed round the valley.

1 exhausted • **2** *prairie* • **3** *culture* • **4** isolated • **5** *trottoir* • **6** *ici, désordonné* • **7** having different colours in different parts • **8** *terne* • **9** lying down • **10** buckets on a wooden bar carried on the shoulders

The Country of the Blind,
H. G. Wells, 1904

A. Read the text. How does Nunez feel when he sees the village and the houses? What strikes him first?

B. How does the narrator emphasise the importance of sight in this part? What other senses does he allude to?

C. Explain the sentence: "*The good man who did that must have been as blind as a bat.*" (l. 34-36)

D. Say what the following sentence shows: "*They followed one another in single file, walking slowly and yawning as they walked, like men who have been up all night.*" (l. 44-47)

E. Sum up the text in your own words.

2 The encounter

A. Read the text. How does the narrator feel as he walks towards the villagers? Why does he feel this way?
B. Why does Nunez repeat "*In the Country of the Blind the One-Eyed Man is King*"? (l. 23-24).
C. Describe the villagers' attitude towards the narrator. Why do they call him "*A strange creature*"?
D. How can you explain Nunez's mood at the end of this part?
E. Go further. Read the last two sentences of the text. What do they reveal about Nunez's attitude, personality and his plans?

Illustration by Claude Allin Shepperson from H.G. Wells' short story "The Country of the Blind", published in *The Strand Magazine* in April 1904

The three men stopped, and moved their heads as though they were looking about them. They turned their faces [...], and Nunez gesticulated with freedom. But they did not appear to see him [...].

"The fools must be blind," he said.

When at last, after much shouting and wrath[1], Nunez crossed the stream by a little bridge, came through a gate in the wall, and approached them, he was sure that they were blind. He was sure that this was the Country of the Blind of which the legends told. The three stood side by side, not looking at him, but with their ears directed towards him, judging him by his unfamiliar steps. They stood close together like men a little afraid, and he could see their eyelids closed and sunken, as though the very balls beneath had shrunk away. There was an expression near awe[2] on their faces.

"A man," one said, "A man it is — a man or a spirit — coming down from the rocks."

But Nunez advanced with the confident steps of a youth who enters upon life. All the old stories of the lost valley and the Country of the Blind had come back to his mind, and through his thoughts ran this old proverb [...]:

"In the Country of the Blind the One-Eyed Man is King."

"In the Country of the Blind the One-Eyed Man is King."

And very civilly he gave them greeting. He talked to them and used his eyes.

"Where does he come from, brother Pedro?" asked one.

"Down out of the rocks."

"Over the mountains I come," said Nunez, "[...] where men can see. From near Bogota [...] where the city passes out of sight."

"Sight?" muttered Pedro. "Sight?"

They startled him by a simultaneous movement towards him, each with a hand outstretched. He stepped back [...].

"Come hither," said the third blind man, following his motion and clutching him neatly.

And they held Nunez and felt him over [...].

"Carefully," he cried, with a finger in his eye, and found they thought that organ, with its fluttering lids, a queer thing in him. They went over it again.

"A strange creature, Correa," said the one called Pedro. "Feel the coarseness of his hair. Like a llama's hair."

"Rough he is as the rocks that begot him," said Correa, investigating Nunez's unshaven chin [...]. "Perhaps he will grow finer."

"He speaks," said the third man. "Certainly he is a man."

[...]

"Let us lead him to the elders," said Pedro. Pedro went first and took Nunez by the hand to lead him to the houses. He drew his hand away. "I can see," he said.

"See?" said Correa.

"Yes; see," said Nunez, turning towards him, and stumbled against Pedro's pail.

"His senses are still imperfect," said the third blind man. "He stumbles, and talks unmeaning words. Lead him by the hand."

"As you will," said Nunez, and was led along laughing.

It seemed they knew nothing of sight.

Well, all in good time he would teach them.

1 anger • 2 amazement and admiration

The Country of the Blind, H. G. Wells, 1904

❷ A one-sided fight

What does it take to be in control?

1 Worlds apart

A. Read the text. How does the relationship between Nunez and the villagers evolve? Why?

B. In your own words, explain the following sentence: "*It was a one-sided fight.*" (l. 30)

C. What makes Nunez and the villagers unable to understand each other?

D. Have your say. Would you say that the Country of the Blind is an inclusive community? Why (not)?

Sense of sight, British artist Annie Swynnerton, 1895

He heard people shouting, and saw a number of figures [...] A crowd of children and men and women (the women and girls he was pleased to note had, some of them, quite sweet faces, for all that their eyes were shut and sunken) came about him, holding on to him, touching him with soft, sensitive hands, smelling at him, and listening at every word he spoke. Some of the maidens and children, however, kept aloof as if afraid, and indeed his voice seemed coarse and rude beside their softer notes. [...] His three guides kept close to him with an effect of proprietorship, and said again and again, "A wild man out of the rocks."

"Bogota," he said. "Bogota. Over the mountain crests."

"A wild man — using wild words," said Pedro. "Did you hear that — Bogota? His mind has hardly formed yet. He has only the beginnings of speech."

A little boy nipped his hand. "Bogota!" he said mockingly. [...]

"He stumbled[1]," said Correa — "stumbled twice as we came hither."

"Bring him in to the elders."

And they thrust[2] him suddenly through a doorway into a room as black as pitch [...]. The crowd closed in behind him and shut out all but the faintest glimmer of day, and before he could arrest himself he had fallen headlong over the feet of a seated man. His arm, outflung, struck the face of someone else as he went down; he felt the soft impact of features and heard a cry of anger, and for a moment he struggled against a number of hands that clutched him. It was a one-sided fight. An inkling of the situation came to him and he lay quiet.

"I fell down," he said; "I couldn't see in this pitchy darkness."

There was a pause as if the unseen persons about him tried to understand his words. Then the voice of Correa said: "He is but newly formed. He stumbles as he walks and mingles words that mean nothing with his speech." [...]

"May I sit up?" he asked, in a pause. "I will not struggle against you again."

They consulted and let him rise.

The voice of an older man began to question him, and Nunez found himself trying to explain the great world out of which he had fallen, and the sky and mountains and such-like marvels, to these elders who sat in darkness in the Country of the Blind. And they would believe and understand nothing whatever that he told them, a thing quite outside his expectation. They would not even understand many of his words. For fourteen generations these people had been blind and cut off from all the seeing world; the names for all the things of sight had faded and changed; the story of the outer world was faded and changed to a child's story; and they had ceased to concern themselves with anything beyond the rocky slopes above their circling wall. [...]

Slowly Nunez realised this: that his expectation of wonder and reverence at his origin and his gifts was not to be borne out[3]; and after his poor attempt to explain sight to them had been set aside [...], he subsided[4], [...] into listening to their instruction.

1 *trébucher* • 2 push • 3 confirmed • 4 become quiet

The Country of the Blind,
H. G. Wells, 1904

❸ A New Citizen

How easy is it to forget about one's roots and start over?

1 A new life

A. Read part 1. In your own words, explain what Nunez plans to do.

B. What game does he play with the villagers? Who eventually wins? Why?

C. Read part 2. Describe Nunez's situation. What did he resort to doing? Why?

D. How do the blind people treat him? Why?

E. Go further. What does the end of the second part show as far as Nunez is concerned?

Part 1

He sat up in the place where they had left him, resting his limbs and turning the unanticipated circumstances of his arrival over and over in his mind. Every now and then he laughed, sometimes with amusement and sometimes with indignation.

"Unformed mind!" he said. "Got no senses yet! They little know they've been insulting their Heaven-sent King and master... I see I must bring them to reason. Let me think. Let me think."

He was still thinking when the sun set.

He heard a voice calling to him from out of the village.

"Yaho there, Bogota! Come hither!"

At that he stood up, smiling. He would show these people once and for all what sight would do for a man. They would seek him, but not find him.

"You move not, Bogota," said the voice.

He laughed noiselessly and made two stealthy[1] steps aside from the path.

"Trample not on the grass, Bogota; that is not allowed."

Nunez had scarcely heard the sound he made himself. He stopped, amazed. [...]

He stepped back into the pathway. "Here I am," he said.

"Why did you not come when I called you?" said the blind man. "Must you be led like a child? Cannot you hear the path as you walk?"

Nunez laughed. "I can see it," he said.

"There is no such word as see," said the blind man, after a pause. "Cease this folly and follow the sound of my feet."

Nunez followed, a little annoyed.

"My time will come," he said.

"You'll learn," the blind man answered. "There is much to learn in the world."

"Has no one told you, 'In the Country of the Blind the One-Eyed Man is King?'"

"What is blind?" asked the blind man, carelessly, over his shoulder.

Four days passed and the fifth found the King of the Blind still incognito, as a clumsy and useless stranger among his subjects.

1 furtive

Part 2

After an unsuccessful attempt to conquer the Country of the Blind, Nunez resigns himself to accepting his fate and live among the villagers.

"I was mad," he said. "But I was only newly made."

They said that was better.

He told them he was wiser now, and repented of all he had done. Then he wept without intention, for he was very weak and ill now, and they took that as a favourable sign.

They asked him if he still thought he could see.

"No," he said. "That was folly. The word means nothing. Less than nothing!" [...]

He expected dire punishments, but these blind people were capable of toleration. They regarded his rebellion as but one more proof of his general idiocy and inferiority, and after they had whipped him they appointed him to do the simplest and heaviest work they had for anyone to do, and he, seeing no other way of living, did submissively what he was told.

He was ill for some days and they nursed him kindly. That refined his submission. But they insisted on his lying in the dark, and that was a great misery.

So Nunez became a citizen of the Country of the Blind, and these people ceased to be a generalised people and became individualities to him, and familiar to him, while the world beyond the mountains became more and more remote and unreal.

The Country of the Blind,
H. G. Wells, 1904

2 Love is blind

A. Read the text. In your own words, say what one of the elders has decided to do.

B. Why did the doctor decide to do this?

C. How does Yacob react? Why?

D. Explain Nunez's reaction.

E. Sum up the conversation between Nunez and Medina-Saroté (l. 52-78) and the choice that he has to make.

F. **Have your say.** What does this part show about tolerance, difference and inclusion in the Country of the Blind?

Blind Love, American artist Chris Steinken, 2011

Months have gone by, and Nunez, as a citizen of the Country of the Blind has fallen in love with his master's youngest daughter, Medina-Saroté.

"You see, my dear, he's an idiot. He has delusions; he can't do anything right."

"I know," wept Medina-Saroté. "But he's better than he was. And he's strong, dear father, and kind — stronger and kinder than any other man in the world. And he loves me — and, father, I love him."

Old Yacob was greatly distressed to find her inconsolable, and, besides — what made it more distressing — he liked Nunez for many things. So he went and sat in the windowless council-chamber with the other elders and watched the trend of the talk, and said, at the proper time, "He's better than he was. Very likely, some day, we shall find him as sane as ourselves."

Then afterwards one of the elders, who thought deeply, had an idea. He was a great doctor among these people, their medicine-man, and he had a very philosophical and inventive mind, and the idea of curing Nunez of his peculiarities appealed to him.

"I have examined Nunez," he said, "and the case is clearer to me. I think very probably he might be cured."

"This is what I have always hoped," said old Yacob.

"His brain is affected," said the blind doctor.

The elders murmured assent.

"Now, what affects it?"

"Ah!" said old Yacob.

"This," said the doctor, answering his own question. "Those queer things that are called the eyes, and which exist to make an agreeable depression in the face, are diseased, in the case of Nunez, in such a way as to affect his brain. They are greatly distended, he has eyelashes, and his eyelids move, and consequently his brain is in a state of constant irritation and distraction."

"Yes?" said old Yacob. "Yes?"

"And I think I may say with reasonable certainty that, in order to cure him completely, all that we need to do is a simple and easy surgical operation — namely, to remove these irritant bodies."

"And then he will be sane?"

"Then he will be perfectly sane, and a quite admirable citizen."

"Thank Heaven for science!" said old Yacob, and went forth at once to tell Nunez of his happy hopes.

But Nunez's manner of receiving the good news struck him as being cold and disappointing.

"One might think," he said, "from the tone you take that you did not care for my daughter."

It was Medina-Saroté who persuaded Nunez to face the blind surgeons.

"You do not want me," he said, "to lose my gift of sight?"

She shook her head.

"My world is sight." Her head drooped lower.

"There are the beautiful things, the beautiful little things — the flowers, the lichens amidst the rocks, the light and softness on a piece of fur, the far sky with its drifting dawn of clouds, the sunsets and the stars. And there is you. For you alone it is good to have sight, to see your sweet, serene face, your kindly lips, your dear, beautiful hands folded together."

"I wish," she said, "sometimes — " She paused.

"Yes?" he said, a little apprehensively.

"I wish sometimes — you would not talk like that."

"Like what?"

"I know it's pretty — it's your imagination. I love it, but now —"

He felt cold. "Now?" he said, faintly. She sat quite still.

"You mean — you think — I should be better, better perhaps —"

He was realising things very swiftly. He felt anger perhaps, anger at the dull course of fate, but also sympathy for her lack of understanding — a sympathy near akin to[1] pity.

"Dear," he said, and he could see by her whiteness how tensely her spirit pressed against the things she could not say. He put his arms about her, he kissed her ear, and they sat for a time in silence.

"If I were to consent to this?" he said at last, in a voice that was very gentle.

She flung her arms about him, weeping wildly. "Oh, if you would," she sobbed, "if only you would!"

1 similar to

The Country of the Blind,
H. G. Wells, 1904

YOUR PROJECT

Imagine and write an ending to H.G. Wells's short story.

- Your story should include the main characters (Nunez, Medina-Saroté, the old doctor and Yacob).
- It should also take into account the general atmosphere and the relationship between them as well as other people's reactions.
- The ending may include a possible moral to the story.

TIPS

Afin de rédiger la fin d'une histoire on peut suivre quelques règles simples :

- Lire ou relire attentivement les extraits proposés de façon à bien identifier et connaître les personnages, leurs relations et les actions qu'ils sont susceptibles de mener ainsi que les conséquences de ces actions, les lieux, les paysages…
- Créer le plan de son intrigue en gardant une évolution cohérente avec le début. On peut s'aider d'un tableau des éléments-clés à compléter avec les éléments imaginés :

	Who?	*When?*	*Where?*	*What?*	*How?*	*Why?*
Extrait 1						
Extrait …						
Ma fin						

- Commencer la rédaction par la phrase finale du dernier extrait.
- Respecter le style de l'auteur : narration, parties dialoguées, descriptions des personnages, de leurs sentiments et réactions…
- Utiliser des connecteurs de temps pour indiquer les moments auxquels les actions se passent (*then, all of a sudden…*) ainsi que les expressions de la simultanéité (*No sooner… than…, hardly… when…*) et les temps du récit, le discours direct / indirect…
- L'histoire doit se terminer en cohérence avec le texte original et elle doit susciter des émotions. Le texte original étant une nouvelle, on peut imaginer une fin avec un rebondissement (*twist*).

LANGUAGE LAB

- Unit's vocabulary
- Audio words
- MP3
- Interactive Test

★ 1. Give synonyms or antonyms of the following elements and make a sentence for each one.

A. disabled ≠ …
B. open-minded ≠ …
C. confident = …
D. isolated = …
E. far away = …
F. strong ≠ …
G. accept sb ≠ …
H. trustworthy ≠ …

★ 2. Rephrase using indirect speech.

A. "You'll learn", the blind man answered.
→ The blind man answered …
B. "There's no such word as "see", said the blind man.
→ …
C. "Why didn't you come when I called you" asked the blind man. → …
D. "I wish you would not talk like that", she said. → …

★★ 3. Match each word with its definition.

A. sharp, acute
B. disregard
C. belittle
1. to portray as less impressive or important than appearances indicate.
2. extremely sensitive to slight details or impressions.
3. to pay no attention to something.

★★ 4. Rephrase as shown in the example.

He had just opened the door when he saw the villager.
→ ***No sooner*** *had he opened the door* ***than*** *he saw the villager.*
→ ***Hardly*** *had he opened the door* ***when*** *he saw the villager.*

A. They had just arrived in the village when they were faced with strange events.
B. She had just got acquainted with the neighbour when it was time to move out.
C. I had just made my point when I realised it was a mistake.
D. We had just started learning the local language when communication became impossible.
E. You had just stopped fearing for the worst when the catastrophe happened.

★★★ 5. Translate into English.

A. *Contrairement aux voyants, les aveugles développent d'autres sens, comme l'ouïe et le toucher.*
B. *Cette nouvelle de H.G. Wells évoque le thème de la tolérance, de l'intolérance et de l'inclusion.*
C. *Nunez essaie de convaincre les aveugles que la vue est un don. Les aveugles, quant à eux, pensent que c'est une maladie.*
D. *Nunez est parfois arrogant et irrespectueux envers les villageois aveugles.*
E. *Il se résigna à rester dans cette communauté et à vivre comme les villageois.*

6. Interactive test! What is your score?

OPEN YOUR EARS!

PHONOLOGY

Écoutez les mots suivants en faisant attention à la prononciation de la graphie « ea » et classez-les dans le tableau. Que remarquez-vous ?

MP3 N°111

meadow • stream • clearer • speak • breast • stealthy • nearer • beneath • smeared • pleased • earflaps • heaven

« ea »		
/i:/	/ɪə/	/e/
…	…	…

• Récapitulons :

- Les prononciations régulières de « ea » sont /i:/ (valeur de base), /ɪə/ (valeur modifiée par « r ») et /e/ (valeur brève).
- La prononciation /eə/ (*bearing*), /ɜ:/ (*heard, learn*) et /eɪ/ (*greatly*) sont exceptionnelles.
- Attention à ne pas confondre « ea » avec l'enchaînement de « e » + « a » comme dans *reassuringly, agreeable, beautiful.*

AUDIO MYSTERY

MP3 N°112

Listen to the recording and solve the mystery!

Quote challenge

★ 3 sentences
★★ 4 to 6 sentences
★★★ 7 sentences and +

Which quote sums up best what you have learnt? Justify!

"The only thing worse than being blind is having sight but no vision."

Helen Keller, deaf and blind political activist and educator (1880-1968)

"We need to make every single thing accessible to every single person with a disability."

Stevie Wonder, American singer, (1950-)

AXE 7

UNIT 23

SHORT CUT

BARBIE GOES INCLUSIVE

How has the iconic doll evolved to embrace diversity in American society?

YOUR PROJECT

Take part in a TV debate about Barbie's influence.

BEFORE CLASS!

Flash to watch!

Watch the video. Be ready to talk about it in class!

Au menu de cette unité :

DÉCOUVERTES CULTURELLES

- Ruth Handler, une entrepreneure visionnaire
- Barbie, une icône mondiale
- La stratégie de Mattel et la culture de l'inclusivité aux États-Unis

OUTILS LINGUISTIQUES

- Les comparatifs / superlatifs
- Le *present perfect*
- La place de l'adjectif
- Les adjectifs composés

❶ The Origins of an Iconic Doll

To what extent does Barbie symbolise female success?

1 The real story of the Barbie doll

A. Read the text. Focus on the creator and her creation. What / Who inspired her?

B. What were the main obstacles to her success?

C. How modern was this doll in the 1950s? Justify by quoting the text.

D. Pick out elements showing that Ruth Handler was a self-made woman who lived the American Dream.

HELP!

Nouns
- entrepreneur /ɒntrəprəˈnɜː/
- self-made woman
- visionary
- persevering

Adjectives
- bold: *audacieux*
- strong-willed: *volontaire*
- clear-sighted: *clairvoyant*
- goal-oriented: *déterminé*

Verbs & Expressions
- come up with an idea
- be intended /ɪnˈtɛndɪd/ for = be targeted at
- launch /ˈlɔːntʃ/ a product

The impact of the Barbie doll on girls' body images and the spread of a stereotypical model of womanhood has been the subject of extended reflections. [...] Yet one story that's much less known is that of Ruth Handler, the creator of Barbie and one of the founders of Mattel.

The first part of Ruth Handler's life is a succession of challenges. Born Ruth Moskowicz in Denver, Colorado, in 1916, she and her family were Polish Jews who had earlier immigrated to the United States. The youngest of 10 children, she could not attend university and initially found work as a secretary. She married Elliot Handler in 1938 and together they traversed the ordeal of World War II, which affected all of the United States. Then came financial hardship[1] for the young couple, living in California with two children. At the time Ruth was 30, but she had a huge ambition for her life and a big vision for the Handler family. [...]

Ruth wanted to make a toy for girls, and knew that she had a test market close at hand, her daughter Barbara. The idea emerged during a trip that the family took to Switzerland in 1956. In the window of a Swiss shop Ruth discovered a sex-symbol doll with a generous shape, Bild Lilli, based on a cartoon character created for the German tabloid *Bild*. Ruth immediately understood the marketing potential of the doll, and took several back to the United States.

In the 1950s, dolls intended for girls were often babies or mother or housewife characters. Ruth Handler's insight[2] was that girls of the 1950s no longer wanted to grow up just to be mothers, and the Barbie doll announced a certain emancipation from the exclusive role of a mother. While we can now see in Barbie the personification of the woman as object, Ruth Handler's idea was to create a toy that reflected women's ability to work and be autonomous. As she stated in her 1994 autobiography: "My whole philosophy of Barbie was that through the doll, the little girl could be anything she wanted to be. Barbie always represented the fact that a woman has choices."

When Ruth Handler presented her new concept to the head of a major American advertising agency, he stated: "It has no chance of succeeding. You're joking". Mattel's executive committee – composed entirely of men except for Ruth – also opposed the idea. She not only imposed the project, she persuaded Mattel's R&D department to make a doll that would be sold at cost, with profits coming from the sale of clothes and accessories. [...]

When the Barbie doll was presented at the New York International Toy Fair in 1959, all the big buyers, including the major American store brands[3] were unimpressed and refused to buy any. While many entrepreneurs would have given up, Ruth Handler decided to sell her doll directly to consumers. A major publicity campaign was launched, which resulted in the worldwide success that we know today.

1 difficulty • 2 understanding • 3 mark

Bertrand Venard, ***TheConversation.com***, 13 June 2019

❷ An Ever-Changing Model

How can Barbie be reinvented?

1 The doll that became a star

A. Read the text and list Barbie's activities.

B. Say why her life can be considered as a modern success story.

C. Comment on the last sentence (l. 15-16).

D. Have your say. How does the painting illustrate the article? Justify.

Andy Warhol, *Barbie*, 1985

At 60 years old, Barbie has transcended the toy store shelf (or the Amazon warehouse). She stars in a Netflix series, "Barbie Dreamhouse Adventures," and has almost 40 animated films to her name. In January, it was announced that Margot Robbie will play Barbie in a live-action movie. She's also a certified social media icon. On her most popular Instagram, @barbiestyle, she shares her outfits, street-style shots and "candid" photos of her hanging out with friends. With 2 million followers, she's on par with some of the bigger social media influencers. On YouTube, where she posts animated vlogs with titles like "Finding Your Voice," "What's In The Box Challenge!" and the Halloween-themed "Lion Makeup Tutorial With Ken," she has almost 6 million subscribers.

On both platforms, the main character is white, blonde and slim.

Emily Dixon, ***edition.cnn.com***, 9 March 2019

2 Impossible standards?

A. Observe the still and guess what the message is.

B. Watch the video and check your guess.

Turn to Worksheet n°43 for help.

C. Have your say. Do you agree that doll makers influence children's self-perception?

VIDEO N°41

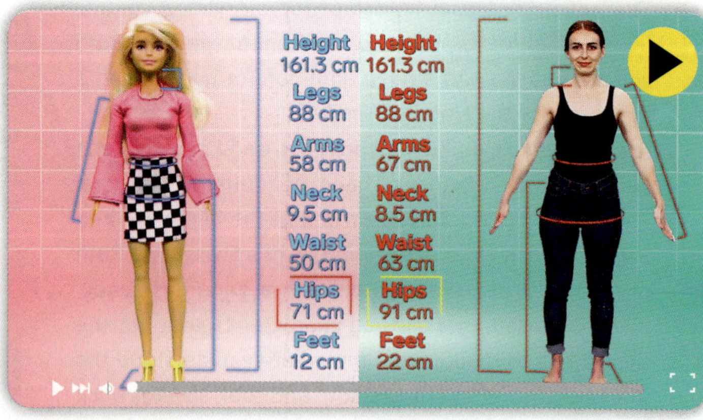

3 Lammily

A. Browse the Internet. Find who Lammily is.

B. Compare Lammily and Barbie.

C. Have your say. Do you agree with the statement "Average is beautiful"?

HELP!

Nouns
- dissatisfaction /dɪssætɪs'fækʃn/
- body esteem /ɪ'stiːm/
- average /'ævərɪdʒ/ = standard

Adjectives
- unrealistic /ʌnrɪə'lɪstɪk/
- damaging /'dæmɪdʒɪŋ/
- curvy /'kɜːvi/ ≠ thin
- chubby /'tʃʌbi/ ≠ slim
- distorted /dɪ'stɔːtɪd/ = false
- healthy /'helθi/ = fit

Expression
- meet standards = respect a norm

4 Adwoa Aboah

A. Imagine why Adwoa Aboah has been made into a doll.
B. Watch the video. What is Aboah's opinion on the project?
C. Account for Lisa McKnight's explanations.
D. Have your say. Give your opinion about the project.

VIDEO N°42

5 Barbie as a role model for girls

A. Observe the two pictures.
Take the quiz on Worksheet n°44
and test your knowledge of these women.
B. Browse the Internet to find other iconic women who were made into Barbie dolls.
C. Go further. You work in a think tank and you must choose the next role model in the English-speaking world. Who would you pick? Why?

6 The Dream Gap Project

A. Imagine what the "Dream Gap Project" is.
B. Watch the video. Explain what the project is (target, objective).
C. What happens when girls turn 5? Why?
D. List the figures and facts.
E. Have your say. Do you think the project is effective? Why (not)?

VIDEO N°43

YOUR TURN! 7 React on a forum

React to the following opinion on a forum: "*In a society where there's all kinds of people, our toys should reflect that.*"

HELP!

Adjectives
- impressive = amazing
- inspiring
- gifted = clever

Verbs & Expressions
- lose confidence
- close the gap = bridge the gap = reduce inequalities
- realise one's full potential
- stay true to oneself
- stand up for = defend
- stand up against = revolt
- be more likely to = have more chances of

❸ Disability, the Last Frontier

How can Barbie dolls create a culture of acceptance?

1 Wheelchair Barbie long overdue

A. Read the text. What motivated Mattel's new creation?

B. Account for Jay Ruderman's declaration (opinion, impact of the model, reasons).

C. Focus on lines 25-39. How symbolic is the story of Becky (model, problem, consequence, meaning)?

D. Have your say. Read the last paragraph and say whether you agree with the journalist.

Mattel unveiled two new Barbies as part of its Fashionista line: Barbie in a wheelchair[1] and Barbie with a prosthetic leg[2]. Kim Culmone, Vice President of Barbie Design, told Teen Vogue that one of the most frequent requests Mattel received was for a doll in a wheelchair. In addition to listening to its customers, the company worked with people with disabilities[3] to bring the dolls to life in the most accurate[4] way possible. [...]

Jay Ruderman, President of the Ruderman Family Foundation, which works to advance the inclusion of people with disabilities throughout society, celebrated the move. "Mattel's announcement — is such a huge step forward. It is not only empowering for young girls with disabilities, but it will break down stereotypes developed at a young age that will help remove stigmas adversely impacting people with disabilities" [...].

This is particularly important because people with disabilities are traditionally either underrepresented or misrepresented [...] even though they make up 19% of the US population [...]. "Kids need to see examples of humans that are different from themselves, but also be able to see toys, movie characters, and other figures that remind them of themselves," Rachel Wright, a New York-based psychotherapist, told me. "If everyone can be represented, it creates a culture of acceptance, rather than one of ignorance, fear, and hate."

[...] This isn't the company's first attempt at inclusion. In 1997, the company introduced Barbie's friend Becky, who was in a wheelchair. But despite several redesigns, her wheelchair never fit in the Barbie Dreamhouse, and she was eventually discontinued[5].

The symbolism here is rich [...]. People with disabilities are expected to conform to the able-bodied world, or risk being cast aside[6].

"Becky's departure matters, because the truth is Becky didn't fit into Barbie's world," disability advocate Karin Hitselberger wrote in a blog post. "Becky's discontinuance reflects how we are often taught to think about disability, in terms of fixing people rather than society. It matters because it echoes a way of thinking that suggests people are problematic when they are different."

Maybe with the new Barbie in a wheelchair, future generations of children with disabilities will come to embrace what makes them different instead of feeling shame. Being disabled profoundly shapes a person's experiences. It's an important part of one's identity, and like Doctor Barbie or Black Barbie, it should be represented and normalized.

1 *fauteuil roulant* • **2** *prothèse de jambe* • **3** *handicap* • **4** *precise* • **5** *arrêt de commercialisation* • **6** *mis de côtés, discriminés*

Melissa Blake, ***edition.cnn.com***, 18 February 2019

YOUR PROJECT

Take part in a TV debate about Barbie's influence over the years. Choose your role (marketing expert, parent, historian, psychologist...) and debate with the help of Worksheet n°45.

LANGUAGE LAB

- Unit's vocabulary
- Audio words
- MP3
- Interactive Test

★ 1. Create pairs of antonyms from the list below.

distorted • thin • curvy • harmless • consensual • chubby • straight • plump • harmful • lean • controversial • truthful

★ 2. Make comparative sentences.

A. Barbie is ... any other doll. *(+ beautiful)*
B. Edith's attitude towards beauty ... is Alfred's. *(= interesting)*
C. Mattel is ... any other toy company. *(+ big)*
D. The Becky doll ... was Barbie. *(- popular)*

★★ 3. Put the adjectives in the right order.

A. Barbie is a ... doll. (blond, tall)
B. Mattel is a(n) ... company. (old, big)
C. Ken represents a ... man. (lean, attractive)
D. She's wearing a ... skirt. (stylish, red, long)
E. He bought some ... trousers. (black, white, worn out)

★★ 4. Match each expression with its synonyms.

A. bridge the gap	1. oppose
B. break down barriers	2. resist
C. stand up for	3. reduce the difference
D. stand up to	4. integrate
E. stand up against	5. defend
F. fit in	6. make equal

★★ 5. Put the verbs in the present perfect.

A. Mattel *(become)* a huge company.
B. She *(wear)* these jeans many times.
C. They *(decide)* to introduce a new doll to their catalogue.
E. We *(seek)* to attract new customers.
D. The sales figures *(grow)* steadily over the last quarter.

★★★ 6. Complete the sentences with the words below.

high-flying • goal-oriented • clear-sighted • strong-willed • self-made

A. Ruth Handler is a real ... woman. She built an empire by herself.
B. She also had to be ... to overcome all the obstacles she had to face.
C. Ruth Handler was a ... creator who always set up great objectives.
D. Moreover as a ... businesswoman she never gave up.
E. As a ... inventor, she made a doll that would still be a hit 60 years after her creation.

7. Interactive test! What is your score?

OPEN YOUR EARS!

PHONOLOGY

• **Les mots en *-ic***

• **Écoutez les mots suivants.** MP3 N°113

iconic • unrealistic • prosthetic • problematic

Que remarquez-vous en ce qui concerne :
- la place de l'accent ?
- la voyelle accentuée ?

• **Récapitulons :** Tous les mots sont accentués sur la syllabe qui précède *-ic*.
Toutes les syllabes accentuées sont réalisées comme des voyelles brèves.

SHOWTIME

L'**accent de phrase** se fait sur la syllabe accentuée du dernier élément lexical de la phrase (en bleu ci-dessous). D'autres mots sont accentués dans une phrase, selon les cas.
Écoutez ces phrases et répétez-les en insistant sur les éléments accentués, en gras. MP3 N°114

*Barbie is one of the most **popular** dolls in **America**.*

→ *Dans le cas de « the most ... », c'est l'adjectif qui est accentué.*

*But that **doesn't mean** that she's loved by **everyone**.*

→ *Un auxiliaire à la forme négative est toujours plus accentué que le verbe qui l'accompagne.*

*For years, women advocates have **criticised** the doll for her **proportions**.*

→ *Un auxiliaire qui n'est pas à la forme négative est généralement non accentué et utilisé à la forme réduite /həv/.*

Quote challenge

★ 3 sentences
★★ 4 to 6 sentences
★★★ 7 sentences and +

Is this quote a good illustration of the unit? Make as many sentences as you can to collect stars!

"My whole philosophy of Barbie was that, through the doll, the girl could be anything she wanted to be. Barbie always represented the fact that a woman has choices."

Ruth Handler, inventor of the Barbie doll (1916-2002)

B1-B2

BACKPACK

Get Ready for your Exam!

UNIT 21

Évaluation

Compréhension de l'oral

"Harriet Tubman on a bill" MP3 n°115

Listen to the audio recording three times and recap what you have understood.

Expression écrite

Choisissez l'un des deux sujets (min. 120 mots).

Question A : In your opinion, how symbolical is it to place the face of a former slave on a dollar bill?

Question B : How can a country deal with its past to make its society more inclusive?

UNIT 22

Évaluation

Compréhension de l'oral

"Celebrating diversity with difference" MP3 n°116

Listen to the audio recording three times and recap what you have understood.

Expression écrite

Choisissez l'un des deux sujets (min. 120 mots).

Question A : How important is the inclusion of disabled people in society?

Question B : How can new technologies make the inclusion of the disabled easier?

UNIT 23

Évaluation

Compréhension de l'oral

"A new Barbie for a new society?" MP3 n°117

Listen to the audio recording three times and recap what you have understood.

Expression écrite

Choisissez l'un des deux sujets (min. 120 mots).

Question A : Do you think the new Barbie dolls will help little girls to develop self-esteem?

Question B : How important are toys to help children to develop creativity?

UNIT 21 Évaluation

Document A

I, too, sing America.
I am the darker brother.
They send me to eat in the kitchen
When company comes,
But I laugh,
And eat well,
And grow strong.
Tomorrow,
I'll be at the table
When company comes.
Nobody'll dare
Say to me,
"Eat in the kitchen,"
Then.
Besides,
They'll see how beautiful I am
And be ashamed—
I, too, am America.

Langston Hughes, *"I, too, sing America"*, 1926

Document B

Toni Morrison, who has died aged 88, was the only African American writer and one of the few women to have received the Nobel prize for literature. The announcement of her 1993 award cited her as a writer "who, in novels characterised by visionary force and poetic import, gives life to an essential aspect of American reality". […] When she started producing fiction, she was editing other writers for the publishers Random House in New York and began to feel the lack of novels which spoke to readers such as herself. Beginning with *The Bluest Eye* (1969), her novels portray the psychic and social lives of African American women, as well as men, covering the trauma of slavery and its economic and psychological consequences during and after the 19th century.

[…] *Song of Solomon* (1977) is wider ranging historically and geographically and, unusually within Morrison's oeuvre, has a black male character, Milkman Dead, as its main protagonist. Here the elements of magic realism […] are developed and Morrison draws on the African American myth of slaves escaping by flying away as an image of Milkman's discovery of his roots in a southern African American tradition. […]

Many readers and critics on both sides of the Atlantic regard her highest achievement to be *Beloved* (1987), the first novel in a trilogy chronicling black American small town and urban communities over the past 150 years. It is based on a factual incident that she uncovered while preparing a historical collection, *The Black Book* (1974), and explores the terrible impact of slavery, its brutality and its dehumanisation, on a young mother who murders her child to prevent her being repossessed by the slave-owner from whom she has escaped. The mother and those who live with her are haunted by the memory of the dead child, and the novel is also a more general representation of the terrible history that continues to haunt African Americans, a history that must be confronted in all its anguish before black people can learn to love themselves and one another.

[…] *Beloved* was awarded the Pulitzer prize for fiction in 1988, although not before a letter signed by more than 40 of America's leading black writers and scholars had decried the lack of recognition for this outstanding novel.

Lyn Innes, *The Guardian*, 6 August 2019

Compréhension de l'écrit Answer the following questions in English, using your own words.

Document A

A. Say who "I" and "they" refer to.
B. What happens to the main character when "company comes" and how does he/she feel about the situation?
C. Comment on l. 16-18 and say if modern America fits this image.

Document B

A. What can you say about the aim of the text and the people involved?
B. How did Toni Morrison portray the lives of African Americans at the time of slavery?
C. Comment on the statement (l. 26-29 "The novel is also…") and say if you share this point of view.

Expression écrite

Choisissez l'un des deux sujets (min. 120 mots).

Question A : Write a conversation between a grandfather/grandmother who lived during segregation and his/her grandchild(ren) who want(s) to know more about the past.

Question B : Would you say that art (films, paintings, music, writing…) can be a form of escape from a hard daily life? Why (not)?

B1-B2

BACKPACK

Get Ready for your Exam!

AXE 7 Évaluation

My name is Harvey Milk and I'm here to recruit you. [...]
About six months ago, Anita Bryant [...] said that the drought in California was because of the gay people. On November 9, the day after I got elected, it started to rain. On the day I got sworn in, we walked to City Hall and it was kinda nice, and as soon as I said the word "I do," it started to rain again. It's been raining since then and the people of San Francisco figure the only way to stop it is to do a recall petition. That's the local joke. [...]
The first gay people we elect must be strong. They must not be content to sit in the back of the bus. [...] They must be above wheeling and dealing. They must be—or the good of all of us—independent, unbought. [...] I will never forget what it was like coming out and having nobody to look up toward. I remember the lack of hope—and our friends can't fulfill it.
I can't forget the looks on faces of people who've lost hope. Be they gay, be they seniors, be they blacks looking for an almost-impossible job, be they Latins trying to explain their problems and aspirations in a tongue that's foreign to them. I personally will never forget that people are more important than buildings. I use the word "I" because I'm proud. I stand here tonight in front of my gay sisters, brothers and friends because I'm proud of you. I think it's time that we have many legislators who are gay and proud of that fact and do not have to remain in the closet. I think that a gay person, up-front, will not walk away from a responsibility and be afraid of being tossed out of office. [...] [In] San Francisco, three days before Gay Pride Day, a person was killed just because he was gay. And that night, I walked among the sad and the frustrated at City Hall in San Francisco and later that night as they lit candles on Castro Street and stood in silence, reaching out for some symbolic thing that would give them hope. These were strong people, whose faces I knew from the shop, the streets, meetings and people who I never saw before but I knew. They were strong, but even they needed hope.
And the young gay people in the Altoona, Pennsylvanias and the Richmond, Minnesotas who are coming out and hear Anita Bryant on television and her story. The only thing they have to look forward to is hope. And you have to give them hope. Hope for a better world, hope for a better tomorrow, hope for a better place to come to if the pressures at home are too great. Hope that all will be all right. Without hope, not only gays, but the blacks, the seniors, the handicapped, the US'es, the US'es will give up. And if you help elect to the central committee and other offices, more gay people, that gives a green light to all who feel disenfranchised, a green light to move forward. It means hope to a nation that has given up, because if a gay person makes it, the doors are open to everyone.
So if there is a message I have to give [...] it's the fact that if a gay person can be elected, it's a green light. And you and you and you, you have to give people hope.

Harvey Milk, *The Hope Speech*, 25 June 1978

Compréhension de l'écrit

Answer the following questions in English, using your own words.

A. After reading the text, what can you say about:
- its nature and its objective?
- the people involved (addresser and addressee)?
- the local joke and its meaning in general?
- the qualities (3 adjectives) necessary once you are elected (and why)?
- how the speaker sees the future?

B. Comment on the following statement and say if you share this point of view or not:
"And if you help elect to the central committee and other offices, more gay people, that gives a green light to all who feel disenfranchised, a green light to move forward." (l. 51-54).

Expression écrite

Choisissez l'un des deux sujets.

Question A : Write a letter to Anita Bryant* to complain about her views on minorities. Use the following sentence as a prompt:
"About six months ago, you said that the drought in California was because of the gay people..."

Question B : Would you say that electing people from minorities to key offices can change the lives of their communities? Why (not)?

*In the 1970s, Anita Bryant (born in 1940), a former miss Oklahoma, became known for strongly opposing gay rights in the U.S.

Évaluation

Observe the documents. According to you, which document best illustrates "Diversity and Inclusion"?

UNIT 21

a "Prejudice is a burden that confuses the past, threatens the future and renders the present inaccessible."

Maya Angelou, *American author* (1928-2014)

b

AXE 7

a "Girls have always been able to play out different roles and careers with Barbie and we are thrilled to shine a light on real life role models to remind them that they can be anything."

Lisa McKnight, Barbie senior vice-president and general manager, in a statement in 2018 when the collection of *Barbie Inspiring Women Series* was first announced.

b "It is never too late to give up your prejudices."

Henry David Thoreau, American poet and philosopher (1817-1862)

The King Arthur statue by Rubin Eynon,
Tintagel, Cornwall, UK

AXE 8

Territory & Memory

AXE 8

UNIT 24

GATEWAYS TO THE USA

Is the United States "the Land of Plenty" for everyone?

YOUR PROJECT

For a naturalisation ceremony, write a poem expressing the happiness and/or hardships of the immigrants.

Au menu de cette unité :

DÉCOUVERTES CULTURELLES

- Le poème *The New Colossus* d'Emma Lazarus
- Les vagues migratoires aux États-Unis aux 19e et 20e siècles
- L'histoire d'Ellis Island et d'Angel Island
- Le *Chinese Exclusion Act*
- Des poèmes de migrants
- Les poèmes retrouvés d'Angel Island

OUTILS LINGUISTIQUES

- L'obligation au passé (*had to*)
- Le discours direct et indirect

BEFORE CLASS!

Flash to watch!

Watch the video and get ready to talk about it in class!

VIDEO N°44

❶ The Promised Land

Why did the U.S. face such a wave of immigrants in the late 19th century?

1 "The New Colossus"

A. Look at the title and the image. Who does the "New Colossus" refer to?

B. Listen to the poem on **MP3 N°118** while reading it. Quote the expressions referring to the Statue of Liberty. Why is it called that?

C. Read the poem with the help of **Worksheet n°46**.

D. **Have your say.** What makes this poem positive and optimistic? Justify.

Not like the brazen[1] giant of Greek fame,
With conquering limbs[2] astride from land to land;
Here at our sea-washed, sunset gates shall stand
A mighty woman with a torch, whose flame
Is the imprisoned lightning, and her name
Mother of Exiles. From her beacon[3]-hand
Glows world-wide welcome; her mild eyes command
The air-bridged harbor that twin cities frame.
"Keep, ancient lands, your storied pomp[4]!" cries she
With silent lips. "Give me your tired, your poor,
Your huddled[5] masses yearning[6] to breathe free,
The wretched[7] refuse of your teeming[8] shore.
Send these, the homeless, tempest-tost to me,
I lift my lamp beside the golden door!"

The New Colossus,
Emma Lazarus, 1883

1 audacious • 2 *membre* • 3 *(ici) phare* • 4 *grandiose* • 5 gathered around • 6 desire • 7 poor creature • 8 *grouillants*

2 Immigration waves

A. Look at the map. What does it show?

B. Where were the four entrance gates?

C. Where did the immigrants come from? What does it say about the American population?

D. Use the figures and dates to give an oral account of the information given on the map.

E. **Go further.** Explain why so many immigrants decided to flee their native countries to start a new life in America. Use **Worksheet n°47** for help.

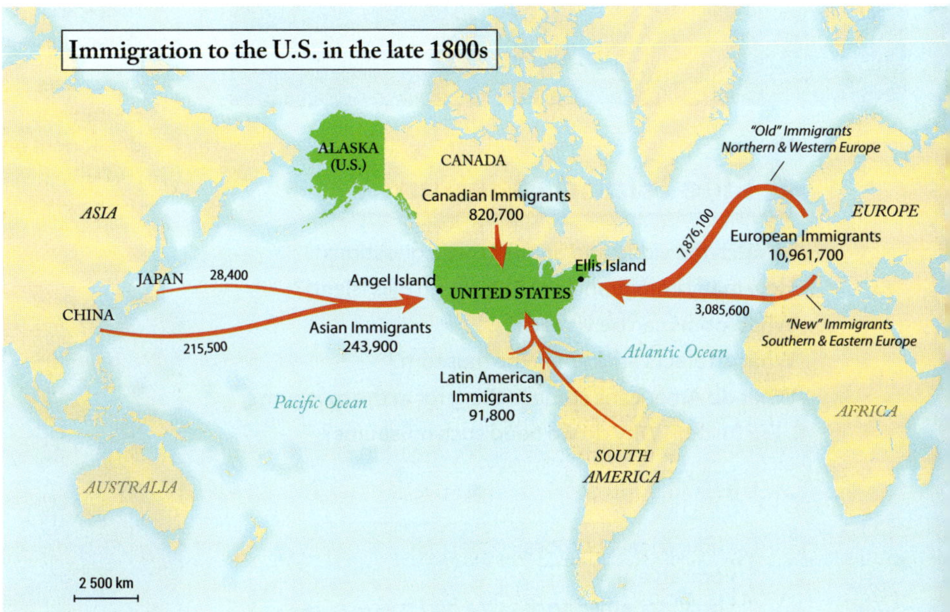

❷ Ellis Island

Why is Ellis Island sometimes referred to as "The Isle of Tears"?

1 A rough journey to the Land of the Free

A. Read the article. Were all passengers treated equally on board? Why?

B. In your own words, describe the living conditions on board for third class passengers.

C. Explain why some immigrants could be considered as "burdens to the state".

D. Go further. Imagine what an "inspection process" was like.

Most immigrants entered the United States through New York Harbor. First and second-class passengers who arrived in New York Harbor were not required to undergo the inspection process at Ellis Island. Instead, these passengers underwent a cursory[1] inspection aboard ship, the theory being that if a person could afford to purchase a first or second-class ticket, they were less likely to become a public charge in America due to medical or legal reasons. The Federal government felt that these more affluent passengers would not end up in institutions[2], hospitals or become a burden[3] to the state. However, first and second-class passengers were sent to Ellis Island for further inspection if they were sick or had legal problems. This scenario was far different for "steerage"[4] or third-class passengers. These immigrants travelled in crowded and often unsanitary conditions near the bottom of steamships with few amenities[5], often spending up to two weeks seasick in their bunks[6] during rough Atlantic Ocean crossings. Upon arrival in New York City, ships would dock at the Hudson or East River piers[7]. First and second-class passengers would disembark, pass through Customs[8] at the piers and were free to enter the United States. The steerage and third class passengers were transported from the pier by ferry or barge to Ellis Island where everyone would undergo a medical and legal inspection.

1 quick and superficial • **2** *(ici) association caritative* • **3** *fardeau* • **4** *entrepont* • **5** *agréments* • **6** *couchette* • **7** *débarcadère* • **8** *douanes*

www.saveellisisland.org

HELP!

Nouns
- **disability** /dɪsə'bɪləti/: *handicap*
- **disease**: *maladie*

Adjectives
- **contagious**
- **dependent on** ≠ **self-reliant** /rɪ'laɪənt/
- **thorough** /'θʌrə/: *rigoureux*
- **uneducated** = **illiterate** /ɪ'lɪtərət/
- **unemployed** = **jobless**

Verbs
- **examine** /ɪg'zæmɪn/
- **lack money**: *manquer d'argent*

2 Ellis Island Museum

A. Watch the video and answer these questions:
- How many immigrants came through Ellis Island?
- What rooms can be visited?
- What artefacts are kept in the museum?
- What do Americans come looking for in the museum?

B. Go further. Why do we need such museums?

HELP!
- educational purpose /'pɜːpəs/
- preserve
- bring together across time and space

VIDEO N°45

3 Immigrants' voices

A. Groupwork. Each group will work on a different poem to explain it to the class.
Use **Worksheet n°48**.

B. What emotions does each poem convey?

Poem #1 MP3 N°119

Unless the officials could pronounce and spell a name, every Eastern European Jew on the ship from Rotterdam became a "Hollander".

Sadie, who was only twelve, wrote each
letter down:
Haych, she said as she wrote it.
Oh, Ell. She had two countries now:
the one rising ahead of her like leavened bread[1]
and the one her father said had saved them
which now would name them.
Out with the bad, in with the good,
her mother said. Chollander
she practiced saying, over and over,
new food in her mouth,
and dropped the name she was born with
like a baby's gummed zwieback[2].
She wrote it down again and again
trying it out like a bride-to-be[3], wondering
who she would become with a name like this
in this place
where she could become it.

1 pain au levain • *2 /ˈzwaɪbæk/: biscotte hollandaise* • *3 future femme*

Ellis Island, September 1907,
Andrea Hollander, 1994

Poem #2 MP3 N°120

Beyond the red brick of Ellis Island
where the two Slovak children
who became my grandparents
waited the long days of quarantine,
after leaving the sickness,
the old Empires of Europe,
a Circle Line ship slips easily
on its way to the island
of the tall woman, green
as dreams of forests and meadows[1]
waiting for those who'd worked
a thousand years
yet never owned their own.
Like millions of others,
I too come to this island,
nine decades[2] the answerer
of dreams.
Yet only part of my blood loves that memory.
Another voice speaks
of native lands
within this nation.
Lands invaded
when the earth became owned.
Lands of those who followed
the changing Moon,
knowledge of the seasons
in their veins.

1 prairie • *2 10 years*

Ellis Island,
Joseph Bruchac, 1979

YOUR TURN! 4 Write a diary entry

Sadie Chollander's diary has been found. Imagine one of her entries. It could be before she left her homeland, on the vessel, on Ellis Island or a few months after her arrival.

HELP!

Nouns & Adjectives
- anger
- excitement
- hardships: *difficultés*
- baffled = confused
- confident
- hopeful
- mesmerising /ˈmezməraɪzɪŋ/: *fascinant*
- seasick: *avoir le mal de mer*
- traumatic: *traumatisant*

Verbs
- be treated like cattle: *être traité comme du bétail*
- land = arrive

❸ Angel Island, the Ellis Island of the West

Journeying to the United States: a promise of freedom?

1 A testimony

A. Read the text. What strategy did the narrator use to get into the country?
B. In your own words, rephrase what a paper father is.
C. Quote the words and phrases revealing the hate of the American staff. Did it reflect the position of the American government?
D. Comment on the narrator's feelings.

It took us 22 days to reach Angel Island from Hong Kong in 1911. The steamship was the *USS Lincoln*[1], named after one of the US presidents. We immigrants slept in steerage[2] and had very little room to move. The smell from the overused toilets was horrible. Many people were seasick. Luckily, I did not mind the rocking of the ship too much. Thoughts of the past and the future kept my mind busy. [...] We had to pay not only my passage but also a special fee[3] to my paper father in the United States. My paper father is not related to me. [...] He agreed to pretend to be my father so I might get into the United States. Those who pay someone in the United States like this are called paper sons. Chinese are not allowed into the country anymore unless they are in a special class, which includes merchants and students. My paper father owns a shop, so he is allowed to vouch for me[4]. [...] But first I must pass my hearing, a meeting where I will be asked many questions before I can enter the country.
The Angel Island Station is on top of a hill. It is a wooden house with a yard fenced in by barbed wire[5]. The others tell me that at the old station the Chinese would escape through the windows and hide in San Francisco, never to be seen again. The fence and US guards in this station keep us from running off. To me it looks like a cage.
I have passed the medical exam. We had to strip and were poked by an angry-faced white man. He checked our teeth and eyes worms[6] and diseases. [...]
I have waited inside the station almost three weeks for my hearing. I do not know why it takes so long. In that time, I have felt both nervous and excited. There is not much to do. [...] The white guards let us outside every morning for an hour. The guards do not like us. I cannot understand what they say, but it is plain in their hard eyes and tight mouths that they think less of us.

1 /ˈlɪŋkən/ • 2 *entrepont* • 3 a sum of money • 4 *se porter garant de qqn* • 5 *fils de fer barbelés* • 6 *vers*

Angel Island Immigration: A History Perspectives Book,
Jamie Kallio, 2014

VIDEO N°46

2 The Chinese Exclusion Act

A. Groupwork.
- **Group A** watches part 1 and takes notes on the narrator, his feelings and the Statue of liberty.
- **Group B** watches part 2 and takes notes on the Exclusion Act.

B. Share your findings with the other group and recap orally.

HELP!

Verbs
- enact a law = pass a law
- fester /ˈfestə/: *s'envenimer*
- languish /ˈlæŋgwɪʃ/ = stay (here)
- single out /ˈsɪŋgəl aʊt/

Adjective
- deep-seated /diːpˈsiːtɪd/ = firmly implanted

3 The lost poetry

A. Read the article. What was found on the walls of the buildings of Angel Island?
B. Why did it take so long to determine what it was?
C. Have your say. It is said that memorial sites aim at giving the next generations a chance to understand their past and shape their future. Discuss this using what you have learnt.

What would-be immigrants couldn't tell their interrogators they inscribed on the walls in the form of classical Chinese poetry—complete with parallel couplets, alternating rhymes, and tonal variations. In 1970, when the buildings of Angel Island were due to be torn down, a park ranger noticed the inscriptions. That discovery sparked the interest of researchers, who eventually tracked down two former detainees who had copied poems from the walls while they were housed on Angel Island, in the thirties. Their notebooks, additional archival materials, and a 2003 study of the walls—which were preserved—turned up more than two hundred poems. (There could be hundreds more buried beneath the putty[1] and paint that the immigration station staff used to cover the "graffiti.") The formal qualities of the poetry—which was written, for the most part, by men and women who had no more than an elementary education—tend to get lost in English translation, but its emotional force comes through.

1 *mastic*

Beenish Ahmed, ***The New Yorker***, 22 February 2017

4 A poem carved on the wall

A. Read the poem while listening to it on **MP3 N°121** .
B. Pick out the words and expressions linked with freedom and imprisonment. What do they reveal about the narrator's situation, feelings and living conditions?
C. What option does he contemplate in the end?

Imprisoned in the wooden building day after day,
My freedom withheld[1]; how can I bear to talk about it?
I look to see who is happy but they only sit quietly.
I am anxious and depressed and cannot fall asleep.
The days are long and bottle constantly empty; my sad mood, even so, is not dispelled.
Nights are long and the pillow cold; who can pity my loneliness?
After experiencing such loneliness and sorrow
Why not just return home and learn to plow[2] the fields?

1 *retenir, cacher* • 2 *labourer*

4 A Resilient Community

What hardships did Chinese immigrants have to face?

1 "Her Story"

A. What did this woman dream of upon landing in America?

B. What really happened to her?

C. Compare the first and last lines of the poem and comment on the role / mission of the poet towards society / towards unknown immigrants.

D. Go futher. Look at the picture of Chinatown and read the ***Cultural fact***. Would you say that it is a thriving community today?

MP3 N°122

Teow Lim Goh imagines English-language versions of the poems that Chinese women detainees might have composed.

I cannot seem to find her story.
She had been lured[1]. by the promise
of a rich man in America,
but when she landed on these shores
she was made to strip
and sold to the highest bidder[2].
Four years she must work without wages
to pay the price of her passage.
She gets ten days off a year,
A month's more work for ten days of sickness,
not enough to cover the days
her blood flows.
She cannot leave
until she pays off her debt.
What happened to her
when the mob[3] came marauding[4]?
Did men beat her,
have their way with her,
a fallen woman
who cannot fall lower?
If I don't tell her story
we cannot see her,
and without a reason for her being,
how will we let her survive?

1 appâter • 2 au plus offrant • 3 foule •
4 a person who moves around looking for sth to distroy or kill

Islanders,
Teow Lim Goh, 2016

Cultural fact

Chinatown: In the mid-1840s, a series of natural disasters occurred across China, which resulted in famine and peasant uprisings. In that context, when the news of a better future in "Gum San" (or "Golden Mountain", the Chinese name for America) reached China, many Chinese took their chances and went to seek their fortune in the Land of Plenty.
"Chinatowns" in the United States are traditionally located in cities like New York City, Philadelphia, Chicago, Boston or San Francisco. They were initially enclaves that facilitated the adaptation of Chinese people to American culture.
Although Chinatowns can now be found across the USA, they originated on the West Coast. Today, Chinatowns are booming and attract thousands of tourists each day.

YOUR PROJECT

For a naturalisation ceremony, write a poem expressing the happiness and/or hardships of the migrants. Then, read it out loud.

LANGUAGE LAB

• Unit's vocabulary
• Audio words
• MP3
• Interactive Test

★ **1. Put these sentences in the preterite.**

A. They must do something about immigration.
B. She must leave her family behind.
C. We must prepare for the long voyage.
D. You must go through the tedious selection process.
E. Immigrants must be pretty strong-willed.
F. Chinese immigrants must face deeply-rooted prejudices.

★ **2. Match the words with their definition.**

1. *emigrant* • 2. *gateway* • 3. *immigrant* • 4. *detained* • 5. *predicament* • 6. *hardship*

A. Something that serves as a means of entry or access.
B. Something that causes suffering or privation.
C. Someone who departs from a country to settle elsewhere.
D. Someone who comes to a country to settle permanently.
E. Kept in custody.
F. A difficult situation in which you do not know what to do.

★★ **3. Put the following sentences in indirect speech.**

A. "You can leave your belongings here." → *She was told* ...
B. "You must prepare your trip meticulously." → *They told him* ...
C. "The American Dream is the root of US immigration". → Jenny told Paul ...
D. "The Chinese Exclusion Act was a mistake." → *The teacher told his students* ...
E. "Immigrants have written beautiful poetry about their predicament." → *He was told* ...
F. "I have waited on Ellis Island for weeks." → *She said* ...

★★ **4. Put the words in the right column. Then, choose a word for each comumn and write a sentence.**

auspicious • *brokenhearted* • *destitute* • *disappointed* • *hopeful* • *disgruntled* • *disillusioned* • *impoverished* • *poverty stricken* • *promising* • *prosperous* • *wealthy*

Rich	Poor	Optimistic / Encouraging	Dispirited / Depressed
...	...	...	...

★★★ **5. Translate these sentences into English.**

A. *Il a dit qu'il ne connaissait rien sur l'histoire de l'immigration.*
B. *Elle leur avait dit qu'ils seraient bien traités.*
C. *Le gouvernement lui avait assuré que tout avait été bien préparé.*
D. *On leur avait dit qu'elles trouveraient un mari aux États-Unis.*
E. *On leur avait promis qu'ils trouveraient un travail facilement.*

6. Interactive test! What is your score?

OPEN YOUR EARS!

PHONOLOGY

La prononciation du son /j/ en anglais américain.

• L'anglais américain ne prononce pas le son /j/ entre certaines consonnes et le son /u:/, comme dans <u>New</u> York.

• **Écoutez les mots suivants et classez-les en fonction de la présence ou de l'absence du son /j/.**

MP3 N°123 *salute* • *music* • *assume* • *suitable* • *consume* • *beauty* • *tune* • *few* • *student* • *dune* • *new* • *cube*

/ju:/	/u:/
...	...

TRAVEL WITH ACCENTS!

Écoutez ce passage dans les deux accents en faisant particulièrement attention à la prononciation.

MP3 N°124 *"My countrymen and myself are <u>ho</u>nored in being thus appealed to as citi<u>zens</u> in the <u>cause</u> of liberty."*

MP3 N°125 *"But the <u>word</u>, liberty, makes me think of the fact that this country is the <u>land</u> of liberty for <u>all</u> men of all nations except the Chinese."*

Picture challenge

★ 3 sentences
★★ 4 to 6 sentences
★★★ 7 sentences and +

How many sentences can you make using what you have learnt? Collect stars!

AXE 8

UNIT 25

MĀORI MEMORY

How can New Zealand embrace the Māori history?

YOUR PROJECT

1 Write and give a speech of reconciliation.

OR

2 Write an article entitled "How can the Māoris revive their culture?"

Au menu de cette unité :

DÉCOUVERTES CULTURELLES

- Le traité de Waitangi
- Le moko, tatouage culturel et mémoriel
- Le rapatriement des restes humains Māoris conservés dans les musées
- Le rapport des Māoris à la terre, la légende de Maui
- Les *stolen generations* en Nouvelle-Zélande et en Australie

OUTILS LINGUISTIQUES

- L'expression de l'exclamation et l'emphase
- *For, since* et *ago*
- Le passif
- Le *present perfect*

❶ Stolen Land

How have Indigenous people's cultures been subjugated?

1 The Treaty of Waitangi

An old Māori chief, Te Tupaea, is talking to his people about their past.

And he was talking in English, tellin em[1] all gathered at his feet, his constantly moving feet, that their inheritance[2] was their past and without the past they were nothing [...].

He told them of great acts of chivalry during the warring with the first white men: of warriors — that's *Māori* warriors — slipping out into the battlefield at night to tend to the wounded[3] enemy, giving the enemy food, drink, even touches of comfort. And the gathering going, Wow, far out, but why? And the chief's eyes with that fighting fire in them saying: So the enemy might have more strength to continue the battle in the morning. And the crowd went, Ooooh! Smiling all over. Thinking: But we never knew that.

No one taught us this at school. They taught us *their* history: English history. They forced us to learn, off by heart, dates and names of great Englishmen and battles fought in a country none of us have ever been to nor are likely to go. And they gave us no marks in our exams when we couldn't remember these dates and funny names and strange-sounding places, and they never understood that to remember things of knowledge ya have to have fire in your belly for it, like the great chief there, or just ordinary passion of wanting to remember it because it, well, it's about yourself, historical knowledge most easily remembered.

And the chief putting into words their vague thoughts, giving their minds a shape they could visualise: We fought em[4] at every turn. We *never* gave up. They came to this land with their queen and kings, and we, the Māori, set up our *own* king in defiance of them. YOU HEAR THIS? And the crowd roared, YESSSSS!!

And when they knew we would never give up they signed a treaty with us. The Treaty of Waitangi[5]. You all heard of that? YESSSS!! You all know what it was? Individuals answering they thought it was an agreement between two peoples to share the land, its resources. *As equals!* their fiery chief exclaiming.

A contract! IT WAS A CONTRACT. Then silence.

And just the coughs and sighs and rustle of movement. Te Tupaea just stood there, legs astride, fists on suited sides. A contract... Whispering it, so the ones at the back had to ask what'd he say, and then their whispering dying down. And Te Tupaea again whispering: Which — they — broke.

1 telling them • 2 patrimony • 3 hurt • 4 them • 5 signed in 1840 between English settlers and tribal chiefs

Once Were Warriors,
Alan Duff, 1995

A. Read the text and say who "he" (l. 1), "(th)em" (l. 27), "the enemy" (l. 8), "their" (l. 28) correspond to. Imagine the situation.

B. What problem about the way history is taught at school does the narrator raise? Give examples.

C. How did the settlers and the Māoris solve the problem of the land?

D. Have your say. Read the last paragraph (l.39-44) and observe the photo. What can you guess about the treaty? Read the *Cultural fact* and explain.

Cultural fact

The **Treaty of Waitangi** was signed in 1840 by the British Crown and Māori chiefs. It intended to establish a British Governor of New Zealand, to recognise Māori ownership of their lands, and to give Māori the same rights as British subjects. However, the English text and the Māori text differ in meaning, particularly in relation to ceding sovereignty. This led to disagreements.
Māori lost control of much of the land they had owned, sometimes through legitimate sale, but often due to unfair land deals or through confiscations.

HELP!

Nouns
- agreement /ə'gri:mənt/
- colonist = settler
- indigenous
- Māori /'maʊri/

Verbs & Expressions
- demand /dɪ'mɑ:nd/
- demonstrate /'demənstreɪt/
- respect ≠ infringe

❷ Preserving Māori Heritage

How can Māori memory live on?

1 Carving one's past: the moko

"The moko is our signature. It is what our ancestors signed their documents with. They used their facial moko when they first traded with the Europeans—the British. Historically, we say that moko comes from the underworld.

The gods associated with the tattooing gave it to the people to bring up to the surface. It is a beautiful metaphor for the revival, because we say that it was underground when it was abolished and there was persecution. We have brought it back up to the surface again like they did in the ancient times. It is not a static art form. It is a breathing, living, growing art form."

Mitchell Ryan, ***National Geographic***, 2014

A. Read the text and answer these questions:
- What does the moko represent in commercial exchanges?
- Where does the moko originate from, according to Māori belief?
- Say what it is a metaphor for.
- Imagine why it was abolished by the Whites.

B. Have your say. What makes the moko a living art form?

2 Read and understand the moko!

A. At home. Do a webquest about the moko and take notes.

B. Select and organise information to explain the meaning of the moko.

C. Present your findings orally.

3 Reinventing bloodline leadership

A. Watch the trailer and be ready to talk about:
- the legend of Paikea ;
- how leadership was organised ;
- what young Paikea Apirana wants ;
- who opposes her and why.
- the objective of the sacred school.

B. Have your say. How vital is it for the Māori to let girls be leaders?

VIDEO N°47

4 Bringing back human remains

Institutions across Europe and the U.S. face growing calls to return art looted[1] during the colonial era. [...] Western institutions have thousands of skulls, skeletons, bone fragments, and even preserved heads of Indigenous people [...]. Typically donated by collectors, missionaries, and colonial officials in the 19th century, these objects are a dark legacy of European's voracious appetite for "curios" of so-called primitive people. Others were collected as evidence of long-discredited, pseudo-scientific theories of white racial supremacy.

[...] Neel—a descendant of the tribes of the Kwakwaka'wakw and vice chair of the First Peoples' Cultural Council in British Columbia—has been working with the Royal British Columbia Museum to help it return hundreds of human remains and sacred cultural objects. "It's about closure[2] and reconciliation," she tells *Artnet News*. Neel stresses how important it is for communities to know that "their grandparents and great grandparents" are reburied[3] with the correct rituals and ceremonies. Many believe that their ancestors' spirits cannot rest until their remains[4] are returned. "It is a form of healing," she says.

[...] Among the most prized "curios" were the preserved tattooed heads of the Māori people. The grim[5] trade began in 1770, when the aristocratic botanist Joseph Banks arrived in New Zealand and traded a pair of linen drawers for the preserved head of a teenage boy. Within 50 years, the trade of human remains was banned[6]. But not before hundreds were sold, many of which ended up in museums in Europe and North America. New York's American Museum of Natural History purchased 35 of them in 1907. The Museum of New Zealand Te Papa Tongarewa estimates that there are remains of at least 600 known Māori and Moriori[7] ancestors, including their preserved heads, in European museums.

Sydney Parkinson, ***Head of Otegoowgoow, Son of a New Zealand Chief,*** 1784

1 stolen • **2** *tourner la page* • **3** give a funeral service again • **4** corpse • **5** sad • **6** forbidden • **7** other Indigenous people from the Chatham Islands in New Zealand

Javier Pes, **www.news.artnet.com,** 29 November 2018

A. Read the article and list what western museums keep in their collections.

B. Explain the way museums obtained these objects and why they collected them.

C. Say how New Zealand tries to bring back these objects.

D. Have your say. How important is it to send back these remains and stolen art in general?

HELP!

Nouns
- **ancestor** /'ænsəstə/
- **facial tattoo** /tə'tu:/
- **work of art**: *œuvre d'art*

Adjectives
- **healing** /'hi:lɪŋ/
- **sacred** /'seɪkrɪd/
- **mummified**

Verbs & Expressions
- **bring back** = **return**
- **carve** = **sculpt**
- **give consent** /kən'sent/

YOUR TURN! 5 Make a banner

Groupwork. Write banners requesting the return of Māori remains. The best ones will be hung on the facade of The Museum of New Zealand.

❸ Mother Land, Mother Nature

How deep is the connection of the Māori with their lands?

1 Venerating Mount Hikurangi

Sculptures to honor Māui and his family

Mount Hikurangi takes its place [...] as the epic manifestation of my mother's mana[1], strength or prestige. Of course, it was not only her mountain, it is the mountain that all Ngāti Porou regard as theirs. She always kept a close eye on Hikurangi whenever we were traveling through the East Coast. This part of Aotearoa [...] was bounded by the sea on the east, and, to the west, the tribal territories [...] As we traversed the massive flanks of the mountain, she would acknowledge it with bowed head. Throughout her life she steadfastly took her bearings from Hikurangi and never showed her back to it.

Mum's awe[2] to Hikurangi was not without foundation [...]. At 1920 metres it was the highest point on the Raukūmara Ranges, but because of her reverence of it, from the very beginning the mountain played an enormous part in my own psychic life, looming over[3] it and through it. Hikurangi's potency came not only from its brooding[4] physical presence but also from the stories attached to it.

For example when Māui[5] went out fishing with his brothers and he dragged Aotearoa up from the sea, it was because his fishhook had caught into one of the crevices of the mountain. When this enormous fish of Māui had finally ceased its struggles and rose through the water, Mount Hikurangi was the first part of the land to broach the surface. [...]

The word Hikurangi means Summit of the Sky, and the mountain is often regarded by Ngāti Porou as a lodstone[6] for the universe. If there were a map of the stars and the planets, the cosmological significance of Hikurangi would be acknowledged by its cardinal appearance. Why? It was the first point on the earth's surface that was touched by the new day. And so I have always liked to think that, if ever you were lost in space, all you would need to do was wait until the sun came up. What would you be waiting for? Why, the flash of sunlight on the sacred mountain! Once you saw that sword of light, then you would calibrate your position.

1 honour, authority, presence or prestige • **2** admiration • **3** *peser sur* • **4** dark • **5** A Māori hero famous for his exploits and cleverness. He is credited with catching a giant fish • **6** *aimant*

Māori Boy: A Memoir of Childhood,
Witi Ihimaera, 2014

A. Read the text and list elements showing that the narrator's mother admired Mount Hikurangi.

B. Say how legends show that people admire the mountain.

C. Go further. Say how important the mountain is to transmission of memory through generations.

HELP!

Nouns
- heritage
- collective memory
- tradition

Verbs & Expressions
- preserve
- keep history alive

2 Māori tales of the sea

Māori have strong spiritual bonds[1] with the land — Papatūānuku (the Earth mother). They regard land, soil and water as taonga (treasures). Māori see themselves as the kaitiaki (guardians) of this traonga, which provides a source of unity and identity for tangata whenua (local people). Not surprisingly, given that New Zealand is surrounded by sea, Māori have a strong affinity with the ocean.

Oral storytelling is a vital element in Māori culture, and the story of demi-god Māui fishing Aotearoa from the sea has been passed down through the generations. The North Island (Te Ika a Māui) was the fish Māui caught and became home to Māui, his family and all Māori. The South Island became the waka (canoe) of Māui through the legend and is known as Te Waka a Māui (the canoe of Māui). Stewart Island, located to the south of the South Island is known as Te Punga a Māui (Māui's anchor).

According to tradition Māori arrived progressively in canoes from Hawaiiki — the ancestral homeland of the Māori, possibly located in or near the Cook Islands. The first waka was captained by Kupe and arrived in the north of the North Island. The tangata whenua (people of the land) of New Zealand have always been great fishers and have special provision[2] to fish under customary[3] fishing regulations. Kaimoana (seafood) caught under the customary fishing regulations cannot be traded or sold.

1 connections • **2** legislation • **3** traditional

media.newzealand.com

A. Read the text and explain Māori people's relation to the sea.

B. Say how the country was formed according to Māori legends.

C. Say why fishing shows that the Māori preserved a part of their traditions.

D. Go further. Use **Worksheet n°49** and label the map according to the legend.

3 Giving legal personhood to nature

A. Online. Watch the video (www.lienmini.fr/htr-tl-25) and take notes about the Māori's strategy to gain national recognition.

B. Prepare your oral recap with a mindmap. Split the task between groups.

C. Have your say. What do you think about giving legal personhood to nature to pass on a culture?

YOUR TURN! 4 Talk about Māori and nature!

Participate in a radio show for the BBC entitled "Māoris people: Guardians of their Lands".

HELP!

Nouns & Adjectives
- guardianship = care
- landscape
- legal personhood = status of "person"
- committed /kəˈmɪtɪd/ = dedicated
- revered /rɪˈvɪəd/ = admired

Verbs & Expressions
- live off the sea = feed on the sea
- reclaim = take back
- worship /ˈwɜːʃɪp/: *vénérer, adorer*

❹ Stolen Generations

How can Indigenous peoples overcome the trauma of their Stolen Generations?

1 Tyrone Marks, welfare home survivor

Former stolen children call for a government investigation into the abuse they suffered (2017)

Throughout English-speaking countries Indigenous peoples saw their children taken away by the state for generations. Most countries have apologized for this shameful past, but New Zealand is still turning a blind eye on its own Stolen Generation. A group now known as Ngā Mōrehu (The Survivors) is currently fighting for the recognition of the Stolen Generation by the state. Tyrone Marks spent eight years in state welfare homes and adult psychiatric institutions. He is the lead claimant in a case taken to the Waitangi Tribunal. The text is based on Tyrone's testimony. He remembers the day a social worker arrived to take him away.

The social worker pretended to be kind to Tyrone Marks. But her act of deception[1] propelled[2] him into an odyssey of abuse. His family was large and poor. But whatever struggles[3] he had growing up paled in comparison to what happened when the social welfare worker turned up in 1967 when Marks was six years old.

"One day they just came, told me they were going to take me out to buy some clothes for me. I even remember the name of the social worker. She made me feel like I could trust[4] her and all she was doing was making sure I had brand new clothes and shoes and stuff. Where everybody else got lunches when they went to school, I didn't. With shoes, I was the last on the list. I never really got any, I had to go to school in bare feet. So this lady was telling me she was buying me some new clothes, so I jumped in the car. I was none the wiser[5] [about] what was going to happen from that point onwards. They said they were buying me some clothes and bringing me back home. But that's not what they were doing at all."

Instead of taking him to get new shoes the social worker drove him to the airport. He was then put on a plane to another part of the country. "These nuns[6] came to pick me up. So I had no idea why I was there. I'd never had anything to do with nuns. I was quite freaked out[7] actually as a kid. It was quite sad. I knew I was a very long way from home; I couldn't just open the door and walk home again. I tried, but I didn't know where I was. That's where it all started from."

For Marks, it was the beginning of an eight-year journey through a number of state welfare institutions. It's an experience more than 100,000 other children endured in New Zealand from the 1940s through to the late 1980s. Most of the children were indigenous Māori.

1 lie • **2** drove • **3** fights • **4** believe in • **5** conscious • **6** *religieuse* • **7** afraid

www.aljazeera.com, 2017

A. Read the first paragraph and give the context of the testimony (name of the man, period, action) (l. 1-5).

B. How did the social worker make the little boy follow her? React.

C. What happened to Marks after he was in the car?

D. Look at the photo above and imagine who the people are and what they are doing.

E. Have your say. Imagine the consequences of this policy on the future of these Māori children.

HELP!

Adjectives
- betrayed
- traumatised /ˈtrɔːmətaɪzd/
- harmful = damaging

Verbs & Expressions
- apologise /əˈpɒlədʒaɪz/
- acknowledge /əkˈnɒlɪdʒ/ = recognise /ˈrekəgnaɪz/

2 "We are the Stolen Generation"

A. Online. Watch the video (www.lienmini.fr/htr-tl-25) and take notes about the Stolen Generation (period, places, people targeted, rule, teaching, objective).

B. What happened to the girl's grandfather (age, place, people, actions and reactions)?

C. Say how some children could hide.

E. Give the number of children kidnapped and the consequences today.

F. Have your say. How important is it to share these stories? Justify.

3 Australia says "sorry"

A. Listen to Australia's former Prime Minister Kevin Rudd on **MP3 N°126** and take notes about:

- how he introduces Aboriginal culture;
- what the Australian nation reflects on;
- what Australian people apologise for;
- what the state plans for the future.

B. Give the objective of the Prime Minister's speech.

C. Have your say. How important is an official apology for oppressed communities?

D. Go further. Compare how Australia and New Zealand tackle the issue of their Stolen Generations.

YOUR PROJECT

1. Write and give a speech of reconciliation.

OR

2. Write an article for National Geographic, entitled "How can the Maori revive their culture?"

HELP!

Nouns
- policy = legislation
- missionary camp /ˈmɪʃnəri/ = religious schools
- grief = extreme sadness
- healing /ˈhiːlɪŋ/ = cure

Adjectives
- forcibly assimilated /ˈfɔːsəbli əˈsɪmɪleɪtɪd/ = integrated by force
- soothing = pacifying

Verbs & Expressions
- mistreat
- take by force = grab = snatch
- resort to /rɪˈzɔːt/ = use
- reflect on
- right the wrongs: *réparer une injustice*
- apologise /əˈpɒlədʒaɪz/

SPICE UP YOUR VOCABULARY

Use the vocabulary below to create your own mind map and add more words if necessary!

Nouns

- ancestor
- apology /ə'pɒlədʒi/
- blemish
- boarding school /'bɔːdɪŋ/
- collective memory
- colonialism /kə'ləʊniəlɪzəm/
- grief /griːf/
- heritage
- indigenous
- knowledge
- land deal
- loss: *perte*
- Māori
- owner /'əʊnə/
- pain
- patrimony
- policy /'pɒləsi/
- reconciliation process
- removal /rɪ'muːvl/
- revival /rɪ'vaɪvl/
- settler = colonist
- sovereignty
- subject
- tattoo /tə'tuː/
- tradition
- trauma /'trɔːmə/
- treaty = legal agreement

Verbs & Expressions

- acknowledge /ək'nɒlɪdʒ/
- apologize /ə'pɒlədʒaiz/
- cure /kjʊə/
- demonstrate
- fade away: *s'effacer*
- fight for one's rights
- have closure: *tourner la page*
- heal /hiːl/
- implement /'ɪmpləment/
- infringe ≠ respect
- mistreat
- reclaim /rɪ'kleɪm/
- revive /rɪ'vaɪv/
- right the wrongs
- sign up
- snatch = grab
- take back
- worship /'wɜːʃɪp/

Adjectives & Adverbs

- abducted /əb'dʌktɪd/
- betrayed /bɪ'treɪd/
- comforting /'kʌmfətɪŋ/
- committed /kə'mɪtɪd/
- dedicated /'dedɪkeɪtɪd/
- harmful
- left behind
- pacifying /'pesɪfaɪɪŋ/
- pain-relieving /rɪ'liːvɪŋ/
- prejudicial /predʒʊ'dɪʃl/ detrimental /detrə'mentl/
- proud /praʊd/
- relief-giving
- resilient = strong
- soothing /suːðɪŋ/
- traumatised /'trɔːmətaɪzd/

RULE THE GRAMMAR!

L'EXPRESSION DE L'EXCLAMATION

• Pour exprimer l'exclamation, on utilise deux structures principales :
- ***How*** + adjectif → ***How horrible!***
- ***What*** + adverbe + nom → ***What lovely trees!***

• On emploie ***a / an*** devant des dénombrables au singulier et l'article Ø devant les indénombrables :

What a nice place!
What Ø dreadful treachery!
Notez les expressions : ***What a shame!*** ***What a pity!***

• Attention dans la forme interro-négative à valeur exclamative, on utilise un point d'exclamation et non un point d'interrogation : ***Isn't it horrible!***

LE *PRESENT PERFECT*

• Le *present perfect* se forme avec l'auxiliaire ***have*** au présent et le **participe passé** du verbe.
• On utilise essentiellement le *present perfect* pour présenter le résultat d'une action débutée dans le passé et qui a des conséquences ou des effets dans le présent.

Māori artefacts have reappeared on the black market.
(Ils sont désormais à nouveau disponibles.)

→ P.299

LANGUAGE LAB

- Audio words
- MP3
- Interactive Test

★ **1. Put the verbs in the appropriate tense (preterite or present perfect).**

A. Ever since colonisation, the Māori ***(be betrayed)*** by the British.
B. James Cook ***(arrive)*** in New Zealand in 1769.
C. Tourists ***(be attracted)*** by New Zealand for many years.
D. Māori ***(fight)*** for their rights with determination for years.
E. The Māori haka dance always ***(frighten)*** rugby players.
F. The Treaty of Waitangi ***(be signed)*** in 1840.

★ **2. In each list, find the odd word out. Justify.**

A. colonist • settler • native • stranger • explorer
B. grief • pain • despair • relief • hopelessness
C. apologise • acknowledge • right the wrongs • repair • deny
D. soothing • pacifying • comforting • traumatising • reassuring

★ **3. Turn the following sentences into exclamations.**

A. This behaviour is outrageous. → How ...
B. This treason was unexpected. → What...
C. This kind of theft is common. → How ...
D. This situation is unbearable. → What ...

★★ **4. Transform the nouns into verbs and the verbs into nouns.**

A. trauma → ...
B. apology → ...
C. acknowledgement → ...
D. revive → ...
E. colonise → ...

★★ **5. Turn these active sentences into passive sentences.**

A. The British annexed both Australia and New Zealand.
B. Europeans states stole local artefacts.
C. Maori people have always worshipped nature.
D. Britain gave independence to Australia in 1942.
E. Colonists treated indigenous people rather badly.

★★★ **6. Match the words with their synonyms.**

A. heal	1. kidnap
B. prejudicial	2. lie
C. betrayed	3. cure
D. reclaim	4. detrimental
E. abduct	5. take back

★★★ **7. Complete the blanks with the words below. Make changes when necessary.**

carve • bring back • healing process • assimilate • own

A. With the Treaty of Waitangi the Māori were dispossessed of the land they ... .
B. Aboriginal children were kidnapped to be ... into white culture.
C. The Māori ... tattoos on their faces to connect to their past.
D. The Māori demand to ... human remains kept in western museums.
E. Returning the remains is part of the ... .

8. Interactive test! What is your score?

OPEN YOUR EARS!

TRAVEL WITH ACCENTS!

1. L'accent néo-zélandais et l'accent australien

• Pour beaucoup d'anglophones, l'accent australien et l'accent néo-zélandais se ressemblent. Il existe un test infaillible pour les distinguer.
Le néo-zélandais dira "*Fush and chups*" /fəʃ ən 'tʃəps/
L'Australien dira "*Feesh and Cheeps*" /fiːʃ ən 'tʃiːps/
La réalité est un peu plus complexe !

2. L'accent australien

• Écoutez les phrases suivantes prononcées par un Australien, puis en anglais standard. Faites attention aux éléments en gras. Quelles différences remarquez-vous ?

MP3 N°127
MP3 N°128

The time has no come for the nation to turn a new page.
A new page in Australia's history by righting the wrongs of the past.

Récapitulons

- Les Australiens et les Londoniens prononcent /aɪ/.
- L'anglais standard prononce /eɪ/.

Picture challenge

★ 3 sentences
★★ 4 to 6 sentences
★★★ 7 sentences and +

How many sentences can you make using what you have learnt? Collect stars!

AXE 8

UNIT 26

SHORT CUT

NEW ORLEANS: A LIVING MUSEUM

Which historical moments have shaped New Orleans?

YOUR PROJECT

Send a video to the mayor of New Orleans proposing a new symbol for the city to replace a Confederate statue.

BEFORE CLASS!

Flash to watch!

Watch this video and be ready to talk about it in class!

VIDEO N°48

Au menu de cette unité :

DÉCOUVERTES CULTURELLES

- Les attraits touristiques de la Louisiane
- L'histoire de la création de la Louisiane
- Les différentes influences culturelles (Afrique, France, Espagne…)
- Le devoir de mémoire du passé esclavagiste (musée, *reenactment*…)

OUTILS LINGUISTIQUES

- Le *past perfect*
- Les modaux au passé
- L'expression de la suggestion (*What about… Let's…*)

❶ A Complex History

How was New Orleans at the heart of changing the United States?

1 The Louisiana Purchase

A. Watch this video and find the answers to the following questions:
- Which countries controlled New Orleans and the Louisiana territory?
- Why did the Americans want New Orleans?
- Why did the French give up the whole territory?
- How much land was in the Louisiana territory?

B. Go further. Imagine what the population of New Orleans must have been like after being governed by so many different countries.

VIDEO N°49

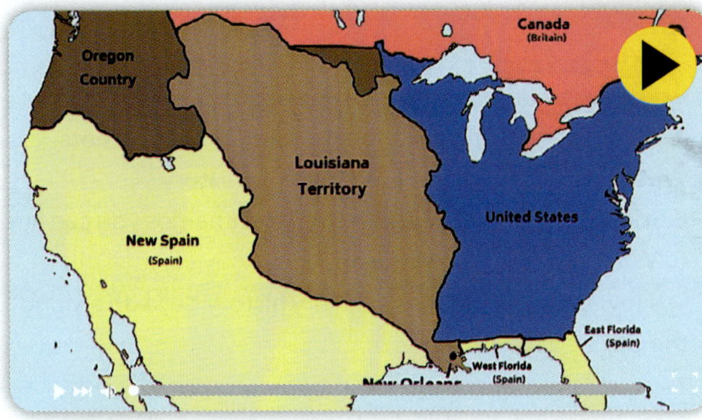

HELP!
- deal = bargain /ˈbɑrgən/: *une bonne affaire*
- bump sth up = to increase the amount of sth
- ratify = make an agreement official

2 Reenacting a slave rebellion

A. Watch the video about the reenactment of the 1811 slave rebellion. Then answer these questions:
- What kind of memorial commemorates the 1811 slave rebellion?
- How and why did artist Dread Scott want to change the way this event is remembered?
- What could have changed if the rebellion had been successful?
- How do the participants feel about this event?

B. Have your say. Do you agree that we should remember the past and think about what *could have* happened?

VIDEO N°50

HELP!
- enslave = turn someone into a slave
- traffic island (n)
- rebel (v) /rɪˈbel/
- rebel (n) /ˈrebəl/
- stuck /stʌk/ = unable to move
- agency = power, ability to act

YOUR TURN! 3 Why reenact the past?

You have been invited to talk about reenactments on *PBS News Hour*. Say if you believe they are something important and what impact they can have on children.

HELP!

Verbs & Expressions
- dress up = wear costumes
- understand
- visualise
- pretend = act out
- experience first-hand
- the value of reenacting the past is…

❷ How New Orleans Acknowledges its Past

How has New Orleans been reevaluating its glorification of certain historical events?

1 Driving through History

A. Read the text and focus on the names of the streets. What does it say about New Orleans's history?

B. Make a list of the categories of street names you can find.

C. What types of names are missing?

D. How can New Orleans's slavery history be seen around the city?

To get around in New Orleans, you drive through history, navigating the dense web of references embedded[1] in the street names. Lasalle. Iberville. Bienville. Orleans. Chartres. Poydras. Ulloa. Galvez. Miro. Carondelet. Claiborne. Lafitte. St. Louis. St. Charles. St. Claude. St. Bernard. Frenchmen. Names New Orleanians negotiate every day. The street map is a time capsule. Unpack[2] all those names, and a lot of the city's history is right there.

Uptown, major thoroughfares[3] are named for the big three of slave-owning presidents: Washington, Jefferson, and Jackson [...].

You can even read history in the street names that aren't there. There's no Lincoln Street. Lincoln was considered the very devil when he ran for president in 1860, and wasn't even listed on the ballot in Louisiana, or anywhere in the South, because he was a threat to four billion dollars of human property—the total estimated on-paper value of slaves in the South. [...]

Mystery, Music, and Pleasure are streets. Piety and Desire, without the latter of which Tennessee Williams[4] would have had no streetcar, are a pair of one-way streets[5] that run in contrary directions.

A series of uptown streets dating from the 1830s commemorates Napoleon Bonaparte, who was the object of a considerable cult in Louisiana. Alongside the major thoroughfare named Napoleon, lesser streets celebrate the battles of his career: Valence, Jena, Milan [...], Austerlitz, Marengo, Constantinople, Cadiz. This is a history that only commemorates victories [...].

For that matter, few New Orleans streets are named after black people. A stretch of Dryades Street (named to honor wood nymphs) was renamed Oretha Castle Haley Boulevard for the civil rights activist who died in 1987. A section of Melpomene [...] — just the part in the ghetto — was renamed Martin Luther King Boulevard while retaining its original name of the muse of tragedy [...]. The entire length of the street wasn't renamed because it would have spoiled the set of nine parallel streets named for muses. ("We have no problems with Dr. King," said the president of the Coliseum Square Association. "It's just that he wasn't a Greek muse.") [...]

In the city's antiquated architecture, slaves' handiwork[6] is everywhere — in the grillwork, the tilework, the mortuary work, and the carpentry [...]. There are plenty of houses standing in New Orleans [...] that were built by enslaved artisans, with the income from slaves' labor. In New Orleans, you can easily see, and feel, that slavery wasn't so long ago.

1 *(ici) ancrées* • 2 examine something in order to understand it • 3 main streets • 4 name of streets in Tennessee Williams's play • 5 *sens unique* • 6 work done skillfully with the hands

The World That Made New Orleans: From Spanish Silver to Congo Square, Ned Sublette, 2008

2 Removing Confederate memorials

Cultural fact
After the Civil War a period known as "Reconstruction" occurred in which Northern troops occupied Louisiana to ensure that slavery had ended. This period lasted until 1877 when Rutherford B. Hayes became president. He permitted certain southern States to take back control of their own governments. This allowed white supremacists back into power and would eventually lead to the installation of segregation.

A. Listen to former New Orleans mayor Mitch Landrieu's speech on MP3 N°129. In your own words, explain why he felt it was important to remove Confederate memorials.

B. What do you think of this initiative? Is this going to help the city or cause more problems?

C. Read the ***Cultural fact*** and say when the Confederate statues were put up and why.

D. Go further. Find information online about other statues celebrating the Confederacy that were removed in 2017.

3 Forcing people to face a dark past

A. Watch this video about the Whitney Plantation and take notes.

B. What made John Cummings decide to turn the plantation into a museum?

C. What was Ibrahima Seck's role in the plantation?

D. What is written next to each slave's name and why?

E. Go further. What effect do the statues and lists of names have on visitors? Is it surprising that this is the first museum of its kind in the USA?

VIDEO N°51

HELP!
- loom: *peser sur*
- cattle (n) : *bétail*
- cull /kʌl/ = collect parts or pieces of sth
- etch: *graver*

YOUR TURN! 4 Give your opinion about memorials

After seeing how the city is trying to reconcile with its slave-owning past, you are inspired to write an opinion piece on nola.com about how memorials to certain people or events can impact citizens.

❸ The Essence of New Orleans

What do New Orleanians like about their city?

1 A city that comes together

A. Groupwork. Listen to what New Orleanians think brings their diverse population together.
- Group A listens to **MP3 N°130** .
- Group B listens to **MP3 N°131** .
- Group C listens to **MP3 N°132** .
- Group D listens to **MP3 N°133** .

B. Share your findings with the other groups. Then get ready to report back to the class.
You can use **Worksheet n°50** for help.

C. In pairs, discuss which symbol of New Orleans you find the most worthy of celebration.

HELP!

Audio 130
- stew (n) /stjuː/: *ragout*
- clash (n) /klæʃ/: *affrontement*
- highs and lows: *des hauts et des bas*
- crime rate: *taux de criminalité*

Audio 131
- active river port
- offshoot: *ramification*

Audio 132
- in the grand scheme of sth: *dans l'ensemble*
- rough /rʌf/ = difficult

Audio 133
- Ash Wednesday: *Mercredi des Cendres*
- float: *char*
- ball /bɒːl/: *bal*
- get dressed to the nines = dress in fancy clothing

YOUR PROJECT

Today there is just an empty pillar where the Robert E. Lee statue was, so the city has asked for replacement ideas to be sent in the form of videos. Create a video explaining and justifying a new unifying symbol. Make sure to say why it is worth remembering and glorifying.

LANGUAGE LAB

- Unit's vocabulary
- Audio words
- MP3
- Interactive Test

★ **1. Fill in the blanks using the words below.**

awareness • *relic of the past* • *vestiges* • *pay tribute to* • *landmark* • *memorialize*

A. The mayor decided that it wasn't right to ... the Confederacy any longer.
B. One of the first steps to change is having an ... of the problem.
C. The statue was used as a ... for decades.
D. NOLA is a city with many ... of its European history.
E. What should the city ... now?
F. The city is hoping that nowadays the Confederacy is a ... .

★ **2. Turn these sentences into suggestions.**

A. Visit New Orleans. → *What about...*
B. Learn Louisiana French. → *Why don't you...*
C. Go and swim in the Bayou. → *Let's...*
D. Learn about Louisiana history. → *Why not...*
E. Study New Orleans jazz. → *What if...*

★★ **3. Choose the correct word.**

A. Do you ***remembrance/remember*** the date of the Louisiana Purchase?
B. My ***recollection/recall*** is that New Orleans became American in 1803.
C. The problem with the statue of Robert E. Lee is that it's a ***reminder/remind*** of slavery.
D. What ***memorials/memories*** should there be in New Orleans that are missing today?

★★ **4. Rewrite these sentences in the past tense, start the sentence with "At the time".**

A. They can buy slaves on the market.
B. He cannot cook French food.
C. In NOLA, you can speak either French or English.
D. They must treat Cajuns with respect.
E. You must be impressed by the varied architecture.

★★★ **5. Put the verbs in the appropriate tense (preterite or pluperfect).**

A. Louisiana ***(be)*** a French territory before it ***(become)*** American.
B. Slavery ***(stop)*** for years before black people ***(obtain)*** equal rights.
C. We ***(realise)*** our family ***(be)*** slave owners in the past.
D. They ***(know)*** about voodoo even before they ***(go)*** to Louisiana.
E. When slavery ***(be abolished)***, slave dealers ***(lose)*** millions of dollars.

6. Interactive test! What is your score?

OPEN YOUR EARS!

PHONOLOGY

La prononciation du « s » grammatical

• Classez les mots dans le tableau en fonction de la prononciation du « s » final puis vérifiez vos réponses avec l'enregistrement. **MP3 N°134**

confederates • *costumes* • *speeches* • *slaves* • *events* • *memorials* • *commemorates* • *judges* • *facts*

/s/	/z/	/ɪz/
...	...	...

SHOWTIME

Say it like the model!

MP3 N°135

Louisi/ana is known around the / world as the home of / Mardi Gras, the / birthplace of / Jazz, and a dis/tinctive cui/sine borne from our rich, abundant / wetlands.

- Écoutez le passage en faisant attention au rythme extrêmement régulier (noté par /). Notez que le rythme s'appuie sur les syllabes accentuées des mots.
- Notez la prononciation de Lousiana /luːˌiːzɪ'ænə/.

Quote challenge

★ 3 sentences
★★ 4 to 6 sentences
★★★ 7 sentences and +

Which quote sums up best what you have learnt? Justify!

"Half of my family has a deep-rooted connection to the South and Louisiana, and for me, New Orleans is one of our most precious, historic communities: visually, emotionally, artistically."

Sandra Bullock, American actress (1964-)

"We wander through old streets, and pause before the age stricken houses; and, strange to say, the magic past lights them up."

Grace King, American writer (1852-1932)

"The past in New Orleans cohabits with the present to an extent not even approximated in any other North American city."

Tom Piazza, American writer (1955-)

B1-B2

BACKPACK

Get Ready for your Exam!

UNIT 24 Évaluation

Compréhension de l'oral

"Angel Island poems" MP3 n°136

Listen to the audio recording three times and recap what you have understood.

Expression écrite

Choisissez l'un des deux sujets (min. 120 mots).

Question A : A descendant of a Japanese man who landed at Angel Island in the late 19th century has found a letter from his/her ancestor in the attic. Imagine and write the letter.

Question B : How does the following statement find an echo in today's America?
"The Angel Island Immigration Center is filled with poems from Chinese and Japanese immigrants. These poems are a cry for freedom and equality that echoes in the shadows of modern America."

UNIT 25 Évaluation

Compréhension de l'oral

"We wear our stories" MP3 n°137

VIDEO N°53

Listen to the audio recording three times and recap what you have understood.

Expression écrite

Choisissez l'un des deux sujets (min. 120 mots).

Question A : A young Māori man/woman speaks with a friend about the necessity to have his/her culture preserved thanks to the Moko. The friend thinks that these tattoos are too visible and unnecessary in modern New Zealand. Imagine and write the conversation.

Question B : Are Māori tattoos an efficient way to pass down traditions and culture from one generation to the next?

UNIT 26 Évaluation

Compréhension de l'oral

"Hurricane Katrina" MP3 n°138

Listen to the audio recording three times and recap what you have understood.

Expression écrite

Choisissez l'un des deux sujets (min. 120 mots).

Question A : Write an entry in the diary of a survivor of Hurricane Katrina. Your entry should start with the following sentence:
"There was a dangerous storm approaching, but residents had no idea what was to come…"

Question B : Comment on the following statement:
"When hurricanes strike and cities flood, people who were already disadvantaged tend to suffer the most. That's because the wind and rain alone do not define the shape of our modern disasters."

UNIT 24 Évaluation

Document A

The story of Chinatown is the story of a neighborhood; an American neighborhood, an old neighborhood, an immigrant neighborhood, where the old country still lives inside the new one. The past and the present are inseparably woven together in this neighborhood defined by Broadway, California, Kearny and Powell streets.
In the mid-1840's, following defeat by Britain in the first Opium War, a series of natural catastrophes occurred across China resulting in famine, peasant uprisings and rebellions. Understandably, when the news of gold and opportunity in far away Gum San (Golden Mountain-the Chinese name for America) reached China, many Chinese seized the opportunity to seek their fortune.
The Chinese were met with ambiguous feelings by Californians. In 1850, San Francisco Mayor John W. Geary invited the "China Boys" to a ceremony to acknowledge their work ethic. However, as the American economy weakened, the Chinese labor force became a threat to mainstream society. Racial discrimination and repressive legislation drove the Chinese from the gold mines to the sanctuary of the neighborhood that became known as Chinatown. The only ethnic group in the history of the United States to have been specifically denied entrance into the country, the Chinese were prohibited by law to testify in court, to own property, to vote, to have families join them, to marry non-Chinese, and to work in institutional agencies.
The success and survival of Chinatown depended a great deal on the family and district benevolent associations which served as political and social support systems to newcomers. The members strove to meet the basic needs of the community, and represented a united voice in the fight against discriminatory legislation process.
"Chinatown" offers a revealing look at how a group of people bound geographically, culturally, linguistically and economically during hostile times has flourished to become a vibrant, courageous and proud community for Chinese Americans and greater San Francisco, referred to as Dai Fao (Big City) in Chinese.

www.pbs.org

Document B

Today, San Francisco's Chinatown has developed cultural autonomy which sustains many activities: dance, music groups, a children's orchestra, artists, a Chinese Culture Center, and the Chinese Historical Society of America. A result of the community's commitment to excellence in education is its involvement in the legal debates of affirmative action vs. school desegregation for Asian-American youth. "Viewed within the context of the City of San Francisco, Chinatown is one of many culturally distinct neighborhoods that together make up the backbone of the City. Viewed within the context of America, Chinatown is an American working class community that has been a partner in building this nation with every other American working class community. Like all other American neighborhoods, Chinatown has been developed by the will and energies of immigrants."

www.pbs.org

Compréhension de l'écrit

Answer the following questions in English, using your own words.

Document A

A. What is the main topic of the text?
B. How was "Chinatown" born in the USA and across the World?
C. How has "Chinatown" lasted?

Document B

A. What can you say about:
– Chinatown and the consequence of its development?
– the cultural importance of "Chinatown" in San Francisco today?
B. Comment on the sentence lines 5-9.

Documents A et B

To what extent do these two texts illustrate the notion of "Territory and memory"?

Expression écrite

Choisissez l'un des deux sujets (min. 120 mots).

Question A : The Oakland Chinatown Street Festival is on again this year! Write a promotional leaflet to attract tourists and locals to the event.

Question B : Comment on the following statement:
"The reality of Chinatown is that there are two Chinatowns:
One belongs to the locals,
the other charms the tourists."

B1-B2 **BACKPACK**

Get Ready for your Exam!

UNIT 25 Évaluation

Document A

A group of Maori landowners is vowing to fight a plan that will strip them of their ancestral land in Papamoa. SAVE Tumu Kaituna have grave fears that more than 4000 Maori landowners will be cut out of 55 hectares of their land if a proposal by Tumu Kaituna 14 Trust, Tauranga City Council, developers and neighbouring non-Maori landowners to sell the land goes through.

"It's about fair process and whether the proposed development benefit the collective Maori owners and future generations of Maori," says SAVE Tumu Kaituna co-spoksperson Karen Stowers.

"Maori land is more valuable than money—never sell it. The proposed development could provide new housing for 15,500 people, but we have seen no plans that provide housing for the Maori landowners.

We also must consider if it really is the best use of the land, for our people and the environment, and an over populated urban city," says Karen.

SAVE Tumu Kaituna co-spokesperson Rawiri Bhana says the plan lacked Maori values including intergenerational thinking and the trustees needed to get back to the table with their people or get off the table.

"A lot of our people are really hurt that those they have put their faith in could potentially sell what little land they have left," says Rawiri.

"The lack of transparency behind the proposed development and the trust's minimal consultation with Maori landowners is a real cause for concern.

There is no evidence to show the Trust are putting the owners aspirations and needs first."

A post on the Tauranga City Council website says council are working with landowners to create a new coastal community in Papamoa East, "to help support our city's future growth".

Te Tumu is a place of great historic and cultural wealth, both for Tangata Whenua and European settlers. Bounded by the Pacific Ocean to the north, the Kaituna River and farmlands to the south, Te Tumu is well-positioned to connect the city to these resources.

Tauranga City Council is working closely with landowners, iwi and hapu to collaboratively decide what the future of Te Tumu might look like.

www.sunlive.co.nz, 13 June 2019

Document B

New Zealand in 2017 became the first country to grant a specific river legal rights, followed by the Indian state of Uttarakhand. This year, the city of Toledo, Ohio, passed what is known as the Lake Erie Bill of Rights to protect its shores, making it one of several U.S. communities to have passed legislation recognizing the rights of nature.

Yet, the idea of what these laws hope to accomplish is where the similarities stop, as their legal bases and the [...] problems they're meant to solve vary from country to country. Many of the laws have also been met with resistance from industry, farmers and river communities, who argue that giving nature personhood infringes on their rights and livelihoods.

Ashley Westerman, *www.npr.org*, 3 August 2019

Compréhension de l'écrit

Answer the following questions in English, using your own words.

Document A

A. After reading the text, what can you say about:
- its main topic?
- the people involved?
- their opinions on the topic?

B. Explain the following statement. Could it apply to other native peoples?
"Maori land is more valuable than money—never sell it." (l. 12)

Document B

A. After reading the text, what can you say about:
- its main topic?
- the people involved?
- their opinions on the topic?

B. Explain the lines 13-14.

Documents A et B

Explain why these two texts have been put together.

Expression écrite

Choisissez l'un des deux sujets (min. 120 mots).

Question A : Write a letter to New Zealand's Prime Minister in which you defend the project to give nature personhood. Choose who you want to be: a Maori or a non-Maori.

Question B : How do you react to the fact that New Zealand has been granting legal rights to natural elements like mountains or rivers?

Évaluation

Observe the documents. According to you, which document best illustrates "Territory and Memory"?

UNIT 24

a "Everywhere immigrants have enriched and strenghtened the fabric of American Life".

John F. Kennedy, former President of the United States (1917-1963)

b "Once I thought to write a history of the immigrants in America. Then I discovered that the immigrants were American history."

Oscar Handlin, American historian (1915-2011)

c

Detention Barracks on Angel Island

UNIT 25

a "If the land is well
and the sea is well,
the people will thrive"

Maori proverb

b "The moko is my voice; it is my visible presence in this time and in this space. It is my rite of passage to the past and to the future. It is the revolving door to my *tupuna* [ancestors] and my descendents. My children and grandchildren will not suffer the oppression of intolerance because I have asserted my *tino rangatiratanga* [sovereignty, autonomy]."

Tuhipo Maria Rapido Kereopa
in *Dedicated by Blood: Renaissance of Ta Moko*, Patricia Steur and Gordon Toi Hatfield, 2002

UNIT 26

a "The New York that Frank Sinatra sang about, people will never know that place. The New Orleans that Louis Armstrong sang about is the New Orleans that's still there — it's preserved."

American Actress **Blake Lively**

b "We wander through old streets, and pause before the age stricken houses; and, strange to say, the magic past lights them up."

Grace King, Louisiana Author (1851-1932)

c

Congo Square sculpture in Louis Armstrong Park, New Orleans, by Adewale Adenle

PRÉCIS GRAMMATICAL

Autour du verbe

Glossaire général

- **Base verbale* (= BV) :** forme du verbe à l'infinitif (sans *to*) : *eat, open...*
- **Proposition* :** constituant de la phrase qui se compose d'un sujet et d'un groupe verbal.
La proposition principale ne dépend d'aucune autre dans une phrase.
- **Valeur aspectuelle* :** manière dont un évènement est perçu. Il peut être perçu dans son déroulement (*-ing*) ou encore par rapport à la fin de sa réalisation (*-en*).

Autour du nom

Autour de la phrase

Éléments de phonologie anglaise

1. LES AUXILIAIRES *BE, HAVE, DO*

Le français utilise les auxiliaires « être » et « avoir » pour construire certains temps.

L'anglais en utilise trois, *be*, *have* et *do*. Tout comme « être » et « avoir », *be*, *have* et *do* sont à la fois des verbes et des auxiliaires.

1 • *Be*

• **Formation**

Forme affirmative	Forme interrogative	Forme négative
I ***am*** *You* ***are*** *He / She / It* ***is*** *We / You / They* ***are***	***Am*** *I?* ***Are*** *you?* ***Is*** *he / she / it?* ***Are*** *we / you / they?*	*I* ***am not*** *You* ***are not*** *He / She / It* ***is not*** *We / You / They* ***are not***

Attention

Be forme son prétérit singulier en ***was*** (*strong* /wɒz/ ; *weak* /wəz/), son prétérit pluriel en ***were*** (*strong* /wɜː/; *weak* /wə/) et son participe passé en ***been*** (*strong* /biːn/; *weak* /bɪn/).

• **Emplois**

- On utilise l'auxiliaire *be* pour former le présent *be* + *-ing*.

She ***is doing*** *her best.* Elle fait de son mieux.

- On utilise aussi l'auxiliaire *be* pour construire le passif.

The thief ***was caught*** *by the police.*

Le voleur a été arrêté par la police.

- On utilise *be* précédé de *there* pour poser l'existence de quelque chose, là où le français utilise « il y a ».

- L'anglais utilise parfois *be* quand le français utilise « avoir ». Il faut donc connaître les usages suivants :

Be	Avoir
To be 10 (years old)	*Avoir 10 ans*
To be hungry / thirsty	*Avoir faim / soif*
To be cold / hot	*Avoir froid / chaud*
To be afraid	*Avoir peur*
To be sleepy	*Avoir sommeil*
To be right / wrong	*Avoir raison / tort*
To be lucky	*Avoir de la chance*

Attention

- Ne pas confondre avec le « il y a » français qui signifie « depuis ».

There is *a man in the garden.* Il y a un homme dans le jardin.

- On accorde *be* avec l'élément à droite de la structure alors que le français reste invariable.

There are *problems.* → ***There is*** *a problemØ.*

Il y a des problèmes. → Il y a un problèmeØ.

2 • *Have*

• **Formation**

Forme affirmative	Forme interrogative		Forme négative	
	Forme avec *got*	Forme avec *do*	Forme avec *got*	Forme avec *do*
I / You / We / They ***have got*** *He / She / It* ***has got***	***Have*** *I / you / we / they* ***got****?* ***Has*** *he / she / it* ***got****?*	***Do*** *I / you / we / they* ***have****?* ***Does*** *he / she / it* ***have****?*	*I / You / We / They* ***have not got*** *He / She / It* ***has not got***	*I / You / We / They* ***do not have*** *He / She / It* ***does not have***

Have forme son prétérit et son participe passé en *had* /hæd/.

L'anglais britannique préfère la forme avec *got* pour les formes négatives et interrogatives, là où l'anglais américain préfère la forme avec *do*.

• **Emplois**

- ***Have* auxiliaire** est utilisé pour former le *present perfect* et le *pluperfect* (plus-que-parfait).

I have done it. → I had done it.

Je l'ai fait. → Je l'avais fait.

- *Have* peut avoir le sens de « prendre », « faire », « consommer », « obtenir ».
Il faut connaître les expressions suivantes :

Have	« Prendre », « faire » ou autre verbe
To have a bath / a shower	*Prendre un bain / une douche*
To have a swim / a walk / a chat	*Nager / se promener / bavarder*
To have a holiday	*Prendre des vacances*
To have a good / bad time	*Passer du bon temps / un mauvais moment*
To have a good / bad trip	*Faire un bon / mauvais voyage*
To have a break / a rest	*Faire une pause / se reposer*
To have a try / go	*Essayer*
To have a look	*Jeter un coup d'œil*
To have a nervous breakdown	*Faire une dépression*
To have an operation	*Subir une opération*
To have a dream	*Faire un rêve*
To have a meal (lunch / breakfast / dinner)	*Prendre un repas*
To have something to eat / to drink	*Manger quelque chose / boire quelque chose*
To have a shave	*Se raser*
To have a party	*Organiser une fête*

3 • *Do*

• **Formation**

Forme affirmative	Forme interrogative	Forme négative
I / You / We / They ***do*** /du:/ *He / She / It* ***does*** /dʌz/	***Do*** *I / you / we / they?* ***Does*** *he / she / it?*	*I / You / We / They* ***do not*** *I / You / We / They* ***don't*** *He / She / It* ***does not*** *He / She / It* ***doesn't***

Do forme son prétérit en *did* et son participe passé en *done* /dʌn/.

• **Emplois**

- On se sert de *do* pour former le présent simple et de *did* pour le prétérit.
Quand *do* est utilisé comme verbe (dans le sens de « faire »), il se construit avec l'auxiliaire *do*.

He does not do it on purpose. → He did not do it on purpose.

Il ne le fait pas exprès. → Il ne l'a pas fait pas exprès.

- L'anglais a deux verbes pour traduire « faire ». Il ne faut pas confondre *do* et *make*.
Il convient d'apprendre les expressions suivantes :

Do	Faire
To do business	*Faire des affaires*
To do the shopping	*Faire des courses*
To do sport	*Faire du sport*
To do an exercise	*Faire un exercice*
To do the cooking	*Faire la cuisine*
To do one's best	*Faire de son mieux*
To do good	*Faire du bien*
To do harm	*Faire du mal*

Make	Faire
To make a bed	*Faire un lit*
To make an effort	*Faire un effort*
To make a mistake	*Faire une erreur*
To make a noise	*Faire du bruit*
To make some tea / coffee	*Faire du thé / du café*
To make money	*Faire de l'argent*
To make a fuss	*Faire des histoires*
To make progress	*Faire des progrès*
To make love	*Faire l'amour*
To make peace / war	*Faire la paix / la guerre*
To make a profit	*Faire un bénéfice*

2. LE PRÉSENT SIMPLE

1 • Formation

Forme affirmative	Forme interrogative	Forme négative
I ***eat*** *You* ***eat*** *He / She / It* ***eats*** *We / You / They* ***eat***	*Do I* ***eat****?* *Do you* ***eat****?* *Does he / she / it* ***eat****?* *Do we / you / they* ***eat****?*	*I* ***do not eat*** *You* ***do not eat*** *He / She / It* ***does not eat*** *We / You / They* ***do not eat***

• Modifications orthographiques

- Quand la **base verbale*** se termine par *-s*, *-x*, *-z*, *-ch*, *-sh* ou *-on*, on ajoute **-es** à la 3e personne du singulier.

Pass → *I pass* → *He / She / It pass**es**.*

Catch → *I catch* → *He / She / It catch**es**.*

Push → *I push* → *He / She / It push**es**.*

- Quand la **base verbale*** se termine par un *-y* précédé d'une consonne, on écrit **-ies**.

Fly → *I fly* → *He / She / It fl**ies***

• Prononciation (→ Phonologie p. 320)

-es se prononce /ɪz/ derrière une consonne (*passes, catches, pushes*).
-s se prononce soit /s/ soit /z/ en fonction du son qui le précède : /z/ dans, *plays, opens, applies* et /s/ dans *talks, looks, takes*.

! Attention

does a une prononciation irrégulière : en effet *do* /də/, /du:/ mais *does* /dʌz/.

2 • Emplois

• Exprimer une vérité générale

Tomorrow never dies.
Demain ne meurt jamais. (titre d'un James Bond)

Water boils at 100 degrees Celsius.
L'eau bout à 100 degrés.

The sun rises in the East.
Le soleil se lève à l'est.

Time and tide wait for no man.
Le temps n'attend pas. (proverbe)

It never rains but it pours.
Un malheur n'arrive jamais seul. (proverbe)

• Rendre compte d'un comportement habituel

Dans ces cas, les énoncés sont souvent accompagnés d'adverbes comme *often, always*, mais aussi *never* ou *rarely*, etc.

She plays baseball ***every*** *Sunday.*
Elle joue au baseball tous les dimanches.

She ***never*** *plays baseball on Sundays.*
Elle ne joue jamais au baseball le dimanche.

Alexander ***often*** *goes shopping with his friends.*
Alexander va souvent faire du shopping avec ses amis.

Alexander ***rarely*** *goes shopping with his friends.*
Alexander va rarement faire du shopping avec ses amis.

• Donner les caractéristiques d'un sujet

Zoey teaches English. (= *Zoey is an English teacher.*)
Zoey enseigne l'anglais.

Peter likes long walks in the country.
(= *Peter is a walker.*)
Peter aime les longues promenades dans la campagne.

• Raconter une histoire

Traditionnellement, le temps de la narration en anglais est le prétérit mais, de plus en plus, à l'oral comme à l'écrit, on utilise le présent simple.

He opens the door and ***discovers*** *that he's not alone in the house. Then he* ***goes*** *outside and* ***sees*** *the frightening dog…*
Il ouvre la porte et se rend compte qu'il n'est pas seul dans la maison. Puis il sort et voit le chien terrifiant…

• Exprimer le futur (quelque chose de programmé)

My train leaves at 3 p.m. tomorrow.
Mon train part à 15 heures demain.
(→ l'expression du futur p. 303)

3. LE PRÉSENT *BE + -ING*

La forme *be + -ing* ajoute une *valeur aspectuelle** au verbe. Il s'agit toujours du présent mais la présence de la forme en *be + -ing* ajoute une information supplémentaire.

1 • Formation

• On utilise l'auxiliaire *be* au présent **simple** et on ajoute *-ing* à la *base verbale**.

Forme affirmative	Forme interrogative	Forme négative
*I **am** reading* *You **are** reading* *He / She **is** reading* *We **are** reading* *They **are** reading*	***Am** I reading?* ***Are** you reading?* ***Is** he / she reading?* ***Are** we reading?* ***Are** they reading?*	*I **am not** reading* *You **are not** reading* *He / She **is not** reading* *We **are not** reading* *They **are not** reading*

Les formes contractées sont normalement utilisées à l'oral.
Pour la négation, on remarque qu'on a le choix entre :
- la forme entière : *You **are not** reading.*
- la forme mixte : *You'**re not** reading.*
- la forme contractée : *You **aren't** reading.*

• L'auxiliaire *be* est aussi utilisé pour former le présent *be + -ing* du verbe *be*.

*He **is being** silly.* Il fait l'imbécile. (= état temporaire)

*He **is** silly.* C'est un idiot. (= état permanent ou présenté comme tel)

Attention

La forme négative *ain't* /eɪnt/ issue de l'argot américain (qui donnerait ici *You ain't reading = you are not reading*) utilisée à toutes les personnes, est à proscrire car trop familière malgré une utilisation très fréquente (par exemple dans la chanson *I Ain't Your Mama* de Jennifer Lopez).

2 • Emplois

• Parler d'une action en train de se dérouler

*He'**s watching** a video.*
Il regarde une vidéo (au moment où je vous parle).

*"**Are** you **talking** to me?"*
C'est à moi qu'tu parles ? (réplique de *Taxi Driver*)

• Indiquer le positionnement physique ou spatial de quelqu'un

C'est pour cela que l'on utilise la forme *be + -ing* pour décrire une image ou un tableau.

*It looks like Mona Lisa **is smiling** at us.*
On dirait que Mona Lisa nous sourit.

He's standing at the door.
Il est à la porte. (En français, on ne précisera pas forcément que la personne est debout.)

He's sitting at the back of the class.
Il est (assis) au fond de la classe.

• Exprimer son agacement

*My uncle is always **asking** stupid questions.*
Mon oncle pose toujours des questions idiotes.

Ici, la présence de l'adverbe *always*, qui indique le caractère récurrent, peut inciter à utiliser le présent simple : *My uncle always asks stupid questions.* Cette forme est elle aussi tout à fait possible mais la forme en *be + -ing* indique, en plus, que cela nous agace !

• Renvoyer à un moment futur (→ p. 303)

*Tomorrow, I'**m having** a huge meal with Barbara.*
Demain, je ferai un bon repas avec Barbara.

• Exprimer une volonté ou un refus

*I'**m** not **eating** with him!*

Je refuse de manger avec lui !

Attention

Selon le contexte, cet énoncé peut signifier « Je ne mange pas avec lui au moment où je parle ». Il faut donc être particulièrement attentif(ve) au contexte.

• Rupture avec une habitude

*I usually cook dinner but tonight we'**re going** to the restaurant!*
D'habitude je cuisine mais ce soir nous allons au restaurant !

Attention

- Certains verbes (de sentiment, d'état mental, d'apparence et de perception) sont peu compatibles avec la forme *be + -ing*.

I know what you mean.
Je vois ce que tu veux dire.

I love you. Je t'aime.

It seems difficult. Cela a l'air difficile.

- *Look*, par exemple, peut être utilisé avec la forme *be + -ing* quand il signifie « regarder » mais pas quand il signifie « avoir l'air » :

She is looking at him. Elle le regarde.

He looks stupid. Il a l'air bête.

4. LE *PRESENT PERFECT*

Même si ce temps ressemble au passé composé français, il n'en est pas l'équivalent anglais. Comme son nom l'indique, le *present perfect* est un temps du présent !

1 • Formation

Le *present perfect* se construit avec l'auxiliaire *have* au présent et le participe passé du verbe.

• Verbes réguliers

Le participe passé se forme de la façon suivante : base verbale* + *-ed*.

Forme affirmative	Forme interrogative	Forme négative
I ***have*** *decided* *You* ***have*** *decided* *He / She / It* ***has*** *decided* *We / You / They* ***have*** *decided*	***Have*** *I decided?* ***Have*** *you decided?* ***Has*** *he / she / it decided?* ***Have*** *we / you / they decided?*	*I* ***have not*** *decided* *You* ***have not*** *decided* *He / She / It* ***has not*** *decided* *We / You / They* ***have not*** *decided*

• Verbes irréguliers

Pour la formation du participe passé des verbes irréguliers → p. VI.

Forme affirmative	Forme interrogative	Forme négative
I ***have forgotten*** *You* ***have forgotten*** *He / She / It* ***has forgotten*** *We / You / They* ***have forgotten***	***Have*** *I* ***forgotten****?* ***Have*** *you* ***forgotten****?* ***Has*** *he / she / it* ***forgotten****?* ***Have*** *we / you / they* ***forgotten****?*	*I* ***have not forgotten*** *You* ***have not forgotten*** *He / She / It* ***has not forgotten*** *We / You / They* ***have not forgotten***

2 • Emplois

• Présenter le résultat d'une action débutée dans le passé

He ***has broken*** *his watch. → His watch is now broken.*

Il a cassé sa montre. → Sa montre est cassée.

The wall was green. I ***have painted*** *the wall. → The wall is now yellow.*

Le mur était vert. J'ai peint le mur. → Le mur est jaune.

Pour le même évènement passé, on peut choisir d'utiliser le prétérit ou le *present perfect*.
Avec ce dernier, on trouve souvent des adverbes de temps qui font le lien avec le présent dans des énoncés au *present perfect* comme *already, ever, never, yet, over…*

She ***finished*** *her lunch.* Elle a terminé son repas.

She ***has already finished*** *her lunch.*

Elle a déjà terminé son repas.

• Parler d'une action débutée dans le passé qui se prolonge dans le présent

I've studied *English for five years.*

Cela fait cinq ans que j'apprends l'anglais.

I've known *Teresa since 2004.*

Je connais Teresa depuis 2004.

• Renvoyer à un passé récent avec l'adverbe *just*

I ***have just turned*** *16.* Je viens d'avoir 16 ans.

I've just bumped *into Paul at the supermarket.*

Je viens de tomber sur Paul au supermarché.

En anglais américain, la tendance est d'utiliser le prétérit dans les énoncés passés avec *just*. Il convient de réserver cet usage au contexte américain. Cette forme est souvent considérée comme fautive par les Britanniques.
I ***just saw*** *your mother.* (US) / *I* ***have just seen*** *your mother* (GB) Je viens de voir ta mère.

3 • Le *present perfect be + -ing*

- Le *present perfect be + -ing* insiste encore plus sur le résultat, les traces, dans le présent, d'une activité passée qui se prolonge.

You're all sweaty! ***Have you been*** *running?*

Tu es en nage ! Tu as couru ?

- Le *present perfect* et le *present perfect be + -ing* sont souvent interchangeables. Selon le sens des verbes, le contexte et la nuance que l'on veut apporter, on privilégiera l'une ou l'autre forme. En effet, la nuance est mince entre *I've studied English for five years* et *I've been studying English for five years.*
Dans les deux cas, on traduira par « Cela fait cinq ans que j'apprends l'anglais ».

5. LE PRÉTÉRIT

Le prétérit est un temps du passé.
Il peut correspondre au **passé composé**, au **passé simple**, à l'**imparfait**, voire au **plus-que-parfait** français.

1 • Formation

a. Verbes réguliers

À la forme affirmative, on ajoute *-ed* à la base verbale à toutes les personnes (*work**ed***).
Aux formes interrogative et négative, on utilise l'auxiliaire *did* avec la **base verbale*** (sans *-ed*).

Forme affirmative	Forme interrogative	Forme négative
*I work**ed*** *You work**ed*** *He / She / It work**ed*** *We / You / They work**ed***	***Did** I **work?*** ***Did** you **work?*** ***Did** he / she / it **work?*** ***Did** we / you / they **work?***	*I **did not work*** *You **did not work*** *He / She / It **did not work*** *We / You / They work **did not work***

• **Modifications orthographiques**

- Quand un verbe se termine par un *-y* après une consonne, il devient *-i*.

*cry → cri**ed***

Attention
Quand un verbe se termine par une voyelle + *-y*, il n'y a pas de modification : *convey → convey**ed***.

- Quand une consonne finale suit une voyelle et que la syllabe est accentuée, on redouble la consonne.

*pop → pop**ped***
*prefer → prefer**red***

Attention
Il n'y a pas de modification orthographique quand une autre syllabe est accentuée : *develop → develop**ed***. Ici, c'est l'avant-dernière syllabe qui est accentuée.

• **Prononciation** (→ Phonologie p. 320)

b. Verbes irréguliers

À la forme affirmative, on utilise la forme irrégulière (voir la liste de verbes irréguliers → p. VI).
Aux formes interrogative et négative on utilise l'auxiliaire *did* avec la **base verbale***.

Forme affirmative	Forme interrogative	Forme négative
*I **ate*** *You **ate*** *He / She / It **ate*** *We / You / They **ate***	***Did** I **eat**?* ***Did** you **eat**?* ***Did** he / she / it **eat**?* ***Did** we / you / they **eat**?*	*I **didn't*** (did not) ***eat*** *You **didn't*** (did not) ***eat*** *He / She / It **didn't*** (did not) ***eat*** *We / You / They **didn't*** (did not) ***eat***

2 • Emplois

• **Récit**

Le prétérit est le **temps du récit** (temps de la narration). Les mots qui indiquent une répétition ou une succession d'évènements dans le passé ou encore un repère passé (*last year, yesterday*, etc.) sont le signe que le prétérit est probable.

*Alfred **took** his exam last month and then **spent** a weekend in Dublin with Sarah.*

Alfred a passé son examen le mois dernier et a ensuite passé un week-end à Dublin avec Sarah.

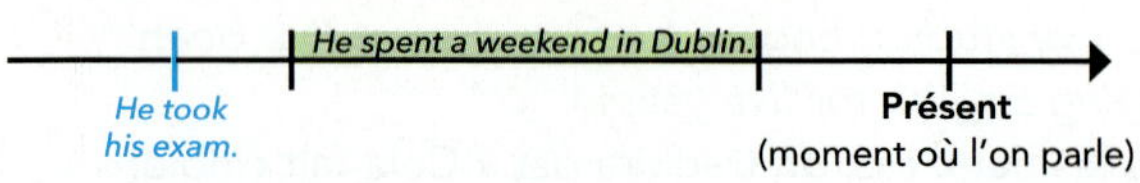

• **Action passée et terminée**

a. L'action peut avoir été ponctuelle.

*Yesterday, Bob **fell** in his garden.*

Hier Bob est tombé dans son jardin.

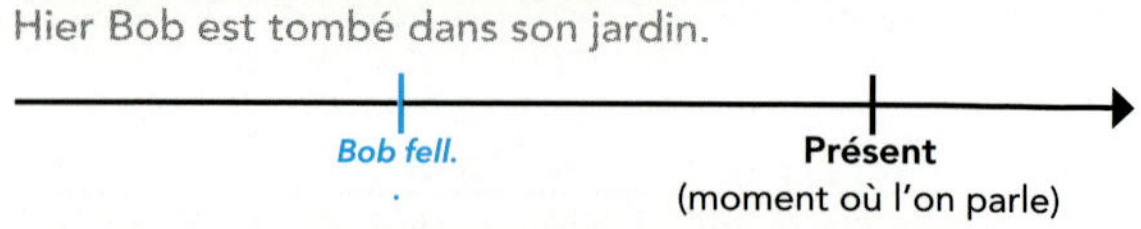

b. L'action peut s'être inscrite dans la durée.

*He **practiced** judo for ten years when he was young and then he **decided** to quit.*

Il a fait dix ans de judo dans sa jeunesse et a ensuite laissé tomber.

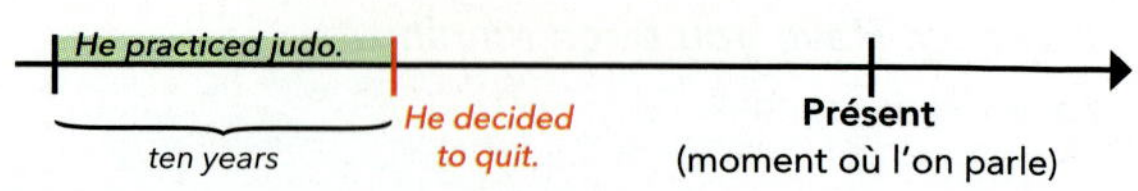

c. L'action peut s'être répétée.

He often cried as a child. Enfant, il pleurait beaucoup.

L'essentiel n'est pas la durée de l'évènement ni même sa répétition mais le fait qu'il soit **terminé et perçu dans sa globalité**. C'est pour cette raison que pour le prétérit, on parle souvent de **rupture avec le présent**.

- ***Used to* /'justu/**

Attention à ne pas confondre avec *be used to* + BV-*ing* prononcé /'ju:ztu/.

I used to get up at 6. (= I don't get up at 6 anymore.)
≠ I am used to getting up at 6. (= I still get up at 6.)
Avant je me levais à 6 heures ≠ J'ai l'habitude de me lever à 6 heures.

On retrouve, avec *used to*, la même valeur de rupture qu'avec le prétérit (on retrouve d'ailleurs *-ed*) mais on insiste encore un peu plus qu'avec le prétérit sur le fait que ce qui est décrit **n'est plus vrai**.
Cela se remarque clairement dans les traductions.

*She **used to practise** MMA (Mixed Martial Arts).*
Avant, elle faisait du MMA.

*She **practised** MMA when she was young.*
Elle faisait du MMA dans sa jeunesse.

*He **used to play** the cello.*
Avant, il jouait du violoncelle.

*He **played** the cello for one year in the 80's.*
Il a fait un an de violoncelle dans les années 80.

On remarque qu'en français, selon les cas, on utilise **l'imparfait**, le **passé composé**, ou le **passé simple**. Il faut donc comprendre les différentes valeurs des temps de l'anglais et se garder de toute association systématique entre un temps du français et un temps de l'anglais.

- **Prétérit *be + -ing***

On utilise le prétérit à la forme *be + -ing* quand on oppose un évènement en cours de déroulement dans le passé à un évènement ponctuel (prétérit simple), toujours dans le passé.

*He **was getting** ready for the party when his mobile **rang**.*
Il se préparait pour la fête quand son portable se mit à sonner.

Ago / For / Since

Ago

- *Ago* s'utilise après un complément de temps et n'est possible qu'avec le **prétérit**. Il a en effet le **même rôle qu'une date**. En français, *ago* se traduit en général par « il y a + durée ».

*He passed his driving license **3 years ago**.*
Il a eu son permis de conduire il y a 3 ans.

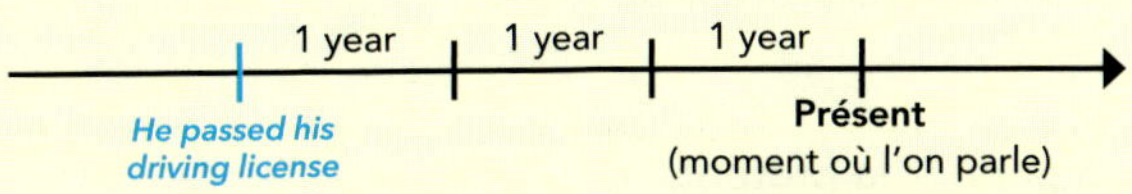

Si l'on est en 2020, cette phrase est équivalente à :
He passed my driving license in 2017.

*We went to the States **4 months ago**.*
Nous sommes allés aux États-Unis il y a 4 mois.

Si l'on est en avril, cette phrase est équivalente à :
We went to the States in January.

- Avec *ago*, on calcule le laps de temps qui nous sépare d'un évènement passé **par rapport à la situation présente.**

Si le contexte est **passé**, on utilisera ***before*** à la place de ***ago*** et l'utilisation du ***pluperfect*** signale que l'on calcule la durée **par rapport à un moment passé**.

*When he had his accident, he had passed his driving license 3 years **before**.*

*He **had passed** his driving license **3 years before he had** his accident.*
Il avait eu son permis de conduire 3 ans avant son accident. / Ça faisait 3 ans qu'il avait son permis de conduire quand il a eu son accident.

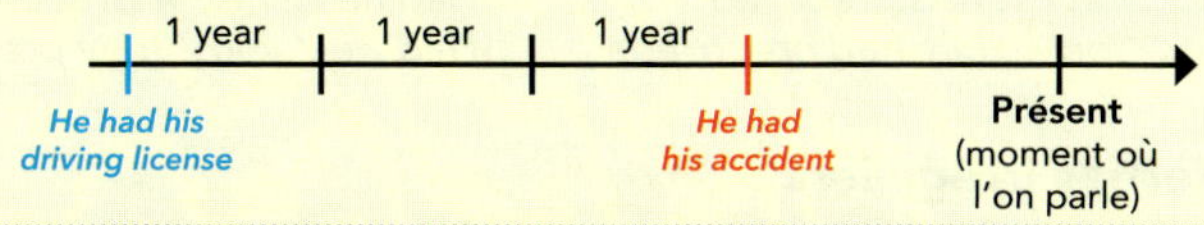

For

For peut s'employer soit avec le prétérit, soit avec le *present perfect*. Dans les deux cas, il exprime **une durée**.

a. Avec le **prétérit**, cette durée **n'a aucun lien avec la situation présente** (valeur de base du prétérit).

*I stayed in the Navy **for 10 years**.*
J'ai passé 10 ans dans la Marine (= c'est terminé).

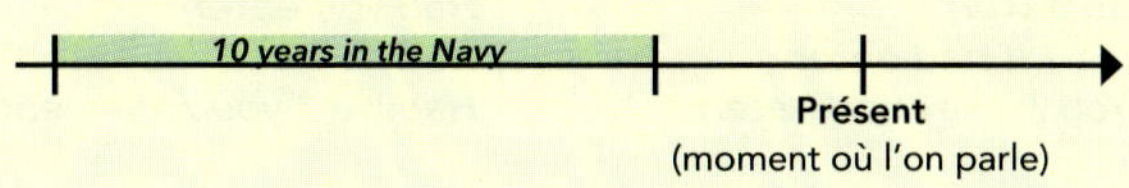

b. Avec le ***present perfect***, *for* exprime toujours **une durée** mais celle-ci est en **lien avec la situation présente.**

I've been** in the Navy **for 10 years.

Cela fait 10 ans que je suis dans la Marine (= j'y suis toujours).

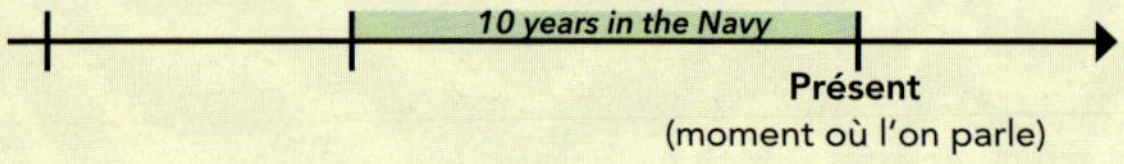

C'est donc le temps de la phrase, prétérit ou *present perfect*, qui détermine si ce qui est décrit est en lien ou non avec le présent. ***For***, dans les deux cas, exprime simplement la durée.

À la forme *be* + *-ing*, le fonctionnement est le même.

*Alysson **has been playing** chess **for 3 hours**.*

Cela fait 3 heures qu'Alysson joue aux échecs.

Since

Since exprime un point de départ. Il peut être suivi d'une date (*Since 1945…*) ou d'un repère temporel (*Since Brexit…*). Ce repère temporel marquant le début d'une action ou d'une période peut très bien être un verbe au prétérit.

Since Brexit = Since the U.K. left the E.U.

Le verbe de la *proposition principale** est toujours au *present perfect*.

*The member states **have been worried since** the U.K. left the E.U.*

Les membres de l'Union sont inquiets depuis que le Royaume-Uni a quitté l'U.E.

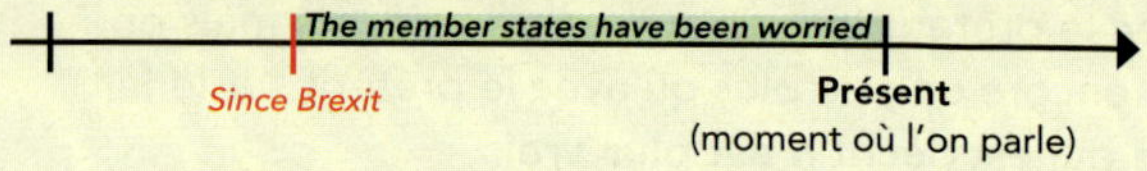

Pour résumer

	Valeur	Temps de la proposition principale
Ago	- date dans le passé - temps écoulé depuis un évènement passé	prétérit
For	durée	- prétérit si cette durée est détachée du présent - *present perfect* si cette durée fait le lien avec le présent
Since	point de départ dans le passé	*present perfect*

6. LE *PLUPERFECT*

Le *pluperfect*, aussi appelé *past perfect*, correspond en de nombreux points au plus-que-parfait français (auxiliaire être ou avoir à l'imparfait de l'indicatif + participe passé = j'avais révisé).

1 • Formation

Le *pluperfect* se forme avec l'auxiliaire *have* au prétérit (*had*) et avec le verbe au participe passé.

• Verbes réguliers

Pour le participe passé des verbes réguliers, c'est la même forme *-ed* que pour le prétérit.

Forme affirmative	Forme interrogative	Forme négative
*I **had** prepar**ed*** *You **had** prepar**ed*** *He / She / It **had** prepar**ed*** *We / You / They **had** prepar**ed***	***Had** I prepar**ed**?* ***Had** you prepar**ed**?* ***Had** he / she / it prepar**ed**?* ***Had** we / you / they prepar**ed**?*	*I **had** not prepar**ed*** *You **had** not prepar**ed*** *He / She / It **had** not prepar**ed*** *We / You / They **had** not prepar**ed***

• Verbes irréguliers

Pour le participe passé des verbes irréguliers, il s'agit de la troisième colonne de la liste (→ p. VI).

Forme affirmative	Forme interrogative	Forme négative
*I **had eaten*** *You **had eaten*** *He / she / it **had eaten*** *We / You / They **had eaten***	***Had** I **eaten**?* ***Had** you **eaten**?* ***Had** he / she / it **eaten**?* ***Had** we / you / they **eaten**?*	*I **had** not **eaten**.* *You **had** not **eaten**.* *He / she / it **had** not **eaten**.* *We / You / They **had** not **eaten**.*

• **À l'oral**

À l'oral, on utilise souvent la forme contractée de *had* (*'d*) et de *had not* (*'d not* ou *hadn't*).

*I**'d prepared** the table before they arrived.*

J'avais préparé la table avant leur arrivée.

*I**'d not prepared** the table before they arrived.*
*I **hadn't prepared** the table before they arrived.*

Je n'avais pas préparé la table avant leur arrivée.

Attention

'd est la contraction de *had* mais aussi de *would* !
Would (→ p. 306) est suivi de la **base verbale*** alors que *had* est suivi du verbe au *participe passé*.

*I knew he**'d arrive** late. (would) / I knew he**'d arrived** late. (had)*
Je savais qu'il arriverait en retard. Je savais qu'il était arrivé en retard.

2 • Emplois

• **Exprimer l'antériorité dans le passé**

On utilise le *pluperfect* pour exprimer l'antériorité d'un évènement passé par rapport à un autre moment passé.

***She had already finished** her homework when her father came back from work.*

Elle avait déjà terminé ses devoirs quand son père est rentré du travail.

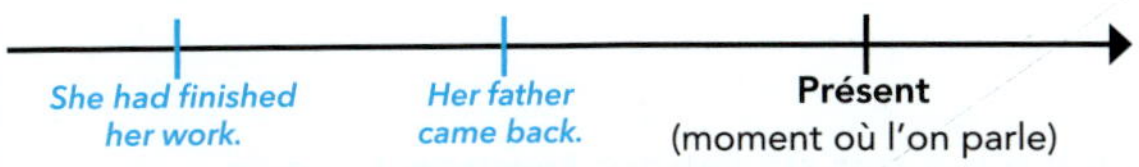

Comme le *present perfect* (→ p. 299), on trouve souvent le *pluperfect* associé à des adverbes du type *already, before, always, ever*. La différence est qu'avec le *pluperfect*, on est dans un contexte passé.

• **Narration au passé**

Dans une narration au passé, on utilise le *pluperfect* pour faire des retours en arrière.

*When **she arrived** at her office, she noticed **she had left** all her files at home.*

Quand elle arriva au bureau, elle remarqua qu'elle avait laissé tous ses dossiers à la maison.

• **Le *pluperfect be + -ing***

Il se forme avec *had* + *been* + verbe + *-ing*.

Avec le *pluperfect be + -ing*, on insiste sur le fait que l'évènement passé antérieur a duré.

*He **had been practicing for hours** when he decided to take a break.*

Il s'était entraîné pendant des heures quand il décida de faire une pause.

7. L'EXPRESSION DU FUTUR

Il n'y a pas, à proprement parler, de temps futur en anglais. On exprime le futur en utilisant l'auxiliaire modal *will* (→ p. 306), une périphrase (*be going to*), le présent *be* + *-ing* ou encore le présent simple.

1 • *Will*

• **Formation**

On utilise l'auxiliaire modal *will* et la base verbale.

Forme affirmative	Forme interrogative	Forme négative
*I **will** decide* *You **will** decide* *He / She / It **will** decide* *We / You / They **will** decide*	***Will** I decide?* ***Will** you decide?* ***Will** he / she / it decide?* ***Will** we / you / they decide?*	*I **will not (won't)** decide* *You **will not (won't)** decide* *He / She / It **will not (won't)** decide* *We / You / They **will not (won't)** decide*

- À la forme affirmative, on utilise généralement la forme contractée à toutes les personnes (*'ll*).

- À la forme négative, on a le choix entre : *will not, 'll not* et *won't*.

À la première personne du singulier ou du pluriel, on trouve encore *shall* avec la même valeur même si cette utilisation est de plus en plus rare et réservée à l'anglais britannique.

***I'll** decide. / I **shall** decide.* Je déciderai.

Dans les deux cas, c'est le verbe et non le modal qui est accentué. Cela explique d'ailleurs que *will* est souvent utilisé sous sa forme contractée.

• **Emplois**

a. Prévoir la réalisation d'une action

Pour l'expression du futur avec *will*, on parle parfois de futur neutre (*colourless future*). On prévoit qu'**une action va se réaliser dans l'avenir** (c'est le cas le plus fréquent).

*It **will be** sunny tomorrow.* Il va faire beau demain.

*He'**ll leave** the party immediately after the cake.*
Il va quitter la soirée directement après le gâteau.

*I'**ll** always **love** you.* Je t'aimerai toujours.

b. Prendre une décision soudaine

On utilise aussi *will* dans le cas où l'on prend une **décision au moment où l'on parle.**

I'm hungry, I'll go and buy a hamburger.

J'ai faim, je vais aller m'acheter un hamburger.

2 • L'expression du futur avec *be going to*

• **Formation**

On utilise *be* au présent suivi de *going to* à toutes les personnes.

*I'm **going to** be sick.*
Je vais être malade.

***Am I going to** be sick?*
Est-ce que je vais être malade ?

*I'm **not going to** be sick.*
Je ne vais pas être malade.

• **Emplois**

a. Renvoyer à un avenir en lien avec le présent

On utilise *be going to* pour renvoyer à un avenir plus ou moins lointain mais qui a **un lien avec la situation présente.**

*Look, it's **going to** rain.* Regarde, il va pleuvoir.

C'est parce qu'on voit les nuages arriver que l'on utilise cette forme, notre prédiction est donc plus sûre. Avec *will*, dans la rubrique précédente, on se contente de faire une prévision.

b. Quand il n'y a pas de repère temporel précis

On peut aussi utiliser *be going to* quand il n'y a pas de repère temporel précis.

*Your exhibition **is going to** be a success!*
Ton exposition va être un succès !

L'utilisation de *will* n'est pas exclue et la nuance est fine :

*Your exhibition **will** be a success!*
Ton exposition va être un succès !

3 • L'expression du futur avec le présent *be + -ing*

• **Formation** (→ p. 298)

• **Emplois**

On utilise le présent *be + -ing* pour exprimer le futur quand quelque chose est **planifié** et qu'on est **sûr de sa réalisation**. On fait « comme si » on voyait déjà l'action en train de se dérouler.

*Tomorrow, I'**m selling** my car.*
Demain, je vends ma voiture.

C'est parce qu'il n'y a pas de **planification de la part de celui** qui parle qu'on ne peut pas dire :
~~*It's snowing tomorrow*~~.
Alors que l'on peut dire :
It will snow tomorrow ou *It's going to snow tomorrow.*

4 • L'expression du futur avec le présent simple

• **Formation** (→ p. 297)

• **Emplois**

On emploie le présent simple pour exprimer le futur quand on renvoie à un **programme**, à quelque chose de **planifié**.

*The concert **starts** at 8 p.m. tomorrow.*
Le concert débutera à 20h demain.

8. L'EXPRESSION DE L'IRRÉEL

Comme l'imparfait en français, le prétérit anglais ne renvoie pas toujours à des évènements qui se sont déroulés dans le passé : il peut servir à renvoyer à des **évènements non encore réalisés ou hypothétiques**. On appelle cela « **l'irréel** », que l'on exprime en français avec le conditionnel ou le subjonctif.

He told her yesterday.
Il lui a dit hier.
(= Cela s'est vraiment passé.)

If he told her, she would be happy.
S'il le lui disait, elle serait heureuse. (= Cela ne s'est pas passé mais on en évoque l'hypothèse.)

L'anglais a un fonctionnement très proche du français pour les trois types d'hypothèses possibles.

1 • Formation

• Hypothèse sur un fait présent

If + présent + *will* + base verbale*

***If** you **go** out now, you **will** ('ll) be cold.*
Si tu sors maintenant, tu vas avoir froid.

On peut bien sûr inverser l'ordre des propositions :

*You'll **be** cold **if** you **go** out now.*

• Hypothèse irréelle portant sur un fait présent

If + prétérit + *would* + base verbale*

***If** you **opened** the window, it **would** ('d) **be** cooler.*
Si tu ouvrais la fenêtre, il ferait plus frais.

Comme précédemment, on peut avoir :

***I'd be** cooler **if** you **opened** the window.*

• Hypothèse irréelle portant sur un fait passé

If + had + -en + would + have + -en

***If** he **had opened** the window, he **would** not (wouldn't) **have been** so hot.*
S'il avait ouvert la fenêtre, il n'aurait pas eu aussi chaud.

Comme précédemment :

*He **wouldn't have been** so hot **if** he **had opened** the window.*

2 • L'expression du souhait et du regret

• Certaines tournures déclenchent aussi l'utilisation du prétérit pour renvoyer à quelque chose d'irréel ou de non encore réalisé. C'est typiquement le cas pour exprimer des regrets ou des souhaits avec des tournures comme *if only, I'd rather, I'd sooner, it's (high) time, I wish…*

***If only** you **could** be more pleasant with your brother.*
Si seulement tu pouvais être plus agréable avec ton frère.

***It's time** you **started** preparing for the exam.*
Il est temps que tu te mettes à travailler pour ton examen.

Notez qu'il est aussi possible d'avoir la structure suivante, sans perte de sens :

***It's time for you to start** preparing for the exam.*

***I wish** you **were** here with me.*
J'aimerais que tu sois là avec moi.

***I wish** she **was / were** here with me.*
J'aimerais qu'elle soit là avec moi. (Ici, on a le choix entre *was* et *were*).

***I'd rather** you **came** alone.*
Je préfèrerais que tu viennes seul(e).

***I'd sooner** you **came** alone.*
Je préfèrerais que tu viennes seul(e).

• Quand le sujet du verbe est le même que celui de *'d rather*, on utilise la base verbale* et non le prétérit :

***I'd rather spend** the evening alone.*
Je préfèrerais passer la soirée seul(e).

• *'d rather, 'd sooner* sont des contractions de *would rather* et *would sooner*. Les formes non contractées sont rarement utilisées.

• La forme *'d better*, utilisée pour exprimer un conseil, est la contraction de *had better* et est suivie de la base verbale* :

***You'd better spend** the evening with some friends.*
Tu devrais passer la soirée avec des amis.

9. LA MODALITÉ

La modalité est la manière dont l'énonciateur exprime sa subjectivité (souhait, capacité, degré de certitude) dans le discours. En anglais comme en français, la modalité peut être exprimée à l'aide d'un **adverbe** (il est **possible** que : *it's **possible** that*) ou d'une **forme** verbale (il se **peut** que : *it **may** be*).

1 • Les modaux

En anglais, on utilise des auxiliaires de modalité ou « modaux ».

Présent	Prétérit
Can /kæn/	*Could* /kʊd/
May /meɪ/	*Might* /maɪt/
Must /mʌst/	
Need /niːd/	
Shall /ʃæl/	*Should* /ʃʊd/
Will /wɪl/	*Would* /wʊd/

• Fonctionnement

Les modaux ont un fonctionnement particulier :
- Ils ne prennent **pas de -*s* à la troisième personne** du singulier au présent.
- Ils s'utilisent **sans *do* / *did*** pour former la forme interrogative ou négative.
- Ils ne sont **jamais précédés ou suivis de *to***.
- Ils n'ont pas d'infinitif ni de participe passé.
- Ils ne s'utilisent **jamais avec -*ing***.
- Il ne peut y avoir qu'un seul modal dans un groupe verbal et il est placé en tête.

2 • Formations simples et composées

	Forme simple (Modal + base verbale)	Forme *be* + *-ing*	Forme *have* + participe passé	Forme *been* + *-ing*
Forme affirmative	*He **must** work harder.*	*He **may** be **working** harder.*	*He **could have worked** harder.*	*He **might have been working** harder.*
Forme interrogative	***Must** he work harder?*	***May** he be **working** harder?*	***Could** he **have worked** harder?*	***Might he have been working** harder?*
Forme négative	*He **must not (mustn't)** work harder.*	*He **may not** be **working** harder.*	*He **could not have worked** harder.*	*He **might not have been working** harder.*

3 • Emplois

On peut considérer qu'il y a deux grands types de modalité en anglais : **la modalité du savoir (probabilité)** et la **modalité de l'action (capacité, permission, obligation)**. Souvent, le même modal est utilisé avec deux sens différents.

- Modalité du savoir :
*He **must** be at home.* Il doit être chez lui.
(= Je crois savoir qu'il y a de fortes chances pour qu'il soit chez lui. Je me prononce sur cette probabilité.)

- Modalité de l'action :
*You **must** rest for a while.* Tu dois te reposer un moment.

Le même modal (*must*) est utilisé en anglais (et le même verbe en français « devoir »), mais dans le 2e cas (modalité de l'action), on ne se prononce pas sur une probabilité (modalité du savoir) : on incite son interlocuteur à faire quelque chose.

• La modalité du savoir (probabilité)

a. La gradation

On exprime son opinion sur le caractère plus ou moins certain d'une action ou d'un fait.
Dans le schéma ci-contre, il faut bien comprendre que la modalité se situe entre l'absolument certain (*John is at home*) et l'absolument impossible (*John is not at home*).
On a donc la gradation suivante :

John is not at home.	(100 % sûr qu'il n'y est pas)
John might be at home.	(25 % sûr)
John may be / could be at home.	(50 % sûr)
John must be / will be at home.	(75 % sûr)
John is at home.	(100 % sûr qu'il y est)

Les pourcentages ne sont bien sûr qu'indicatifs mais permettent de choisir le bon modal en fonction du contexte.

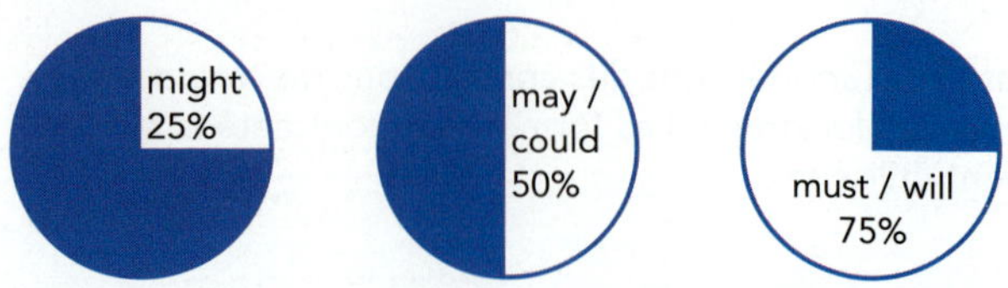

b. La négation

Attention

Il faut faire attention au sens de la négation :

*He **might be** at home.* Il se peut qu'il soit à la maison.

*He **might not be** at home.*
Il se peut qu'il ne soit pas à la maison. (= La probabilité est faible qu'il n'y soit pas.)

Cas particulier : avec *must*, on utilise *can't* à la forme négative pour exprimer la modalité du savoir.

*He **must** be at home.*
Il doit être chez lui.

*He **can't** be at home.*
Il ne doit pas (« peut pas ») être chez lui.

*You **must** be joking!*
Tu plaisantes !

*You **can't** be serious!*
Tu plaisantes !

- **La modalité de l'action**

La modalité de l'action est plus complexe que la modalité du savoir car elle se décline en différents sens. Chaque sens est associé à un modal particulier.

a. La capacité / l'incapacité : *can / can't*

Il s'agit d'exprimer une capacité physique, intellectuelle, etc. On le traduit souvent par « savoir » ou « pouvoir » en français.

*I **can** speak Chinese.* Je sais parler chinois.

***Can** you swim?* Est-ce que tu sais nager ?

*You **can't** have your cake and eat it!*
On ne peut pas avoir le beurre et l'argent du beurre !

b. La permission / l'absence de permission : *may / may not*

*You **may** come in.* Tu peux entrer. (On insiste sur le fait que l'on donne une autorisation)

*You **may** not enter the room when the class has started.*
Il n'est pas permis d'entrer dans la classe quand le cours a débuté.

*Mum, **may** I go to the cinema tonight?*
Maman, est-ce que je peux aller au cinéma ce soir ?

Dans la langue courante, *may* (plus soutenu) est souvent remplacé par *can* (plus courant).

***Can** I go to the cinema tonight?*

Si la réponse est *Yes, you may*, la mère insiste sur le fait que c'est elle qui décide et qui accorde la permission.

c. L'obligation / l'interdiction : *must / mustn't*

*You **must** do as you are told.* Tu dois faire ce qu'on te dit.

*You **mustn't** tell your little sister that Father Christmas doesn't exist.* Tu ne dois pas dire à ta petite sœur que le Père Noël n'existe pas.

***Must** you always contradict me?*
Faut-il toujours que tu me contredises ?

d. Le conseil : *should / shouldn't*

*You **should** always make the most of everything.*
Il faudrait toujours profiter de tout.

*You **shouldn't** talk to her like that!*
Tu ne devrais pas lui parler sur ce ton !

***Should** I ask him now or wait after the class?*
Dois-je lui poser la question maintenant ou attendre la fin du cours ?

e. La volonté / le refus : *will / will not / won't*

He won't talk to me. Il refuse de me parler.

Will you marry me? Yes, I will.

Veux-tu m'épouser? Oui, je le veux.

f. La nécessité / l'absence de nécessité : *need / need not / needn't*

Need I explain the reasons why?
Dois-je expliquer mes motivations ?

You needn't work so hard. Il est inutile de travailler autant.

Remarque : le modal *need* est de plus en plus souvent remplacé par le verbe *need* qui se construit comme un verbe classique (avec *do*) : *You don't need to work so hard.*

4 • Les équivalents des modaux

Au passé et au futur, on utilise ces **équivalents** de préférence aux modaux :

must → have to	*can → be able to*	*may → be allowed to*
*You **must stop** worrying about her.* Tu dois arrêter de te faire du souci pour elle. *You'll **have to** stop worrying about her.* Il faudra arrêter de te faire du souci pour elle.	*He **can** speak English fluently.* Il parle anglais couramment. *Next year, he'll **be able** to speak English fluently.* L'année prochaine, il saura parler anglais couramment.	*You **may** leave now.* Vous pouvez partir maintenant. *She told me I **was allowed to** leave.* Elle m'a dit que je pouvais partir.

Les énoncés ci-dessus sont quasi équivalents en termes de modalité.

10. LES NOMS

Les noms communs anglais sont répartis en deux catégories : **les dénombrables** et **les indénombrables**. La même distinction existe en français mais ce ne sont pas nécessairement les mêmes mots qui sont indénombrables dans les deux langues.

1 • Les indénombrables

Les indénombrables ne peuvent pas être comptés et représentent un ensemble considéré comme un tout.

• Quelques indénombrables

Ils appartiennent généralement à une des catégories suivantes :

Des noms de matériaux : *cotton* (coton), *silk* (soie), *iron* (fer), *steel* (acier), *wood* (bois), *tea* (thé), *coffee* (café), *food* (nourriture), *milk* (lait), *water* (eau), *oil* (huile), etc.

Des noms renvoyant à des ensembles : *furniture* (des meubles), *hair* (les cheveux, mais attention : *hairs* → des poils), *luggage* (des bagages), *garbage*, *rubbish* (des détritus), *toast* (pain grillé), *fruit*, *money*, etc.

Des noms abstraits : *accommodation* (le logement), *advice* (des conseils), *business* (les affaires), *damage* (des dégâts), *traffic* (la circulation), *evidence* (des preuves), *growth* (la croissance), *information* (des renseignements), *knowledge* (le savoir), *honesty* (l'honnêteté), *news* (des nouvelles), *nonsense* (des absurdités), *research* (la recherche), *trouble* (des ennuis), *weather* (la météo), *work* (emploi), etc.

• Emplois

Les indénombrables ne se mettent pas au pluriel et le verbe reste au singulier.

*No news **is** good news.* Pas de nouvelles, bonnes nouvelles.

*Where **is** my luggage?* Où sont mes bagages ?

Ne pas utiliser l'article indéfini (*a* / *an*) devant un indénombrable.

That's Ø good advice! C'est un bon conseil !

Attention *Thanks for **all the good** advice!* Merci pour tous les bons conseils !

Si l'on veut dénombrer des indénombrables pour des raisons de précision, il faut utiliser des expressions comme *a piece of*, *an item of*. Attention à ne pas abuser de ces formes !

*She gave me **an interesting piece of** information.* Elle m'a donné un renseignement intéressant.

*That's **an odd item of** news.* C'est une nouvelle étrange.

2 • Les dénombrables

Il est possible de compter les dénombrables (*one cat, two cats, an apple, two apples*) et on peut donc les mettre au pluriel.

• La plupart des noms anglais font leur pluriel en ajoutant *-s* ou *-es*.

cat → *cats* *peach* → *peaches* *house* → *houses*

• Certains mots qui se terminent en *-f* ou *-fe* ont un pluriel en *-ves*.

calf (veau) → *calves* *wolf* (loup) → *wolves*
knife (couteau) → *knives* *half* (la moitié) → *halves*
wife (épouse) → *wives* *life* (vie) → *lives*
leaf (feuille) → *leaves* *thief* (voleur) → *thieves*
self (le moi) → *selves* *shelf* (étagère) → *shelves*

Attention *handkerchief* (mouchoir en tissu) a son pluriel en *-s* : *handkerchiefs*.

• Certains mots ont un pluriel irrégulier.

child → *children* *ox* (bœuf) → *oxen*
man → *men* *woman* → *women*
foot → *feet* *goose* (oie) → *geese*
tooth (dent) → *teeth* *louse* (pou) → *lice*
mouse (souris) → *mice*

• Certains dénombrables ne changent pas de forme au pluriel.

deer (daim), *fish* (poisson), *sheep* (mouton), *aircraft* (avion)… Ainsi, on dit :

*There is **a sheep** in the field.* Il y a un mouton dans le pré.

*Look at the **flock of sheepØ**.* Regarde le troupeau de moutons.

• Les noms collectifs

- Les noms collectifs sont utilisés pour renvoyer soit au groupe soit aux individus qui composent ce groupe. On a donc le choix entre un accord au singulier ou au pluriel. Voici les principaux :

army (armée) ; *audience* (spectateurs) ; *cast* (distribution) ; *company* (société, entreprise) ; *crew* (équipage) ; *crowd* (foule) ; *family* (famille) ; *government* (gouvernement) ; *group* (groupe) ; *public* (public) ; *press* (la presse) ; *staff* (personnel) ; *team* (équipe).

- Certains noms collectifs s'accordent toujours au pluriel.

cattle (le bétail) *people* (les gens)
management (la direction) *police* (la police)

***The police have** arrested the thieves.*
La police a arrêté les bandits.

- Ces noms peuvent être comptés.

***Ten people have** passed the exam.*
Dix personnes ont réussi l'examen.

3. Les dénombrables ou indénombrables

• Certains noms indénombrables peuvent avoir un fonctionnement dénombrable dans certains contextes avec, bien sûr, un changement de sens.

indénombrable	dénombrable
business (les affaires)	*a business* (une entreprise)
coffee (du café)	*a coffee* (un café)
country (la campagne)	*a country* (un pays)
glass (du verre)	*a glass* (un verre)
hair (les cheveux)	*a hair* (un poil)
work (le travail)	*a work* (une œuvre)
people (les gens)	*a people* (le peuple)

• Certains noms portent la marque du pluriel et s'accordent au pluriel alors qu'ils sont souvent singuliers en français. Il s'agit souvent d'objets « doubles ».

Pluriel en français et en anglais

glasses (lunettes) *binoculars* (jumelles) *scissors* (ciseaux)

Pluriel en anglais mais pas en français

bermudas (un bermuda) *trousers* (un pantalon) 🇬🇧
pyjamas (un pyjama) *pants* (un pantalon) 🇺🇸
jeans (un jean)

*His trousers **are** too short!*
Son pantalon est trop court !

4. Les noms propres

- Les noms de pays au pluriel s'accordent toujours au singulier.

*The United States **is** bigger than Switzerland.*
Les États-Unis sont plus grands que la Suisse.

- Contrairement au français, les noms de famille portent la marque du pluriel.

*I've invited the Packer**s** and the Hunter**s**.*
J'ai invité les Packer et les Hunter.

11. LES ARTICLES

Les articles font partie de la famille des déterminants. À ce titre, ils indiquent comment le nom qui les suit est perçu par l'énonciateur.

1 • Fonctionnement général

a. L'article défini *The*

• Prononciation

- Devant un son consonne (→ p. 320), on prononce /ðə/ :
The dog → /ðə dɒg/ *The university* → /ðə juːnɪˈvɜːsəti/

- Devant un son voyelle, on prononce /ði/ :
The orange → /ði ˈɒrɪndʒ/

• Emplois

On emploie l'article défini *the* quand on parle d'éléments **bien définis**, au singulier ou au pluriel.

- Cette définition peut être liée au contexte immédiat :

***The teacher** told me I did very well this term.*
Le professeur m'a dit que j'avais bien travaillé ce trimestre.

Il s'agit d'un professeur que celui ou celle qui parle connaît bien et dont l'identité est connue de la personne à qui il ou elle s'adresse. Ce fonctionnement est le même qu'en français.

*Look at **the horses**, they are beautiful.*
Regarde les chevaux, ils sont magnifiques.

On sait de quels chevaux il s'agit (ceux que l'on est en train de regarder). Comme en français, on utilise l'article défini.

- Cette définition peut venir de la syntaxe :

***The girl** who is wearing a yellow jumper is very bright.*
La fille qui porte un pull jaune est très douée.

Tout ce qui se trouve à droite du nom (*girl* / fille) vient préciser de quelle fille on parle et justifie l'utilisation de l'article défini.

- Cette définition peut venir de la connaissance universelle (ce que tout le monde sait) :

The Earth (la Terre), *the Moon* (la Lune), *the government* (le gouvernement), etc.

b. L'article indéfini *A / An*

• Prononciation

On utilise *a* devant un son consonne (→ p. 320) :

A dog → /ə dɒg/ *A university* → /ə juːnɪ'vɜːsəti/

Devant un son voyelle, on utilise an /an/ :

An orange → /ən 'ɒrɪndʒ/

• Emplois

- On utilise l'article indéfini (*a, an*) pour désigner un élément parmi d'autres. L'article indéfini n'existe qu'au singulier et seulement devant un nom que l'on peut dénombrer.

He's got a dog. Il a un chien.

Attention

Certains mots anglais commencent par un *h* muet, donc par un son voyelle. Devant ces mots, on utilisera soit *an* soit *the* /ði/ :

hour, hourly, heir (héritier), *heiress* (héritière), *heirloom* (héritage), *honour, honourable, honourably, honorary, honorific, honest, honesty, honestly*

c. L'article Ø

On utilise généralement l'article Ø (« article zéro ») pour désigner des **éléments parmi d'autres.**

L'article Ø est généralement traduit en français par « des » :

There were Ø boys and Ø girls in the audience

Il y avait des garçons et des filles dans le public.

2 • Emplois particuliers

a. Exprimer une généralité

Pour exprimer une généralité, on utilise l'article Ø pour les **dénombrables au pluriel** et les **indénombrables.**

• Les dénombrables au pluriel

Betty doesn't like Ø dogs. Betty n'aime pas les chiens.

Attention à ne pas calquer le français :

Betty doesn't like ~~the~~ dogs.

Si on parle des chiens en général, l'article *the* est impossible. En revanche, cette phrase est possible s'il s'agit de chiens en particulier.

*Betty doesn't like **the dogs** that she saw yesterday.*

Betty n'aime pas les chiens qu'elle a vus hier.

Il faut donc veiller à ne pas traduire *le, la, les* français par *the* pour renvoyer à une généralité.

• Les indénombrables

Avec des indénombrables, on n'utilise pas d'article pour exprimer une généralité, contrairement au français :

Ø Time flies.

Le temps passe très vite.

Ø Love is everywhere.

L'amour est partout.

His actions are motivated by Ø passion.

Ses actions sont motivées par la passion.

b. Emplois particuliers de *The*

• Devant un instrument de musique avec le verbe *play*

*Thomas plays **the** cello.* Thomas joue du violoncelle.

• Devant des adjectifs désignant des groupes

The English (les Anglais) *The homeless* (les sans-abris)

Attention

Ø *English people* désigne un groupe de nationalité mais ne prend pas d'article défini !

• Devant les noms de pays au pluriel

The United States (Les États-Unis)

The United Kingdom (Le Royaume-Uni)

Ici, il s'agit d'un singulier mais qui renvoie à une réalité plurielle : les différents pays qui composent le Royaume-Uni.

Attention

Les autres noms de pays sont généralement précédés de l'article Ø, contrairement au français :

Ø France, Ø England, Ø Italy, Ø Japan

la France, l'Angleterre, l'Italie, le Japon

c. Emplois particuliers de *A / An*

• **Devant un nom de profession**

On utilise *a / an* devant un nom de profession alors que le français utilise l'article Ø :

*Paul is **a** dentist.* Paul est Ø dentiste.

• **Pour exprimer des mesures**

On utilise *a / an* quand on exprime des mesures par rapport à une variable (temps, espace, poids, etc.).

*It's £3 **an hour**.* Cela coûte 3 livres par heure.

*He can see his dad twice **a week**.*
Il peut voir son père deux fois par semaine.

d. Emplois particuliers de l'article Ø

• **Devant des noms abstraits**

Ø Poverty is a real problem these days.
La pauvreté est un réel problème de nos jours.

• **Devant des noms de lieux**

You go to Ø school. Tu vas à l'école.

She went to Ø Inverness. Elle est allée à Inverness.

• **Devant un nom de personne titrée**

Contrairement au français, on utilise l'article Ø devant un nom de personne précédé par un titre.

Ø Prime Minister Theresa May.
La Première ministre Theresa May.

Ø Queen Elizabeth II. La reine Elisabeth II.

Attention

To go to prison → aller en prison en tant que prisonnier.

To go to the prison → aller à la prison (pour rendre visite à quelqu'un par exemple).

12. LES QUANTIFIEURS

Les quantifieurs servent à délimiter une quantité (de la plus petite à la plus grande). Les usages sont différents selon que l'on parle de noms dénombrables ou indénombrables.

1 • *Some / any* : une certaine quantité de

• **Forme affirmative**

On peut utiliser *some* avec des dénombrables ou des indénombrables à la forme affirmative.

*There are **some** apples in the kitchen.*
Il y a des pommes dans la cuisine.

*There's **some** milk on the table.*
Il y a du lait sur la table.

Dans ces deux cas, on prononce *some* avec sa forme réduite (non accentuée) : /səm/.

• **Forme interrogative**

À la forme interrogative, on utilise *any* /'eni/ (la lettre « a » a une prononciation irrégulière, (→ p. 319).

*Is there **any** milk in the house?* Est-ce qu'on a du lait ?

*Are there **any** apples in the kitchen?*
Y a-t-il des pommes dans la cuisine ?

Toutefois, quand on offre quelque chose à quelqu'un, on utilise *some* :

*Would you like **some** tea?* Vous prendrez du thé ?

La même question avec *any* serait moins polie.

*Would you like **any** tea?* Vous ne prendrez pas de thé ?

2 • *Not any / no* : quantité nulle

On peut utiliser *not any* et *no* avec des dénombrables ou des indénombrables.

• **Construction négative : *not any***

*There **isn't any** milk left.* Il ne reste pas de lait.

*There **aren't any** apples left.* Il ne reste pas de pommes.

• **Construction affirmative : *no***

*There **is no** milk left.* Il ne reste pas de lait.

*There **are no** apples left.* Il ne reste pas de pommes.

3 • Peu de, un peu de, beaucoup de...

• Peu de

- Avec un **dénombrable,** on utilise ***few*** :

*There are **few** apples.* Il y a peu de pommes.

- Avec un **indénombrable,** on utilise ***little*** :

*There is **little** milk left.* Il reste peu de lait.

• Un peu de

- Avec un **dénombrable,** on utilise ***a few*** :

*There are **a few** apples left.* Il reste quelques pommes.

- Avec un **indénombrable,** on utilise ***a little*** :

*There is **a little** milk left.* Il reste un peu de lait.

• Beaucoup de

- Avec les **dénombrables,** on utilise ***a lot of*** ou ***many*** :

Many se prononce /'meni/ (pour la prononciation de la lettre « a », (→ p. 319).

*There are **a lot of / many** apples.*

Il y a beaucoup de pommes.

- Avec les **indénombrables,** on utilise ***a lot of*** ou ***much*** :

*There is **a lot of / much** milk.*

Il y a beaucoup de lait.

Dans la langue courante, on utilise plus généralement *a lot of* dans les phrases affirmatives et *much* ou *many* dans les phrases interrogatives et les négatives.

4 • Autres quantifieurs

• *One* / *one of them* : un / un seul

One child was awake.

Un seul enfant était réveillé.

• *Both* / *both of them* : les deux

Attention à la prononciation de *both* : /bəʊθ/

Both friends won the prize.

Les deux amis remportèrent le prix.

• *Each* / *every* : chaque

Each child was happy. Every child was happy.

À noter également, la construction idiomatique :

Each and every child was happy.

• *All* : tous, tout, toute, toutes

All the milk had disappeared.

Tout le lait avait disparu.

All the flowers had blossomed.

Toutes les fleurs avaient fleuri.

• *The whole* /həʊl/ : la totalité de (seulement devant un dénombrable singulier)

The whole class cracked up laughing.

Toute la classe se mit à rire.

• *Most* /məʊst/ / *most of* : la plupart de

Most people like watching football on television.

La plupart des gens aiment regarder le foot à la télé.

Most of the players played well.

La plupart des joueurs ont bien joué.

• *Either* /'aɪðə/ : l'un ou l'autre

***neither* /'naɪðə/ :** ni l'un ni l'autre

*I like both dresses: you can wear **either**.*

J'aime les deux robes: tu peux porter l'une ou l'autre.

*He hesitated between tea and coffee and in the end he had **neither**.*

Il hésitait entre le thé et le café et en fin de compte il n'a pris ni l'un ni l'autre.

5 • Les composés de *some / any / no / every*

some	any /'eni/	no	every
someone / somebody quelqu'un	*anyone / anybody* n'importe qui, quelqu'un / quiconque	*no one / nobody* personne	*everyone / everybody* tout le monde
something quelque chose	*anything* quelque chose, rien, n'importe quoi	*nothing* /'nʌθɪŋ/ rien	*everything* tout
somewhere quelque part	*anywhere* quelque part, n'importe où	*nowhere* nulle part	*everywhere* partout

13. LES ADJECTIFS

1 • Emplois

Les adjectifs anglais sont invariables, ils ne s'accordent ni en genre ni en nombre :

These earrings are beautiful. Ces boucles d'oreilles sont très belles.

Il existe deux sortes d'adjectifs :

- les adjectifs **épithètes** (directement rattachés au nom) se placent avant le nom :

A red table. Une table rouge.

- les adjectifs **attributs**, qui se placent après un verbe d'état (comme *be*).

He is asleep.	*She is glad.*	*They are cross.*
Il est endormi.	Elle est heureuse.	Ils sont fâchés.
She is alive.	*We are afraid.*	*He is ill.*
Elle est vivante.	Nous avons peur.	Il est malade.

2 • Ordre des adjectifs

- Quand il y a plusieurs adjectifs placés avant le nom, comme dans *a big black car*, on les place du plus subjectif au plus objectif. Ainsi, on dira plus volontiers :

A nice tall man (un homme grand et gentil)

que *A tall nice man*.

La taille est un critère plus objectif que le fait d'être gentil.

Attention

Cette règle est un repère mais n'est pas une règle absolue. Parfois, pour des raisons euphoniques (harmonie sonore), l'ordre des adjectifs est modifié.

- **TACOM** est un moyen mnémotechnique pour pouvoir décider de l'ordre des adjectifs en anglais :

Taille / Âge / Couleur / Origine / Matière

An enormous new bright French stone house.

Une énorme maison de pierre française, récente et de couleur vive.

On voit que le français est moins tolérant en ce qui concerne le nombre d'adjectifs possibles avant le nom. À vrai dire, ces accumulations sont certes possibles en anglais mais restent rares car peu élégantes.

3 • Les comparatifs et les superlatifs

• Le comparatif de supériorité

adj. court + *-er* + *than*
more + adj. long + *than*
} = plus + adj. + que

- **Les adjectifs d'une syllabe (courts) :**

on ajoute *-er* à l'adjectif + *than*.

His car is nicer ***than*** *mine.*

Sa voiture est plus belle que la mienne.

- **Les adjectifs de trois syllabes ou plus (longs) :**

on utilise *more* + adjectif + *than*.

This picture is ***more*** *beautiful* ***than*** *the one in the hall.*

Cette photo est plus belle que celle qui est dans le hall.

On voit que dans le cas des adjectifs longs, on peut calquer sur le français.

- **Les adjectifs de deux syllabes suivent l'une des deux règles ci-contre :**

Les adjectifs en *-er*, *-y* ou *-ly* suivent la règle des adjectifs courts :

clever → cleverer *pretty → prettier* *silly → sillier*

Les autres suivent la règle des adjectifs longs :

obscure → more obscure

doubtful → more doubtful

• Le comparatif d'égalité

as **+ adj. +** ***as*** = aussi + adj. + que

He is ***as clever as*** *his friend.*

Il est aussi intelligent que son ami.

• Le comparatif d'infériorité

less **+ adj. +** ***than*** = moins + adj. + que

He is ***less clever than*** *his friend.*

Il est moins intelligent que son ami.

• Récapitulatif

	A > B	A = B	A < B
Adjectifs courts	*He's smart**er** **than** Paula.*	*He's **as smart as** Paula.*	*He's less **smart than** Paula.*
Adjectifs longs	*He's **more intelligent than** Paula.*	*He's **as intelligent as** Paula.*	*He's **less intelligent** than Paula.*

• Pour traduire « de plus en plus »

- Avec les adjectifs courts :

*It's getting dark**er** and dark**er**.*

Ça devient de plus en plus sombre.

- Avec les adjectifs longs :

*It's getting **more and more** interesting.*

Ça devient de plus en plus intéressant.

• Pour traduire « de moins en moins »

On utilise *less and less* avec les adjectifs longs et courts.

*It's getting **less and less** dark.*

C'est de moins en moins sombre.

*It's getting **less and less** interesting.*

C'est de moins en moins intéressant.

• Le superlatif

the **+ adj. court + -*est*** = le + plus + adj.

the **+ *most* + adj. long** = le + plus + adj.

The biggest. Le plus grand.

The most interesting. Le plus intéressant.

Attention

Comparatifs et superlatifs irréguliers :

adjectif	comparatif	superlatif
bad	*worse*	*worst*
far	*farther / further*	*farthest / furthest*
good	*better*	*best*
little	*less*	*least*
old	*older / elder*	*oldest / eldest*

- ***Farther / farthest*** ne s'utilise qu'avec son sens spatial alors que ***further / furthest*** s'accommode aussi d'un sens métaphorique ou figuré :

*She lives **farther / further** away.* Elle vit plus loin.

*Please contact me if you need any **further** information.*

N'hésitez pas à me contacter pour davantage d'informations.

- ***Eldest*** s'utilise uniquement pour des êtres humains alors que ***oldest*** peut s'utiliser avec des êtres humains et des êtres inanimés :

*Paul is the **eldest**.* Paul est le plus vieux.

*The Major Oak is the **oldest** oak in Britain.*

Le Major Oak est le plus vieux chêne d'Angleterre.

14. LE GÉNITIF

(LE CAS POSSESSIF)

On utilise le « génitif » pour indiquer que quelque chose appartient à quelqu'un. En français, on peut avoir recours à la structure avec « de » pour marquer la possession. L'équivalent anglais peut être la structure en *of* : La voiture de mon père.

The car of my father.

Si cette construction est parfois possible en anglais, on préfère utiliser *'s* : *My father's car.*

Le génitif est une construction très ancienne et très fréquente, commune aux langues germaniques. On la retrouve dans certains mots courants sans se rendre compte qu'il s'agit d'un ancien génitif, comme par exemple *tradesman, craftsman, Wednesday* (*Wodan's day, Wodan* étant un ancien dieu germanique !).

1 • Formation

Pour construire le génitif, on inverse l'ordre des mots par rapport au français.

La voiture de mon père

My father's car

Le génitif est un déterminant du nom, c'est-à-dire qu'il joue le même rôle qu'un article. On ne répète donc pas ce dernier : *My father's ~~the~~ car.*

• Pour un nom au singulier, on ajoute *'s*.

*The woman**'s** computer.*

L'ordinateur de la femme.

• Pour un nom au pluriel, on ajoute simplement l'apostrophe.

*The students**'** pens were all broken.*

Les stylos des étudiants étaient tous cassés.

2 • Emplois

• Exprimer la possession (utilisation principale)

Jane's room is really big.

La chambre de Jane est très grande.

• Exprimer la durée

It's ten minutes' walk from College.

C'est à dix minutes à pied de l'Université.

• Exprimer une relation spatiale ou temporelle

Last night's events were unexpected.

Les évènements de la nuit dernière étaient inattendus.

London's streets are always very busy.

Les rues de Londres sont toujours très fréquentées.

• Pour parler de groupes d'individus

The Parliament's decisions were appreciated.

Les décisions prises par le Parlement furent appréciées.

• Pour parler de magasins spécialisés

I've got to go to the butcher's shop.

Je dois aller chez le boucher.

Attention

Dans le cas des magasins spécialisés, on omet souvent le deuxième nom :

*I've got to go to the butcher's **(shop)**.*

Ainsi on dira :

To go to the dentist's. Aller chez le dentiste.

To go to the hairdresser's. Aller chez le coiffeur.

Par extension, pour désigner un nom de lieu, on peut omettre le deuxième terme quand il est évident :

To go to St. Paul's (Cathedral).

Aller à (la cathédrale) Saint-Paul.

We're having a party at Tom's (place).

Nous avons une soirée chez Tom.

15. LES PRONOMS

Le fonctionnement des pronoms en anglais est comparable à ce qui se passe en français : un pronom est utilisé pour **remplacer un nom.** (Pour les pronoms relatifs (→ p. 316))

Pronoms sujets	Pronoms compléments	Pronoms possessifs	Pronoms réfléchis
I	*me*	*mine*	*myself*
you	*you*	*yours*	*yourself*
he	*him*	*his*	*himself*
she	*her*	*hers*	*herself*
it	*it*	*its own*	*itself*
we	*us*	*ours*	*ourself/ourselves*
you	*you*	*yours*	*yourselves*
they	*them*	*theirs*	*themselves*

Attention

Les pronoms possessifs ne doivent pas être confondus avec **les déterminants possessifs** (*my, your, his, her, its, our, your, their*), qui indiquent à qui appartient le nom qui suit.

*This is **your** book. This book is **yours**.*
déterminant — pronom

1 • Les pronoms et déterminants possessifs

• Les déterminants possessifs s'accordent avec le « possesseur », contrairement au français qui les accorde avec le « possédé » :

He likes his sister a lot.

Il aime beaucoup sa sœur.

She likes her brother a lot.

Elle aime beaucoup son frère.

- On peut renforcer le déterminant possessif à l'aide de *own* :

*She's got a mansion with **its own** pool.*

Elle possède une demeure qui a sa propre piscine.

- Pour les parties du corps, on utilise les déterminants possessifs là où le français utilise les articles définis :

*She had **her** hands in **her** pockets.*

Elle avait les mains dans les poches.
(et non « ses mains dans ses poches »)

• **Pour dire « un de... »,** on utilise la structure avec *of* + pronom possessif :

*She's a good friend **of mine**.* C'est une de mes bonnes amies.

*It's a stupid idea **of his**.* C'est l'une de ses idées idiotes.

2 • Les pronoms réfléchis

Pour insister sur une personne ou un objet, on utilise les pronoms réfléchis. Le sujet et l'objet sont la même personne :

*Ask him **yourself** if you're so impatient.*
Demande-lui toi-même si tu es si impatient.

*She is talking to **herself**.*
Elle est en train de parler toute seule.

Contrairement au français, certains verbes anglais se construisent sans pronom réfléchi. On estime que le sens du verbe est suffisamment explicite. Par exemple : se laver (*wash*), se sentir (*feel*), se raser (*shave*), se rencontrer (*meet*), s'excuser (*apologise*), se lever (*stand up*).
He shaved. Il s'est rasé. Et pas : ~~He shaved himself.~~

3 • Les pronoms réciproques

Pour indiquer un échange entre plusieurs personnes, on utilise *each other* (deux personnes) et *one another* (plus de deux personnes) pour indiquer un échange entre ces personnes :

*These football players never win because they hate **one another**.*
Ces joueurs de foot ne gagnent jamais car ils se détestent.

*The **two boys** can't stand **each other**.*
Les deux garçons ne se supportent pas.

En anglais, il n'est pas indispensable de préciser qu'ils sont deux car cela est sous-entendu par l'emploi de *each other* :

*These babies love **each other**.*
Ces deux bébés s'adorent.

16. LA VOIX PASSIVE

En utilisant le passif, on met l'accent sur l'action plus que sur celui qui la fait (l'agent).
Voix active : *The owners cherish their pets.*
Voix passive : *The pets are cherished by their owners.*

1 • Formation

• **On utilise l'auxiliaire *be* et le verbe au participe passé :**

*The pets **are fed** with top notch food.*
Les animaux de compagnies sont nourris avec de la nourriture de première qualité.

Pour réintroduire l'agent, on utilise *by* :
*The pets **are fed** with top notch food **by** their owners.*

• **C'est le même fonctionnement quel que soit le temps utilisé :**

*The pets **were fed** with top notch food.*
Les animaux de compagnies ont été nourris avec de la nourriture de première qualité.

*The pets **have been fed** with top notch food.*

*The pets **will be fed** with top notch food.*

• **La double complémentation (C.O.D.)**

Certains verbes comme (*ask, show, tell, teach, offer, send, lend*, etc.) se construisent avec deux compléments directs.

- Voix active :

Tom gave <u>me</u> <u>some money</u>

complément 1 → *me* ; complément 2 → *some money*

- La voix passive peut alors se construire de deux façons :

Some money was given to me.

I was given some money. (forme la plus fréquente)

- En français, on est obligé d'avoir recours à la structure en « on » : On m'a donné de l'argent.

17. LES PROPOSITIONS SUBORDONNÉES RELATIVES

Une *proposition** subordonnée relative est un constituant de la phrase composé d'un « sujet + groupe verbal » et introduit par un pronom relatif.
Elle joue le même rôle qu'un adjectif.

*He met a **sporty** girl.* Il a rencontré une fille sportive. → adjectif

*He met a girl **who was sporty**.*
Il a rencontré une fille qui était sportive.
→ proposition subordonnée relative

1 • Les pronoms relatifs

En anglais, les pronoms relatifs font la distinction entre humains et non-humains. Ils peuvent avoir différentes fonctions : **sujet, complément (direct ou indirect)** ou **complément du nom**.

Fonction des pronoms	Pronoms relatifs pour des humains	Pronoms relatifs pour des non-humains
Sujet	*who*	*that / which*
Complément direct ou indirect	*that / who / whom / Ø*	*that / which / Ø*
Complément du nom	*whose*	*of which / whose*

• Le pronom sujet

Il se place juste avant le verbe de la proposition subordonnée relative.

- On utilise *who* pour un humain :

*The girl **who** came yesterday is the neighbours' daughter.*
La fille qui est venue hier est la fille des voisins.

- On utilise *that* ou *which* pour un non-humain :

*You need a car **that / which** isn't too expensive.*
Il te faut une voiture qui ne soit pas trop chère.

• Le pronom complément (direct ou indirect)

Il se place avant le sujet du verbe de la proposition subordonnée relative.

- On utilise *that, who, whom* ou Ø pour un humain.

*This is the teacher **that / who(m)** / Ø I saw yesterday.*
C'est le professeur que j'ai vu hier.

*This is the teacher **that / who(m)** / Ø I told you about yesterday.*
C'est le professeur dont je te parlais hier.

Whom est de nos jours très formel et réservé à l'écrit.
La forme la plus fréquente est celle avec Ø.

- On utilise *that* ou *which* pour un non-humain :

*The DVD **that / which** / Ø you bought is rubbish.*
Le DVD que tu as acheté est nul.

*The DVD **that / which** / Ø I told you about is rubbish.*
Le DVD dont je t'ai parlé est nul.

• Le complément du nom

- On utilise *whose* avec les humains et on le place avant le nom de la proposition relative :

*The pupil, **whose** uniform was not the right colour, had to buy another one.* L'élève dont l'uniforme n'était pas de la bonne couleur a dû en acheter un autre.

- On utilise *whose* ou *of which* pour les non-humains :

*The shoes **whose** heels are too high are not allowed in the school.* Les chaussures dont les talons sont trop hauts ne sont pas autorisées à l'école.

Attention

La construction *of which* se place après le nom de la proposition relative : *The shoes **the heels of which** are too high are not allowed in the school.*

Cette tournure reste présente à l'écrit mais n'est plus guère utilisée à l'oral.

2 • Ce qui / ce que

• *What*

On utilise *what* pour annoncer quelque chose dont on va parler :

***What** happened yesterday is simply unacceptable.*
Ce qui s'est passé hier est tout bonnement inacceptable.

• *Which*

On utilise *which*, **précédé d'une virgule,** pour reprendre le contenu de la proposition qui précède :

*He told me he wanted to quit, **which** is ludicrous.*
Il m'a dit qu'il voulait démissionner, ce qui ne rime à rien.

3 • Où

Contrairement au français qui emploie « où » dans tous les cas, en anglais on utilise *where* pour un lieu et *when* pour le temps.

*This is a time **when** a coffee would be appreciated.*
C'est le moment où un café serait le bienvenu.

*This is the place **where** I was born.*
C'est l'endroit où je suis né(e).

18. LE STYLE INDIRECT

Quand on passe du style direct (paroles prononcées) au style indirect (paroles rapportées), on observe les mêmes règles de concordance des temps qu'en français. Ce passage entraîne des modifications du verbe, des pronoms et de l'ordre des mots.
Pour passer au style indirect, on utilise un verbe de « rapport de paroles » tel que *say* ou *tell*.

« I'm doing my homework. » → He said (that) he was doing his homework.

« Je fais mes devoirs. » → Il a dit qu'il faisait ses devoirs.

On remarque qu'en français « que » est obligatoire alors que *that* est facultatif en anglais.

1 • Style indirect et concordance des temps

- Le présent simple au discours direct devient un prétérit au discours indirect :

*"I don't like Peter." → He said (that) he **didn't like** Peter.*

« Je n'aime pas Peter ».→ Il a dit qu'il n'aimait pas Peter.

- Le *present perfect* au discours direct devient un *pluperfect* au discours indirect :

*"**I've** never **liked** her." → He said (that) he **had** never **liked** her.*

« Je ne l'ai jamais aimée ». → Il a dit qu'il ne l'avait jamais aimée.

- Le prétérit au discours direct devient un *pluperfect* au discours indirect :

*"I **bought** some food yesterday." → He said (that) he **had bought** some food the day before.*

« J'ai acheté de la nourriture hier ». → Il a dit qu'il avait acheté de la nourriture le jour précédent.

On constate que, comme en français, certains repères temporels sont modifiés.
(*yesterday → the day before*)

2 • Style indirect et auxiliaires modaux

- Au style indirect, certains modaux sont utilisés à leur forme au prétérit.

*"I **will** never leave you." → He said (that) he **would** never leave her.*

« Je ne te quitterai jamais ». → Il a dit qu'il ne la quitterait jamais.

*"I **can** do it for you if you wish." → He said (that) he **could** do it for her if she wished.*

« Je peux le faire pour toi si tu veux. » → Il a dit qu'il pouvait le faire pour elle si elle le souhaitait.

*"**May** I open the window?" → She asked her whether she **might** open the window.*

« Puis-je ouvrir la fenêtre? » → Elle lui a demandé si elle pouvait ouvrir la fenêtre.

- Au style indirect, certains modaux ne changent pas de forme.

*"You **must** remain quiet during the concert." → He said (that) she **must** remain quiet during the concert.*

« Tu dois rester calme pendant le concert. » → Il lui a dit qu'elle devait rester calme pendant le concert.

(au style indirect, on peut aussi utiliser *was to* ou *had to* à la place de *must*.

*"You **could** go out tonight." → She told me (that) I **could** go out tonight.* « Tu pourrais sortir ce soir. » → Elle m'a dit que je pourrais sortir ce soir.

*"It **might** rain tomorrow." → She said (that) it **might** rain tomorrow.* « Il se peut qu'il pleuve demain. » → Elle a dit qu'il se pourrait qu'il pleuve demain.

*"You **should** call your Mum more often." → He said (that) she **should** call her Mum more often.*

« Tu devrais appeler ta mère plus souvent. » → Il a dit qu'elle devrait appeler sa mère plus souvent.

3 • Les phrases interrogatives indirectes

Les phrases interrogatives indirectes se construisent après des verbes du type *ask, wonder, know*, etc.
La seconde proposition est alors introduite par un mot interrogatif du type *what, which, who, when, where*, etc.

***Where** is my pen? → He **asked where** his pen was.*

Où est mon stylo ? → Il a demandé où était son stylo.

Attention

Contrairement au français, il n'y a pas d'inversion sujet / verbe en anglais :

*I wonder where **Paul is**.*

Je me demande où est Paul.

*He asked her where **the museum was**.*

Il lui a demandé où était le musée.

ÉLÉMENTS DE PHONOLOGIE ANGLAISE

Remarques sur la transcription phonétique :

- Les transcriptions sont données en anglais britannique standard (SBE), ou R.P. (*Received Pronunciation*).
- L'apostrophe avant une syllabe signifie que celle-ci est accentuée : *nature* → /'neɪtʃə/.

1 • La transcription

• Les voyelles

Les voyelles sont produites par l'air expulsé des poumons qui fait vibrer les cordes vocales. L'air ainsi expulsé ne rencontre presque pas d'obstacles quand il traverse l'appareil phonatoire (la bouche).

Symbole phonétique	Exemple	Transcription
/iː/	sheep	/ʃiːp/
/ɪ/	ship	/ʃɪp/
/e/	bet	/bet/
/æ/	bat	/bæt/
/ɑː/	bath	/bɑːθ/
/ɒ/	cot	/kɒt/
/ɔː/	court	/kɔːt/
/ʊ/	look	/lʊk/
/uː/	cool	/kuːl/
/ʌ/	bud	/bʌd/
/ɜː/	bird	/bɜːd/
/ə/	about	/ə'baʊt/

• Les diphtongues

Les diphtongues sont des voyelles qui commencent par un son et se terminent par un autre (deux sons vocaliques).

Symbole phonétique	Exemple	Transcription
/eɪ/	name	/neɪm/
/aɪ/	shine	/ʃaɪn/
/ɔɪ/	boy	/bɔɪ/
/əʊ/	no	/nəʊ/
/aʊ/	now	/naʊ/
/ɪə/	here	/hɪə/
/eə/	care	/keə/
/ʊə/	pure	/pjʊə/

• Les consonnes

- Les consonnes sont des sons qui rencontrent un obstacle (la langue, les dents, les lèvres…) quand ils traversent l'appareil phonatoire.
- Les consonnes peuvent être « sourdes » (pas de vibration des cordes vocales) ou « sonores » (vibration).

a. Consonnes sourdes :

/p/ ; /t/ ; /k/ ; /f/ ; /θ/ ; /s/ ; /ʃ/ ; /tʃ/

Astuce : si l'on pose des doigts sur sa gorge en prononçant ces sons, on ne sent pas de vibration.

b. Consonnes sonores :

/b/ ; /d/ ; /g/ ; /v/ ; /ð/ ; /z/ ; /ʒ/ ; /dʒ/

Astuce : si l'on pose ses doigts sur sa gorge en prononçant ces sons, on sent une vibration.

Symbole phonétique	Exemple	Transcription
/p/	pig	/pɪg/
/b/	big	/bɪg/
/t/	tip	/tɪp/
/d/	dip	/dɪp/
/k/	cane	/keɪn/
/g/	gain	/geɪn/
/m/	mean	/miːn/
/n/	need	/niːd/
/ŋ/	thing	/θɪŋ/
/f/	fox	/fɒks/
/v/	vixen	/'vɪksən/
/θ/	thanks	/θæŋks/
/ð/	that	/ðæt/
/s/	soot	/sʊt/
/z/	zoo	/zuː/
/ʃ/	shine	/ʃaɪn/
/tʃ/	chain	/tʃeɪn/
/ʒ/	measure	/'meʒə/
/dʒ/	jeep	/dʒip/
/r/	run	/rʌn/
/h/	house	/haʊs/
/w/	want	/wɒnt/
/j/	young	/jʌŋ/
/l/	lot	/lɒt/

2 • Prononciations particulières : *-ed* et *-s* grammatical

• *-ed*

La terminaison grammaticale *-ed* sert essentiellement à former le prétérit et le participe passé des verbes réguliers.

-ed se réalise comme une consonne **sonore** /d/ ou **sourde** /t/ selon le contexte.

a. Quand *-ed* suit une consonne sourde, on utilise sa forme sourde /t/.

laughed /lɑːft/ — *licked* /lɪkt/
hoped /həʊpt/ — *hissed* /hɪst/

b. Quand *-ed* suit une consonne sonore ou une voyelle, on utilise sa forme sonore /d/.

sobbed /sɒbd/ — *lagged* /lægd/
heaved /hiːvd/ — *judged* /dʒʌdʒd/

c. Quand -ed suit un *t* ou un *d*, on utilise la prononciation /ɪd/.

Un problème se pose si l'on applique les deux premières règles aux cas où la consonne qui précède est un *t* ou un *d* :

- le verbe *part* + *-ed* donnerait /pɑːt + t/, ce qui est difficile à prononcer et encore plus difficile à percevoir auditivement.

- le verbe *end* + *-ed* donnerait *end + d/.

Dans les deux cas, la désinence (terminaison) serait mal perçue. Pour remédier à ce problème, on insère un son voyelle /ə/ ou /ɪ/ entre la consonne finale et la désinence.

Granted /'grɑːntɪd/ — Parted /'pɑːtɪd/
Ended /'endɪd/ — Fainted /'feɪntɪd/

! Attention

-ed se prononce aussi /ə/ ou /ɪ/ dans *hatred* (la haine), *wicked* (méchant), *naked* (nu) et *sacred* (sacré).

• -*s* grammatical

Le -*s* grammatical concerne :
- la marque du pluriel (*dogs*) ;
- la troisième personne du singulier au présent simple (*he sings*) ;
- les cas possessifs (*Paul's car*).

Le -*s* grammatical se réalise comme consonne **sonore** /z/ ou **sourde** /s/.

a. Le -*s* grammatical se prononce /s/ quand il suit les phonèmes suivants : /p/ ; /t/ ; /f/ ; /θ/ ; /k/

tops /tɒps/ — *cats* /kæts/
clocks /klɒks/ — *sniffs* /snɪfs/

b. La désinence -*s* se prononce /z/ après une consonne sonore ou une voyelle.

man's /mænz/ — *boys* /bɔɪz/
pains /peɪnz/ — *pigs* /pɪgz/
Jane's /dʒeɪnz/

c. -*s* se prononce /ɪz/ ou /əz/ quand il suit *s, z, sh, ch* ou *g*.

Un problème se pose si l'on applique les règles précédentes aux cas où le mot se termine par /s/, /z/, /ʃ/, /tʃ/, /dʒ/. En effet, ces sons sont trop proches de /s/ et de /z/ et ces derniers ne seraient pas clairement perçus.

On insère donc un son voyelle /ɪ/ ou parfois /ə/ entre la fin du mot et la désinence :

buses /'bʌsɪz/ — *judges* /'dʒʌdʒɪz/
barrages /'bærɑːʒɪz/ — *passages* /'pæsɪdʒɪz/
bushes /'bʊʃɪz/ — *messages* /'mesɪdʒɪz/
riches /'rɪtʃɪz/

L'ajout du -*e* orthographique est un bon moyen de se souvenir de cette règle.

MÉTHODOLOGIE
SOMMAIRE

Réussir le bac !

MÉTHODOLOGIE FICHE 1

COMPRENDRE UN DOCUMENT ORAL

Modalités de l'épreuve

La compréhension de l'oral au baccalauréat est évaluée à partir d'un **document audio ou vidéo** dont la durée n'excède pas **1 minute 30**. Le document est **écouté trois fois, les écoutes étant espacées d'une minute**. Durant les écoutes, les candidats peuvent prendre des notes. À l'issue de la troisième écoute, les candidats utilisent le temps dont ils disposent comme ils le souhaitent **pour rendre compte du document oral, en français, de manière libre ou guidée**.

Les outils de réussite

- Les modalités de l'épreuve
- Les critères d'évaluation

9 CONSEILS POUR COMPRENDRE UN DOCUMENT AUDIO OU VIDÉO

Avant l'écoute

1. Anticipez le contenu.

→ À partir du titre ou de la source, imaginez quel(s) sujet(s) sera/seront abordé(s) dans le document, ou de quelle nature sera ce document (*speech? interview?* etc.)

→ Commencez à mobiliser mentalement le lexique autour de vos hypothèses.

Lors de la première écoute

2. Visez une compréhension globale.

→ Nature du document audio / vidéo (interview, débat, émission radio, reportage, etc.) ?

→ Nombre de locuteurs, identité, spécificités (homme, femme, enfant, adulte) ?

→ Indices sonores (musique, bruits de fond…) ?

3. Décidez de la prise de note adaptée, selon le type de document. Trouvez la méthode qui vous convient le mieux. Voici quelques idées :

- S'il y a plusieurs intervenants → Créez des colonnes pour chacun d'entre eux.
- S'il y a beaucoup de dates → Construisez une frise chronologique.
- S'il y a plusieurs thèmes évoqués → Faites une carte mentale avec des boîtes par thème, ou utilisez plusieurs couleurs.

Cette méthode vous évitera de nombreux contresens.
Lors des 2e et 3e écoutes, complétez vos notes.

Lors des deux dernières écoutes

4. Prenez des notes. Utilisez des symboles et abréviations pour plus d'efficacité.

5. Écrivez directement en anglais ! Ne perdez pas de temps à traduire en français ce que vous entendez. Vous aurez le temps de traduire vos notes plus tard si nécessaire.

6. Repérez les informations importantes.

a. Les mots accentués, les mots porteurs de sens ;
b. Les dates, les chiffres et les noms propres ;
c. Les indicateurs de temps et les mots de liaison.

À la fin des écoutes

7. Réfléchissez et déduisez. Si vous avez pu identifier des thèmes, alors beaucoup de mots prendront du sens. Que pouvez-vous déduire de certains mots, selon le contexte ?

8. N'inventez pas ! Déduire et inventer sont deux choses distinctes. Si la raison pour laquelle vous pensez que le document traite d'un sujet simplement parce qu'un mot vous y fait penser, vous risquez de faire fausse route. Pour déduire correctement, il faut des indices concrets : par exemple, le ton des intervenants + un bruitage. Recouper les informations. Et si c'est une vidéo, appuyez-vous sur les images (expressions des locuteurs…).

9. Synthétisez l'information. À la fin des écoutes, vous devrez être en mesure de répondre à ces questions : *Who? When? Where? What? How? Why?* Vérifiez que tout est logique et que vous n'avez pas fait de contresens. N'oubliez pas de vous relire.

Niveau attendu

A. Identification du contexte et de la situation d'énonciation

B2 : Peut identifier la richesse d'un contexte ou d'une situation d'énonciation, y compris en relevant le cas échéant des éléments implicites.

B. Identification des réseaux de sens

B2 : Peut identifier la cohérence globale d'un document ou dossier : identifier les principales raisons pour ou contre une idée ; reconstituer une chronologie d'événements dans un récit ; repérer des sauts ou retours en arrière, etc.

C. Identification des stratégies de communication

B2 : Peut repérer une intention en distinguant l'expression d'un point de vue de l'exposé de faits. Peut identifier des éléments implicites de l'articulation entre des documents.

MÉTHODOLOGIE FICHE 2

COMPRENDRE UN DOCUMENT ÉCRIT

Les outils de réussite

- Les modalités de l'épreuve
- Les questions de guidage
- Les critères d'évaluation

Modalités de l'épreuve

La compréhension de l'écrit est évaluée à partir d'un ou deux textes. Les candidats en **rendent compte dans la langue cible (en anglais)**. Ils sont guidés par des questions qui portent également sur la compréhension de l'ensemble du dossier constitué par les documents supports de l'évaluation de la compréhension de l'oral et de l'écrit. La longueur cumulée des textes est comprise entre 2 500 et 4 500 signes, blancs et espaces compris.

6 CONSEILS POUR COMPRENDRE UN TEXTE

Préparez-vous

1. Anticipez le contenu.

→ Regardez le titre et/ou la source. S'agit-il d'un texte documentaire, informatif ? D'un récit ? D'une fiction ?

→ Si le questionnaire sur le texte est donné (comme lors d'un contrôle), lisez les questions en premier. Cette stratégie est efficace, car les questions donnent déjà beaucoup d'indices sur le sujet général du texte, les personnages et/ou les lieux.
Si vous savez ce que vous devez chercher avant même de lire le texte, vous éviterez de nombreux contresens.

2. Observez le texte, effectuez les repérages sur la forme. Y a-t-il des éléments qui ressortent tels que :

→ Des dialogues entre guillemets ?

→ Des passages soulignés, en *italique* ou en **gras** ?

→ Des majuscules qui pourraient indiquer des noms propres (personnages, lieux, adjectifs de nationalité…) ?

→ Des dates, nombres ou chiffres ?

→ Des mots ou expressions qui reviennent plusieurs fois ?

Lisez et déduisez

3. Lisez le texte et revenez sur les passages repérés pour comprendre à quoi ils correspondent exactement.

→ Qui parle dans les dialogues ?

→ Attention, ce n'est pas parce qu'un nom est cité que cette personne intervient dans la scène.

→ À quels événements correspondent les dates ?

→ À quoi se réfèrent les données chiffrées ?

4. Appuyez-vous sur les mots connus et les mots transparents. Ne perdez pas trop de temps à essayer de déchiffrer tous les mots que vous ne comprenez pas. Il ne faut pas interpréter sans indices. Déduisez, mais n'inventez pas.

Astuces pour inférer le sens d'un mot inconnu

a. **Interrogez-vous sur sa nature : s'agit-il d'un nom, d'un verbe, d'un adjectif… ?**

b. **Observez le contexte dans lequel le mot est utilisé.**

c. **Prêtez attention à sa composition. S'agit-il d'un mot composé ? Connaissez-vous sa racine ? Y a-t-il un préfixe (*dis-, un-, post-, pro-, il-…*) ou un suffixe (*-ful, -less, -ly, -ship…*) ?**

Exemples :
hair ***(cheveux)*** **+ cut** ***(couper)*** **= haircut** ***(coupe de cheveux)***
un + happy ***(content(e))*** **= unhappy** ***(malheureux/euse)***

5. Découpez le texte en plusieurs parties lorsqu'il vous semble un peu long.

Utilisez des indicateurs (mots de liaison, marqueurs de temps) pour trouver différentes parties dans le texte. Souvent, ces parties correspondent aux paragraphes. Beaucoup d'autres changements peuvent intervenir :

→ Les personnages changent de lieu ;

→ Le point de vue n'est plus le même ;

→ Le sujet est différent.

Donnez à ces parties des titres, pour naviguer plus facilement dans le texte lorsque vous y chercherez des informations plus précises.

Résumez

6. Posez-vous les 6 questions-clés : *Who? When? Where? What? How? Why?*

Si vous répondez à ces questions, vous avez déjà fait une grande partie du travail !

Réussir le bac !

MÉTHODOLOGIE FICHE 3

LE COMPTE RENDU

Les outils de réussite

- Les modalités de l'épreuve
- Les critères d'évaluation

RESTITUTION ÉCRITE EN FRANÇAIS D'UN DOCUMENT AUDIO / VIDÉO

Lors de l'examen, il vous appartient de définir le temps que vous souhaitez consacrer à la restitution. Toutefois, il ne faut pas oublier que vous devez également réaliser une production écrite. Nous vous conseillons d'y consacrer 10 minutes. Voici quelques conseils pour optimiser votre temps.

1. Ayez en tête les critères d'évaluation.

En effet, la précision de votre compte rendu permet à l'examinateur de savoir ce que vous avez compris. Vous pouvez consulter les critères d'évaluation détaillés en flashant le code QR ci-dessus.

A1 = mots isolés, dates, chiffres

A2 = les informations essentielles

B1 = comprendre comment s'organise le contenu, articulation des points de vue, cohérence du discours

B2 = implicite, pourquoi ce document est intéressant et ce qu'il apporte de nouveau

2. Votre compte rendu doit préciser :

→ la nature du document (extrait d'un film, une publicité, une campagne de sensibilisation, une interview radiophonique, un discours, etc.),

→ le thème principal,

→ les informations sur les intervenants (sexe, âge, occupation, etc.),

→ les arguments échangés et les partis pris,

→ le ton employé par les interlocuteurs (ton neutre, humour, colère, etc.),

→ le but de ce document (sensibiliser, informer, dénoncer, promouvoir, interroger, etc.).

3. Lors de la rédaction, veillez à :

→ barrer au fur et à mesure vos notes pour ne rien oublier,

→ soigner la présentation et l'orthographe,

→ utiliser du vocabulaire précis,

→ éviter les anglicismes,

→ utiliser des connecteurs logiques (car, puisque, en effet, effectivement, ainsi, donc, grâce, par conséquent, à cause de, etc.),

→ ne pas donner votre avis.

4. Relisez-vous pour vérifier la cohérence et corriger les fautes.

RESTITUTION ÉCRITE EN ANGLAIS D'UN TEXTE

1. Les critères d'évaluation

A. Identification du contexte et de la situation d'énonciation

B2 : Peut identifier la richesse d'un contexte ou d'une situation d'énonciation, y compris en relevant le cas échéant des éléments implicites.

B. Identification des réseaux de sens

B2 : Peut identifier la cohérence globale d'un document ou dossier : identifier les principales raisons pour ou contre une idée ; reconstituer une chronologie d'événements dans un récit ; repérer des sauts ou retours en arrière, etc.

C. Identification des stratégies de communication

B2 : Peut repérer une intention en distinguant l'expression d'un point de vue de l'exposé de faits.
Peut identifier des éléments implicites de l'articulation entre des documents.

2. Lors de la rédaction de votre compte rendu :

→ Aidez-vous des éventuelles questions guidées pour structurer le contenu.

→ Dégagez les points principaux et les détails significatifs du/des document(s) (idées, points de vue similaires et/ou différents, arguments, exemples, etc.).

→ Utiliser des mots de liaison et des connecteurs logiques (*furthermore, moreover, besides, also, instead of, notwithstanding, whereas, while*, etc.).

→ Utilisez un ton impersonnel.

→ Si l'épreuve comporte deux documents, précisez s'ils sont complémentaires ou contradictoires, ainsi que la raison pour laquelle ils ont été associés.

→ Établissez une relation entre le(s) texte(s) et l'axe étudié.

3. Relisez attentivement

→ Vérifiez la cohérence et la clarté.

→ Corrigez les fautes.

MÉTHODOLOGIE FICHE 4

EXPRESSION ORALE EN CONTINU

Parler en continu, c'est parler sans interruption, seul(e) devant un auditoire. Il s'agit d'une compétence dont vous aurez besoin dans la plupart des matières, notamment au grand oral du baccalauréat, ainsi que plus tard, dans votre vie professionnelle. Il faut donc vous préparer dès maintenant à bien maîtriser cet exercice. Pour vous expliquer comment procéder, nous allons nous concentrer sur la technique du discours : les conseils donnés peuvent s'appliquer à tous les types de production orale en continu.

20 CONSEILS POUR RÉUSSIR SA PRODUCTION ORALE

Préparez votre message

1. Respectez bien les consignes (sujet, temps, syntaxe…).

2. Décidez du message que vous voulez transmettre.

3. Selon le sujet, faites une liste du vocabulaire étudié et choisissez les termes et expressions que vous allez employer. Veillez à utiliser un lexique riche et varié.

4. Trouvez des formulations fortes et percutantes. Vous pouvez par exemple sélectionner une ou deux citations inspirantes en lien avec votre sujet, et les apprendre par cœur.

5. Préparez une fiche avec vos notes, c'est-à-dire les mots-clés, les idées principales, la trame de votre discours.

Travaillez votre élocution

6. Inspirez-vous de conférences de personnalités anglophones. Vous pouvez par exemple regarder quelques discours de Barack ou Michelle Obama sur YouTube. Vous pouvez aussi aller sur le site TED.com, qui est une mine de conférences très vivantes, souvent passionnantes, sur tous les sujets.

7. Soignez votre prononciation : dès que vous avez un doute sur la prononciation d'un mot, **vérifiez avec un dictionnaire en ligne.**

8. L'anglais est une langue très accentuée et très rythmée alors **exagérez l'accentuation** : n'hésitez pas à en faire trop, cela vous aidera à bien prononcer !

9. Pour insister sur une idée et être persuasif/ve, vous pouvez **utiliser la même expression** plusieurs fois.

10. Répétez votre discours à voix haute, à l'aide de votre fiche de notes, pour bien le connaître, sans avoir à le lire.

11. Ralentissez le débit : pour trouver le bon rythme, vous devez avoir l'impression de parler lentement. Sur votre fiche de notes, vous pouvez indiquer des signes (//) aux endroits où vous marquerez une pause.

12. Chronométrez-vous pour être sûr(e) que votre discours n'est ni trop long, ni trop court.

13. Filmez-vous avec votre portable ou une tablette pour vérifier votre posture et votre prononciation. C'est un très bon exercice pour prendre conscience des points à améliorer.

Le jour J

14. Soignez votre posture : tenez-vous bien droit(e) pour montrer que vous êtes sûr(e) de vous. Même si votre niveau de stress est élevé, cela ne doit pas se voir. Dites-vous que votre auditoire ne le sait pas. L'apparence est très importante, n'oubliez pas de sourire !

15. Respirez ! Avant de prononcer le tout premier mot : prenez une profonde inspiration, sans monter les épaules. Respirez le plus bas possible (gonflez votre bas-ventre), puis respirez lentement.

16. Regardez vos auditeurs. Ce contact visuel est fondamental. Vous pouvez aussi choisir plusieurs points au fond de la classe en hauteur, pour ne pas avoir à croiser le regard de vos camarades si vous êtes trop intimidé(e).

17. Prenez votre temps, respirez entre chaque phrase, faites des pauses pour créer du suspense et de l'attente chez les auditeurs ou utilisez des *gap fillers*.

18. Insistez sur certains mots : les idées importantes que vous voulez transmettre doivent être mises en valeur.

19. Parlez assez fort pour être entendu(e) jusqu'au fond de la classe.

20. À la fin de votre discours, **remerciez votre auditoire** pour son écoute attentive.

Réussir le bac !

MÉTHODOLOGIE FICHE 5

LIRE UN SUJET ET CONSTRUIRE UN PLAN

Les questions des sujets de dissertation vous invitent à vérifier votre compréhension du sujet mais aussi à faire état de vos connaissances culturelles sur le sujet donné. Il est donc important de comprendre dès le début ce que l'on attend de vous. Voici quelques conseils pour vous aider à décrypter le sujet et pour construire un plan.

Les outils de réussite

- Les modalités de l'épreuve
- Les questions de guidage
- Les critères d'é valuation

Lire et comprendre le sujet

Identifiez le type de sujet. Le sujet peut vous inviter à :
- → Commenter une citation ou une opinion donnée ;
- → Exprimer votre propre opinion sur un thème ;
- → Répondre à une question générale / une problématique ;
- → Comparer deux éléments ;
- → Donner libre cours à votre créativité.

Repérez et définissez les mots-clés du sujet (souvent rattachés à la thématique de l'axe étudié).

Sujet de dissertation :

Survivalism is everywhere these days, in literature, podcasts, films and TV shows. How can you explain that the survivalist movement has been gaining ground over the past few years to become mainstream in the USA?

Mot-clés 1 → donner une définition de ce qu'est le mouvement « survivaliste » et l'ancrer aux États-Unis.

Mot-clés 2 → montrer par vos lectures et culture médiatique que ce sujet est présent dans la fiction depuis longtemps.

Mot-clés 3 → définir *inequalities* (par rapport à l'appartenance / l'origine sociale / le genre…)

Construire le plan

1. Notez vos idées générales sous la forme de mots-clés, de schémas. Illustrez chaque idée principale à l'aide un ou deux exemples. À ce stade, inutile de faire des phrases, au risque de perdre du temps et de ne pas finir dans le temps imparti. Lorsque vous avez noté toutes vos idées, vous pourrez les organiser en plan.

2. Organisez vos idées dans un plan.

a. Exemple de sujet : *Does affirmative action towards Dalits help to reduce social inequalities?*

Pour un tel sujet, dit « fermé » (= il n'y a pas un nombre infini de réponses), vous pouvez adopter un plan en trois parties. Pour schématiser (mais il faudra argumenter vos positions !) :

I. = Oui II. = Non III. = Nuances.

Vous pouvez aussi poser le sujet dans son contexte en deux ou trois parties.

I. = Faits / Causes

II. = Application / Conséquences / Perspectives d'avenir…

b. Exemple de sujet : *Would you like to take part in a mission to Mars?*

Pour un tel sujet, où l'on vous demande votre avis, vous pouvez recourir à un plan plus libre. Exemple de plan :

I. = Le rappel historique / contexte

II. = Votre avis / vos enjeux / l'avenir de l'humanité…

3. Connectez vos idées à l'aide de mots de liaison. Ceci permettra à votre texte d'être bien structuré et donc à votre lecteur de suivre le cheminement de vos idées.

- **Pour introduire le sujet :** First / First of all / Initially / To start with…
- **Pour enchaîner les idées :** Firstly / Secondly / Thirdly… / Then / After that / Next / In addition (to) / as well / also… / on the one hand… on the other hand… / Besides / Moreover / As a matter of fact… / Indeed / Beyond…
- **Pour exprimer la cause :** Because / For that reason / This is why… / Due to… / Since
- **Pour exprimer le but :** In order to / so that…
- **Pour comparer :** In the same way / Like… / Unlike… / Let's compare… / Whereas… / On the other hand…
- **Pour exprimer l'opposition :** But / However / Nonetheless / Nevertheless / Despite… / In spite of… / On the contrary… / Although…
- **Pour conclure :** Finally / Last but not least / Eventually / As a conclusion / To put it in a nutshell / To sum up / In short /

4. Rédigez et relisez votre copie.
- → Présentez votre sujet dans votre introduction.
- → Écrivez des paragraphes clairs (un paragraphe = une idée + un exemple).
- → Illustrez vos idées par des exemples précis.
- → Terminez par une brève conclusion.
- → Relisez votre copie et supprimez les fautes !

MÉTHODOLOGIE FICHE 6

CONSEILS POUR ÉCRIRE UN (BON) ARTICLE !

Voici les 5 éléments indispensables que votre article doit comporter.

1. Un titre court clair et percutant : le lecteur doit savoir tout de suite de quoi vous allez parler.

2. L'introduction (= le chapeau) sert à expliciter le titre et annonce les points forts de l'article. Elle doit fournir en partie une réponse aux 5 W (*who / what / where / when / why?*). Elle fait environ deux ou trois phrases, bien détachées du reste du texte (sautez une ou deux lignes entre l'introduction et le corps de l'article).

3. Le corps de l'article

→ Il faut toujours avoir votre cible en tête pour savoir comment vous exprimer : posez-vous la question de savoir à qui s'adresse l'article et adaptez le ton.

→ Captez l'attention de votre public : ajoutez une touche d'humour, des exemples parlants, des citations pertinentes, des statistiques inattendues, ou encore interpellez directement le lecteur.

→ Le texte doit être aéré pour être agréable à lire. Sautez une ligne entre chaque paragraphe. Et n'oubliez pas : 1 idée = 1 paragraphe.

4. La conclusion

Vous écrivez avec un but en tête : assurez-vous qu'il a bien été atteint à la fin de l'article (avez-vous bien transmis tous les messages que vous vouliez ?).
La conclusion peut aussi inviter le lecteur à continuer à se renseigner sur le sujet ou à répondre à une question qui demeure non résolue.

5. La signature

N'oubliez pas d'indiquer votre nom et le nom du journal / du magazine pour lequel vous travaillez, ainsi que la date de parution de votre article. Cela apportera une touche d'authenticité !

CONSEILS POUR ÉCRIRE UNE LETTRE

1. Identifier la situation de correspondance

Lisez attentivement les consignes pour savoir ce que l'on attend de vous. En effet, le ton et le vocabulaire employés ne seront pas les mêmes si l'on s'adresse à un proche ou si l'on rédige un courrier formel.

2. Mise en forme

→ Le nom et l'adresse du destinataire vont à gauche ;
→ La date en haut à droite ;
→ Le nom et l'adresse de l'expéditeur en bas à gauche sous la signature ;

3. Le corps du texte

N'oubliez pas de faire un paragraphe par idée et d'utiliser des mots de liaison pour structurer vos propos.

Évitez toute familiarité et n'employez pas de contractions avec des personnes lointaines ou inconnues : cela serait impoli.

4. Formule de clôture

→ À quelqu'un qu'on ne connaît pas : *Yours sincerely, Yours truly, Yours faithfully, Respectfully, Best regards…*
→ À un proche : *Love, Hugs from…, Take care…*

CONSEILS POUR ÉCRIRE UN DIALOGUE

1. Identifiez les différents intervenants (nom, fonction dans l'histoire, leur psychologie, leur opinion, etc.).

2. Rédigez une brève introduction rappelant le cadre de départ, la situation.

3. Établissez une liste de verbes introducteurs et des verbes de mouvement. Pensez également à inclure des adverbes de manière. Ex : *He replied angrily… Janet considered the man's words, then after hesitating, she said… She nodded…*

4. Utilisez des didascalies pour préciser l'attitude, les émotions, les mouvements des personnages et la mise en scène.

5. Privilégiez un langage oral. Les formes contractées, les *tags*, les réponses courtes, les *gap fillers*, etc. rendront le dialogue vivant et réaliste.

6. Les guillemets sont de rigueur. Pensez à les ouvrir et à les fermer à chaque réplique et passer à la ligne à chaque fois qu'un personnage différent parle.

Relisez-vous avec attention

Faites au moins deux relectures, en vous concentrant à chaque fois sur un élément différent. Par exemple, relisez-vous en vérifiant d'abord la cohérence des temps.

MÉTHODOLOGIE FICHE 7

ÉVALUATION DE L'EXPRESSION ORALE

Les outils de réussite

- Les modalités de l'épreuve
- Les critères d'évaluation

Modalités de l'épreuve

L'épreuve orale dure **10 minutes, sans temps de préparation.**
Le candidat a le choix **entre trois axes culturels du programme proposés par l'examinateur.**
En tenant compte du choix du candidat, l'**examinateur propose des pistes de discussion : deux documents iconographiques**, ou **deux citations**, ou **un document iconographique et une citation.**
Le candidat explique en langue cible pendant cinq minutes maximum quel document ou quelle citation illustre à son sens le mieux l'axe qu'il a choisi et pourquoi.

L'entretien est élargi à des questions plus générales, portant par exemple sur le travail réalisé par le candidat sur l'axe choisi.

VOICI QUELQUES CONSEILS POUR VOUS AIDER LORS DE L'ÉPREUVE

Le choix de l'axe

- Choisissez l'axe dans lequel vous avez le plus de connaissances et d'exemples ancrés dans la sphère anglophone.
- Il faut que vous maîtrisiez le champ lexical de l'axe pour pouvoir commenter le document et dire en quoi il illustre l'axe choisi.

Le choix du document

- Il n'y a pas de bon ou de mauvais choix dans cette épreuve. Vous ne pouvez pas vous tromper. Toute réponse ou tout argument, toute idée donnés au cours de cette épreuve sera recevable à condition qu'il/elle soit cohérent(e). Seuls sont pris en compte dans la notation les critères d'évaluation ci-après.

La présentation du document

- Lors de votre prise de parole appuyez-vous sur le document mais également sur vos connaissances personnelles.
- N'hésitez pas à comparer les deux documents entre eux pour justifier votre position.
- Si c'est une image décrivez-la rapidement avant de l'analyser. Pour apprendre à décrypter une image, n'hésitez pas à consulter la fiche « Comment commenter une image » p. 330.
- Pour une citation, regardez attentivement :
  - qui en est l'auteur ;
  - d'où est extraite la citation (livre, film, discours politique, etc.) ;
  - dans quel contexte ces propos ont été tenus ;
  - l'auteur est-il/elle du même avis que la majorité ou a-t-il/elle un avis dissident ?
  - le ton employé (humour, ironie, etc.) ;
  - quels sont les mots-clés qui permettent de la rattacher à l'axe.

Quelques expressions que vous pouvez utiliser lors de votre présentation

This document shows that...
On this document we can see...
We can clearly distinguish that...
Everything makes us think that...
Every detail seems to indicate that...
This image/document is probably intended to...
It may be asserted that this document illustrates well the topic...
I'll take another example...

Interaction pendant l'entretien

- Écoutez attentivement les questions de votre interlocuteur : celles-ci ont pour objectif de vous faire préciser / expliciter / approfondir ce que vous avez pu dire. Il n'y a pas de pièges ! Elles sont aussi posées pour vous faire compléter / étayer vos propos en vous suggérant de nouvelles pistes, par exemple.
- Rebondissez sur ce qui est dit pour montrer que vous pouvez prendre l'initiative et que vous êtes à l'écoute.
- N'hésitez pas à faire répéter la question en cas de doute : *Could you please repeat?*
- Ou à reformuler pour vous assurer de bien avoir compris : *If I understand well, you ask me to… / Just to make sure I get your point, you want me to…*

Cas pratique

Document A

Document B

"While it has its benefits, social media should not be the primary platform for the #MeToo campaign as activist movements based online can often become trivialized, diverting from their original goals."

Bami OKE, American journalist for *The Brown Daily Herald*, 2017

Si vous choisissez le document A

This picture is a good example to illustrate "Citizenship and Virtual Worlds". Indeed, it insists on the dangers of virtual worlds. The picture is a good way to make children, teenagers and adults aware that those who are on the other side of your screen may not be who you think they are. Instead, they may want to steal your personal data, hack into your bank account or even steal your identity to commit malicious acts by using your name and address. This picture could be a campaign to warn citizens against websites that could do you a lot of harm.

Si vous choisissez le document B

This quote is a good illustration of "Citizenship and Virtual Worlds". Indeed, when reading it we could think of social media as a form of counter power that could right the wrongs of our society. Social media like Twitter, Facebook or Instagram could help citizens to denounce the ills of our society and make governments react. Yet, were social media invented to that end? Could they become the only source of information that citizens would turn to? This quote insists on the role of citizens, who should be careful not to use social media as the only channel to make their voices heard.

Réussir le bac !

MÉTHODOLOGIE FICHE 8

COMMENTER UNE IMAGE

LES 3 ÉTAPES POUR COMMENTER UNE IMAGE

Pour analyser une image, il y a trois phases essentielles :

Identifier la nature de l'image ➜ Décrire l'image ➜ Interpréter le message.

Décrire et interpréter une image

1. Pour décrire une image, il faut **dire ce que l'on voit**, partez du point focal et décrivez ce que vous voyez. Soyez précis(e) : imaginez que vous devez décrire l'image à quelqu'un qui ne l'a pas sous les yeux et qui doit la dessiner en suivant les instructions ! Faites le test avec un(e) camarade !

2. Après avoir décrit ce que vous voyez, vous **devez expliquer le message.**

Appuyez-vous sur ce que vous savez du document :
- si c'est une publicité → l'annonceur veut influencer le consommateur (avec de belles images, un slogan accrocheur, un jeu de mots…)
- si c'est un film → le producteur veut intéresser son public potentiel (science-fiction, aventure, etc.)
- si c'est un tableau figuratif → le peintre donne à voir une situation réelle, veut créer de l'émotion (ou pas) par la composition, les couleurs, les lignes de force…
- si c'est une photographie d'actualité → le photographe veut témoigner d'un évènement
- si c'est une caricature → l'illustrateur tourne en dérision un fait …

3. Dans certains cas, vous pouvez aussi **faire part des émotions que vous ressentez** face à l'image :

peur / tristesse / colère / dégoût / surprise / amusement / admiration / joie / sérénité…

Expliquez à quoi vos émotions sont dues :
- au cadrage (gros plan ? ...)
- à la composition (symétrique ? …)
- aux couleurs (chaudes ? froides ? harmonieuses ? ...)

❶ Lexique

Description

There is… / There are…
The picture represents… is from…
The scene takes place in…
The document dates back to…
The picture is composed of… /
It's made up of…
It looks like a…
It portrays…
We are shown a…
In the picture, the … + be + -ing

Couleurs / Atmosphère

cold, dark, gloomy, dusky, obscure, colourless

pale, washed out, faded, dull

warm, bright, vibrant, colourful, flashy, vivid

Interprétation

It seems… / It represents… /
It means … / It symbolises…
It embodies… / It's a metaphor of…
It warns us about… /
It criticises … /
It conveys the impression that…
It shows… / It reminds me of…

❷ Images

Comment identifier la nature d'une image ?

Chaque nature de document répond à un objectif différent et revêt une forme qui lui est propre.
En voici quelques exemples :

A film poster	***A book cover***	***An ad / an advertisement***	***A cartoon / a comic strip* (plusieurs cases)**
	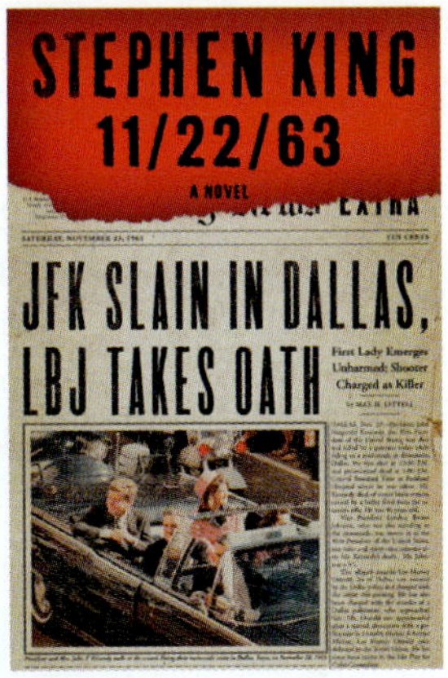		

Éléments à repérer

- Le titre *(the title)* - Les noms des acteurs/trices *(the actors / actresses)* - Le/La réalisateur/trice *(the director)* - Le/La producteur/trice *(the producer)* - Des logos / noms de studios (*logos / studios names*) - Les crédits *(the credits)* - La phrase d'accroche *(the catchphrase)* - Parfois des citations de presse *(endorsements)* - Un visuel *(visuals)*	- Le titre bien en évidence, parfois une phrase d'accroche *(a tagline)* ou un sous-titre *(a subtitle)* - Le nom de l'auteur(e) *(the author, the writer)* - Parfois une illustration (photo ou dessin) *(a picture, a drawing)* - Toujours : le nom ou le logo de la maison d'édition *(the publisher)* - Parfois un bandeau publicitaire (prix littéraire…) *(a belly band)*	- Le logo de la marque *(the logo)* - Une phrase d'accroche / un slogan commercial *(a catchphrase)* - Le nom du produit *(the product)* - Un slogan *(the slogan)* - Un visuel souvent retouché *(an edited picture / image)* **Remarque** : Ce sont les mêmes éléments à repérer sur une affiche de prévention. Les deux veulent inciter le public à faire quelque chose.	- Des dessins, souvent à but humoristique - Des cases *(frames)* - Des bulles de dialogue *(speech bubbles / balloons)* ou une légende *(a caption)* - La signature de l'auteur(e) *(the cartoonist's signature)* **Remarque** : *a comic strip (at least 2 frames)* = dans un journal ; *a comic book* ou *a graphic novel* = un livre

Réussir le bac !

MÉTHODOLOGIE FICHE 9

VOCABULAIRE PAR AXES

AXE 1 Identity & Exchanges

- abroad
- belong somewhere
- bond = link
- citizenship
- conflict
- conform to
- cultural diversity
- culture shock/gap
- disappear = wear off = fade
- diversity
- economic
- economic exchanges
- expat
- fit in = adapt to
- foreign = alien
- foreign-born
- frontier = border
- global village
- globalization
- heritage
- identity
- inclusiveness/inclusion
- lifestyle
- open/close borders
- outcast
- overcome
- partnership
- preserve
- protectionism
- root
- selective immigration
- share
- tourism
- touristic
- tradition(al)
- welcome/greet sb

AXE 2 Private Space & Public Space

- activist
- assert one's rights/power over sb
- be confined to
- be on an equal footing with sb
- break the glass ceiling
- courageous = intrepid
- dedicate/devote oneself to sb/sth
- demonstrate
- demonstration
- emulate
- equality
- female empowerment
- feminism
- fulfil one's dream
- gender
- influential
- liberated
- male-dominated
- pioneer
- public/private space/life
- role model
- self fulfilment
- sex discrimination
- shelter
- strong-willed/determined
- struggle/fight
- survivalism/survivalist
- survive
- women's rights

AXE 3 Art & Power

- ad(vertisement)
- address an issue
- address/catch an audience
- advertise
- aim at sth/Ving
- brand
- censored
- censorship
- commercial
- committed art
- convey a message
- counter culture/counter power
- creative
- defend = advocate
- denounce = condemn
- give/make/deliver a message/ speech
- harmful = destructive
- (il)legitimate
- imaginative
- make a difference/change
- manipulate
- power
- provocative
- raise awareness
- spread the word
- stand for/represent
- street art/land art
- striking = impressive
- take action
- target

AXE 4 Citizenship & Virtual Worlds

- artificial intelligence
- break into a system/computer
- break the law ≠ comply with the law
- censorship
- commitment
- concern
- condemn
- counter power
- cyber bullying
- deceive
- denounce
- (dis)connected
- face-to-face interaction
- facial recognition
- fake news
- freedom of speech/expression
- gather personal data/information
- grant access to sb
- hacker
- hacktivism
- highly-skilled
- (home) security
- identity theft
- intrusive
- invade one's privacy
- isolated
- lawbreaker
- manipulation
- modern = up-to-date
- online safety/etiquette

- personal data
- private life
- social media/network
- socialize
- spy on sb/sth
- teleworking
- the media
- track/follow one's movements
- virtual reality
- virtual worlds
- walls have ears
- whistleblower
- wiretap = bug

AXE 5 Fictions & Reality

- antihero/antiheroine
- belief
- dystopia ≠ utopia
- dystopia(n)
- embody
- escape from reality
- fiction ≠ reality
- fictional ≠ real
- fictitious
- hero/heroine
- imaginary
- legend
- literature
- make believe
- myth
- pretend
- reenact(ment)
- science-fiction
- storytelling
- villain

AXE 6 Scientific Innovations & Responsibility

- achievement = exploit
- advocate for sth
- be allowed to ≠ be forbidden to
- bioengineer
- bioprinting
- breakthrough
- carry out an experiment
- cloning
- discovery
- (un)ethical
- enhance
- eradicate = erase
- ethics
- exoskeleton
- experiment
- experiment on sb/sth
- genetic research
- genetically engineer
- groundbreaking = revolutionary
- immortality
- improvement
- invention
- life-changing
- moral responsibility
- mutation
- push back the limits
- reach the point of no return
- robot
- robotics
- scientific research
- scientist
- sustainable development/energy
- testing
- theoretical
- theory
- transhumanism
- vaccine
- visionary

AXE 7 Diversity & Inclusion

- able-bodied
- cliché = stereotype
- demonstrate = take to the streets
- denigrate/disparage
- disability
- disabled
- discriminate against sb
- discrimination
- equality
- fit in/adapt to
- hatred
- include ≠ exclude
- inclusion/integration ≠ exclusion
- (in)tolerance
- minority
- protest
- racism
- stare at sb
- strong-willed
- Civil Rights movement
- Freedom fighters

AXE 8 Territory & Memory

- ancestor
- collective memory
- colonialism
- colonist = settler
- deeply-rooted = deep-seated = firmly implanted
- descendant
- duty of remembrance
- heritage
- historic
- historical
- indigenous
- infringe on ≠ respect human rights
- land deal
- make history
- memorial
- memory
- prejudicial to
- rebel
- reclaim = take back
- recognize
- reconciliation
- reenact the past
- reflect on sth
- resilient
- right the wrongs
- sovereignty
- traditions
- trauma
- traumatic
- traumatized

Crédits iconographiques

Couverture : Ferrantraite / Istockphoto - **p. 12 :** Pilgrim Hall Museum - **p. 14 :** Bastiaan Slabbers/Istock/Getty Images ; Photo12/Alamy/George Sheldon - p. 16 : COLLECTION CHRISTOPHEL © New Line Television - **p. 17 :** Courtesy E. Eicher/D.R - **p. 19 :** Jeff Greenberg/Getty Images - **p. 20 :** © Eliza Southwood - **p. 21 :** Gilbert Bellamy/REUTERS - **p. 22 :** Janine Wiedel Photolibrary/Alamy/Photo12 - **p. 23 :** © Brinkhoff-Moegenburg ; Sutton Hibbert/REX/Shutterstock/SIPA - p. 24 : Kiran Gidda Courtesy of Charlie Brinkhurst-Cuff - **p. 25 :** Sutton Hibbert/REX/Shutterstock/SIPA - **p. 27 :** Anwar Hussein/Getty Images - **p. 28 :** darekm101/Istockphoto ; ACHPF/Shutterstock - p. 30 : Photo12/Alamy/Megapress - **p. 37 :** © 2020 King Features Syndicates, Inc. ; Chris Jackson/Getty Images - **p. 38 :** © Kip Evans Photography - **p. 40 :** Everett / Bridgeman images ; COLLECTION CHRISTOPHEL © PolyGram Filmed Entertainment - **p. 42 :** National Portrait Gallery, London/ Bridgeman Images ; Photo Philip Mould Ltd, London / Bridgeman Images; National Portrait Gallery, London/Bridgeman Images - **p. 43 :** COLLECTION CHRISTOPHEL © Universal Pictures ; COLLECTION CHRISTOPHEL © universal pictures - **p. 46 :** COLLECTION CHRISTOPHEL © Gather Films - Picturesque Films - **p. 47 :** Bauman Rare Books - **p. 48 :** © ABC/Andia.fr - **p. 49 :** Terravivos.com ; Terravivos.com; Terravivos.com - **p. 50 :** Photo12/Alamy/Maurice Savage ; Photo12 / Alamy / Nancy Kaszerman / ZUMA Wire - **p. 51 :** GARY DOAK / Photo 12 - **p. 53 :** COLLECTION CHRISTOPHEL © National Geographique - **p. 54 :** © Ashley smith Wide eyed Studios - **p. 56 :** Peter Barritt/Alamy/Photo12 - **p. 57 :** Collection Christophel © Keep your head / MICA Entertainment - **p. 58 :** © Archives Charmet / Bridgeman Images - p. 59 : Gillian K. Willman - p. 61 : COLLECTION CHRISTOPHEL © Benaroya Pictures - H Films - Raslan Company of America - p. 63 : Photo12/Alamy/UrbanZone - **p. 64 :** Anthony Asael/Art in All of Us /Getty Images - **p. 69 :** Look and Learn / Bridgeman Images ; Jacky Fleming - **p. 70 :** Banksy/DR - **p. 72** : Photo12/Alamy/Peter Horree - **p. 73 :** The Coca-Cola Company / Printed by permission of the Norman Rockwell Family Agency - **p. 76 :** TopFoto / Roger-Viollet /ADAGP Paris, 2020 - **p. 77 :** adblockbristol.org.uk - **p. 78 :** Photo12/Alamy/northshoot - Food - **p. 79 :** Brand: Van Heusen, Origin: USA, Decade: 1940s, Image type: Magazine Advert ; plastikstudios.com - **p. 80 :** Surfers against Sewage – www.sas.org.uk - **p. 81 :** Surfrider Foundation Australia - **p. 84 :** Cavan Images/Istockphoto ; Prod DB - **p. 86 :** Steve Greenberg/ Cagle Cartoon ; David Horsey/Tribune Content Agency; Paresh/Cagle Cartoon - **p. 87 :** Glen Le Lievre ; Kenneth Catalino - **p. 88 :** © Marvel / Twentieth century fox / Collection Christophel ; Everett Collection/ Aurimages - **p. 90 :** Storms Media Group/Alamy/Photo12 - **p. 91 :** Photo12/Alamy/Martin Shields - p. 93 : Docs Anciens/docpix.fr ; Lisa Poole/AP/SIPA PRESS; Photo12/Alamy - **p. 96 :** Noam Galai/Getty Images - **p. 99 :** Marie Baronnet ; Ian Witlen/Shutterstock - **p. 100 :** R. Kikuo Johnson - **p. 102 :** chrisdorney/Shutterstock - **p. 103 :** Prod DB © BBC Wales - Hartswood Films - Masterpiece Theatre / DR - **p. 104 :** Kelvin Chan/AP/SIPA - **p. 105 :** John Darkow/Cagle Cartoon - **p. 106 :** Alan Pearce - p. 110 : Gabriel Olsen/FilmMagic/Getty Images - **p. 112 :** Drama/DR - p. 113 : IstockPlus/ Getty Images - **p. 114 :** Gorodenkoff/Shutterstock ; Photo12/Alamy/AF archive - **p. 115 :** Signe Wilkinson Editorial Cartoon used with the permission of Signe Wilkinson, the Washington Post Writers Group and the Cartoonist Group. All rights reserved ; Nath Paresh/Cagle Cartoon - **p. 116 :** Clay Bennet Editorial Cartoon used with the permission of Clay Bennett, the Washington Post Writers Group and the Cartoonist Group. All rights reserved - **p. 117 :** Oli Scarff/Getty Images ; Nate Beeler/Cagle Cartoon - **p. 127 :** Reprinted with permission from The Chronicle Herald ; David Becker/Getty Images - **p. 128 :** Prod DB - **p. 130 :** Jillian Meyer Photo/Getty Images ; Paramount / The Kobal Collection / Aurimages - **p. 131 :** Everett Collection / Aurimages ; Prod DB - © Zentropa Entertainments - Forward Films - Spier Films/DR; The Kobal Collection/Aurimages; Prod DB/DR - **p. 132 :** Christie's Images / Bridgeman Images - **p. 133 :** AKG Images / North Wind Picture Archives ; DR - **p. 134 :** Bettmann /Getty Images - **p. 135 :** Everett Collection / Bridgeman Images ; Zuma Press / Aurimages - **p. 137 :** Everett Collection / Aurimages ; Prod DB © Evenstar Films - Film Science - Harmony Prod. - Primitive Nerd; Everett Collection / Aurimages; BBQ_DFY / Aurimages - p. 139 : Zuma Press / Aurimages - p. 140 : © Leonard Beard - p. 141 : Tate, Londres, Dist. RMN-Grand Palais / Tate Photography ; Photo12/Alamy/Jeff Morgan 09 - **p. 142 :** Pictorial Press Ltd/Alamy/Photo12 - **p. 143 :** Bridgeman Images ; Gary Doak /WriterPictures/Leemage/Bridgeman Images - **p. 144 :** COLLECTION CHRISTOPHEL © WGN America -/Twentieth Century Fox Television - **p. 145 :** COLLECTION CHRISTOPHEL © Twentieth Century Fox ; Richard Meek/The LIFE Images Collection via Getty Images/Getty Images - **p. 146 :** Theo Cottle ; Stephan Readmond - **p. 147 :** Scott Eisen/Getty Images/AFP ; Photo12/Alamy/Ethel Wolvovitz - **p. 148 :** The Egremont Collection / National Trust Photographic Library/Derrick E. Witty / Bridgeman Images - **p. 149 :** Kate Oleska www.kateoleska.com ; Jesse Wild/Future Publishing/REX/SIPA PRESS - **p. 150 :** Collection Christophel © Walt disney ; Collection Christophel © Columbia TriStar - **p. 151 :** Collection Christophel © The WB Network ; COLLECTION CHRISTOPHEL © Netflix - Archie Comics Publications - Warner Bros. Television - **p. 152 :** Julia Kuntzle ; Aurimages - **p. 155 :** Matt Cardy/Getty Images - **p. 156 :** Collection Christophel © Upside Down Films / Les Films Upside Down - **p. 157 :** Collection Christophel © Temple Hill Entertainment / TSG Entertainment ; Collection Christophel © LAMF / STX Entertainment - **p. 158 :** Christian Ganet/ArtComPress/Leemage ; David M. Benett/Dave Benett/Getty Images - **p. 159 :** Southampton City Art Gallery/Bridgeman Images - **p. 160 :** Alamy/Photo12/ © Moviestore Collection Ltd ; Portrait Essentials/Alamy// Photo12 - **p. 161 :** The Picture Art Collection/Alamy/Photo 12 ; Colport/Alamy/Photo12 - **p. 162 :** Albert L. Ortega/Getty Images - **p. 164 :** CHRISTOPHEL © BBC Studios - Amazon Studios - Narrativia - Salt River Studios - The Blank Corporation / DR ; Collection Christophel © Atlas Entertainment / DC Comics / Lin Pictures / Warner Bros - **p. 166 :** HOUSE OF CARDS (Serie TV-2013-S6-Aff. US) 01 ; Collection Christophel/ © AMC - **p. 167 :** Collection Christophel © Aggressive Mediocrity / DC Entertainment / Jerry Bruckheimer Television - **p. 168 :** COLLECTION CHRISTOPHEL © Paré / United Artists ; Colin Willoughby / ArenaPAL - **p. 169 :** © Tate, Londres, Dist. RMN-Grand Palais / Tate Photography - **p. 170 :** COLLECTION CHRISTOPHEL © Warner Bros. / Heyday Films ; Collection Christophel © Marvel Studio 2017; Collection Christophel © Castle Rock Entertainment / Nelson Entertainment - **p. 171 :** COLLECTION CHRISTOPHEL © Groucho II Film Partnership / Silver Pictures ; COLLECTION CHRISTOPHEL © Warner Bros; Collection Christophel © Marvel studios - **p. 175 :** Lutetia/Société Lyonnaise de Production de Films (SLPF)/Société d'Exploitation Lyon-Bordeaux (SELB) / Photo © United Archives/Cinema Collection / Bridgeman Images - **p. 181 :** MGM/Cinerama / The Kobal Collection / Aurimages - **p. 182 :** Prod DB © Universal Pictures-Amblin Entertainment - Legendary Entertainment - Apaches Entertainment / DR - **p. 184 :** Photo12/Alamy/Mark Kerrison - **p. 187 :** Vitaliy Ankov / Sputnik ; Gabriel Olsen/Getty Images - **p. 189 :** SVEN HOPPE / DPA / dpa Picture-Alliance - **p. 191 :** WENN Rights Ltd / Alamy Stock Photo - **p. 192 :** © National Geographic (April 2017) - **p. 193 :** Photo12/Alamy/UPI ; SIPANY/SIPA - **p. 194 :** Bettmann/Getty Images ; Everett Collection / Bridgeman Images; Ian Gavan/Getty Images - **p. 196 :** Capital Press Agency / Rex Features/Sipa Press - **p. 198 :** Prod DB/ DR ; Prod DB / DR - **p. 199 :** Prod DB/DR - **p. 203 :** peepo/Istockphoto - **p. 206 :** Showtime/BBQ_DFY/Aurimages - **p. 208 :** Prod DB/Universal/DR - **p. 209 :** Twentieth Century Fox/Entertainment Pictures/Zuma Press/Aurimages ; FineArtImages/Leemage - **p. 210 :** Arcturus Holdings Limited - **p. 211 :** Prod DB/The National Theatre/Rex Features/DR ; Prod DB/The National Theatre/Rex Features/DR - **p. 212 :** Universal/The Kobal Collection/ Aurimages - **p. 213 :** 2014 by Stone Arch Books, a Capstone imprint. All rights reserved. - **p. 215 :** Stephanie Mac Millan - **p. 216 :** COLLECTION CHRISTOPHEL © NBC - Universal Television - Sony Pictures Television - MiddKid Productions - Kripke Enterprises - Davis Entertainment ; COLLECTION CHRISTOPHEL © Universal Pictures - **p. 217 :** Science Photo Library / Shockey, Gwen - **p. 218 :** © 2018 - 2020 AlanGutierrezArt - **p. 219 :** © 2011 - 2020 Unita-N - **p. 220 :** From 11/22/63 by Stephen King. New York: Scribner, 2011. Reprinted with the permission of Scribner, a division of Simon & Schuster, Inc. All rights reserved. - **p. 221 :** ERIC FEFERBERG / AFP - **p. 223 :** COLLECTION CHRISTOPHEL © BBC Studios - British Broadcasting Corporation (BBC) - **p. 227 :** Donald Iain Smith/Istockphoto - **p. 228 :** Diarmuid Greene /Getty Images - **p. 230 :** Jay Mallin/ZUMA Wire/ Alamy /Photo 12 - **p. 231 :** The Australian Human Rights Commission - **p. 232 :** Underwood Archives/Leemage ; Elliott Erwitt/Magnum Photos - **p. 233 :** ullstein bild/akg-images ; Keystone/Gamma-Rapho - **p. 234 :** Beowulf Sheehan/PEN/Opale/Leemage - **p. 235 :** Pete Souza/Official White House - **p. 236 :** The Granger Coll NY / Aurimages - **p. 237 :** Matt Heron/Take Stock/TopFoto ; David Redfern/Redferns/Getty Images - **p. 238 :** Hulton Archive/Getty Images ; Van Es/AP Photo/Sipa Press - **p. 239 :** UPPA / Aurimages ; Stanley Weston/Getty Images - **p. 240 :** Cavan / Alamy/ Photo12 - **p. 241 :** REUTERS/Joshua Lott - **p. 245 :** © Joe Fournier - **p. 246 :** Prod DB / DR ; Prod DB / DR - **p. 247 :** Christie's Images / Bridgeman Images ; George C. Beresford /Getty Images - **p. 249 :** Bridgeman Images - **p. 251 :** © Chris Steinken - chris-steinken.pixels.com - **p. 254 :** © Mattel.

BARBIE and associated trademarks and trade dress are owned by, and used under license from, Mattel. The views and opinions expressed in this section are those of the authors and do not necessarily reflect the opinion or position of Mattel ; GAMMA-RAPHO - **p. 255 :** RICKERBY/SIPA - **p. 256 :** © Mattel / ADAGP Paris, 2020 - **p. 257 :** Frédéric REGLAIN / Divergence - **p. 258 :** © Mattel. BARBIE and associated trademarks and trade dress are owned by, and used under license from, Mattel. The views and opinions expressed in this section are those of the authors and do not necessarily reflect the opinion or position of Mattel - **p. 260 :** MPI/Getty Images - **p. 263 :** David Horsey/Tribune Content Agency - **p. 264 :** Photo12/ Alamy/Gary E Perkin - **p. 266 :** Granger / Bridgeman Images - **p. 267 :** Gabriel Ramos/Shutterstock ; Granger / Bridgeman Images - p. 268 : COLLECTION CHRISTOPHEL © Memento Films Production / DR - **p. 269 :** Chris Felver / Bridgeman Images ; mikhail/Shutterstock - **p. 270 :** The Granger Collection, New York/ Coll. Christophel - **p. 271 :** Photo12/Alamy/ZUMA Press, Inc. - **p. 272 :** Teow Lim Goh ; Michael Urmann/Shutterstock - **p. 273 :** Photo12/Alamy/Stacy Walsh Rosenstock - **p. 274 :** Photo12/Alamy/Blaine Harrington - **p. 275 :** Stanislas Fautré/Only france - **p. 276 :** Becky Nunes - **p. 277 :** Photo12/Alamy/World History Archive - **p. 278 :** Photo12/Alamy/Hana Sladeckova ; GL Portrait / Alamy / Hemis - **p. 279 :** Maurie Hill / Dreamstime.com ; Beerpixs/Istockphoto - **p. 280 :** Tuputau Lelaulu/Handout via REUTERS - **p. 281 :** Justin McManus/The Sydney Morning Herald - **p. 284** : iStock Editorial - **p. 286 :** iStockphoto - **p. 287 :** AP Photo/Scott Threlkeld)/Sipa Press - **p. 288 :** Istockphoto ; Photo12/Alamy/Ron Buskirk; Icon Sportswire / Getty Images; REUTERS/Jonathan Bachman - **p. 293 :** The Image Bank Unreleased/Getty Images ; Photo12/Alamy/RM USA - **p. 329 :** Pedro Jr / IlustraDesign / www.pedrojr.com.br - **p. 331 :** Everett Collection / Aurimages ; From 11/22/63 by Stephen King. New York: Scribner, 2011. Reprinted with the permission of Scribner, a division of Simon & Schuster, Inc. All rights reserved.

Crédits textes

p. 17 : *Leaving My Amish World: My True Story* (2019) Eirenne Eicher © Fearless Publishing House - **p. 18 :** © 2017 The New York Times Company. All rights reserved. Used under license. - **p. 21 :** Copyright Guardian News & Media Ltd 2020 - **p. 22 :** "Happy Jamaican Independence Day 2019: How the iconic Caribbean island got its flag" (06/08/2019) Georgia Chambers © The Evening Standard - **p. 23 :** *Small Island* (2004) Andrea Levy © Headline - **p. 24 :** *Mother Country: Real Stories of the Windrush Children* (2018) Charlie Brinkhurst-Cuff © Headline ; "Bristol to strengthen cultural and economic links with Jamaica" (01/11/2018) Esme Ashcroft © The Bristol Post - **p. 25 :** *"Back to My Own Country," Six Stories and an Essay* (2014) Andrea Levy © Tinder Press - **p. 29 :** "Creating Middle Class Jobs: A Federal Tourism Growth Strategy" © Government of Canada - **p. 30 :** "Canada aims to attract more international students by expanding presence overseas" (14/04/2019) Andy Blatchford © GlobalNews.ca - **p. 31 :** "WWOOFing Canada – Essential Tips From A Host" (28/01/2018) Yrene Dee © BackCountryCanadaTravel.com https://backcountrycanadatravel.com/wwoofing-canada/ - **p. 32 :** OCDE (2019), Recruiting Immigrant Workers: Canada 2019, Recruiting Immigrant Workers, Éditions OCDE, Paris / OECD.org - **p. 35 :** Copyright Guardian News & Media Ltd 2020 - **p. 36 :** "Long before multiculturalism, Canada had always been a country of immigrants" (27/09/2019) Dan Archer © AssiniboiaTimes.ca - **p. 41 :** *The Lady Elizabeth* (2008) Alison Weir © Ballantine Books, Penguin Random House / DR - **p. 42 :** © BBC - **p. 44 :** "Bet You Didn't Know: Witches," "Queen Elizabeth I Biography, and "The Gold Rush of 1849" © 2020, A&E Television Networks, LLC, available respectively at https://www.history.com/topics/halloween/history-of-witches-video, https://www.biography.com/royal ; "Historical Notes: Why did Elizabeth I never marry?" © Independent.co.uk (09/06/1998) - **p. 47 :** "Watch a Cold War Era Video That Advises You How to Survive a Nuclear Attack" (29/09/2016) Mariana Zapata © AtlasObscura.com https://www.atlasobscura.com/articles/watch-this-cold-war-era-video-that-teaches-you-how-to-survive-a-nuclear-attack - **p. 48 :** Reprinted from Climatewire with permission from E&E News. Copyright 2019. E&E provides essential news for energy and environment professionals at www.eenews.net. - **p. 49 :** © The Vivos Group, Del Mar, California https://www.terravivos.com/secure/reserve.htm - **p. 50 :** Excerpt(s) from EDUCATED: A MEMOIR by Tara Westover, copyright © 2018 by Second Sally, Ltd.. Used by permission of Random House, an imprint and division of Penguin Random House LLC. All rights reserved. - **p. 51 :** Excerpt(s) from STATION ELEVEN: A NOVEL by Emily St. John Mandel, copyright © 2014 by Emily St. John Mandel. Used by permission of Alfred A. Knopf, an imprint of the Knopf Doubleday Publishing Group, a division of Penguin Random House LLC. All rights - **p. 55 :** How to Climb Mont Blanc in a Skirt (2011) Mick Conefrey © Oneworld Publications - **p. 57 :** © Republished with permission of John Wiley & Sons - Books, from Complex locations : women's geographical work in the UK, 1850-1970, Avril Maddrell, 2011; permission conveyed through Copyright Clearance Center, Inc. - **p. 58 :** "The lady explorers with a sense of adventure" (16/20/2011) Giulia Rhodes © Express.co.uk - **p. 59 :** 'Published with the permission of Cambridge Scholars Publishing' - **p. 62 :** Excerpt(s) from DEAR IJEAWELE, OR A FEMINIST MANIFESTO IN FIFTEEN SUGGESTIONS by Chimamanda Ngozi Adichie, copyright © 2017 by Chimamanda Ngozi Adichie. Used by permission of Alfred A. Knopf, an imprint of the Knopf Doubleday Publishing Group, a divisio - **p. 66 :** "Young, female and powerful: Was Elizabeth I a feminist?" (16/11/2017) Kate Wilkinson © RMG.co.uk / DR - **p. 67 :** Evan Osnos / The New Yorker © Condé Nast - **p. 68 :** © Telegraph Media Group Limited 2017 ; Evan Osnos / The New Yorker © Condé Nast - p. 73 : "THE ART OF NORMAN ROCKWELL" © NRM.org - **p. 74 :** "Apple's holiday ad is an animated short film" (20/11/2018) Romain Dillet © TechCrunch.com ; "Storytelling And Advertising: How To Bring The Two Together" (16/01/2019) Patrick Foster © TheNextAd.com - **p. 75 :** "The resurgence of hand-painted mural advertising" (14/11/2017) Greg Spraker © Grafik.Agency - **p. 76 :** "Art and Advertising: friends or foes?" (12/08/2014) Joe Turnbull © Apollo-Magazine.com - **p. 77 :** "Art and Advertising: friends or foes?" (12/08/2014) Joe Turnbull © Apollo-Magazine.com - **p. 78 :** "Using Satire and Parody to Make Your Content Humorous" (30/08/2018) Andrew M. © WriterAccess.com - **p. 79 :** "Photographer Reverses Gender Roles In Sexist Vintage Ads" (2018) Hidreley © BoredPanda.com - **p. 85 :** "NRA rewrites Brothers Grimm fairy tales – with guns" (29/03/2016) Andrew Buncombe © Independent.co.uk - **p. 91 :** From The New York Times. © 2019 The New York Times Company. All rights reserved. Used under license. - **p. 92 :** "The Science of Storytelling: What Listening to a Story Does to Our Brains" Leo Widrich (01/02/2016) © Buffer.com - **p. 93 :** Speech at the Democratic Party of Wisconsin Founders Day Gala, Barack Obama, (16/02/2008) - **p. 97 :** "Once upon a time ... a guide to digital storytelling" (25/09/2019) Kevin Courtney © IrishTimes.com - **p. 98 :** Fantasyland: How America Went Haywire: A 500-Year History (2017) Kurt Andersen © Penguin Random House - **p. 103 :** Copyright 2012 Smithsonian Institution. Reprinted with permission from Smithsonian Enterprises. All rights reserved. Reproduction in any medium is strictly prohibited without permission from Smithsonian Institution - **p. 104 :** "Man fined for refusing to show his face to police face recognition software" (01/02/2019) Martine Berg Olsen © Metro.co.uk - **p. 105 :** From The New York Times. © 2019 The New York Times Company. All rights reserved. Used under license. - **p. 106 :** The Sherlock Holmes Handbook for the Digital Age: Elementary Cyber Security (2016) © Alan Pearce - **p. 109 :** "Will virtual reality and AI help us to find love or make us lonelier?" (12/09/2019) Martin Coulter © FT.com - **p. 110 :** © 2018 The Atlantic Media Co., as first published in The Atlantic.Com All rights reserved. Distributed by Tribune Content Agency - **p. 111 :** "Online dating isn't a game. It's literally changing humanity." (13/02/2019) Chris Taylor © Mashable.com - **p. 112 :** "iPride & Prejudice: Tinder-swiping Mr Darcy will star in a reworking of Jane Austen's classic love story as literary experts update passages from three classics 'for the digital age'" (08/02/2018) Alisha Rouse © DailyMail.co.uk - **p. 115 :** "About Kevin Mitnick: CEO, Team Leader, and Chief White Hat Hacker" © MitnickSecurity.com - **p. 118 :** Andy Greenberg, Wired (c) Conde Nast ; © The Economist Group Limited, London (03/07/2010) - **p. 119 :** Engineering a Traitor (2018 ed.) Brian David Johson © Army Cyber Institute at West Point and the Threatcasting Lab at Arizona State University - **p. 120-123** : Engineering a Traitor (2018 ed.) Brian David Johson © Army Cyber Institute at West Point and the Threatcasting Lab at Arizona State University - **p. 125 :** "Online dating isn't a game. It's literally changing humanity." (13/02/2019) Chris Taylor © Mashable.com - **p. 126 :** "Anonymous took the hacktivism community with them when they died" (19/05/2019) Isaiah Mayersen © TechSpot.com - **p. 132 :** From CLASSZONE.COM Copyright © by Houghton Mifflin Harcourt Publishing Company. All rights reserved. Used by permission of the publisher. Any further duplication is strictly prohibited unless written permission is obtained from Houghton Mifflin Harcourt - **p. 133 :** The Searchers (2016 reprint) Alan LeMay © Kensington Publishing. All rights reserved. Reprinted by arrangement with Kensington

Dépôt légal : avril 2020 – n° éditeur : MAGSI20200728
Achevé d'imprimer en août 2020
par Aubin Imprimeur en France

IMPRIM'VERT
Votre imprimeur agit pour l'environnement

PEFC
10-31-1601
Certifié PEFC
pefc-france.org